The Matter of Araby in Medieval England

Meeting (Asamblea): A Christian lord pledges friendship with a Muslim. A fourteenth-century painting on the ceiling of the Sala de los Reyes, Palacio de la Alhambra, Granada.

The Matter of Araby in

Medieval England

Dorothee Metlitzki

New Haven and London, Yale University Press, 1977

Copyright © 1977 by Yale University.
All rights reserved. This book may not be
reproduced, in whole or in part, in any form
(except by reviewers for the public press),
without written permission from the publishers.

Designed by John O. C. McCrillis
and set in Baskerville type.
Printed in the United States of America by
The Murray Printing Co., Westford, Massachusetts.

Published in Great Britain, Europe, Africa, and Asia
by Yale University Press, Ltd., London.
Distributed in Latin America by Kaiman & Polon, Inc.,
New York City; in Australia and New Zealand by Book & Film
Services, Artarmon, N.S.W., Australia; in Japan by
Harper & Row, Publishers, Tokyo Office.

Library of Congress Cataloging in Publication Data

Metlitzki, Dorothee.
    The matter of Araby in medieval England.

    Includes index.
1. English literature—Arab influences. 2. English
literature—Middle English, 1100–1500—History and
criticism. 3. Literature, Comparative—English and Arab.
4. Literature, Comparative—Arab and English. I. Title.
PR128.M4   820'.9'001   76–23678
ISBN 0–300–02003–1

To the memory of my parents
Israel Yosifovich Metlitzki and Rosa Rachel Malbin

and to my daughter Ruth Grdseloff

Contents

Illustrations

Preface

This study was begun many years ago at the University of London with the encouragement of my teachers, the late Charles Jasper Sisson and the late Sir Hamilton Gibb. It was resumed at the University of California at Berkeley under the impetus of a Fellowship of the American Council of Learned Societies, to which I express my thanks. My friends and colleagues at Yale University, Stephen Barney, Marie Borroff, Lowry Nelson, Jr., and Fred Robinson read the entire manuscript and made comments and suggestions for which I am grateful. I also wish to thank Howard Garey, for his help in translating Old French, and Charles Fineman, who provided invaluable assistance in technical matters and bibliographical research.

I am grateful to the A. Whitney Griswold Faculty Research Fund of Yale University for defraying the cost of preparing the manuscript for publication and to my editors Ellen Graham and Charles Grench of the Yale University Press for turning it into a printed book.

Parts of chapter 3 in part 1 of the book have previously appeared in the form of articles: "On the Motion of the 'Heart' in *The Owl and the Nightingale*," *Neuphilologische Mitteilungen* 71 (1970): 621–35; "The Code of Chaucer's 'Secree of Secrees' Arabic Alchemical Terminology in *The Canon's Yeoman's Tale*," *Archiv fuer das Studium der Neueren Sprachen und Literaturen*, Heft 4, Band 207, Jahrgang 122 (1970): 260–76; "The Celestial Origin of Elpheta and Algarsyf in Chaucer's Squire's Tale," *Euroasiatica* 4 (1970): 3–13. I wish to thank the editors of these publications for permission to reprint the material.

When I have used Arabic words and names in the text I have either left them in familiar English forms or transliterated them without full diacritical marking. An exact transliteration is provided in the index. I have supplied modern English renditions along with the Middle English excerpts, for the benefit of Arabists, but I have not considered it necessary to translate Latin, as most of it is incorporated in paraphrase in the English text and does not present special problems.

Dorothee Metlitzki

New Haven
August 1976

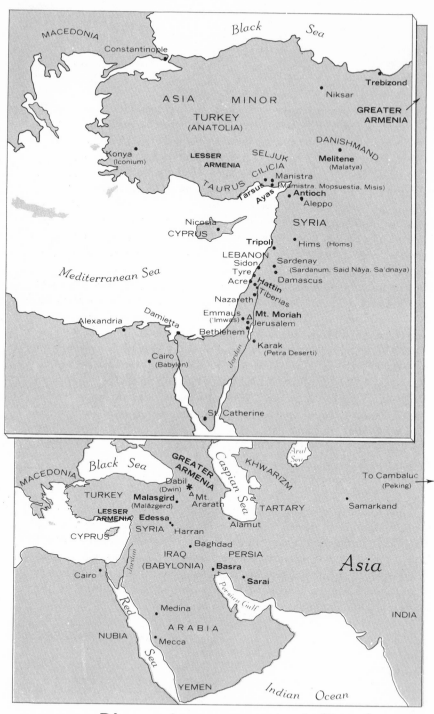

Places Associated with People and

Europe

∗   archeological evidence

△   mountains

Events relating to the Matter of Araby

Part One: Scientific and Philosophical Learning

1

The Transmission

The people who contributed to the formation of what, in the Middle Ages, was known as "Saracen"[1] culture were of the most varied ethnic origins. They were Greeks, Persians, Indians, Copts, Nestorians, Zoroastrians, and Jews, whole populations living in a vast expanse of territories extending from the Indian Ocean to the Atlantic which the spread of Islam from the heart of the Arabian peninsula had engulfed with lightning speed. These indigenous peoples were the heirs of old and brilliant civilizations which had been consolidated in the Byzantine and Persian Empires. Yet under the influence of their Arab conquerors they were molded into a new cultural unity that expressed itself in a new *Arabian* way of life. The dominating force in this new culture was Islam, the official religion; its medium of expression was Arabic, the language of the Koran. Thus, Arabic literature, in the Middle Ages, is "the enduring monument of a civilization, not of a people."[2] It is the product of diverse older civilizations, Syrian, Persian, and particularly Greek, which in the course of the expansion of the Arab Empire in the seventh and eighth centuries had been merged, transposed, and translated by a genius of assimilation peculiar to the medieval world. During the period when elements of this composite Arabian culture began to penetrate the Latin West, France was the seat of Latin civilization, and its schools occupied the leading position in the cultural life of the Latin world. Englishmen were at the heart of this "Gallic" territory. From the time of Alcuin of York, the first French minister of education, the activity of English teachers and students at the French schools was ever increasing, and in the diffusion of Saracen learning throughout the West, English scholars were the pioneers.

THE CRUSADES

It would be natural to assume that the first impact of Arabian culture on Latin Europe was brought about by the most dramatic confrontation of East and West in the Middle Ages—the Crusades. There is, indeed, a school of thought which regards the whole phenomenon of the Crusades as a reflection of the Muslim jihād, the holy war against the infidels—a defensive countermovement to the spectacular victories of the Muslims in Europe.[3]

The cultural effect of the Crusades on medieval Europe was thoroughly examined ninety years ago by Hans Prutz whose work, *Die Kulturgeschichte der Kreuzzuege,* has not been superseded in its scope and detail. The staggering wealth of material accumulated by Prutz shows the extent of Arab influence on a wide range of Frankish activities, on military technique, on vocabulary, on food, clothing, and ornamentation.[4] In scholarly fields, especially astronomy and mathematics, Prutz recognized the supremacy of the influence coming from Muslim Spain and its flourishing centers of learning on which modern scholars have focused their attention. To Prutz, however, the historical and cultural significance of the Crusades was unsurpassed. He compared the penetration of the Crusaders to the Orient to the triumphant progress of Alexander the Great. He saw Frankish knights opening the wonders of the East to an astonished Europe and, like Alexander, bringing about the marriage of Orient and Occident.

Since the days of Prutz, the historical evaluation of the Crusades has undergone a radical change or, rather, has come full circle. We find Steven Runciman, in the middle of the twentieth century, essentially returning to the opinion of Herder who, in 1787, considered the Crusades a wild episode—"nichts als eine tolle Begebenheit"—which cost Europe "a few million men" but did not bring any "enlightenment."[5] "Seen in the perspective of history the whole Crusading movement was a vast fiasco," writes Runciman. "The almost miraculous success of the First Crusade set up Frankish states in Outremer; and a century later, when all seemed lost, the gallant effort of the Third Crusade preserved them for another hundred years. But the tenuous kingdom of Jerusalem and its sister principalities were a puny outcome from so much energy and enthusiasm."[6]

In the perspective of Europe's intellectual history, the cultural contribution of the Crusades was also puny. They helped to accelerate tendencies already at work in Sicily and Spain, but their importance as a leaven in thought is intangible and difficult to assess. The Crusaders were military men of action. If they were interested in anything of the superior civilization of the Saracens which it was their aim to destroy, it was in new techniques of siege and fortification, in military instruments, in trade, transportation, and the use of money. But even here, as Heeren recognized a hundred and seventy years ago, whatever they learned from the Saracens was in spite of themselves.[7] "The intellectual life of Outremer was, in fact, that of a Frankish colony," concludes Runciman. "The Courts of the Kings and Princes had a certain cosmopolitan glamour; but the number of resident scholars in Outremer was small; and wars and financial difficulties prevented the institution of real centres of study where native and neighbouring learning could have been absorbed. It was the absence of these centres that made the cultural contribution of the Crusades to western Europe so disappointingly small."[8]

The journey of Adelard of Bath to Syria in the early twelfth century might be considered as a sign that Latin scholars in the East were not inactive. Antioch, which Adelard visited on his journey, had a brilliant tradition of translation from Greek and Syriac into Arabic.[9] But there is nothing to indicate that Adelard carried any texts away with him as his younger contemporary, Daniel of Morley, did from Spain. The amount of translation from the Arabic in Palestine and Syria was surprisingly small, and even the new geographical learning filtered very slowly indeed into the annals of the thirteenth century, as we know from Haskins.[10] In the most important literary activity of the crusading Franks, the writing of history, there are signs of some acquaintance with Arabic sources.[11] But the total effect of Muslim culture on the Crusaders seems to have reduced itself to a general aspiration to copy the comforts and luxuries of Oriental life, which indeed are richly depicted in medieval romance.

The serious interest in Islamic civilization began in the *West* and was due to the penetration of Latin clerics into the cultural realms of the Saracens, in the wake of professional interests in which scholarly pursuits were deeply embedded.

In the eighth century, when Alcuin was writing, the Arabs had already set their cultural stamp on North Africa and Latin had been ousted by Arabic. Even before the Muslim occupation, North Africa was the channel through which Eastern learning had been carried to the Latins for centuries. Now it served as a springboard for the Muslim conquest of Sicily and Spain. Within a decade of Tariq's landing at Gibraltar in 711, the language of the Koran was used among the Christians of Spain. In the lifetime of Bede, as early as 724, John, bishop of Seville, translated the Bible into Arabic.[12]

A hundred years later the state of arabization among the Christians of Spain was such that Alvaro, bishop of Cordova, despaired of the future of Christian youth:

> Who to-day among our faithful laymen is able to understand the Holy Scriptures and the books which our doctors have written in Latin? Who is there inspired with love of the Gospel, the Prophets, the Apostles? Are not all our young Christians . . . most conspicuous for their foreign erudition and perfected in Arabic eloquence? They eagerly study Arabic books, read them intently, and discuss them with ardour. . . . Alas! Christians are ignorant of their own language, the Latins do not care for their own tongue!
>
> Scarcely one in a thousand can be found in the Christian community who is able to compose a well-written Latin letter to a friend. But there are a great many among them who can expound the Arabic pomposity of language with greatest erudition, and adorn the final clauses of verses more elegantly than the Arabs themselves![13]

Bad as it was from the point of view of Christianity, the cultural assimilation of the "would-be Arabs," the Mozarabs (Christians living under Muslim rule) played a vital part in the transmission of Arabic learning
to the West and may well have left traces in early England which still
elude us.

Islam began to be treated seriously first by missionaries, Cluniac,
Franciscan, and Dominican, who felt that the Muhammadan "heresy"
could not be fought unless understood. It was a missionary concern which
led Peter the Venerable, abbot of Cluny, to engage the Englishman
Robert of Ketton on the first Latin translation of the Koran in 1141, not
without "entreaty and a high fee."[14]

The pleas for the peaceful conversion of the Saracens accompanied the
crusading movement from the very beginning.[15] They increased in volume
in proportion to the Frankish military defeats and became commonplace
when the hope for the recovery of the Holy Land had vanished and the
whole of Eastern Christendom was being lost to Muslim rule. The failure
to defeat the Saracens in the East by force of arms, apparent to all even
before the loss of Jerusalem to Saladin in 1187, intensified the missionary
activities in the West that moved in the wake of the Christian reconquest
of Spain. The local ecclesiastical authorities encouraged the rummaging
in Muslim "armaria," the libraries attached to mosques and courts. It
is to them that Western scholars busily flocked in the footsteps of local
Mozarabs like Mark of Toledo, another translator of the Koran, who
describes himself as "Toletum rediens . . . in armariis Arabum studiose
queriens."[16] The penetration into the Arab "treasure-chests" of learning
in northern Spain brought about the excited discovery that it was the
Arabs who were the true representatives of classical knowledge and the
giants on whose shoulders Latin science and philosophy had to be placed.
Both in Sicily and Spain the direct contact with Arabian scholarship was
weak while the countries were still under Saracen rule and political isolation emphasized the religious differences and prevented any natural
mingling. At the time of at least partial Christian domination, however,
the barriers came down and Latin scholars were free to visit the centers of
Muslim learning and work with Arabs, Mozarabs, and Jews. In Spain this
stage was reached after the Christian conquest of Toledo in 1085; in
Sicily about the time when Robert Guiscard took Salerno, in 1077, "with
the help of Latins, Greeks, and Saracens."[17]

ARABIAN CULTURE IN SICILY

Of the rich flowering of Arabian culture in Sicily very little has survived
and the exact pattern of its composition is still uncertain beyond the general impression of the brilliance and versatility that marked the Sicilian

way of life. Sicily was under Arab domination from 902 to 1091. But it was only after the Norman conquest, especially under the rule of its "two baptized sultans,"[18] Roger II (1130–54) and his grandson Frederick II (1215–50), that Arab influence began to permeate Latin medieval life from this region of Europe. The history of Sicily has been described as the story of Western civilization in miniature. A center of Greek, Roman, Visigothic, Byzantine, and Arab civilization, Sicily was the natural meeting place of the three main elements which composed medieval culture: Greek, Arab, and Latin.

In his description of the Sicilian court the Arab geographer Ibn Jubair is full of praise for the Norman king, William II (1166–89), who could read and write Arabic and had a Muhammadan bodyguard.[19] Roger II suggested the preparation of the silver plate map of al-Idrisi which contained seventy-one maps and was known as "the book of Roger" among the Arabs. But the representative man of medieval Sicily was Frederick II. "O fortunate Emperor!" wrote his court astrologer, Michael Scot, another British pioneer in the exploration of Arabian knowledge, "I verily believe if ever a man in this world could escape death by his learning, thou wouldst be the one. . . ."[20] The environment that shaped this king, acclaimed both as Antichrist and "stupor mundi" by his contemporaries, depicts the Arabian splendor of medieval culture in Europe.

> At eight and nine years old the young king wandered about without let or hindrance, and strolled unchecked through the narrow streets and markets and gardens of the semi-African capital at the foot of the Pellegrine. An amazing variety of peoples, religions and customs jostled each other before his eyes: mosques with their minarets, synagogues with their cupolas stood cheek by jowl with Norman churches and cathedrals, which again had been adorned by Byzantine masters with gold mosaics, their rafters supported by Greek columns on which Saracen craftsmen had carved in Kufic script the name of Allah. Round the town lay the pleasure palaces and fountains of Norman kings in the exotic gardens and animal preserves of the Conca d'oro, the delights of which had inspired the Arab poets. In the market-places the people went about their business in many-coloured confusion: Normans, and Italians, Saracens, Jews and Greeks.[21]

Frederick conducted a learned correspondence with Arabic scholars in Egypt, Syria, Iraq, Arabia, Yemen, Morocco, and Spain. He sent questions bearing on geometrical, philosophical, and astronomical problems to the provinces of the caliphate and exchanged books with their emirs.

A Sicilian teacher of Arabic dialectics accompanied the emperor to Palestine on the Third Crusade, and Frederick's Arabic conversation on philosophy with the Sultan al-Kamil's envoy, Fakhr ad-Din, probably had greater bearing on the issue of the political negotiations than did the military operations.

The Norman court at Palermo continued the splendid tradition of Saracen Sicily with its rich and complex civilization. Nowhere else did Latin, Greek, and Arab live side by side in peace and toleration; nowhere else was the spirit of humanism more deeply expressed in the actual policy of its rulers. These rulers were Normans and their heirs. As in England, they adopted no policy of suppressing native culture. They were concerned with political administration and, above all, law. The result was that the cultural productivity encouraged by this policy of law and order included Arabs and Jews and was particularly rich and many-sided. In the education of a Sicilian prince and nobleman an admiration of Arabian culture was as natural an element as the cultivation of French at the court of medieval England. "In the twelfth century," writes Haskins, "it is significant that the two most advanced states from the point of view of administrative organization, England and Sicily, should be precisely those in which literature and learning are most fully developed in relation to the royal court." There was a constant to-and-fro between Norman England and Norman Sicily. Royal policy encouraged the presence of Englishmen at the Sicilian court and there was continuous interchange in administrators, clerks, and scholars among whom Peter of Blois as the common teacher of both William II and Henry II holds a special place. Even the most famous Anglo-Norman institution, the Exchequer and its Pipe Rolls, may have had its beginnings in the Sicilian *duana* (Arabic *dīwān*), which was largely staffed by Saracen officials, kept voluminous registers, and "seems plainly to go back to Saracenic antecedents."[22]

At the Sicilian court, royal charters and registers were composed in three languages: Greek, Latin, and Arabic. The result was that translation was an easy and natural function and the most distinguished translators were officials of the royal administration and members of the royal household. An Englishman, Robert of Salesby, stood at the head of King Roger's chancery. He was not a great scholar himself, as we know from John of Salisbury. But his lavish hospitality to visiting Englishmen, which delighted John of Salisbury when he was his guest in the summer of 1150, must have surely helped those who had literary and scientific interests like John of Salisbury himself—he studied with a "Graecus interpres" in Apulia.[23] A "quidam magister natione Anglus" described by Gervase of Tilbury, himself for a time a member of the Sicilian household, appeared before Roger II in quest of Virgil's tomb. Gervase praises him as a man "summe literatus, in trivio et quadrivio potens et acutissimus, in physica operosus, in astronomica summus."[24]

The pioneer of Arabic studies in England, Adelard of Bath, came to his "Arabum studia" by way of Sicily: "What the Gauls do not know those beyond the Alps reveal; what you cannot learn among the Latins, abundant Greece will teach you."[25] We know that he visited Salerno and Magna Graecia (southern Italy) where he met a Greek philosopher and discoursed on medicine and the nature of the universe.

In Sicily, texts were translated from the original Greek side by side with versions from the Arabic. "Vir tamen grecae quam arabicae linguae peritissimus, latinae quoque non ignarus," is the description of Eugene of Palermo, admiral of King Roger's fleet and translator of Ptolemy's *Optics* from the Arabic. It is given in the preface to a Sicilian Latin translation of Ptolemy's *Syntaxis Astronomica* known throughout the Middle Ages by its Arabic name of *Almagest*.[26] A *Greek* codex of the Almagest was brought to the Sicilian court in 1158 by Henricus Aristippus, a member of the royal household and himself a translator of Plato, on his return from a diplomatic mission to Constantinople.[27] The codex was turned from the Greek into Latin—a decade before the Latin version from the Arabic— by a visiting scholar, a Salerno student who braved Scylla and Charybdis and the lava of Etna to see it. The name of the translator and the identity of the"vir mentis serenissime" to whom the Latin version is dedicated are unknown.[28] But the translation has been connected with an Englishman and may well constitute the most significant link in the close relationship between Sicily and England. Henricus Aristippus, bearer of the Almagest, was the close friend of an English scholar as we know from his preface to Plato's *Phaedo*. The Englishman, "Roboratus fortunatus," was about to return home, but Aristippus tried to keep him in Sicily by reminding him that it was a scholar's paradise. There were libraries, the writings of great philosophers, and learned friends: "Why are you in a hurry? Why are you getting ready to go home?" To the wise man, as Virgil says, "omne solum patria est, ut volucri vacuo quicquid in orbe patet."[29]

The influences that were transmitted from "the tripartite culture of Sicily" flourished in England and were encouraged by royal patronage as is clear from the many learned and scientific works dedicated to Henry II, including Adelard of Bath's treatise on the astrolabe. "Your king is a good scholar, but ours is the better," writes Peter of Blois to Walter Opha- mil, archbishop of Palermo, another ecclesiastic from England. "I am well acquainted with the abilities and the performance of both. With the English king there is daily study, constant conversation with the best scholars and eager discussion of all questions."[30] No wonder that the English court under Henry II and Eleanor of Aquitaine reflected a new cosmopolitan culture in which the Saracen strain is an unmistakable fiber in both romance and scholarship.

ARABIAN CULTURE IN SPAIN

The disintegration of the caliphate in the East, bad as it was for the political power of Islam, played an important part in stimulating the cultural flowering of the Muslims of Spain, where the Latin "intelligentsia" came into closest contact with Islamic society. Just as Baghdad had deprived Byzantium of its supremacy in the East, the Fatimid, Aghlabid, and Umayyad rulers of the independent Arab provinces were anxious to outshine the Abbasid capital in cultural achievements. In the West, Cordova, the seat of the Umayyad dynasty of Spain, had become the center of a brilliant civilization in the tenth century.

We have the accout of Sa'id ibn Ahmad, qadi of Toledo (d. 1070), who describes the flourishing culture of Cordova under al-Hakam II, second Umayyad caliph of Spain (961–76):

> The Sultan Al-hakem . . . having ascended the throne, the cultivation of letters received a new impulse, and by his encouragement of all sorts of studies, by his unwonted liberality towards the learned, whom he invited to his capital from Baghdad, Cairo, and other distant countries, and, above all, by his exquisite taste for literature, which he had cultivated with success during his father's lifetime, the torch of science shone brighter than ever. . . . He caused all sorts of rare and curious books to be purchased by his agents in Cairo, Baghdad, Damascus, Alexandria, and other great cities in the East; and no work on ancient or modern science was discovered that was not immediately procured at any cost and sent to him. By these means he collected a richer and more extensive library than the Khalifs of the Abbasid dynasty ever did during the whole period of their reign, and the learned of Andalus devoted their attention to the study of the sciences contained in the books of the ancients. . . .[31]

With the rise of the petty dynasties after the fall of the Umayyads in the eleventh century, the cultivation of learning was intensified. According to ash-Shaqundi (d. 1231), "the cause of science and literature, instead of losing, gained considerably . . . when, after the breaking of the necklace and the scattering of its pearls, the kings of small states divided among themselves the patrimony of the Beni Umeyyah." For "the usurpers disputed with each other the prize of prose and poetical composition, and overstocked the markets with all departments of science. . . ."[32]

The conquest of Toledo by Alfonso VI in May 1085 was thus one of the most important events not only in the political but in the intellectual history of medieval Europe. At one stroke the Christian world took possession of a civilization next to which the Latin West, to quote Daniel of Morley, seemed "infantile,"[33] provincial, and barbaric. While France and England were agrarian, monastic, and feudal, Islamic society resided in the cosmopolitan sophistication of its cities and courts whose lifeline spanned the most ancient centers of civilization along the Mediterranean which, in the famous words of Henri Pirenne, was a Muslim lake.[34] The conqueror of Toledo himself had married an Arab. He admired the culture of Jews and Muslims to whom he extended his patronage, so that for two generations at least Toledo remained the seat of the most important Moorish community in Christian Europe.

The Toledo fountains which Daniel of Morley admired and which "varied in fulness with the moon's phases and contained salt water although distant six days' journey from the sea,"[35] were from the time of its most famous ruler, al-Ma'mun (1043–75), who had taken the "by-name" of the great Baghdad caliph and whose palace and fountains were the wonder of the Muslim world. A decade before the Christian conquest he had turned Toledo into an intellectual center equal to Seville and Cordova. In the tradition of the Arabs, its learning was concentrated at court and at the great mosque which, in July 1085, barely two months after the Christian conquest, was turned into a cathedral.

It was there that the "armaria Arabum," the rich library cabinets of the Arabs, were situated to which northern scholars soon began to flock and which enabled Peter the Venerable to boast that Christian scholars had finally penetrated the secrets of the Arabs.[36] The fanaticism of the Cluniac monks violated Alfonso's agreement with the Muslim population which included the preservation of the mosque as an Islamic place of worship. But the Church continued Islamic tradition in encouraging the teaching and translation of mathematical, astronomical, and philosophical works at the cathedral itself which "in forma mezquitae a tempore Arabum adhunc stabat."[37] (Daniel of Morley still saw the mosque and it was not subjected to the usual Christian alterations until 1226.) Indeed the foundation of the college that emerges from the picture drawn by Daniel of Morley is attributed to the primate, Don Raimundo, whose term of office was from 1126 to 1152. The first sign of a systematic activity of translation is found in the collaboration of Yohannan ben David (Johannes Hispalensis), a Spanish Jew, and the archdeacon of Segovia, Domingo González (Dominicus Gundissalimus) who expressly state that they worked at the bidding of Raymond, archbishop of Toledo and primate of Spain.[38]

"Dixit translator: et ego complevi eius translationem ex arabico in latinum . . . apud urbem Toletanum."[39] There are a great number of manuscripts which show that for a hundred years, from about 1150 to

1250, Toledo was the center of an extraordinary movement of translation from Arabic into Latin that proceeded with the help of Jews, Mozarabs, and occasional Muslims. In character, though not in scope, this under-taking was comparable to the original work of translating from Greek and Syriac into Arabic which, in the eighth century, had been started by Caliph al-Mansur at Baghdad.[40] At first the activity of the Latin trans-lators was sporadic. We find them, like Robert of Ketton and Herman the Dalmatian, in various places in northern Spain and southern France: Barcelona, Segovia, León, Pamplona; Toulouse, Béziers, Narbonne, Marseilles. In the second quarter of the century the focus becomes Toledo and crystallizes into what may be considered a "school," like the famous "Bait al-Hikma" (House of Science) at Baghdad which flourished in the reign of the Abbasid Caliph al-Ma'mun (813–33) and was engaged in the copy and translation of manuscripts.[41] It is with the school of al-Ma'mun that al-Khwarizmi, the first Arabic astronomer to be discovered by the Latins, was connected. He makes his Latin entry in England, in a revised Spanish version of his astronomical tables made by Maslama ibn Ahmad al-Majriti and translated by Adelard of Bath.

2

"Arabum studia" in England

When Adelard of Bath, *philosophus anglorum,* returned to England about 1120 from extensive travel in southern Europe and the Levant, he echoed the complaint of another famous English translator made three hundred years before his time.[1] The state of affairs and learning in England was in a lamentable condition. From what his friends told him on arrival, Adelard gathered that "violence ruled among the nobles, drunkenness among the prelates, corruptibility among the judges, fickleness among the patrons, and hypocrisy among the citizens; mendacious promises were given lightly, friends were invidious, and almost all whom one met courting favour."[2] The coming anarchy of the reign of Stephen was on its way. Nothing seemed more distasteful to Adelard than to submit to "this misery." Being unable to avert "this moral degeneration," he decided to ignore it: "Unica enim malorum irrefragabilium medicina est oblivio."[3] But Adelard had brought back a unique consolation—his enthusiasm for *Arabum studia.* He is the first Latin translator of al-Khwarizmi's astronomical tables and Euclid's *Elements* from the Arabic.

King Alfred had complained of the English ignorance of Latin, the language of literature and moral culture. Adelard could not endure the prejudice against modern science which in his time was synonymous with Arabian scholarship. He had spent seven years in study and travel in order "to investigate the learning of the Arabs as best he could."[4] As a youth he studied at Tours and later taught at Laon, the school which Anselm, the pupil and namesake of Anselm of Canterbury, had made famous. But Adelard was not impressed with what he had found there: "Quod enim Gallica studia nesciunt, transalpina reserabunt, quod apud Latinos non addisces, Graecia facunda docebit."[5] "Graecia facunda" meant Salerno and Syracuse, Tarsus and Antioch, which he says he visited, and the centers of learning in northern Spain which he does not mention. All were concerned with the transmission of Greek knowledge from Arabic versions and commentaries.

What did medieval England know about the Arabs before Adelard of Bath made his plea on behalf of Arabian learning in the first decades of the twelfth century?

The Venerable Bede died in 735. Only three years before, Charles

Martel at the battle of Tours had finally stemmed the Muslim thrust into Europe. Bede had been fully aware of the Saracen danger that threatened France since the occupation of Narbonne in 720. An Arab army had crossed the Pyrenees even earlier. This is what we find in the *Ecclesiastical History of the English Nation*:

> The 729th year of the Lord's incarnation there appeared two comets about the sun and struck great terror into the beholders thereof. For one went before the sun at his rising in the morning; the other followed the setting of the sun in the evening, both presaging as it were terrible destruction to the east as well as the west. . . . and they appeared in the month of January, and continued about two weeks. At what time the Saracens, like a very sore plague, wasted France with pitiful destruction, and themselves not long after were justly punished in the same country for their unbelief.[6]

Bede and his Carolingian contemporaries have been praised for the lack of rancor in their remarks about the Saracens[7] but what, perhaps, is more surprising is the lack of curiosity about a colorful enemy who had entrenched himself in the heart of their world. The fundamental indifference about each other afflicted both Christians and Saracens. Even at the height of Muslim power, when Christian embassies from countries beyond the Pyrenees arrived at Cordova, they were welcomed as a manifest sign of Umayyad prestige. But the Arab chroniclers tell us nothing about the reasons that might have prompted the Latins to send embassies to the Muslim court. To the Arabs all northerners were *majūs*—pagans and idolators to be either ignored or conquered.[8]

Bede's awareness, an unusually historical one for his time, did not concern itself with the Saracens beyond the feeling that they were a visitation, a sore plague like other misfortunes which had befallen the Christian world for its sins. There is no trace of information about the nature and origin of these unbelievers who beset Christendom from their base in Spain. When he speaks of the Saracens Bede strikes the keynote of the unvaried theme which resounded throughout the Middle Ages and persisted to the Renaissance: the Saracens must be punished for their unbelief. The nature of this unbelief and of its professors did not stir a flicker of interest in the most comprehensive mind of the time in Latin Europe.

York, which under Egbert (Bede's pupil and friend) superseded Jarrow as the cultural center of the West, had truly international connections and an exceptionally rich library. The manuscripts which Egbert collected were burned by the Danes in 867. The attempt to rebuild the library after the Norman conquest was equally doomed. Every trace of it vanished in 1137 when a great fire consumed the cathedral and most of the town.[9]

Alcuin, who directed the cathedral school and library following his master Aelbert, has left us enthusiastic verses in praise of the library in which he enumerates some of its treasured possessions. A French scholar has concluded from this "catalogue" that the York library, in the eighth century, had owned books in Greek, Hebrew, and Arabic.

> There shalt thou find the volumes that contain
> All of the ancient fathers who remain;
> There all the Latin writers make their home
> With those that glorious Greece transferred to Rome,—
> The Hebrews draw from their celestial stream,
> And Africa is bright with learning's beam.[10]

It is doubtful that Alcuin's line "Africa lucifluo vel quidquid lumine sparsit" (or, what Africa has spread abroad with light-giving lamp) warrants an assumption of Arabic manuscripts in England at so early a date. But, significantly, it shows an awareness of African learning as distinct from Latin, Greek, and Hebrew which need not necessarily be interpreted as referring only to the Christian theologians of Rome and Byzantine Africa. In the early Middle Ages, Africa, quite literally, fed the luminaria, the lamps of churches, schools, and libraries by the olive oil that it produced and exported.[11] The Muslim conquest may have put an end to commercial activities if we follow Henri Pirenne.[12] Yet the metaphor of the lamp fed by African oil was still vivid in Alcuin's mind and probably expressed an actually continuing intercourse, the Arab raids notwithstanding.

Alcuin was, of course, aware of Arab Africa when he was writing his verses on the saints of the archbishopric of York. In one of his letters from the court of Charlemagne written in 790, he mentions the rule of the Saracens: "The leaders and officers of our Most Christian King have taken a great part of Spain from the Saracens, about three hundred miles along the seacoast. But, the shame of it! Those same accursed Saracens, also called Agarenes, hold control all over Africa and much of greater Asia."[13]

So far as we know, the Carolingian court was unaffected by the intrusions of the East on its doorstep beyond the military and political encounters. Alcuin's designation of the Saracens as "Agareni ab Agar" is taken from the *Etymologies* of Isidore of Seville[14] and, like the rest of Carolingian "new" learning, followed the beaten path of patristic literature. More interesting is Alcuin's reference, in a letter to the emperor from Tours, to a reported disputation between the heretical Spanish bishop Felix of Urgel and a Saracen, a first hint of an interest in Islam.[15] Inevitably, there were new stimuli in the air which stirred into new life the standard questions about the nature of the universe contained in Isidore.

The "Codex Toletanus" of Isidore's *Etymologies* contains glosses in Arabic that date from the eighth century.[16]

There is a restless spirit of inquiry in Alcuin and the school of York which foreshadows the peregrinations of Adelard of Bath that finally led him to his *Arabum studia*. Quite literally, Adelard's way began at Laon, a school which owed its existence to Alcuin. An uncommon interest in astronomy is characteristic of York. Alcuin writes of Aelbert: "My master very often used to say to me, 'They were the wisest of men who discerned these arts [the zodiac and calculations of astronomical time] in Nature. It is a great disgrace for us to let them die out in our time!'"[17] It is virtually certain that texts on astronomy, medicine, and natural science other than Pliny were available at the York library.[18] "You asked me about the tides of the sea and their action on the soil," writes Coena, archbishop of York (767–81) to Raymond Lull in Germany—an earlier namesake of the famous Lull—who has asked him for books on natural science, "nothing can be ascertained about this, and all is uncertain. The books on cosmography have not yet come to hand. . . ."[19]

When Coena was writing, the translations from the Greek had begun at the court of al-Mansur. Ptolemy's cosmography was translated into Arabic about 800;[20] it took another four hundred years for it to reach and dominate Western thought as the most important acquisition of Arabian science.

WALCHER OF MALVERN AND PETRUS ALFONSI

> And dost thou not see that the stars in the heavens are without number, and yet none of them but the sun and the moon are subject to eclipses?
>
> [*Disciplina Clericalis*]

The influence of *Arabum studia* in the West begins with the names of stars and astronomical instruments, as is evident from the earliest Latin-Arabic glossary.[21] Like all civilizations in the history of mankind, medieval Europe desired an accurate calendar "and when the astrolabe was introduced from the Arabs it was immediately recognized as a measuring instrument which could be used to correct old and inaccurate data."[22] The *Liber de astrolabio* ascribed to Gerbert, the philosopher-pope Sylvester II, in the second half of the tenth century, has Arabic terminology. In his letters Gerbert expressly mentions treatises that, partly at least, were translations from the Arabic. If one is to believe William of Malmesbury, whose *Gesta regum* appeared about 1125, Gerbert studied mathematics at Barcelona and penetrated as far as Cordova "*causa sophiae*."[23] In the eleventh century Lorraine had established itself as the chief center for the study of astronomy and the abacus, the first knowledge of which, according to William of Malmesbury, Gerbert also brought from the Saracens. In England, the abacus was known to members of the curia regis under William the Conqueror and William Rufus and was introduced by Lotharingian abacists who were promptly appointed to ecclesiastical positions to relieve the "sweating calculators."[24] (See figure 1.)

The earliest example of Arabic astronomy in England casts its light far ahead into the future on two particularly significant landmarks in English literature and thought: Malvern, the priory of William Langland, author of *Piers Plowman*, and Chaucer's treatise on the astrolabe.

In 1092, Walcher, prior of Malvern, observed the eclipse of the moon and fixed it accurately by means of the astrolabe, one instrument of Arabic astronomy already in his possession. Walcher was using the instrument in its Moorish form as devised in Toledo. It consisted of a single tablet with two small subsidiary pieces and was named after az-Zarqali, a contemporary eleventh-century Arab astronomer in Spain. In the excited account of his new experiment Walcher mentions three of the instrument's points by their Arabic names, Almagrip, Almeri, and Almucantaraz, which in Chaucer, explaining the astrolabe to little Lewis three hundred years later, appear as "aziumtz, almury and almycanteras."[25]

Walcher was a Lotharingian by birth and had traveled in Italy in 1091 where he also saw an eclipse. But it is clear that the astrolabe came into his hands only in England, for in Italy he had not even a clock (horologium) to determine the exact time. All he knew was that he saw the eclipse in the *western* part of the sky shortly before dawn.[26] On his return from the Continent, he compared notes with another monk who had seen the eclipse in the *east*, still before midnight. There was therefore a considerable difference in the measuring of time between Italy and "this our island of England."[27]

The observation of an eclipse of the moon and the ensuing discussion of a difference in time between two geographical points are stages of the greatest significance in the introduction of Arabian science into Europe.

> The Arab astronomers devoted special attention to the exact calculation of the frequency of eclipses . . . , as they made use of it to ascertain the difference in longitude between two places on the earth. They worked out tables (based on Ptolemy) which gave the times of the beginning and ends of the eclipse for various parts of the earth as well as the area of the moon's disc covered.[28]

Walcher of Malvern's experiment in the use of the astrolabe is the earliest recorded in the West. It is strictly in line with the whole Arabian tradition of the astronomical sciences.

The accurate determination of time and place by the moon and stars naturally flourished in a Near Eastern civilization whose religious law required five prayers a day at regular intervals in the direction of Mecca and whose calendar followed the lunar year. Bede, too, in "the earliest and fullest account which we possess of any native Teutonic calendar," explains that the Angli calculated their months by the course of the moon and therefore called them "monaþ."[29] Walcher's newly found method, the "eclipse method," of calculating astronomical time was therefore at the very heart of the new learning acquired from the Arabs and first brought to England before its general adoption in the West. It continued to be the most popular way of finding latitudes and longitudes until the sixteenth century.

Walcher is also the first "translator" of Petrus Alfonsi, physician, astronomer, philosopher, best known as the author of the *Disciplina Clericalis*, a converted Spanish Jew by the name of Moshe Sephardi, whose sojourn in England in the reign of Henry I is still mysterious. The *Disciplina Clericalis*, which "Petrus Alfonsus, a servant of Christ Jesus" wrote for the benefit of Christians, is the first collection of oriental tales composed in the West for Westerners (see below, chapter 5). Peter says that divine inspiration prompted him to "translate" the book into Latin. He composed it partly from the sayings of philosophers, partly from Arabic proverbs and Arabian tales both in prose and verse, and partly from fables of birds and animals. The moral purpose of the *Disciplina* is contained in its name—a rule of life. It is drawn from the worldly wisdom of an Arab who admonishes his son before his death and also contains advice from a master to his pupil. The moral is embedded in tales and connecting links of dialogue between the narrator and his listener. The illustrating tales and exempla are of oriental origin, some of them biblical. But Petrus says he has endeavored to exclude everything "that is contrary to our belief or different from our faith."[30]

The importance of Petrus Alfonsi's *Disciplina Clericalis* as a milestone in the development of medieval literature cannot be exaggerated. Its influence swept Europe with the force of new life. The *Disciplina* created a new kind of fiction, the medieval tale, and inspired collections of wise sayings and exempla; it opened the way for a stream of oriental stories, themes and motifs, and introduced the frame tale to Western Europe.[31] When Chaucer, in the *Canterbury Tales*, quotes "Piers Alphonce,"[32] he points to the true source from which much of his own material was derived, though indirectly, through French and Italian translations, Latin adaptations, and an infinite variety of versions that incorporated free-floating fragments of Petrus Alfonsi's literary masterpiece.

The fame of the *Disciplina Clericalis* rests on secure foundations. What, however, is not yet clearly visible to students of medieval literature is its author's unique stature as an émigré scholar and scientist whose native education comprised the whole range of the Arabo-Hebraic culture of Spain and his extraordinary function in bringing this heritage directly to England. The Wife of Bath's healthy reliance on experience versus authority indirectly stems from the work of Piers Alphonce who, in the first half of the twelfth century, flung the principles of Arab experimental science directly into the lap of England and her wandering scholars in France.

The story of Arabic science in England is centered around Petrus Alfonsi. His connection with the first Latin translation of al-Khwarizmi's astronomical tables by Adelard of Bath, Walcher's and Petrus Alfonsi's contemporary, has, in recent years, come more and more to the fore, particularly in the work of the Spanish scholar Millás Vallicrosa.[33] Moses the Spaniard, alias Petrus Alfonsi, royal physician at the court of Henry I, emerges as the first teacher of Arabian astronomy in England whose influence between 1092, the year of Walcher's experiment, and 1126, the date of Adelard's tables, transformed the Lotharingian aptitudes imported from the Continent into truly original accomplishments whose far-reaching ramifications in the scientific and intellectual development of Europe are still embedded in a complex maze.

Petrus Alfonsi is one of the line of brilliant Jewish physicians who served caliphs, kings, and emperors both in Orient and Occident. Moshe Sephardi was converted to Christianity in his forty-fourth year, at Huesca, on St. Peter's day, June 29, 1106, and was named after his godfather, the king of Aragon, whom he calls "the glorious emperor of Spain."[34] His sponsor was Alfonso I, el Batallador, who aspired to the throne of Castile after his marriage to a Castilian princess who succeeded her father in 1109. Alfonso I of Aragon is therefore sometimes called Alfonso VII of Castile. We know that Petrus Alfonsi was Alfonso of Castile's physician, but it may have been that Alfonso VI of Castile, conqueror of Toledo, Alfonso of Aragon's father-in-law, also employed him.

Moshe Sephardi became a Christian at the height of his career and prestige. His conversion may have been due to the influence of Cluniac monks. Their missionary zeal in Spain, particularly strong at the court of Alfonso VI who had an Arab wife and was therefore especially susceptible to religious pressure, led to the first translation of the Koran by the Englishman Robert of Ketton.

At the time of Moshe Sephardi's conversion only ten years had passed since Huesca had been reclaimed from the Muslims. Until 1096, when he was thirty-four, Petrus Alfonsi had spent his life in the midst of a flourishing Muslim environment. His godfather Alfonso of Aragon conquered Tudela on the Ebro and in 1115 signed an agreement with the Jews of the town in which he specified under what conditions they would enjoy his protection.[35] A similar charter of protection to Jews ("or at least to certain individuals")[36] was issued by Henry I of England whose physician Petrus Alfonsi subsequently became.

Apparently Petrus left Spain soon after his conversion. We discover him as the author of a polemical treatise *Contra Judaeos* composed soon after his baptism. The *Dialogue of Peter and Moses* shows the state of dissension between his two selves, the Jew Moses and the Christian Peter:

> Librum autem totum distinxi per dialogum, ut lectoris animus promptior fiat ad intelligendum. In tutandis etiam Christianorum rationibus nomen quo modo Christianus habeo, posui: rationibus vero adversarii confutandis, nomen quod ante baptismum habueram, id est Moysem.[37]

The work is a violent rejection of Judaism and its interpretation of the prophetic books—an attack whose echoes resounded in the Hebrew literature of medieval Spain, especially in the work of Petrus Alfonsi's younger contemporary and fellow countryman, the Jewish astronomer Abraham bar Hiyya Sephardi, of Barcelona.[38]

The treatise, however, also devoted an entire dialogue to a polemic against Islam, for the question is asked why Petrus, living among Muslims, did not become a Muslim. Petrus Alfonsi's exposition is thus the source from which most of the *accurate* information about Islam first entered the Latin world, for example, the dazzlingly sensuous picture of the Muslim paradise—a Land of Cockayne—which became so popular with medieval writers (see below, chapter 6).

Petrus establishes the pagan origin of the Kaaba, the holy black stone in Mecca which is the center of Muhammadan worship, and connects the hajj, the duty of pilgrimage, with a pagan festival of the sun—statements on which later medieval writers built their idea of Islam as idolatry.[39] Petrus Alfonsi himself never questioned the genuine monotheism of Islam, but he rightly attributed it to the influence of Judaism and Christianity. He expanded the Bahira legend, known from Islamic tradition —that Muhammad as a youth had been instructed in Christianity by a Nestorian monk—to include the idea that a heretical Jew had also influenced the founder of Islam. We do not know what written sources he used for his statements but they are as authoritative and accurate as his insistence on the Hebrew text of the Bible.[40]

The "Dialogus Petri cognomento Alphonsi, ex Judaeo Christiani, et Moysi Judaei" exercised a considerable influence in England,[41] though Petrus is entirely unrepresentative of later polemical writers who made use of him. The work was imitated and drawn upon in the frequent disputations against Jews that are standard medieval fare, both in the form of dialogues with Jews and dialogues on the subject of Judaism between master and pupil, a safe form of debate from the Christian point of view as the antagonist did not have to be made dramatically convincing and knowledge from the inside like Petrus Alfonsi's could be conveniently ignored. The first reference in England is in the *Dialogus* of Bartholomew of Exeter, "but it is to be noted that Bartholomew had already got away from this form of a dispute between Christian and Jew."[42] Petrus Alfonsi's influence is clearly marked in Peter of Cornwall (1197–1221), fourth prior of the Augustinian Priory of Holy Trinity, Aldgate, in London, who wrote the "Disputation of Peter of Cornwall against Symon the Jew." Several passages that show a knowledge of Hebrew and the literature of the Jews have been taken from Petrus Alfonsi's *Dialogus*.[43] Peter also quotes Petrus Alfonsi directly and, most important, mentions another work by him, *Humanum proficuum*, which has not yet been identified and which contains references to the *Secret of Secrets*.[44]

There is, however, one important difference between Petrus Alfonsi and the Christian theologians who imitated him. Petrus Alfonsi was a scientist and a truly learned man addressing himself to other learned men, Christians, Jews, and Muslims alike—a new stance in Western scholarship. Like all Jews living in medieval Spain, he considered a familiarity with Islam as a normal part of his heritage. He was thoroughly versed in Hebrew and Arabic, took care to separate the factual elements from the critical, and imbued his polemics with a range of philosophical and scientific learning whose repercussions on the intellectual history of medieval Europe, and in particular England, have not yet been fully gauged (see below, chapter 5). Apart from the knowledge of Islam from original sources, Petrus's *Dialogus* contains much rabbinic and cabbalistic material which became fully available to the West only in later forms.[45] Petrus Alfonsi was the first to give Christians an insight into these writings—a useful tool in the increasingly bitter and threatening polemics against the Jews. Most significantly, however, the twelve dialogues between Peter and Moses reflect the astronomical learning of the Arabs which Petrus was the first to bring to the attention of the Latins on their own ground.

Thus, an interpretation of a biblical passage turns into an astronomical exposition in which Peter subjects Moses to various mathematical calculations that are later taken up in Petrus Alfonsi's astronomical work. Moses rises to the new knowledge with surprising alacrity—to the pleasure of lecturing master Peter: "Laetor te rei capere veritatem."[46]

The passage is 2 Esdras 9 : 6: "Exercitus coeli supplicat tibi" (the host of heaven adores thee). In the Hebrew text, which Peter undoubtedly had in mind, the meaning is explicit: the hosts of heaven bow to thee.[47] Peter's comment on this is an excellent example both of his familiarity with an uncommon rabbinical tradition, probably transmitted by Babylonian Jews who went to Spain, and his original application of the new astronomy to biblical exegesis. He derides the literal-mindedness and ignorance of Jewish scholars—"vestri doctores"—who take the text to mean that God's abode is in the West. For the stars (the hosts of heaven) descend to the West, they say, and thus bow to God. Peter explains that "west" and "east" are not absolutes. They are not the same to all men. What is "east" to one may be "west" to another. In addition, the hours of sunset and sunrise vary in different regions and the problem is how to calculate these differences in time and how to determine the longitudes of different locations. Peter then puts Moses through an elaborate series of calculations of different times at cities 30° east and 30° west of the hypothetical city of Arin,[48] the sort of Arabian knowledge that, as we know from the *Quaestiones Naturales*, particularly aroused the admiration of Adelard of Bath.

The city of Arin itself is a new contribution to the cosmological learning of the West. Petrus Alfonsi was also the author of a climate-map (see figure 2). It shows the mythical "civitas" Arin, "the zero meridian of Hindu astronomy," considered as the navel of the world by medieval Arab geographers; it gives the south at the top above the city of Arin, the seven habitable climates below, and the extreme northern zone, "uninhabitable from the cold," at the foot—all characteristic features of Arab cartography.[49] In the *Dialogus* Petrus Alfonsi seems to be the first writer among the Latins to show the conceptions of Arab cosmography, which had its origin in Greek science and particularly in Ptolemy, whom astronomers like al-Khwarizmi, working at the court of the caliph al-Ma'mun in Baghdad, had improved and corrected. Bede, who describes the five climates or zones that encircle the world, was following Macrobius.[50]

We know what Petrus Alfonsi thought of Macrobius from a "letter" which he addressed to the peripatetics throughout France (per Franciam) —the only copy of which is found in England as a preface to an astronomical treatise by "Petrus Alfonsi, servant of Jesus Christ and translator of this book." Petrus condemns the lazy reliance on old authorities of which the Latins are guilty and addresses himself to the wandering scholars in search of astronomical learning. He describes himself as their brother and fellow student (frater eorum et condiscipulus) but points out that astronomy is an art with which "all of the Latins generally" are unfamiliar, though he himself has been diligently occupied with it for a long time. He rebukes those among the Latin scholars who are content to base their studies on old Latin authorities like Macrobius instead of following where their own observations and experiments lead. If they do not heed his advice, it is only because of pride and laziness, says Petrus. He is willing and eager to teach them. What he proposes to do is to bring astronomy to them in their own land and save them the hardship of travel in distant regions in pursuit of that rare and precious science. His aim in writing the book is both scholarly and moral. To the "peripatetics nourished by the milk of philosophy everywhere throughout France" he wants to reveal the beauty of Arabic astronomy. For himself, he wishes to prepare "a perpetual name after death."[51]

It is precisely after rehearsing the uses of old learning, grammar, dialectic, arithmetic, and logic that Petrus Alfonsi extols the glories of Arabic astronomy. Even medicine is dependent on astronomy, says the royal physician, for living bodies are affected by change and the revolution of time that it is the business of astronomy to observe and measure. In Petrus's letter and treatise there are no allusions to any previous Latin translation of any other astronomical work. They were probably written before 1126, the date of Adelard's preface to his translation of al-Khwarizmi's tables.[52] In Adelard we find the idea of the city of Arin uncritically adopted as fact. He emphasizes that the chief places in every country might be determined by the meridian of Arin, as had been done by the Saracens.[53] By now there are signs of enthusiasm for Arabic science at Western schools and there are enough students of the new astronomy to require a textbook.

We do not know when or under what circumstances Petrus Alfonsi came to England. He is described as the "medicus" of Henry I and probably settled there ten years after Henry's accession, in the year 1110, which, because of his disappearance from Spanish records, is the reported year of his death.[54] It is clear that Petrus Alfonsi left Spain soon after his conversion, and it may well be that he could not bear the opprobrium of the Jewish community of his native land of which he must have been a distinguished member and which his baptism and his *Dialogus* had outraged. The manner in which he carried his knowledge of Spanish-Arabian science to the heart of the Latin world reminds one of the most distinguished contemporary Jewish scholars. Abraham bar Hiyya of Barcelona and Abraham ibn Ezra of Tudela considered it their mission to spread the new learning among the Jews of France and England for whom they made Hebrew translations of Arabic mathematical and astronomical treatises. In his book *Megilat ha-Mgaleh* (Scroll of the Revealer) written in 1129, Abraham bar Hiyya refutes the type of arguments against Judaism and its prophetic books which we find in Petrus Alfonsi's *Dialogus*. Like Petrus, he is prompted by the feeling that the ignorant have to be educated in Arabic science.[55] In the preface to his cosmographical treatise *Tsurat ha-Arets* (The Shape of the Earth), Abraham bar Hiyya explains that he felt called upon to spread the knowledge of Arabic science among Hebrew readers in France.[56]

Abraham bar Hiyya is closely associated with the work of translating from the Arabic that was concentrated in Provence, at Toulouse and Béziers.[57] The most famous Jewish astronomer of the time, Abraham ibn Ezra of Tudela, was in Narbonne in or shortly before 1139; he stopped in

the town of Béziers. In 1158 he was in England. "'Twas in the year 4919/
1158 A.D. at midnight, on Sabbath eve, the 14th of Tebeth/Dec. 7th that
I, Abraham Ibn Ezra, a Spaniard, was in one of the cities of the island
called the 'corner of the earth' Angle-terr for it is in the last of the seven
divisions of the inhabited earth. . . ."[58]

Petrus Alfonsi's relationship to other Jewish scholars in Spain before his
conversion is completely obscure. But the feeling that the ignorant have to
be educated in Arabic science must have had its roots in his knowledge of
the activities of Jewish scholars among Jewish communities outside Spain.
Petrus Alfonsi is the first Christian to express a sense of mission in spreading Arabic astronomy among the Latins in the land of the Franks.

Walcher must have come across Petrus Alfonsi in England between
1112 and 1120. For the lunar tablets that accompany Walcher's account
of the lunar eclipse of October 1092 "are worked out by the clumsy methods of Roman fractions."[59] This treatise, "De experientia scriptoris,"
was written between 1108 and 1112. The second treatise, written in England in 1120, is the one which claims to be a Latin translation of Petrus
Alfonsi: "Sententia Petri Ebrei cognomento Anphus de dracone quam
dominus Walcerus prior Malvernensis ecclesie in latinam transtulit linguam."[60] Here Walcher has already adopted the Arabic methods of
astronomical calculation and has transposed them to the meridian of
England, the country in which he lives. Most important, as Millás Vallicrosa has pointed out, he has translated Arabic terminology: "draco,
caput et cauda draconis" (dragon's head and dragon's tail), which both in
Arabic and Hebrew designate the path of ascent and descent of the
moon.[61] Indeed, a copy of "De dracone" is found together with the *Disciplina Clericalis* in a manuscript that ascribes both works to Petrus alone.
There is also an allusion to Petrus Alfonsi's use of astronomical tables
which seems to be connected with the contemporary Latin translation of
al-Khwarizmi's astronomical tables by Adelard of Bath.[62]

The personal relation between Walcher and Petrus is emphasized at
the end where Walcher tells of certain questions which he put to Petrus
Alfonsi and the answers which he received. Most convincing is the sadness
of his "master" Petrus, which Walcher reports, at having left his books
with all the new knowledge behind in a country across the sea, which can
only be Spain (". . . dicebat et codices suos in quibus de his et de aliis
pluribus omnia certa habebat se trans mare tunc temporis reliquisse").[63]
Petrus was therefore the teacher who showed Walcher the position of the
sun, moon, and nodes at noon on April 1, 1120.

The work of Petrus Alfonsi in England is also seen in a set of astronomical tables common in treatises based on the Arabic which indicate the
date of October 1, 1116. The tables are part of an astronomical treatise
preserved in a twelfth-century manuscript at Corpus Christi College,

Oxford.[64] The work is "undoubtedly," according to Neugebauer, based on the astronomical tables of al-Khwarizmi in the version generally attributed to Adelard of Bath. The text contains an introduction in which the author identifies himself in the familiar way of the *Disciplina Clericalis*: "Dixit petrus anfulsus seruus ihesu christi translatorque huius libri." He says that he has labored hard—"magno labore . . . et summo studio"— to translate the work from Arabian, Persian, and Egyptian sources for the benefit of the Latins. The treatise contains four chronological chapters by Petrus Alfonsi, presents the Arabic names of three Muslim months in a Spanish pronunciation, and has frequent references to Petrus Alfonsi both in the body of the text and in later marginal comments. Several groups of the later marginal notes relate the manuscript to the abbeys of Winchester and St. Albans. The annotator apparently had access to a work by Petrus which gave the date as October 1, 1116.[65]

The close agreement with the Latin version of al-Khwarizmi's tables by Adelard of Bath is the most extraordinary aspect of the treatise in the Oxford manuscript. As was noted by Haskins, "there can be no question of two independent versions, for in the explanatory portions the verbal coincidence is exact."[66] Moreover, the work is identical with the astronomical treatise, also in the name of Petrus Alfonsi, which is preceded by his letter to his Latin "fellow students" in France, the only copy of which is also of the twelfth century. In fact, as the text clearly shows, Petrus's introduction in the Oxford manuscript is only an excerpt from the much longer address to the peripatetics to whom he offers his learning.[67]

The problem of authorship and annotation in Corpus Christi 283 is unclear and complicated. Neugebauer has found "that the bulk of the tables is based on a rather unskillful adaptation to non-Islamic conditions: all the Arabic years and months are replaced by Julian years and months" and the manuscript is "not nearest to the Islamic original but on the contrary farthest removed from it."[68] However, Petrus is certain to have composed the tables for the date of October 1, 1116, and to have concerned himself with astronomical calculations in England based on al-Khwarizmi before Walcher's translation of the "Sententia Petri Ebrei . . . de dracone," written in 1120, and before Adelard's translation of al-Khwarizmi's tables in 1126. In the opinion of Millás Vallicrosa the astronomical treatise of 1116 "Dixit Petrus Anfulsus" is the beginning of a translation or a free version of al-Khwarizmi's work by the royal physician, later revised by Adelard of Bath.[69]

Walcher of Malvern's standing as the first student of Petrus Alfonsi poses an interesting question about the knowledge of Arabic in medieval England. We hear that he "translated" Petrus Alfonsi: "in latinam transtulit linguam." The style of the work is that of a translation from the Arabic.[70] But Walcher's statement, according to Haskins, "must be plainly taken in the general sense of a paraphrase rather than as meaning a version which would require knowledge of Arabic on Walcher's part."[71] We know that "the medieval conception of translation had in general been that of paraphrase."[72] But a paraphrase of what? Petrus Alfonsi's Arabic, Hebrew, or Latin? What made an "Arabist" in medieval English eyes? We know that the occurrence of occasional Greek words in an author seemed to medieval writers sufficiently impressive evidence for a knowledge of Greek, so that Alcuin's knowledge of Greek, for instance, was overestimated, and Bede's, on the other hand, seems exceptional for his time. Even at the height of medieval humanism in the twelfth century, John of Salisbury, who studied Greek in Apulia, shows little knowledge of the language, appealing to John Saracen for help with patrological texts as late as 1166.[73] A knowledge of Hebrew was much more frequent, thanks to the continuing popularity of St. Jerome (who insisted on the need of knowing the Bible in its original text) and to the physical presence of Jews. Hebrew books were much commoner than Greek books in medieval English libraries.[74]

Whatever knowledge of Arabic or Arabic terminology Walcher had was evidently transmitted to him by Petrus Alfonsi. But it must have been a most extraordinary accomplishment nevertheless. We conclude that Walcher was the first native student of Arabic learning in England just as Roger Bacon—"a-t-il lu les livres arabes?"[75]—was the first Latin critic of the work of translation from the Arabic.

ADELARD OF BATH

The official authorship of the first Latin translation of a scientific work made from the Arabic is well known: "Ezich Elkaurezim per Athelardum bathoniensis ex arabico sumptus."[76] The translator, Adelard of Bath, was English and, like Walcher, a contemporary of Petrus Alfonsi; he was also apparently in England at the time. Contrary to traditional opinion, Millás Vallicrosa does not think that Adelard ever went to Spain where he could have worked from the Arabic,[77] though the Latin version of al-Khwarizmi's tables is based on the Spanish edition made by Maslama ibn Ahmad al-Majriti. It retains Cordova as the basic meridian and the Hijra as the basic era. There are also a number of Arabic words, again in a Spanish transliteration, which were left untranslated in the body of the Latin text.[78] Adelard's version was later adapted to the meridian of London by Robert of Ketton, the translator of the Koran and Adelard's younger contemporary. Robert also "set it in order"[79] by translating some of the Arabic words which had been retained and omitting others altogether.

"Conceivably Adelard may have used Peter as an interpreter, after the fashion of the later translators from the Arabic," is the opinion of Haskins.[80] Millás Vallicrosa is more emphatic: he considers Moshe Sephardi (Petrus Alfonsi) as Adelard's collaborator.[81] It was, then, the Spanish physician who initiated a new stage in the writings of Adelard. There is no trace of Arabic material in Adelard's earlier writings, in the Platonic treatise *De eodem et diverso*, or in the *Regulae abaci*, an introduction to arithmetic which is dedicated to "H. suo," probably his young pupil Henry Plantagenet at the court of Henry I.[82] As in Walcher of Malvern, the stage of the fusion of Lotharingian tradition with Arabic influences is clearly discernible. The *Regulae abaci* traces the path marked by the introduction of the abacus into the English exchequer. The translation of al-Khwarizmi's tables is dated 1126, and it seems to have been accomplished in England, on Adelard's return from abroad, following an encounter with Petrus Alfonsi who would then have been sixty-four years old.

What we know of Adelard of Bath has been gathered from his own writings with one single exception. An entry in the Pipe Roll of 1130, the first year when Pipe Roll records began to be kept, states that the sum of 4s 6d was paid to "Adelardus de Bada" from the revenues of Wiltshire. The sum represents a pardon of a collective murder fine imposed by royal writ and is the kind of favor customarily granted to those in the employment of the court.[83]

Earlier writers, like Pits, Leland, and Tanner, report that "Athelardus Badunensis" was a "monachus" (probably confusing him with Adelard of Blandinium who wrote a Life of St. Dunstan a century earlier), and say that he traveled in France, Germany, Italy, Spain, Egypt, and Arabia, taught at Laon, lived in the reign of Henry I, and died in 1130[84]— obviously as inaccurate a statement as the reported death of Petrus Alfonsi in 1110.

Adelard depicts himself as wearing a green cloak and an emerald ring, and gives us the following details of his curriculum vitae: his "patria" was England, his "natale solum" Bath. While still a "iuvenis" he traveled to the Norman kingdom of Sicily in pursuit of knowledge.[85]

His first search therefore was for Greek philosophy and natural science, the sort of learning which flourished in Sicily and, in 1158, reached its apex when Henricus Aristippus brought the original Greek text of Ptolemy's *Almagest* from Constantinople.

Adelard visited Salerno and southern Italy and met "quendam philosophum Graecum, qui prae ceteris medicinae naturasque rerum disserebat. . . ."[86] The *De eodem et diverso*, from which these passages are taken, was written before 1115 and apparently composed in Syracuse. It has the form of a letter from Adelard to his nephew and is dedicated to William, bishop of Syracuse—"naturally a Norman"—who occupied the office from 1105 to 1115.[87] The scene is laid in Tours where Adelard had

parted from his nephew the year before, to the nephew's great conster-
nation: he disapproved of his uncle's decision to travel in search of learning and accused him of "levity and inconstancy." We have the familiar
setting of medieval allegory: a conversation with a wise old man with
whom Adelard discusses astronomical questions, a solitary walk far from
the madding crowd by the bank of the Loire soothed by the perfume of
flowers and the sound of the river, and, finally, a meeting with two allegorical ladies and their companions, Philosophia and Philocosmia, who
engage him in a discussion of the one and the many, the spirit versus the
senses. The work is permeated by Plato's *Timaeus* and Boethius's *Consolation of Philosophy* and there is no trace of Arabic science. There are a few
Greek but no Arabic words. Adelard had already traveled but he had not
gone farther than Sicily.

A continuation of his journey, reported in the *Quaestiones Naturales*, took
Adelard to the heterogeneous Christian civilizations of the East, to Tarsus
in Cilicia, Antioch in Syria, and a little Armenian town called Manistra
in the district of Antioch where he experienced an earthquake. Apparently he also reached Jerusalem where he made an experiment on
Mount Moriah, if, indeed, he is the anonymous author who describes how
he determined the place where the sun was directly overhead on "Mount
Amor" about the time of the summer solstice and how he found the center
of the earth. The anonymous record of this experiment gives us a chronological indication that fits Adelard to perfection: "Et tempore quo men-
suravi hoc est annus. xxxviiii. et vinum non bibi, oculi mei somno satiati
non fuerunt, ne exuperaveram in eo quod inquirebam."[88] If Adelard is
speaking here—an assumption which is strengthened by allusions to the
Platonic *De eodem et diverso* and Salerno medical doctrine which also
appears in the *Quaestiones Naturales*—he must have been thirty-nine years
old in 1115, for the same manuscript contains tables for the lunar cycle of
the years 1136 to 1154. Adelard, then, may have been born in 1076, which
would have made him fourteen years younger than Petrus Alfonsi. However, all we can do with any certainty is to adopt the opinion of Haskins:
"The painstaking character of the experiment is interesting, and it falls
in with Adelard's habit of mind and his known travels in Syria."[89]

The extension of Adelard's study tour to Cilicia and Syria was probably due to the realization that had come to him in Sicily: the search for
Greek science led farther to the East and ultimately to the Arabs. There
is, however, no reason to suppose that his travels took him outside the
realm of Norman influence. There is no evidence that Adelard ever went
to Spain. He does not mention such a journey—an omission that is unlikely had he been there—and the name "Goth" which is applied to him
in some manuscripts[90] and has been taken to refer to a stay in northern
Spain is probably a corruption of "Bath." Adelard's work bears clear

imprints of Spanish Arabic scholarship, but, as has already been pointed out, these may have been acquired in England.

Adelard returned to England "in the reign of Henry, son of William," having evidently left it before 1100. The state of affairs that he found there filled him with misery. We know this from his outburst in the *Quaestiones Naturales* which he composed, again for the benefit of his nephew, in praise of Arabic learning.

The *Quaestiones Naturales*, in the form of a dialogue between uncle and nephew, is essentially a report of Adelard's grand tour and reflects his excitement at the new scientific outlook of the Arabs which had left the Latin schools far behind. There is as yet no crystallization of any specific knowledge that Adelard may have acquired in astronomy or mathematics or any other branch of learning beyond a general enthusiasm for the experimental methods of Arabic science. Adelard was primarily a mathematician, as we know from his praise of the bishop of Syracuse for his outstanding mathematical learning and from Adelard's own preoccupation with Euclid. He may well have been an officer of the Exchequer for a time who became tutor to the future Henry II. The personal relationship to the royal court and Henry is seen in a book on falconry—a royal sport—that he composed,[91] and especially in one of his last works which marks the consummation of Adelard's development as a scholar. It is a book on the astrolabe, written for Henry, "Heynrice, cum sis regis nepos," between 1142 and 1146. Henry, to whose "infantia" Adelard refers, was living in his uncle's household at Bristol between the ages of nine and thirteen.[92] This *Libellus magistri Alardi bathoniensis de opere astrolapsus* is a true reflection of the whole range of development which Adelard and Western learning had undergone.

The brilliant tradition which he has discovered "among the Arabs" is being passed on: "Inde fit ut non solum ea que Latinorum scriptis continentur intelligendo perlegas, sed et Arabum sententias super spera et circulis stellarumque motibus intelligere velle presumas."[93] The admonition addressed to Latin scholars by Petrus Alfonsi has become part of the Western heritage and is being handed down to a young Englishman of royal blood.

The intriguing question about Adelard's connections with his younger English contemporaries, Robert of Ketton and Daniel of Morley, who did go to Spain, cannot yet be answered. The nature of Adelard's relations with foreign scholars both abroad and in England is also completely obscure. Aside from Petrus Alfonsi there is the link with Berachyah ha-Nakdan who translated Adelard's *Quaestiones Naturales* into Hebrew a generation later and who was probably of English origin.[94]

The dependence on the Spanish schools of Arabic learning, reinforced by actual residence in Spain and a knowledge of Arabic, is clearly seen a generation later when the transmission of Arabic science to England is in full swing with Robert of Ketton, Daniel of Morley, Roger of Hereford, Alfred of Sarechel, and Michael Scot who continued Adelard's aim of "Arabum studia scrutari." Most of these Englishmen went to Spain in search of astronomical and mathematical treatises and took an active part in the systematic work of translation in which Latin, Mozarab, and Jewish scholars collaborated at Toledo and other seats of learning in the valley of the Ebro and the region of the Pyrenees. For by the middle of the twelfth century the beginning disintegration of Muslim rule in Spain had finally brought the Latin and Islamic worlds into intimate contact.

ROBERT OF KETTON

The first Englishman whom we find in Spain pursuing the work of translation from the Arabic is Robert of Ketton, as a contemporary twelfth-century manuscript calls him,[95] of Ketton in Rutland, who revised Adelard's version of al-Khwarizmi's astronomical tables for the meridian of London and is the first Latin translator of the Koran.

When we first meet him in northern Spain, in the region of the Ebro, Robert identifies himself as "Angligena."[96] In later manuscripts of his alchemical, mathematical, and astronomical works he appears as "Robertus Cestrensis," of Chester—a connection that is still unexplained.[97]

What we know of him has been gleaned from his own writings, the works of his friend and collaborator Herman the Dalmatian, and particularly from the correspondence and prefaces of Peter the Venerable, the Cluniac abbot.

In 1141, while on a tour of inspection of Cluniac monasteries in Spain, Peter, on the lookout for Latins with a knowledge of Arabic—"contuli ergo me ad peritos linguae arabicae"—discovered Robert of Ketton and Herman the Dalmatian (or Slav), a particularly gifted "scholasticus," in the region of the Ebro. The two friends were "students of the art of astrology" and both expert in Arabic, as Peter described them to Bernard of Clairvaux.[98] He persuaded them "with entreaty and a high fee" to abandon their studies in the interest of a higher good: the fight against "the vile heresy of Mahomet," a thorough knowledge of which they would make available to equip the ignorant Latins for their missionary work.

Peter the Venerable's account of his visit to Spain is the first notice we have of Robert of Ketton. In 1143, writing to Bernard of Clairvaux on completion of the corpus of treatises on Islam and Muhammad which he had initiated, he refers to Robert, "nunc" archdeacon of Pamplona. Robert is described in the same way by Peter of Poitiers, the abbot's secretary and editorial assistant, who accompanied the abbot to Spain and stayed behind to arrange and edit the translated material in the rendering of which he was also an active collaborator.[99] It is clear that Peter the Venerable felt a great urgency in the matter. Again and again he mentions the trouble and expense—"magno studio . . . et impensis"—which he had to undergo to get the work done. He had convinced himself, evidently from viewing the missionary activity of Cluny on the spot, that a knowledge of the Koran and Islamic theological literature had become imperative to Christians.

Peter proceeded in the skilled way of all good propagandists, sparing neither effort nor money and enlisting the aid of first-rate scholars, though their zeal in disclosing the treasures of Muslim libraries, as we know from Robert's and Herman's prefaces,[100] had a very different origin and aim. It sprang from the thirst for Arabic science that we find in Adelard. Once harnessed in the service of Christian polemics, however, they out-Petered Peter in professing the contempt for Islam and its ways which was expected from every good Christian. In spite of the precious and self-consciously "literary" style that Robert displays in his letters to Peter the Venerable and which has jarred the sensibilities of French scholars,[101] he can hardly be accused of showing less tolerance towards Islam than the abbot of Cluny. His disgust at "the detestable history of Mahumet" and "the stagnant swamp" of the Saracen "sect"[102] is no doubt an echo of Peter's, but it is probably also an expression of his suppressed anger at having had to spend his time on religious doctrine and theology instead of on what really concerned him—astronomical and mathematical science.

The partnership of the two scholars in Spain, the Englishman and the Slav, was close and long-standing. In the preface to his translation of the astrologer al-Kindi's *Judicia* Robert addresses "mi Hermanne" as the one who suggested the work and as an astronomer second to none among the Latins. The form of address is still formal—"vestris nutibus," "voto vestro serviens transtuli."[103] Herman, in his introduction to the astrology of Albumasar, uses "tu" and speaks warmly of the advice given him by Robert about the organization and composition of his work.[104] Robert was obviously the greater stylist, and this may have been the reason why he was chosen to translate the pièce de résistance, the Koran. He may also have been the younger of the two, and his "vester" is a sign of respect. In 1144 he speaks of himself as "iuvenis" and marvels at his own temerity to have undertaken so difficult a task as Arabic-Latin translation.[105]

The abbot of Cluny could not have made a better choice for his purpose. Not only were Robert of Ketton and Herman the Dalmatian well versed in Arabic—"periti utriusque linguae"—but they had access to the intimate "chests"—armaria—of the Arabs from which they had gathered an abundance of material. We know from Robert himself that he was deeply engrossed in astronomical and geometrical study when he was

interrupted by Peter. He had "gladly sweated" over Euclid and Theodosius in order to achieve the main aspiration that had prompted both him
and his friend in their journey to Spain—a knowledge of Ptolemy's *Almagest*. Herman, we know, had been in Spain for several years at the time
of Peter the Venerable's visit, for in 1138, he translated from the Arabic
a treatise by the Jewish astrologer Saul ibn Bishr or, as he calls him,
Zael.[106] He must indeed have been "peritissimus" in Arabic by the time
Peter engaged his services. That Robert's knowledge of Arabic was equally good is clear from the fact that it was he who undertook the most difficult and most ambitious portion of Peter the Venerable's enterprise.
While Robert was still rendering the first "authorized" version of the
Koran, Herman had freed himself to continue the pursuit of Ptolemy
which he brought to realization in France. On June 1, 1143, we find him
there finishing a translation of Ptolemy's *Planisphere* from the Arabic text
of Maslama al-Majriti, which he dedicated to his master, Thierry of
Chartres.[107] The importance of the "astrological" work that was post-
poned at the insistence of Peter the Venerable or at the command of
religion, as Robert put it, is seen from the fact that Herman's translation
is the only text of the *Planisphere* which has come down to us. The original,
both in Greek and Arabic versions (including that of Maslama), has been
lost. In the same year, at Béziers, in Languedoc, Herman wrote his only
original composition, *De essentiis*, a philosophical treatise which like his
earlier translation of Albumasar (Abu Ma'shar Ja'far al-Balki) is dedicated to Robert of Ketton: "tu mihi studiarum omnium specialis atque
inseparabilis comes rerumque et actuum per omnia consors unice, mi
Rodberte."[108]

Robert of Ketton makes it quite clear that he was not at all enthusiastic
about sacrificing his scientific preoccupation in order to place his knowledge of Arab "treasures" at the disposal of polemicists. Only a high price
could persuade him to "expose" the Saracen "heresy" to full view, though
he dutifully protests that he was induced to undertake the task by "the
wisdom and spiritual light" of the Cluniac abbot. Like Adelard of Bath
and Walcher of Malvern before him, Robert seems, above all, a man of
reason, fanatical only on request.

In assessing his stature as an Arabist we must also remember that he
was the sole Latin translator of the Koran, the opus magnum in the
Cluniac body of works designed to condemn Islam out of its own mouth.
The researches of Marie Thérèse d'Alverny have made it possible to gain
a clear picture of this collection, for whose composition Peter also engaged
a Mozarab and a Spanish Muslim.

The Mozarab, Petrus Toletanus, knew both Latin and Arabic, but his
Latin was weaker, and the abbot therefore assigned his secretary, Peter of
Poitiers, to help the Mozarab with the Latin and become his "socius."[109]

Petrus Toletanus is responsible for the translation of the "Risalah" of al-Kindi, a "letter" professing to be a contemporary account of a ninth-century controversy on the values of Islam and Christianity and one of the most important documents on early Islam. Petrus Toletanus's version of the Risalah, or Apology, as it is called, "was in fact the greatest Cluniac contribution to the biography of Muhammad and to the history of early Islam."[110]

Among the Arabic writings found by the Christians in Spanish Muslim armaria were, of course, several copies of Muhammad's genealogy as found in the earliest Muslim biography of the Prophet by Muhammad ibn Ishaq and the traditions (ḥadīth) of the life of Muhammad. These entered Peter the Venerable's collection both in a version of Robert of Ketton and a translation by Herman the Dalmatian, "scholasticus subtilis & ingeniosus."[111] Herman's version is entitled "De generatione Machumet et nutritura eius" and was rendered into Latin at León, Spain. Herman was also the translator of the well-known apocryphal "dialogue with Abdia the Jew," an imaginary conversation between Muhammad and four Jewish scholars—"principes Iudaeorum, & magistri in Israel"—led by one Abdia ben Salon. As the Latin preface points out, this "dialogue" had great authority with the Arabs, and Herman is justly praised as "peritissimus utriusque linguae, Latinae scilicet atque Arabicae."[112]

In a twelfth-century manuscript of the Paris Arsenal (no. 1162, see figure 3), which d'Alverny considers the original manuscript of Peter the Venerable's collection, the corpus of translations is opened by Robert of Ketton. It is preceded by an introductory "Summa" of the "heresy and diabolical sect of the Saracens" by Peter the Venerable and his letter to Bernard of Clairvaux "de translatione sua qua fecit transferri ex arabico in latinum."[113]

A letter of Robert of Ketton to Peter introduces the first work of translation proper which is glossed as "Fabule Saracenorum" in the manuscript and is a treatise on the origin of Islam and the life of Muhammad and seven of his successors, including a genealogy, which is not identical with the version of Herman the Dalmatian but is drawn from a similar source and covers similar ground. This work, translated by Robert of Ketton, appears elsewhere as "Chronica mendosa & ridiculosa Saracenorum, de vita Mahometis & successorum eius."[114] Robert thus holds the visible place of honor in the collection. Evidently, he attacked his task by first translating the *Chronica* independently of Herman and then tackled the Koran, a feat which is an extraordinary accomplishment even under the most favorable conditions. His only aid in elucidating the frequent linguistic obscurities of the Koran which still puzzle scholars must have been the Muslim, Muhammad, whom Peter engaged to bear witness to the faithfulness of the commissioned translation—"ut translationi fides plenissima non deesset." Peter mentions the Saracen only once, in the preface to his own "Contra sectam Saracenorum": "Christianis interpretibus etiam Sarracenum adjunxi."[115] As he does not specify his role, it may be assumed that Muhammad was the replica of Peter of Poitiers on the Arabic side: Peter polished and glossed the Latin; Muhammad helped with the Arabic. Robert says that the abbot of Cluny himself helped him with formulations, though this assistance must have been more of a gesture of encouragement and supervision than anything else. At any rate Peter the Venerable was back in France when the translation was finished, having left Peter of Poitiers to collect the material, do the editing, and gloss it to his heart's content.

We know exactly when the translation of the Koran was completed, for Robert's relief was evidently so great that he indulged in a rhetorical explicit:

> Explicit liber legis diabolice Sarracenorum, qui arabice dicitur Alchoran, id est Collectio capitulorum siue preceptorum.
>
> Illustri gloriosissimoque uiro Petro Cluniacensi abbate precipiente, suus angligena Robertus Ketenensis librum istum transtulit, anno Domini millesimo centesimo quadragesimo tercio, anno Alexandri millesimo quadringentesimo tercio, anno Alhigere quingentesimo tricesimo septimo, anno Persarum quingentesimo undecimo.[116]

The work, then, was completed between June 16, the beginning of the Persian year, and July 15, 1143, the beginning of the year 538 of the Hijra. Robert the Englishman was appointed archdeacon of Pamplona before the end of that year.

The next step in Robert's work of translation is a treatise on the composition of alchemy by one Morienus Romanus, who according to the *Fihrist*, the Arabic Book of Chronicles which is the classic medieval dictionary of biographies, was the teacher of the Umayyad prince, Khalid ibn Yazid (635–704) for whom he composed the book at Alexandria.[117] Robert's version is dated February 11, 1144. He says that he has decided to translate the treatise "since what alchemy is and what is its composition, your Latin world does not yet know truly."[118] Robert's preface to this work sheds a clear light on his real feelings about the collaborative enterprise into which he was persuaded and which is now behind him:

> Nomen autem meum in principio Prologi taceri non placuit, ne aliquis hunc nostrum laborem sibi assumeret, et etiam ejus laudem et meritum sibi quasi proprium vendicaret. Quid amplius? humiliter omnes rogo et obsecro, ne quis nostrorum erga meum nomen mentis livore (quod saepe a multis fieri consuevit) tabescat.[119]

He rightly feels that in the difficult work of translation from the Arabic credit should be given where it is due. Was Robert annoyed at the general character of the accolade and the ambiguity of credit given by Peter the Venerable in his prologue to the body of work in which Robert unquestionably had the lion's share? Peter dutifully enumerates the translators by name and praises them for their knowledge of languages and erudition but he fails to attribute each part of the translation—the genealogies, the dialogue with Abdia, the Risalah—clearly to its author and, what is particularly striking, also fails to single out Robert as the main translator of the Koran which, aided by Muhammad and possibly at times by the Mozarab Petrus Toletanus, he was, as we know from his own preface.[120]

At any rate, by 1145 Robert was again deeply engaged in mathematical and astronomical work, for in that year we find him in Segovia translating al-Khwarizmi's *Algebra* which, like his translation of the Koran, broke completely new ground for Latin Europe. The *Book of Algebra and Almucabola*[121] (of "making whole" and "balancing") introduced the name and function of a new branch of mathematics—algebra, from Arabic *jabara*, to restore. The name of the author, al-Khwarizmi, was itself becoming a new concept from the opening sentence ("Dixit algoritmi") of another of his works, the *Arithmetic*. The concept is algorism, Chaucer's "augrim."

Although Robert did not translate al-Khwarizmi's important preface to his work, probably because of the reference to Muhammad, the Prophet—Peter the Venerable's diabolical "heretic"—he had no compunction about translating the usual invocation to the deity at the beginning of the Muslim treatise: "In nomine dei pii et misericordis incipit liber Restaurationis et Oppositionis numeri quem aedidit Mahomet, filius Algaurizin. Dixit Mahomet, Laus deo creatori, qui homini contulit scientiam inueniendi vim numerorum."[122] The practical importance of the *Algebra* to the West is clear from the explicit: "This, then, is the method by which all proposed problems concerning commercial transactions or weights and measures and all related problems are to be solved."

> Praise be to God, beside whom there is no other. Here ends the book of restoration and opposition of number which in the year 1183 [Spanish era] Robert of Chester in the city of Segovia translated into Latin from the Arabic.[123]

Two years later, in 1147, Robert is back in London, writing, like Adelard, a treatise on the astrolabe which by now is the standard trademark of every English "Arabist."[124]

DANIEL OF MORLEY

When Daniel of Morley, the second English scholasticus whom we can follow to Spain, went to Toledo, it was a capital whose first lady was Eleanor, daughter of Henry II of England and wife of Alfonso VIII of Castile, later the victor of the battle of Las Navas de Tolosa (1212) which caused the exodus of half a million Arabs from Spain.[125] The presence of the English queen may have enhanced the attraction of Toledo to English scholars, but the star of its school was a Lombard, Gerard of Cremona (1114–87), the translator of the *Almagest* from the Arabic and "fons lux et gloria cleri."[126] He is called "the father of translators" by Roger Bacon, to whom he was "qui fuit antiquior inter illos."[127] Gerard of Cremona spent most of his life in Toledo. He is named "Toletanus" like John of Spain, who originally hailed from Seville and was one of the Jews "qui ibi erant ex antiquis temporibus."[128] John of Spain, as has already been mentioned, is known for his collaboration with the archdeacon of Segovia, but we also hear that he was composing a treatise on the conversion of Arabic years into Roman at the request of two Englishmen, Glauco and William, of whom there is no other trace.[129]

We learn that Gerard of Cremona came to Toledo in search of Ptolemy's great work on astronomy—"amore tamen almagesti quem apud Latinos minime reperit, Toletum perrexit"[130]—which, as we also know from Robert of Ketton,[131] was the magnet that drew Latin scholars to Spain. But while others came and went, or were interrupted by Peter the Venerable, Gerard remained and dedicated his entire life to the pursuit of *Arabum studia* which, like Chaucer's ideal clerk, he would gladly learn and gladly teach. The stature of his work and of his person among his colleagues remind one of Shakespeare's. He never signed his versions from the Arabic, and a list of his translations was arranged after his death by his faithful "socii" in order to ensure that no strange name was affixed to his books: "cum nulli eorum nomen suum inscripsisset . . . ne libris ab ipso translatis infigatur alienus."[132] Daniel tells us that Gerard was born under the sign of Jupiter, as he learned from his own lips, and therefore considered himself a free man of royal independence and a born king of the spirit. When Daniel speaks of him in 1177, Gerard is already famous as the translator of the *Almagest*—"qui Almagesti latinavit"—his chef d'oeuvre which was to bring the name of Ptolemy's *Syntaxis* within the reach of even the Wife of Bath.

While Daniel was in Toledo, Gerard had begun a series of expositions and translations which were as crucial as the *Almagest* to the development of Western thought. He was engaged in translating Aristotle as interpreted by the Arabs. Daniel of Morley, the Englishman, is the first Latin to mention four previously unknown Aristotelian treatises which he seems to have brought with him among "a multitude of precious books" that he says he acquired in Spain. Three of these works by Aristotle were translated by Gerard of Cremona "Gallipo mixtarabe interpretante," like the *Almagest*.[133]

It was Gerard's fame as a teacher and expounder of Arabic science that gave Toledo its international stature and fame. Daniel found him lecturing to a body of students, like his Muslim predecessors, at the Toledo mosque, which shows that Toledo was the first de facto university in Christian Spain, though it was not an official *studium generale*. Daniel's eyewitness account of the proceedings is a unique medieval document, the effects of which on the intellectual climate of medieval England have not yet been fully probed.

Who was Daniel of Morley? All we know of him is what he says about himself in the only work by him which is extant: "Philosophia magistri danielis de merlai ad iohannem Norwicensem episcopum." He was a native of Morley in Norfolk in the diocese of Norwich, whose bishop, John of Norwich (1175–1200), was his mentor and friend. It is to the bishop that Daniel sings the praises of the Arabs and of Toledo. Like Adelard a generation before him, Daniel went abroad "causa studii." At first, of course, to Paris—of which he paints a most extraordinary picture indeed: "Brutes" occupy university chairs "with grave authority." They have nothing to teach their students. All they do is read from volumes which cannot be carried because of their weight, hold leaden pencils in their hands, and mark books with asterisks and obeli. They stand in their places like statues "because of their ignorance" but nevertheless wish to appear wise on account of that very silence. Finally, when the Paris professors made an attempt to say anything at all, Daniel found them most childish—"infantissimos."

The English scholar fled in horror, and hastened to hear "wiser philosophers of the universe" at Toledo where "the teaching of the Arabs . . . was greatly famous in those days."[134]

Unlike Gerard of Cremona, his master, Daniel must have been born under the sign of Saturn, for his disposition appears to have been choleric. He reports how he heckled Gerard of Cremona and even tried to hide his admiration for the master's knowledge and skill—an attitude to his teachers that Daniel's most distinguished German biographer characterizes as "Respektlosigkeit."[135] It did not seem to have troubled Gerard of Cremona, however, for we find him conducting his collegium like a Muslim faqih, anticipating counterarguments and sharpening his points in a lively encounter with his students.

The scene that Daniel describes took place about 1175 when Gerard, with the help of Ghalib the Mozarab, was completing his version of the *Almagest* and was lecturing on Ptolemy's view of astrology and the fatal influence of the stars. When Gerard of Cremona started on his translation he had probably very little, if any, knowledge of Arabic. The burden of authenticity must therefore have lain on the Mozarab who, we hear from Daniel in the body of his *Philosophia*, translated the Arabic into the vernacular, "in lingua toletana," whence Gerard turned it into Latin. The importance of the Mozarab's oral Castilian rendering decreased in proportion to Gerard's progress in Arabic, but it is this looseness of responsibility and the inevitable inaccuracies proceeding from this method that incurred Roger Bacon's violent criticism of the Toledan translators.

In Thorndike's view "Daniel's little trickle of learning from Toledo" does not represent a considerable advance over Adelard of Bath.[136]. But his treatise presents clearer proof of the manner in which the "doctrina Arabum" passed directly to England. In Birkenmajer's interpretation of the Berlin manuscript of the *Philosophia*, the seat of learning to which Daniel intended to repair on his return from Toledo was Northampton, and he probably met his spiritual father, the bishop of Norwich, at Oxford on the way to that town, for he says he met him "in ipso itinere." (See figure 4.) According to Birkenmajer, Daniel wished to introduce reforms at the school of Northampton, and if this suggestion could at all be established it would give Daniel's Arabic studies a local habitation of considerable significance.[137] We have such a local focus in Hereford, the native town of the astronomer Roger of Hereford, Daniel of Morley's contemporary.

ROGER OF HEREFORD,   ALFRED THE ENGLISHMAN, AND ROGER BACON

Urbs Herefordensis multum tibi competit, in qua
Proprius est trivii quadriviique locus,
Floruit et floret, in hac specialiter urbe
Artis septenae praedominatur honos.

[Poem addressed to Gerald of Wales
inviting him to come to Hereford][138]

The fame of medieval Hereford rests on its map of the world, designed by Richard of Haldingham, a prebendary of Hereford cathedral. The *mappa mundi* dates from about 1300 and is mainly based on Orosius. It was entirely unaffected by the new mathematics or astronomy.[139] Yet there is evidence that Hereford, already a hundred years before the composition of the map, was a center of Arabic science. The town harbored a school and masters who maintained that even theology had much to learn from astrology and astronomy.[140]

The state of learning in medieval Hereford may be gathered from the catalogue of the cathedral library which, in the twelfth century, owned

Petrus Alfonsi's *Dialogue against the Jews* and a mathematical treatise with roughly drawn diagrams and ten lines of verse on the subject of Arabic numerals.[141] In 1178, Roger of Hereford adapted the astronomical tables that existed for Toledo and Marseilles to the meridian of the city of Hereford, using the Christian calendar "because the years of the Arabs and their months are difficult to our people who are not accustomed to them." Roger also tells us that the time of the eclipse of September 12, 1178, was observed in three cities, Hereford, Marseilles, and Toledo, and that their longitudes in relation to Arin, the world center, were determined in that way.[142]

The identity of Roger of Hereford is uncertain. We find a separate account under three different names: Rogerus Henofortensis or Herefordensis, Rogerus Herefordus, and Rogerus Yonge, alias Puer or Infans.[143] There are also several twelfth-century Rogers at Hereford, most notably a Roger Capellanus mentioned in the catalogue of the cathedral library, and a Roger, "Larderer" to the king. on whom Henry I bestowed the bishopric of Hereford but who died before he was consecrated.[144] In 1185, however, according to the Pipe Roll, Roger, clerk of Hereford, acted as itinerant justice together with Walter Map, another of Hereford's distinguished citizens.[145]

Whatever his official function at Hereford, Roger of Hereford was a twelfth-century astronomer and mathematician whose intellectual circle encompassed Alfred the Englishman and, most likely, Alexander Neckam. Roger's signature is found in various treatises that incorporate the new science; his adaptation of the Toledan tables to Hereford is linked with Robert of Ketton's revision of the tables of al-Khwarizmi.[146] Roger of Hereford's chief work, the *Compotus*, criticizes the work of Latin computists as compared to that of the Hebrews and Chaldeans. It is dedicated to Gilbert, most probably Gilbert Foliot, bishop of Hereford from 1148 to 1163, and then bishop of London (1163–87). A connection is also established in Gilbert's letters and charters in which Roger of Hereford attested the bishop's documents.[147]

The perface to the *Compotus* is dated September 9, 1176.[148] Roger describes himself as "a young man who seems presumptuous in rehandling so many writings of the ancients." Yet he would rather consume himself in study than in anything else and devote his leisure to the "regimen scholarum" to which he has already given many years of "sweaty" hard work. He knows how difficult it is to add anything new to a subject that has been dealt with, "saepe et diligenter," by most eminent scholars. He was, however, compelled to write the treatise "at the request of many who were attracted by the excellence of this science."[149]

Another of Roger's astronomical treatises, discussing the properties of planets in different countries, has a characteristically Islamic opening:

"In the name of God the pious and merciful, here opens the book of the division of astronomy and its four parts composed by the famous astrologer Roger of Hereford." Arabia, India, Turkey, Babylonia, and Spain are the countries to which signs and planets are ascribed.[150] The work, it seems, is a translation or adaptation from the Arabic, suggesting that Roger acquired his learning in Spain like Robert of Ketton, Daniel of Morley, and, in particular, his friend, Alfred the Englishman or Alfred of Sareshel. Alfred translated the Arabic version of the pseudo-Aristotelian *De vegetabilibus*, dedicating it to "magistro Rogero de Herfodia."[151] His important treatise on the motion of the heart, *De motu cordis*, is dedicated to Alexander Neckam, who died in 1217.[152]

Alfred the Englishman is known to have visited Spain. He was a famous man in his time. Robert Grosseteste, bishop of Lincoln, mentions him in his *Summa philosophiae*, stating that Alfred belonged to the generation preceding Alexander of Hales.[153] Roger Bacon places him with Michael Scot (between Gerard of Cremona and Herman the German) as one of the translators who "fuerunt temporibus nostris."[154]

The association of Alfred the Englishman with Roger of Hereford raises important questions about the role of Hereford and Herefordshire in the transmission of Arabic learning. What was the intellectual milieu of Alexander Neckam and poets like the anonymous author of *The Owl and the Nightingale*? Is Alfred the Englishman the "magister Alured" cited in the Hereford cathedral library?[155]

Alfred's biographical data, including his place of birth, Sareshel (also, Sarewel, Sarchel, or Sereshel)[156] are obscure. But his work marks a crucial turning point in the intellectual development of medieval England for it passes beyond the mathematical and astronomical preoccupations of Roger of Hereford and brings us into the philosophical currents of Oxford at the beginning of the thirteenth century. In Alfred's writings we have a wealth of Aristotelian citation such as cannot be found in any other Latin author of his time. Alfred's knowledge of the Arab Aristotelians is prominently displayed in his version of three chapters which were a kind of appendix to the fourth book of Aristotle's *Meteorology*. It was made from the Arabic of Avicenna: "tria vero ultima Avicennae capitula transtulit Aurelius [sic] de arabico in latinum."[157]

De motu cordis draws freely on the notions of Arab philosophers and refers to Aristotle's *Physics*, *Metaphysics*, and *Nicomachean Ethics*. Among Alfred's works there is also a lost commentary on Aristotle's *Parva Naturalia* and a commentary on the *Meteorology* used by Roger Bacon.[158] Bacon, in his turn, called Avicenna the most important imitator of Aristotle, the guide and prince of philosophy after him: "Avicenna, dux et princeps philosophiae post Aristotelem, quoniam precipuus eius imitator".[159] However, Bacon's gratitude to his compatriot for his share in the transmission of Aristotle and Avicenna was not unqualified. He ranks Alfred among those translators who "erraverunt in suis translationibus" and strongly condemns the "tanta falsitas in eorum operibus, quod nullus sufficit admirari."[160] In discussing the technique of translation in general, Bacon nevertheless gives us an idea of Alfred's skill as a translator and the method by which some words and idioms of the original were retained. We learn of a famous example: *belenum*, the Spanish word for henbane (*beleño*), the Latin "semen cassilaginis," used by Alfred of Sareshel in his translation of *De vegetabilibus* which he dedicated to Roger of Hereford. We hear that the word was believed to be Arabic by "omnes doctores," and Bacon himself had taken it for such until he realized his mistake through the reaction of his Spanish students who openly laughed at him at one of his lectures when he proceeded to explain *belenum* as the original Arabic form.[161]

The treatise on the plants is not the only one of Alfred's translations to contain a Spanish word: the Spanish measure *arrova* appears in Alfred's version of Aristotle's *Meteorology*.[162]

The occurrence of Spanish words in translations from the Arabic is a singularly important factor in understanding the procedure of medieval Arabic-Latin translation. Like John of Spain and Domingo González before him, Alfred evidently worked to the dictation of a Mozarab or Jew, turning the text into Latin while the whole or part of it was read and explained to him in the vernacular Spanish from the Arabic copy that was being used as the original.[163] Bacon and "omnes doctores" at the schools of England and France, knowing the translation to have been made from the Arabic, blithely considered the strange words retained in the Latin as Arabic. Thus Roger Bacon himself hardly reached the linguistic standard he prescribed for others. His severe criticism does not detract from the truly impressive achievement of his pioneering countrymen.

MICHAEL SCOT

The translator on whom Roger Bacon bears down most severely is Michael Scot, scholar-in-residence to Frederick II, known to legend as one "qui fuit astrorum scrutator, qui fuit augur, / qui fuit ariolus, et qui fuit alter Apollo."[164] According to Bacon, Scot ascribed to himself many translations and knew neither languages nor science: "Similiter Michael Scotus ascripsit sibi translationes multas. Sed certum est quod Andreas quidam Judaeus, plus laboravit in his. Unde Michaelus, sicut Heremannus, retulit, nec scivit scientias neque linguas."[165] Bacon's information on the translators in general and on Michael Scot in particular was evidently drawn from Herman the German whose own translations of Averroes and Aristotle date from 1240 and 1254.[166] Herman may well have been Bacon's teacher; we know that he enlightened Bacon on the meaning of *belenum* in Alfred's translation of *De vegetabilibus*: "Hermannus translator mihi dixit."[167] It is a valuable piece of information on the method which Latin scholars used at Toledo that Michael worked with the help of a Jewish interpreter called Andrew who labored more than he. Herman's strictures, however, are attenuated by Pope Honorius III who, in 1224, wrote Stephen Langton, archbishop of Canterbury, recommending Michael Scot for a benefice as one "who flourishes among other men of learning with a singular gift of science." In 1227, we have the testimony of Gregory IX who praises Scot's knowledge of Hebrew and Arabic and his wide familiarity with Latin learning.[168]

A closer acquaintance with Michael's writings has proved Bacon's harsh criticism to be unjustified. Scot's numerous treatises "show a knowledge of medicine, natural philosophy, and music, as well as a familiarity with the various branches of astronomy and its medieval applications."[169] Given the oral method of translation at Toledo, we are unable to judge the extent of Scot's knowledge of languages, but he seems to have been at one time associated with Jacob Anatoli, the Hebrew translator of Averroes and Ptolemy.[170] This in itself gives some indication of his interest in Hebrew. As to Arabic, he could not possibly have been so ignorant of it as Bacon would have it: the earliest date in Michael's life which has come down to us is 1217 when we find him already at Toledo, translating an astronomical treatise of al-Bitruji.[171]

There is no evidence concerning the date and place of Michael Scot's birth and very little is known of his career, though much has been conjectured with the help of legend, a few historical facts, his association with the Sicilian court at Palermo, and, above all, his writings.[172] The various accounts of Scot's studies at Durham, Oxford, and Paris are a matter of pure guesswork. Michael's sojourn in Spain, which is certain, was not confined to Toledo. He also visited Cordova—as we learn from a note in a fifteenth-century manuscript[173]—most likely in order to gain a nearer acquaintance with the writings of Averroes, which he was the first to introduce to the Latin West. The chief work accomplished in Spain is Scot's version of Aristotle's *Liber animalium*: "Completus est liber Aristotelis de animalibus, translatus a magistro michaele in tollecto de arabico in latinum."[174]

The translation is cited in Alexander Neckam's *De naturis rerum* and was probably made about 1210.[175] In 1260, William of Moerbeke completed another translation of the work directly from the Greek, but it was the version of Michael Scot from the Arabic that was used in the universities in the age of Chaucer and "all abbreviations and summaries of the Aristotelian zoology stem from it."[176]

The translation of Aristotle's *De coelo et mundo* as well as *De anima*, both in the commentary of Averroes, indicates Scot's intense activity in Spain. The Arabic text of Ibn Rushd's "great commentary" has not been found but we have Scot's Latin translation.[177]

Michael's preface to *De coelo et mundo* mentions the translation of al-Bitruji's *On the Sphere* and was consequently composed after 1217. The preface is addressed to Stephen of Provins and is a significant feature, for in 1231 this Stephen, canon of Rheims, was named by Pope Gregory X as a member of a commission appointed to examine and censor the translations of Aristotle's books on natural science.[178]

In 1220 Michael was at Bologna. There is a manuscript note to the *Liber animalium*, dated October 21, 1220, stating that "ego michael scotus" was staying at the house of a prominent widow ("uxor alberti galli") and practicing medicine. There is also a detailed description of a medical case in the neighborhood about which Scot was consulted by a discreet and wise woman called Mary who was brought to him by his landlady.[179]

This, it seems, was Scot's first appearance in Italy. It may have been the year of Scot's first meeting with Frederick of Hohenstaufen, for we know that the emperor visited Bologna about that time. Four years later, in 1224, Michael Scot is found enjoying the patronage of the papal curia.[180] From 1224 to 1227 the papal registers show a series of entries referring to Michael. Their contents indicate that he must have been a cleric of some prominence and distinction: the first entry, the letter of January 16, 1224, in which Pope Honorius III recommends Scot to Stephen Langton, had no immediate effect in procuring a benefice for Michael in the province of Canterbury. In March of the same year a license was granted to magister Michael Scotus authorizing him to hold "two benefices with cure of souls." In May, 1225, this was supplemented by an indult permitting him to hold "one additional benefice with cure of souls in England and two in Scotland."[181] Moreover, the pope had procured Scot's election to the archbishopric of Cashel in Ireland in the previous year, which, however, was rejected by Michael on the ground that he was ignorant of the Irish tongue.[182] But he seems to have known Anglo-Saxon. A list of Anglo-Saxon names of the months, similar to that in Bede, is found in Scot's *Liber introductorius*, an astronomical treatise addressed to Frederick II.[183]

The last item in the register referring to Scot is dated April 28, 1227, and is contained in one of the first bulls issued by the successor of Honorius. We find Pope Gregory soon after his accession urging Langton to carry out the papal mandate and confer an ecclesiastical living in his province on Master Michael, a man "hec contentus littera tantum erudiri latina, ut in ea melius formaretur, hebraice ac arabice insudavit laudabiliter et profecit."[184]

The year 1228 finds Scot as one of the scholars of the "academic republic" fostered by Frederick II. Leonardo of Pisa's *Liber abaci*, in its revised edition of that year, is addressed to "domine mi magister Michael Scotte, summe philosophe." Leonardo's preface is a testimony to the dignity of medieval teaching and scholarship:

> You have written to me, my lord Master Michael Scottus, supreme philosopher, that I should transcribe for you the book on numbers which I composed some time since. Wherefore, acceding to your demand and going over it carefully, I have revised it in your honour and for the use of many others. In this revision I have added some necessary matters and cut out some superfluities. In it I have given the complete doctrine of numbers according to the method of the Hindus, which method I have chosen as superior to others in this science. . . . This book indeed regards practice more than theory. So those who wish by it to know well the practice of this science, should engage in its practice by continuous usage and prolonged exercise, so that, knowledge through practice having become habitual, memory and intellect so concord with hands and figures, that as it were by one impulse and breath in one and the same instant they work together in every respect about the same thing. And when a pupil has once attained this habitude, he can gradually come easily to perfection therein.[185]

There are only two more specific dates in Scot's career: 1232, when a copy of Michael's *Abbrevatio Avicennae* was made at the emperor's request from Frederick's own original by Henry of Cologne at Malfi,[186] and 1235 or 1236, the year of Scot's death. We learn from a poem by Henry of Avranches, court poet to the emperor, that "sic accusator fatorum fata subivit." Henry of Avranches does not say when Michael died but the poem was composed for Frederick II shortly before his campaign against the Lombards, and Henry's reference to the court astrologer, the denouncer of fate who himself submitted to fate, implies Scot's death shortly before the poem was written.[187] Legend has it that Michael was killed by a falling stone in accordance with his own prediction and that he was buried in Scotland.[188]

Michael Scot's place in medieval literature does not reflect his singular importance in the history of medieval thought. In Dante and Boccaccio, he owes his "dreaded fame" to his reputation as court astrologer to Frederick II, the challenger of popes and lover of Saracen learning, who, in 1227, was excommunicated for failure to embark on the Crusade. Like Doctor Faustus, Scot is depicted as a wizard and devil's disciple, endowed with mysterious supernatural powers. In the inferno of the *Divine Comedy* he is "truly a master of every magical art"; in the *Decameron* we hear of the "great master of necromancy" in Bologna.[189] Some Scottish tales about the "wondrous" Michael are mentioned by Sir Walter Scott in the *Lay of the Last Minstrel*. We find in one of Scott's notes that in his own day "in the south of Scotland, any work of great labour and antiquity, is ascribed, either to the agency of Auld Michael, of Sir William Wallace, or of the devil."[190]

Michael's own learning, through his wide acquaintance with books on magic, alchemy, and astrology, brought him to the view that the art of magic was something "not found nor received in philosophy, because it is the mistress of all iniquity and evil, often deceiving and seducing the souls of its practitioners and injuring their bodies." In the *Liber particularis*, a supplement to the *Liber introductorius* addressed to the emperor, we learn that the astrolabe is sometimes used in invoking demons, a practice "which the Roman Church condemns and forbids to every good Christian under the penalty of anathema. The reason is lest they make free with the name of the stars to perpetrate evil, since the stars do not have the power to work any evil. But there are on their surface certain very wise spirits, who are assigned to certain works of malignity."[191]

The wording of Michael Scot's definition of magic bears close resemblance to what we find in the *Didascalicon* of Hugh of St. Victor (1096–1141): "Magic is not accepted as a part of philosophy, but stands with a false claim outside it."[192] The Islamic view is represented by Ibn Khaldun, the most authoritative medieval Muslim historian: "These sciences are forbidden by the various religious laws, because they are harmful and require their practitioners to direct themselves to beings other than God, such as stars and other things." Jabir ibn Hayyan, "the chief sorcerer of Islam," is condemned by Ibn Khaldun, because "he lengthily discussed both sorcery and the craft of alchemy which goes together with sorcery, because the transformation of specific bodies from one form into another is effected by psychic powers, and not by a practical technique." Maslama ibn Ahmad al-Majriti abridged and corrected these books, says Ibn Khaldun, for astrology, sorcery, and talismans are sciences related to the mathematical disciplines.[193]

In other words, Michael Scot, the "magician" of the Western world, was the same type of "sorcerer" as Jabir ibn Hayyan and Maslama al-Majriti, two giants of Arab scholarship, without whom the scientific knowledge of the Latin medieval world would have taken a radically different course. The intellectual evolution of England in the twelfth and thirteenth centuries is unthinkable without Michael Scot and the group of Latin translators whose lives have been outlined above and whose place in the history of science has been established since the authoritative investigation of Haskins. The problems of the texts of the translations and their Arabic originals have increasingly engaged the labors of modern students of medieval philosophy and science. What is being attempted here is, first, to make the connection with these translators for students of medieval English literature so as to illuminate sources of imagery and secondly, to trace general currents of thought as they reached England in some of their works.

3

"Doctrina Arabum" in England

The Introduction of Aristotle

In a well-known passage of the *Opus Majus* Roger Bacon implies that Michael Scot was largely responsible for the most important event in the history of medieval thought: the introduction of Aristotle from the Arabs. "In the time of Michael Scot," says Bacon, "who in the year of the Lord 1230 appeared with some portions of Aristotle's books on Natural Philosophy and Metaphysics, and their authentic commentaries, the philosophy of Aristotle was magnified among the Latins."[1] Until the twelfth century, Aristotle was known to the Latins as logician only, in the translations of Boethius from the Greek.[2] When the influx of Aristotle's writings in natural philosophy and science came about 1200, the principal part of it was conveyed from Arabic versions and commentaries in the interpretation of Avicenna and Averroes. By 1210 the books on natural philosophy and metaphysics had become such a danger to the medieval schools as to incur a special decree of a synod at Paris: "nec libri Aristotelis de naturali philosophia nec commenta legantur Parisius publice vel secreto, et hoc sub pena excommunicationis inhibemus."[3]

In 1212 a special syllabus for the Faculty of Arts was drawn up by the papal legate, Robert of Courçon. It expressly forbade the study of Aristotle's *Metaphysics* and *Natural Philosophy*.[4] The prohibition was repeated by various popes in succession but was a dead letter from the start. Edicts were issued as late as 1263, yet in 1255 all Aristotelian writings were officially accepted by the universities.[5] Commentaries on the prohibited books by the most distinguished teachers began to appear as early as 1230.[6] With Michael Scot's translation of the *Historia animalium*,[7] the entire body of Aristotle's work became generally known. The "wise and absolute" teacher of the Arabs,[8] exalted by Dante, was "the master of those who know."[9]

The impact of Aristotle on the Platonic tradition of Europe may be gauged from a letter of Maimonides:

> The writings [literally, words] of Aristotle's teacher Plato are in parables and hard to understand. One can dispense with them, for the writings of Aristotle suffice, and we need not occupy [our attention] with the writings of earlier [philosophers]. Aristotle's intellect

[represents] the extreme of human intellect, if we except those who
have received divine inspiration.

The works of Aristotle are the roots and foundations of all works
on the sciences.[10]

The emancipation from the influence of Plato was a characteristic
feature of the philosophers of the Arab West, "much less evident in the
Muslim East."[11] It deeply affected the Latin translators of the school of
Toledo. In medieval England, the first exponent of Arab Aristotelian
thought is Adelard of Bath, the apostle of "Arabum sententiae" among
the Latins. His defense of experience versus authority, an Aristotelian
doctrine that he had learned from Arab masters, prepared the way for the
portrait of his famous (imaginary) compatriot, the Wife of Bath: "Experience, though noon auctoritee / Were in this world, is right ynogh for
me. . . . "

Adelard's *De eodem et diverso* is, as we have seen, a Platonic treatise.
Plato is for him the "princeps philosophorum," "familiaris meus," the
teacher whose *Timaeus* dominates the Boethian Aristotle.[12]

Adelard, recalling his own experience as a student at Tours, exhorts
his nephew to a life of study. He recounts an allegorical debate between
philosophy and love of the world which he "witnessed" himself in his
student days. His favorite subject was astronomy—the earliest indication
of the interest that led him to Arabic studies. His venerable teacher had
taken him one night on a walk outside the city wall leaving him to study
the stars in a setting of sweet-smelling flowers by the side of the Loire.
Overwhelmed by the powerful fragrance and the sound of the river,
Adelard, like many another medieval dreamer, suddenly saw two female
figures, one on his right and one on his left: "una quarum *eadem*, altera
vero *diversa* a principe philosophorum appellatur."[13]

The one on his right, Philosophia, was accompanied by seven virgins,
the seven liberal arts; the one on his left, Philocosmia, was attended by
five virgins, the riches and honors of this world.[14] Love of the world opens
the debate but Philosophia, assisted by the seven liberal arts and Adelard
himself, wins the day. Philocosmia makes her impact on the reader, however. She quotes a proverb with Brechtian conviction: "As much bread as
you distribute, so many philosophers will you have."[15]

She also mocks the daily proliferation of Platos and Aristotles who
shamelessly hold forth on subjects they know nothing about, placing their
faith in their own verbosity: "et assidue quidem etiam nunc cotidie
Platones, Aristoteles noui nobis nascuntur, qui aeque ea, quae nesciant,
ut et ea, quae sciant, sine frontis iactura promittant; estque in summa
uerbositate summa eorum fiducia."[16]

Philosophia rebuts Philocosmia by following the argument of the

Timaeus and of Boethius, whom philosophy consoled. There is an attempt to reconcile Plato and Aristotle in the manner of the school of Chartres.[17] But we remain with the Platonic view of the universe: "homo est nomen."[18] The world of the senses is an illusion: "unde nec ex sensibus scientia, sed opinio oriri valet. Hinc est, quod familiaris meus Plato sensus irrationabiles vocat."[19]

De eodem et diverso lacks Adelard's later enthusiasm for experimental science, "though the more concrete temper of the author reveals itself at the end of an explanation of the geometrical determination of the height of a tower and in an account of a debate with a Greek philosopher of southern Italy on topics of natural philosophy."[20]

There is an element in the treatise which is of singular importance for the European reception of the Arabic Aristotle. It is the awakening of the scientific spirit of independent inquiry which Adelard encourages in his nephew.[21] In *De eodem et diverso* all roads worth taking lead *away* from the schools of France to the scholars of "Greater Greece," one of whom Adelard met near Salerno, as he tells his nephew: "Et ego certe, cum a Salerno ueniens in Graecia maiore quendam philosophum Graecum, qui prae ceteris artem medicinae naturasque rerum disserebat, sententiis praetemptarem, causam scilicet quaerens, qua ui et natura magnetes ad se ferrum trahant. . . . "[22] The inquiry about magnetism on the native grounds of Greco-Arabic medical learning gives the direction which Adelard's studies are taking the pull of an almost natural force.

ADELARD'S "QUAESTIONES NATURALES"

The *Quaestiones Naturales*, written in England about seven years (ca. 1120) after *De eodem et diverso* sets forth Adelard's advocacy of Aristotelian thought in deliberate confrontation with traditional "Gallic" learning. The treatise introduces a reference to Aristotle's *Physics*, cites "Aristotelian rules," and attests to a fully developed interest in science which is now characterized as "Arabicorum studiorum sensa."[23]

The *Quaestiones Naturales* is a completely new phenomenon in the literature of the West in its advocacy of the experimental method, its adherence to experience against the claim of authority, and its defense of the "moderns." Adelard's "Arabs," for the first time in the groves of Latin academe, are authoritatively evoked by the side of the traditional triumvirate: Plato, Boethius, Macrobius. Adelard writes:

> When I returned to England not long ago, while Henry, son of William, was ruling the English, having absented myself from my native land for the sake of study for a long time, a convening of friends was both pleasant to me and agreeable. . . . Among those who had come was a certain nephew of mine, one who was more implicated in

the causes of things than he was able to explicate, who asked me to expound something new of Arabic studies [nepos quidam meus, in rerum causis magis implicans quam explicans, aliquid Arabicorum studiorum novum me proponere exhortatus est]. As others assented to his request, I undertook to write down a treatise, which, indeed, I know to be useful to its readers but do not know to be pleasing. For this generation has an inborn vice: it considers nothing worthy of acceptance which is discovered by moderns [Habet enim haec generatio ingenitum vitium, ut nihil, quod a modernis reperiatur, putet esse recipiendum]. Therefore it is necessary, that when I wish to make public my own discovery, I impute it to a stranger saying "Somebody said it, not I." Thus, that I may be heard at all, a certain lord invented all my opinions, not I.[24]

While Adelard makes sure that "Arabic studies" include his own ideas and observations, it is nevertheless clear, in the England of Henry I, that *Arabum studia* is something to be reckoned with. The nephew is sceptical of Saracen learning and especially Adelard's preference for it. But his uncle's interest in the Arabs is nothing new. The nephew has been familiar with it from his first days as a student. Adelard reminds him, somewhat ironically, at the opening of their conversation, that he had left him and other students in Laon while he went to foreign lands to explore the learning of the Arabs:

You remember, nephew, when, seven years ago, I left you, while you were still a boy, and other students of mine, to pursue Gallic studies at Laon, it was agreed among us, that I should investigate the learning of the Arabs to the best of my ability, while you, to no less extent, acquired the inconsistency of Gallic ideas.

[Meministi, nepos, quod, septennio iam transacto, cum te in Gallicis studiis paene puerum iuxta Laudisdunum una cum caeteris auditoribus meis dimiserim, id inter nos convenisse, ut Arabum studia ego pro posse meo scrutater, tu vero Gallicarum sententiarum inconstantiam non minus adquireres].[25]

The nephew immediately seizes the opportunity to challenge his uncle. "I often heard you expounding the views of the Saracens," he says in effect, "but not a few of them seem to be rather futile." He informs his uncle that he may lose patience with his lecturing and attack his views because Adelard disparages the Latins for their "invidious ignorance" while extolling the Arabs ("cum Saracenorum sententias te saepe exponentem auditor tantum notaverim earumque non paucae satis futiles mihi videantur, patientiam meam paulisper abrumpam, teque eas edisserente, ego, sic ubi mihi videbitur, obviabo. Quippe et illos impudice extollis et nostros detractionis modo inscitia invidiose arguis").

Adelard is not surprised at his nephew's attitude. He reproaches him for his impertinence ("protervitati tuae morem geram") and states that he will expound his teaching in such a way as to protect it. He will set forth what he has to say as the views he has gained from Arabic learning so that nobody should accuse him of making up his own out of ignorance: "I have learnt indeed what fall may follow the professors of truth among the vulgar. Therefore it is the cause of the Arabs which I plead, not my own [Novi enim, quis casus veri professores apud vulgus sequatur. Quare causam Arabicorum, non meam agam]."[26]

Adelard's opening exchange with his nephew shows the *unromantic* "matter of Araby" impressing itself on reluctant Latins in medieval England. "Arabum sententiae," from still unspecified sources, is already a battle-cry for new ideas streaming into the schools of "Gaul." The *Quaestiones Naturales* reflects the process of adjustment and assimilation at an early stage, before Adelard began his own work in the systematic transmission of mathematical and astronomical texts from the Arabic. Between 1142 and 1146, his work on the astrolabe, addressed to the future Henry II, is authoritatively specific about "Arabum sententias." He means Arab astronomy:

> Intelligo iam te, Heynrice, cum sis regis nepos, a philosophia id plena percepisse nota. . . . Inde fit ut non solum ea que Latinorum scriptis continentur intelligendo perlegas, sed et Arabum sententias super spera et circulis stellarumque motibus intelligere velle presumas. . . . De mundo igitur eiusque districtione quod arabice didici latine subscribam.[27]

The *Quaestiones Naturales* is an important prelude to Adelard's work as a Latin translator of Arabic treatises. The form of the treatise has an early Arabic analogue: a fragmentary tract of eight "questions on natural things," translated by Hunain ibn Ishaq in the ninth century, and ascribed to Proclus.[28] The subject matter with which Adelard deals in his dialogue has not been traced to specific Arab authors, but "the authority of the Arabs" hovers over it. The Galenic physiological part, on the nature of breathing and sense perception, reflects Adelard's stay at Salerno where Constantine the African (ca. 1015–87) had latinized Arabic medical treatises almost a century before.[29]

The essential element in Adelard's *Quaestiones Naturales* is not discernible new material but a new methodology with which "Arabic studies" are credited. The treatise concerns itself with common problems of natural science but deliberately excludes theological speculation. In this it follows the best traditions of Islamic scholarship.[30] Adelard's proclaimed purpose is to expound "what he has learnt from Arab teachers under the guidance of reason."

Adelard and his nephew discourse on various branches of natural science in the scholastic form of questions and answers. They begin and proceed in the accepted manner of medieval teaching, dealing first with the lower world of plants (questions 1–6); then moving, on an ascending scale, to the nature of animals (questions 7–14) and man (questions 15–47), and finally reaching the discussion of cosmic phenomena, the earth, the sea, and the sky (questions 48–76). Altogether, the nephew puts seventy-six questions, at times in a somewhat provocative manner, taunting his uncle with "the authority of your Arabs" and wondering whether "those Saracens had not ensnared him with subtle nonsense."[31] But the sauciness of the nephew enlivens the dialogue. There is no trace of the formal allegorical convention, in the manner of Boethius and Martianus Capella which Adelard had cultivated seven years before. The style reflects Adelard as a "modern" teacher humorously coping with a headstrong student who refuses to unlearn what has been drilled into him. It is left to the nephew to proclaim, somewhat defensively, that science does not negate divine will: "Scientia etenim mea nulla est, nisi de illo sciam."[32]

Some of the discussion is typical of scholastic speculation: the nephew wants to know why human beings have no horns and why the nose is situated above the mouth.[33] The greater part, however, is concerned with the problems of the natural world which reveal a genuine scientific interest and knowledge derived from experiment.

Adelard knows that the earth is round;[34] he alleges the indestructibility of matter.[35] He has experienced an earthquake while crossing a bridge in the vicinity of Antioch.[36] Together with his nephew he has watched the working of a "magic water jar" at the house of an old enchantress. He saw water in a vessel held up by pressure of air but categorically refused to call the experiment "magic."[37]

We have a discussion of such questions as: why do plants grow without any previous sowing of seed? what is the cause of earthquakes, thunder, lightning? if a hole were made straight through the earth, in what direction would a stone projected into it fall? why if a vessel is full and its lower part open, will water not issue from it unless the upper lid is first removed?[38]

The example of the imaginary stone dropped through the earth's center, which Sir Thomas More took such great pains to explain to his wife, Dame Alice, makes an early appearance in Adelard's dialogue. Before More it reached Vincent de Beauvais who quoted "Adelardus and nepotem" verbatim.[39]

This problem and several others of the *Natural Questions* are discussed in *De naturis rerum* of Alexander Neckam who owed a debt to Arabic teachers as well.[40] Neckam cites Isaac Judaeus, whose works reached the Latins through Constantine the African,[41] and Alfraganus (al-Farghani) who became known through the school of Toledo in Neckam's time.[42] Unlike Roger Bacon a century later,[43] Neckam does not mention Adelard. But Neckam, we know, was a friend of Alfred the Englishman,[44] a representative of the generation that immediately followed in Adelard's footsteps. By that time the learning of Adelard's masters was "greatly famous," and no apologies had to be made for it.

Adelard, "on the authority of his Arabs," emphatically opposes the purely speculative method of the Gallic schools. He rejects the scholastic tendency to argue from mere design: "If you put your premeditated purpose in the place of a question," he tells his nephew in reply to "quare homines cornua non habeant," "I must first get from you some reason, either true or likely, why they ought to have them in your opinion; otherwise a discussion of this kind does not deserve to hold a place among philosophers. I, for one, do not consider it worth the trouble to find causes for all existing phenomena, but only for those things which, according to what reason shows me, ought to be different from what they are."[45] Thorndike suggests that Adelard inserted the question about horns as a topical comment, "a sly hint against the militarism of the feudal age."[46] The nephew is concerned with self-defense: "man, who is of higher rank than the lower animals, has neither natural arms of defense, such as horns or death-dealing tusks, nor speed of flight by which to escape the foe's menace."[47]

Adelard answers in the name of the human intellect in the language of an Aristotelian doctrine that, in the interpretation of Averroes, "created the greatest excitement in the academic world of Western Christendom."[48] His retort to his nephew is probably the earliest example in medieval England of a paean to reason that stemmed from Islamic Aristotelian thought. On the "ambiguous" question of why human beings have no horns, Adelard points out that

> he has what is far better and nobler, I mean reason in which he so pre-eminently excels the brutes that by means of it he can subdue them, put bits in their mouths, and then train them in various exercises. You see then by how much the gift of reason transcends all natural weapons. . . .
>
> Man, being a rational and therefore social animal, is adapted for two operations, action and deliberation, as we call them, war and peace. Daily life teaches him that in the activities of war arms are required, but in time of peace truth teaches him to lay them aside, and remove them far from the innermost chamber of his thoughts. For the one is provoked by wrath, to the other reason gives its sweetness. Consequently, if provided with natural weapons, he would be unable, when engaged in making treatises of peace, to lay them aside.[49]

"Reason" and "experience" are two slogans in Adelard's philosophy which he has brought home as "something new in the way of Arabic learning": "Non Stoicum me, sed Bathoniensem dico. Quare non Stoicorum errata, sed meum intellectum docere debeo."[50]

"If you wish to hear anything further from me, give and take reason," Adelard tells his nephew when the young man's quibbling becomes too much for him, "for I am not the sort of man that can be fed on a picture of a beefsteak."[51]

His emancipation is particularly striking in what he has to say about language divorced from the impact of reality: "the fact is, that the mere word is a loose wanton abandoning herself now to this man, now to that [omnis quippe littera meretrix est, nunc ad hoc nunc ad illos affectus exposita]."[52]

Adelard's "Arabici magistri" have taught him that nature "is not confused and without discretion" and that "human science must be listened to in so far as it has advanced." "Deo non detraho. Quidquid enim est, ab ipso et per ipsum est," says Adelard. But things do not happen without a natural reason: "Voluntas quidem creatoris est, ut a terra herbae nascantur. Sed eadem sine ratione non est." Things should only be referred to God when human knowledge fails altogether: "In quo vero [humana scientia] universaliter deficit, ad Deum res referenda est. Nos itaque, quoniam nondum inscitia pallemus, ad rationem redeamus."

Adelard refuses to enter upon the problem of the existence and nature of God when "I am rather able to reject what is not, than to prove what is." Instead, he concludes the dialogue by putting forward a practical suggestion: "Since we have already spoken at some length about the order of things, let us refresh our minds with well-deserved rest. In the morning, if it suits you, let us meet again and discuss the beginning or beginnings."[53]

The significance of the *Quaestiones Naturales* for the "arabization" of medieval England lies in a passage quoted from it by Roger Bacon: "In Adalardus' book on Questions about Nature the following query is put about weak authority: What else is authority of this kind than a halter? Just as brute beasts are led with any kind of halter whithersoever one wishes, and do not perceive whither they are being led nor why; so not a few, captive and bound by beastlike credulity, mere authority leads off into danger."[54] Roger Bacon proceeds to quote Averroes by the side of his English philosopher. He knew that Adelard's plea had been learnt from Arab masters. Adelard says:

> I have learnt one thing from my Arab masters under the guidance of reason. You, however, captivated by the spectacle of authority, follow your head-stall. For what else is one to call authority but a

head-stall? Just as dull animals are led by a head-stall wherever one wishes, without seeing why and where they are being led, and only follow the halter which leads them, so not a few of you, held and fettered as you are by an animal-like credulity, are led into danger by the authority of writers.

Hence certain people usurping to themselves the title of authorities have employed an unbounded licence in writing, and this to such an extent that they have not hesitated to insinuate to men of an animal-like intelligence the false instead of the true. Why should you not fill sheets of paper, and why not even fill them on both sides, when to-day you can for the most part get readers who require no proof of sound judgement from you, and simply put their trust in the name of a time-worn title?

They do not understand that reason has been given to individuals in order that, with it as chief judge, they may be able to distinguish the true from the false. If reason had not been meant to act as chief judge, it would have been given to them individually to no purpose. It would have been enough if it had been given to the one who draws up the law, be it a single man, or several people. The rest would have been satisfied with their dictatorial ordinances and commands.

"In my opinion authority is a matter of contempt," declares Adelard of Bath over two hundred and fifty years before Chaucer's Wife of Bath gave the idea an equally vigorous poetic expression. We must first search after reason, and when that has been found, but not until then, authority, if attention is drawn to it, may be added as a secondary factor: "Id autem assero, quod prius ratio inquirenda sit, ea inventa auctoritas, si adiacet, demum subdenda."[55]

Adelard's *Quaestiones* paved the way for Daniel of Morley, who, a generation later, returned to England with his "doctrina Arabum que in quadruvio fere tota existit" encased not only in his mind but, as we have seen, in a "multitude of precious books." The direct continuity of the learning Daniel acquired may be also traced in the Wife of Bath: she quotes from the preface to Gerard of Cremona's translation of the Arabic *Almagest* which Daniel witnessed at Toledo (see below, chap. 5).

4

"Arabum sententiae" in Middle English Literature

The literary impact of the translations from the Arabic is revealed in the use of scientific imagery by medieval poets. In England the scholarly focus on "star-wisdom" is reflected in *The Owl and the Nightingale,* a poem composed between 1186 and 1216. Some of the material in the poem in the debate between the birds on various topics seems to be drawn from a contemporary circle of "naturalists" whose intellectual interest in Arabian learning is aligned in a chain of dedications, linking Roger of Hereford, Alexander Neckam, and Alfred the Englishman, all contemporaries of the *Owl* poet. A reminder of the official theologians who sponsored these "Arabists" may lie in the pun on Foliot's name in the poem (l. 868, "Ne singe ih hom no foliot"). Gilbert's connection with Roger of Hereford[1] draws him into a sphere of Arabian science that surrounds *The Owl and the Nightingale.*

The interests that led English scholars to Arabian learning are discernible in the poem in two areas: astrology and Galenic medical thought. Each is represented by the activity of an English translator from the Arabic, contemporary with the *Owl* poet, and pursued, in England, by the leading scholars of the age. The treatment of these subjects in the poem reflects the light of new ideas.

The astrological debate in *The Owl and the Nightingale* has been recognized as the expression of a general interest in astrology under the impact of Arabian science, specifically, as a possible comment on the planetary conjunction of 1186.[2] Its greatest significance, however, in the history of the ideas that affected the masterpieces of Chaucer is its reflection of the *attitude* to astrology which prevailed in medieval England at the end of the twelfth century. The distinctive feature is the consideration of stellar determinism in respect to divine providence and human will. "Al hit itid þurþ Godes wille," says the owl in her astrological debate with the nightingale.[3] Does this statement represent a "Christianization" of astrology as received from the Arabs or an attitude which entered the Latin world *within* the body of the Arabic material itself?

In defending herself against the nightingale, the owl emphatically disposes of the problem of whether prognostication is compatible with the exercise of divine and human will:

Hwanne ich iseo þat sum wrechede
Is manne neh, inoh ich grede,
An bidde inoh þat hi heom schilde,
For toward heom is [harm vnmylde].
Ah þah ich grede lude an stille
Al hit itid purþ Godes wille.

[ll. 1250–56]

[When I see that some trouble is coming, I call out lustily, bidding men earnestly to be on their guard, because a cruel disaster approaches. But though I exclaim both loudly and quietly, it all comes about by the will of God.]

The nightingale has mocked the owl's depressing propensity for prophesying only misfortune:

Dahet euer suich budel in tune
þat euer bodeþ unwreste rune,
and euer bringeþ vuele tiþinge,
an þat euer specþ of vuele þinge!

[ll. 1169–72]

[Bad luck to such a herald amongst men, who is ever proclaiming futile secrets, bringing continually unwelcome tidings, and telling ever of unlucky things!]

But the brunt of the nightingale's attack is not on prognostication, it is on the owl's *competence*.

Ich habbe iherd, & soþ hit is,
þe mon mot beo wel storrewis
þat wite innoþ of wucche þinge kume,
So þu seist þe is iwune:
Hwat canstu, wrecche þing, of storre,
Bute þat þu bihaltst hi feorre?
Alswo deþ mani dor & man
Þeo of swucche nawiht ne con.
On ape mai a boc bihalde,
An leues wenden & eft folde,
Ah he ne con þe bet þaruore
Of clerkes lore, top ne more:
Þah þu iseo þe steorre alswaa
Nartu þe wisure neauer þe mo.

[ll. 1317–30]

[I have heard—and true it is—that he who knows rightly what things are coming, as thou sayest is true of thee, must be well versed in star-lore. But what dost thou know of the stars, thou miserable object! except that thou beholdest them from afar?—as doth many a beast and man, who knows naught about such matters. An ape, for instance, may gaze on a book, turn its leaves, and close it again: but it is unable, all the same, to make head or tail of what is written. And though in like fashion thou gaze at the stars, still art thou none the wiser for it.]

The owl's claim that she knows enough of "bokes lore," as well as the gospel, makes no impression whatsoever on the nightingale. She brands the owl as an ignoramus in scholarly "star-wisdom" ("clerkes lore"). It is because she is *ignorant* that the source of the owl's powers of divination can only be witchcraft.

> "Wat!" heo seide, "Hule, artu wod?
> þu ӡeolpest of seolliche wisdome;
> Pu nustest wanene he þe come,
> Bute hit of wicche crefte were.
> þarof þu, wrecche, moste þe skere,
> ӡif þu wult among manne boe,
> Oþer þu most of londe fleo;
> For alle þeo þat þerof cuþe,
> Heo uere ifurn of prestes muþe
> Amanset: swuch þu art ӡette,
> þu wiecche crafte neauer ne lete."
>
> [ll. 1298–1308]

["What!" she exclaimed. "Owl! art thou mad? Thou art boasting of a strange wisdom, and thou wert ignorant whence it came, unless it came to thee by witchcraft. And of witchcraft, thou wretch, thou must cleanse thyself, if thou art anxious to remain amongst men: otherwise thou must flee the country. For all those, who were skilled in witchcraft, were cursed of old by the mouth of the priest: as thou art still, since thou hast never forsaken witchcraft."]

The treatment of astrology in the poem accurately reflects the respect for the new science in the group of scholars who worked with the Arabic material. We know that the orthodox hostility of the Church Fathers did not affect the enthusiastic acquisition of astrological knowledge. What must be pointed out, however (and this has been consistently missed), is that not only the techniques of the new science but also its philosophical premises were transmitted from the scholars of medieval Islam. The attitude of Muslim scientists, as well as of Christian theologians, is represented in the discussion of prognostication in *The Owl and the Nightingale*.

The English scholars who discovered Arabic science in the twelfth century promulgated astrology as a universal law. "All the observations and measurements of the stars, all the devising of astronomical instruments, all the calculation of astronomical tables, were motivated by the urge to implement the universal law of nature in the service of humanity." This basic principle of international medieval culture set forth "that the entire world of nature was governed and directed by the movement of the heavens and the celestial bodies, and that man, as an animal naturally generated and living in the world of nature, was also naturally under their rule. Astrological medicine was an obvious sequel of this assumption and was free from the objection that prediction of man's fate violated the freedom of the will."[4] Astrology was simply applied astronomy, the science of judging the influence of the stars upon men. It was a natural and indispensable part of astronomy and in human affairs, the road to wisdom and power.

The refutation of astrology that we find in John of Salisbury stems from Augustine and the patristic tradition. The first indication that the patristic view had received a shock under the impact of Arabic science comes in the English translators.

In the preface to his *Compotus* (1176), Roger of Hereford states that even theology, "which is about the knowledge of the creator," has made use of astronomy not only as a necessity for itself but for the whole of life, both public and private.[5] Daniel of Morley, present at Toledo in 1175, tells us how amazed he was to hear Gerard of Cremona maintain the fatal influence of the stars and refute the arguments of Gregory the Great against astrologers. Daniel remained sceptical about the claims of stellar influence at birth: why, then, is it that a king's son and a peasant's son, born under the same constellation, retain their respective stations in later life? Gerard dismissed his question by insisting on the accord necessary between constellation and "nature" (Si uero natura constellationi uel constellatio nature non concordet, constellatio non omnimodum consequetur effectum). If a king's son and a peasant's son are born under the same star, they will both be kings, but not by the same means. The king's son will naturally succeed his father; the peasant's son, however, will reign among peasants because of the strength and superiority of his character. The great master challenged his English disciple directly: "Why are you surprised? I, who speak, am a king." He was born under a royal sign, with the sun in the ascendant and other favorable circumstances. "When I asked him ironically where he reigned," says Daniel, Gerard proudly replied: "In the mind, because I do not serve any mortal."[6] This dramatic affirmation of the sovereignty of man's unconquerable mind brought the discussion to a close. It illustrates the full impact of the intellectual authority which underlay astrological predictions.

What the Latin translators of the twelfth century transmitted in the body of their Arabic texts, in a scientific framework, was an affirmation of prognostication. But it did not imply a denial of divine providence. The philosophical and theological complications relating to Christian doctrine do not acquire momentum until the middle of the thirteenth century, with the process of assimilating the Aristotelianism of Arab and Jewish scholars into the Christian system.

A good example is the attitude of Robert Grosseteste, bishop of Lincoln, who, with Michael Scot, was the leading scientist of the day. In his later works, under the influence of Augustine and Basil's *Hexaemeron*, he condemns astrological teaching "written at the dictation of the devil." In his early works, contemporary with *The Owl and the Nightingale*, "there is no evidence that he had faced, or was aware of the implications of astrology for free will and human dignity."[7]

The representative view of astrology which prevailed among the "naturalists" was that of Michael Scot, a man both intellectual and religious: "Every astrologer is worthy of praise and honour, because he has found favour with God, his Maker, since by such a doctrine as is astronomy he probably knows many secrets of God, and things which few know."[8] Michael Scot's sublime notion of astrology is first found in Albumasar, the author of the first astrological treatise to be transmitted to England from the Arabic: "See how we have reached the Creator who moves things from things apparent and known and apprehended by the senses; it is clear what the everlasting is, the one who has power without end, the immovable and incorruptible, the highest."[9]

The problem of stellar determinism in respect to divine providence was regularly raised in the Arabic astronomical works which the Latin translators studied and adapted. Muslim philosophers had faced it in their own adaptations of Greek scientific works to the theism of Islam. Albumasar discusses the function of divine will in the short work which Adelard of Bath translated about 1133—"Incipit Ysagoge minor Iapharis mathematici in astronomiam per Adhelardum Bathoniensem ex arabico sumpta."[10] The treatise is an abridgement, made by Albumasar himself, of his *Greater Introduction to Astronomy* which, between the years 1133 and 1140, was twice translated into Latin by two other scholars. One of them, Herman of Dalmatia, dedicated his translation to his friend and collaborator Robert of Ketton. Adelard's version of the "Small Introduction" was the first hint in Latin literature of the importance of Albumasar and the beginning of Albumasar's long career as the supreme authority on astrology in the West. In the time of the *Owl* poet, about fifty years later, we have the evidence of Daniel of Morley that Gerard of Cremona lectured on Adelard's "Ysagoge."[11]

By 1180 Daniel of Morley had returned to England convinced, with Albumasar, that he who condemns astronomy destroys science: "Qui igitur astronomiam dampnat, phisicam necessario destruit. Non enim facile curat, qui causas rerum ignorat."[12] Like Adelard, he emphatically relies on the Arabs against the antiquated authority of ancient Christian authors. His two principal sources are Albumasar and Alfraganus who,[13] between 1187 and 1199, appears in Neckam's *De naturis rerum* as well. To Alain of Lille, who had probably read the *Introduction to Astronomy* in the translation of Herman of Dalmatia, Albumasar was the undisputed master of stellar science.[14]

Like the *Owl* poet, Albumasar adjusted the Aristotelian prime mover to the Koranic doctrine of the omnipotence and absolute transcendence of God's will.[15] He "frequently mentions divine will as the originator or the moderator of the course of nature."[16] In the Latin versions of Albumasar's *Introduction to Astronomy*, we accordingly find Deus in place of Allah, as we do in alchemical treatises.[17] Thus the owl's pronouncement on the sovereignty of God's will—"Al hit itid þurþ Godes wille"—is a concession to the omnipotence of God which we find in the most sophisticated Arabic treatises, an assumption transmitted with the original sources and therefore, properly, an integral part of Islamic "star-wisdom."[18]

The association of astrology with magical practices, as in the nightingale's assault on the owl, had a long tradition not only in the Church Fathers, but in medieval Islam as well. The Spanish astronomer Maslama al-Majriti, on whose Cordova revision Adelard based his version of al-Khwarizmi's tables, is described by Ibn Khaldun in the fourteenth century as "the leading Spanish scholar in the mathematical (scientific) and magical sciences."[19] Adelard's contemporaries, Peter Abelard (1079–1142) and Hugh of St. Victor (1096–1141), while accepting the value of astronomical observations in agriculture and medicine, reject the prediction of "contingentia" by means of astronomy as diabolical. "Contingentia" are opposed to "naturalia," natural events which may be deduced from natural causes. What Abelard calls "contingentia" are indeterminate future events which depend on chance, divine providence, or human choice. The act of his lecturing on that specific day is a matter of free will and nobody could have discovered it by astronomy. Those who are expert in the stars and know their nature, says Abelard, can indeed, by great exertion (suas maxime vires exercent), foretell *natural* events; but he who pretends to predict contingent happenings practices sorcery not astronomy. If the predictions of such "divinatores" are right, they have not made them "ex arte" but "ex opinione diabolica instructi."[20]

The question of contingency is thoroughly dealt with by Albumasar in refuting the critics of astrology. Basing himself on the authority of the Philosopher, namely, Aristotle, he establishes three groups of contingents: "natural"—rain most often following the gathering of clouds; "difficult" —a commoner who hopes to become king, the example used by Daniel of

Morley in his astrological challenge of Gerard of Cremona; and "equal"
—a pregnant woman who hopes to give birth to a boy rather than a girl.
He explains contingency in the physical world as stemming from matter
because of its capacity to receive one quality and then its opposite. All the
planets do is to signify the possible happenings. For matter, being formed
of the four elements, is entirely dependent in all its transformations upon
the influence of the heavenly bodies. The totality of contingency in matter
is therefore outlined in advance in the regular motions of the stars but in
such a way as to follow God's disposition. Man's free will constitutes the
first principle of contingency in him but his freedom of choice is circum-
scribed by the matter of which his body is made. This matter, as it does in
all animated beings as well, depends on stellar influence. The crucial
difference, however, is that man has a rational soul that even under the
influence of the stars, has the power of deliberation. Man's body has the
capacity to receive new qualities or affections from the stars. Planetary
influence does not destroy freedom of the will: "as man in contradistinc-
tion to all other animals has the power of deliberating and choosing by
virtue of his reason, and the capacity to receive the impression of different
physical qualities in his body by virtue of the four elements of which it is
composed, human nature is open to a wide range of contingency which,
however, is wholly signifiable by the motions of the planets."

According to Albumasar, the function of astrology was to concern itself
"with the category of the possible not with that of the necessary or the
impossible." The astrologer "does not enquire whether fire burns or not,
or whether snow is cold or not; he is only interested in knowing if such fire
will burn tomorrow such a body which has a disposition to be burned, or if
one particular thing will become frozen, or whether there shall be rain or
no rain, whether this individual man will decide to talk to another or not
to talk, or whether he shall walk tomorrow or not. What the astrologer
does in these cases is to make sure that the thing enquired about belongs
to the possible."[21]

It should be noted that the kinds of misfortunes predicted by the owl
are all possible or "natural" misfortunes: death, loss of property, the
downfall of friends, fire, war, theft, plagues and pestilences, widowhood,
marital strife, famine, the workings of vengeance and malice, hangings,
murder, the outcome of judicial combat. According to the best authorities
of the time, such misfortunes are indeed associated with evil stellar influences of Saturn, Mars, and also of comets. They may be found in the
most respected astronomical treatises as well as in chronicles and literary
works. The owl's foresight specifically includes weather predictions (ll.
1201, 1202, 1205), the most scientific form of astrology at the time. There
are instructions in numerous treatises throughout the Middle Ages on how
to forecast storms, rain, and temperature from the movement of the

planets through the twelve signs of the zodiac and the twenty-eight mansions of the moon.[22]

In condemning prognostication by witchcraft the nightingale does not only agree with Peter Abelard, but also echoes the view of the greatest astrologer of the time, Michael Scot. In *Liber particularis* he warns against the use of the astrolabe in invoking evil spirits "which the Roman Church condemns and forbids to every good Christian under the penalty of anathema. The reason is lest they make free with the name of the stars to perpetrate evil, since the stars do not have the power to work any evil."[23] Thorndike has found, as we have seen, that the wording of Michael Scot's definition of magic closely resembles that which closes the *Didascalicon* of Hugh of St. Victor: "Magic is not included in philosophy, but is a distinct subject, false in its professions, mistress of all iniquity and malice, deceiving concerning the truth, and truly doing harm; it seduces souls from divine religion, promotes the worship of demons, engenders corruption of morals, and impels the minds of its followers to every crime and abomination."[24] The passages in the *Didascalicon* denouncing prognosticators and their cooperation with demons contain an important distinction between "mathematica" and "mathesis." "Mathesis" is not a science but a superstition which attributes the fate of men to the stars.[25] The same alarm is sounded by John of Salisbury: "mathematici" depart from the foundation of sound knowledge and "allured by a false vision of reason, they slip to their own destruction into pseudo-mathesis."[26]

John of Salisbury's attitude has been described as that of the Church Fathers.[27] Living at a time when Arabic science was making its way northward, this pupil of William of Conches and bishop of Chartres (1176–80) was still oblivious to its presence. But "John is visibly embarrassed by the ancient strictures placed on *mathesis* by the Fathers, because much that was linked with *mathesis* has now become the proper concern of the *physicus.* . . . Foreknowledge of the future in particular belongs to the Physicus."[28] John's indictment of evil practitioners of prognostication as diabolical wizards does not deny the legitimate function of astrology:

> If mathematicians were content with the aim of approved mathematics, that of the schools, they would have the power to ascertain the position of the stars and from their signs to presage with sober judgment the character of periods according as they occur in nature and to pluck the ripe fruit of their speculations. But when they make their phylacteries broad and enlarge their fringes by assigning to constellations and planets excessive power, ascribing to them some sort of authority for their work, they end by wronging the Creator. Not knowing the celestial phenomena with which they deal as a sobering influence, they are, according to the apostle, fools."[29]

John of Salisbury's anxiety to ensure that no "wrong is done Him who hath made heaven, earth, and all that is in them"[30] is evident in the Islamic astrologers as well. It is not the sole prerogative of Christian theological thought. What is at issue in *The Owl and the Nightingale* is not the partristic problem of the validity of astrological predictions but the status of the owl as a scientific astrological practitioner. Is she "astronomicus" or "diabolicus"?

Albumasar's exposition makes a good defense of the owl. He emphasizes that uncommon intellectual capacity is required to link all factors concurring in astrological judgment. Even the wisest and most learned astrologers are not infallible. The ignorance or perversion of a deficient practitioner should not be used to criticize the science. No one should despise what knowledge is obtainable. Even a little knowledge is of great benefit, especially in foreseeing future events. As for the astrologer himself, he must have confidence in his science while avoiding interference with the unknown or with that which exceeds the power of reason.[31] In Albumasar's scientific framework there is no room for a discussion of magic or sorcery. But there is an extensive discussion of fortunate and unfortunate stars and the problem of deficient practitioners is considered to be serious.

The nightingale's assault on the owl as practicing witchcraft is thus part of a serious methodological discussion of astrology as a science. In the context of the poem, this discussion is especially pointed, since witchcraft is usually practiced at night when the owl hoots its evil predictions. "Wane þu hauest a niȝt igrad / Men boþ of þe wel sore ofdrad" (ll. 1149–50). It was the owl's claim to be an accredited astrologer that was too much for the nightingale: "Hwat canstu, wrecche þing, of storre / Bute þat þu bihalst hi feorre? / Alswo deþ mani dor & man / Þeo of swucche nawiht ne con" (ll. 1321–24). But the legitimate science of astrology is never questioned. We have moved from the era of Hexaemerons to the astrological cosmology of the Arabs.

Like the astrological debate, there is another topic in *The Owl and the Nightingale* which may reflect newly acquired Arabic learning. At one point, lines 933–52, the nightingale almost loses her self-control. The owl has derided the nightingale's nightly abode—"Par men goþ to here neode" (1. 938)—and this is almost too much for her. But she remembers what she has learnt about anger:

> An sat sumdel & heo biþohte,
> An wiste wel on hire þohte
> Þe wrappe binimeþ monnes red.
> For hit seide þe King Alfred:
> "Sel [d]e e[re]ndeþ wel þe lope,
> An selde plaideþ wel þe wroþe";
> For wrappe meinþ þe horte blod

Þat hit floweþ so wilde flod
An al þe heorte ouergeþ,
Þat heo naueþ no þing bute breþ,
An so forleost al hire liht
Þat heo ne siþ soþ ne riht.
Þe Niȝtingale hi understod,
An ouergan lette hire mod.

[ll. 939–52]

[She therefore remained deep in thought for a time: for she knew well in her heart of hearts, that anger robs a man of wisdom. Alfred the king had already also said it: "Seldom intercedes well the hated man, seldom pleads well the angry man." For wrath stirs up the blood of the heart, so that it flows like a wild flood, overpowering all the heart and leaving to it naught but breath. The heart thus loses all its light, and can discern neither truth nor right. The Nightingale was aware of this, and she let her mood of anger pass.]

Is there evidence of a new psychology and physiology of the *heart* in the above passage?

Atkins renders the lines in the following manner: "For wrath stirs up the blood of the mind, so that it flows like a wild flood, overpowering all the mind and leaving to it naught but passion. The mind loses all its light, and can discern neither truth nor right."[32] The rendering of *heorte* by "mind" and of *breþ* by "passion" raises a series of interesting and complicated questions. For it is precisely in the second half of the twelfth century, in the England of Alfred the Englishman and Alexander Neckam, that the physiology and psychology of the heart, to which the above passage seems to refer, came to be considered in a new light.

The nightingale's meditation on wrath and its effects on reason takes place in her "þohte"; the temperamental effects of wrath which she describes are in the "heorte". If we take *heorte* to mean "heart," i.e., the human or animal heart considered medically or scientifically, the nightingale's trend of thought—her brain has not lost the capacity of cool deliberation in spite of her anger—may be viewed as comprising three elements: first, anger—a distemper—affects the heart through an unnatural change in the vital blood ("horte blod"); secondly, the heart is the seat of the soul and the discerning faculty; thirdly, in a state of anger the heart holds nothing but "breath"—vapor or useless air whose normal flow and function have been obstructed.

The psychological physiology of the heart is the subject of *De motu cordis* by Alfred the Englishman.[33] The treatise on the movement of the heart draws freely on the psychological and physiological notions of Arab Aristotelians in discussing the relationship between the functions of the body and the mind. Alfred sees the heart as the *principium vitae* and the *domicilium animae*.[34] We find the same view in the *De laudibus sapientiae* of his friend and patron Alexander Neckam, a metrical paraphrase of *De naturis rerum* that Neckam composed toward the end of his life.[35]

In *De naturis rerum* itself, wrath degenerating into hatred is said to be the death of the soul (mors animae adest spiritualis). Anger ascends to the mind like the most harmful pestilential fever described by physicians. Like a fire it may be extinguished but it generates smoke noxious to the eyes of the soul—i.e., to the intellect and to reason: "Fumus procreatus ex igne iracundiae valde nocius est oculis animae, scilicet intellectui et rationi."[36]

The thesis that the heart is the physical seat of the intellect or soul can be traced back to Hippocratic writings. It deeply affected the tradition of Aristotelian and Galenic medical thought and its transmission to the West by the Arabs. Alfred, who, as we know from his *De vegetabilibus* had also translated the portions on minerals of Avicenna's *Kitāb ash-Shifā'* (Book of Healing),[37] must have been acquainted with the opinion of the great Arab physician and philosopher:

> It is necessary that the soul should be attached to the first organ in which life takes birth, and so it is impossible that an organ should be alive without the attachment of a psychical faculty to it, or that the first thing attached to the body should not be this principle but a posterior faculty. This being so, the organ to which this principle is attached must be the heart. This theory of Aristotle is opposed to that of the Divine Plato.[38]

The prevailing Western notion of the soul was Platonic, as we find it in Macrobius: "ut autem homo constet et vivum animal sit, anima praestat, quae corpus inluminat, porro inluminat inhabitando et habilitatio eius in cerebro est."[39] In the twelfth century, the Platonic doctrine of the seat of the soul was firmly established.[40] It is particularly noticeable in William of Conches (ca. 1080–ca. 1154), whose theories of the elements and the soul were already undergoing modification under the influence of Arabic medical works adapted by Constantine the African and of the *Introduction to Astronomy* of Albumasar.[41] Constantine's *Liber Pantegni*, where we find the Aristotelian and Galenic ideas of vital spirit ascending from the heart to the brain, is expressly cited by William of Conches.[42] William, however, still speaks of "cerebrum, ubi est sedes animae (non quod ibi solum sit, sed quia ibi discernit)."[43]

The theories of Costa ben Luca (Qusṭā ibn Lūqā, ca. 900), a medical authority known to Constantine the African, are found in a treatise *De differentia animae et spiritus* which Alfred cites in his work on the motion of the heart. Their basis is the belief in the existence of "spiritus," a substance which perishes when separated from the body and operates most of the vital processes such as breathing and the pulsation of the blood. The processes of sensation and movement are directed by spiritus arising in the brain and operating through the nerves. The breathing and the pulse are operated by spiritus arising from the heart which nourishes the spiritus in the brain and enables it to exercise the faculties of cogitation, memory, and "foresight": according to some physicians and philosophers, says Costa ben Luca, there are two chambers in the heart and there is more spiritus than blood in the left ventricle and more blood than spiritus in the right.[44] The quality of the spiritus and its effects on mental processes depend on the health of the body; the more perfect the human body, the more perfect the spiritus and the clearer and more subtle the functions of the mind.

The most authoritative medieval view is found in the *Canon of Medicine* of Avicenna (Chaucer's Avycen):

> Allah created the left side of the heart, and made it hollow in order that it should serve both as a store-house of the breath and as the seat of manufacture of the breath. He also created the breath to enable the faculties of the soul to be conveyed into the corresponding members. In the first place the breath was to be, the rallying-point for the faculties of the soul, and in the second place it was to be an emanation into the various members and tissues of the body (whereby these could manifest the functions of those faculties).[45]

The whole subject is complicated by the close interdependence of medieval theology, philosophy, and science and the various theories of both metaphysicians and physicians.[46] In the second half of the twelfth century, however, Alfred the Englishman approached the discussion in a new way, basing himself on the principles of Galenic medicine which taught that the function of the heart was the creation of vital spirit from a mixture of blood and air.

The importance of *De motu cordis* for contemporary psychology and physiology is clear from Alfred's dedication: he is speaking of the Aristotelian concept of the soul of which

> ergo primum et praecipuum organum cum eiusdem virtutibus et operationibus, nostris adhuc ignotum intemptatumque phisicis, declarare institui, tuoque opus ipsum examini, maxime Alexander, offerendum rectissime censui. . . .[47]

Unlike the theologians, Alfred maintains that body and soul are a complete and integrated whole. The soul can exercise its faculties, including the "intellectus agens," only through the body. The whole existence of the human soul moves within the physical organism of which the heart is the vital center, "the organ of organs" through whose function life is maintained. With Alfred the question of the seat of the soul is equivalent to the question of the seat of bodily life itself: "cor igitur vitae domicilium pronuntio."

The head or brain cannot be the seat of the soul because its activity is not continuous but intermittent. The only organ whose activity is continuous is the heart. Alfred acknowledges the participation of the brain in the exercise of mental and sensory functions but what enables the brain's participation is not a psychical substance located in the brain. It is the operation of the virtues and faculties of the soul which are centralized in the heart and directed from it. The soul cannot change its seat and cannot migrate in the body because if it did so the departure of the vital principle would stop the motion of the heart. It is the heart which is also "principium sensus et motus." The soul is the simple and indivisible principle of life itself, the soul contains heat: "anima calorem continet."[48]

Most strikingly, Alfred compares the heart to the sun whose rays irradiate the whole body, while the brain is a mirror that catches and reflects the rays of the sun: .

> Pervenit virtus ad cerebrum, sicut calor a sole in terrae superficiem . . . ejusdem quoque irradiatio ad totum corpus a cerebro tanquam a speculi superficie resultat. A corde enim virtus exoritur, in cerebro confortata consummatur . . . cerebrum integre irradiationem suscipit, perfecteque refundit, sicut exactissime polita speculi superficies radium.[49]

The work of Alfred represents an important shift in the prevailing ideas on the psychological and physiological relationship of head and heart. The "spiritus animalis," regarded as operating the functions of the brain, is seen as a subtle distillation of the "spiritus vitalis" in the heart. Alfred considers psychological and mental phenomena as a continuing sublimation of the substantive content of the arteries.

Alfred's philosophy of the soul is grounded in a detailed exposition of the anatomy and physiology of the heart, of breathing, and of blood circulation. Like Avicenna, Alfred distinguishes four principal organs: the heart, the brain, the liver, and the genitals. The brain is the seat of the mental faculties, sensation, and movement; the liver governs the nutritive or vegetative faculties; procreation depends on the generative organs. But while the activities of these three may be safely interrupted without stopping life, the motion of the heart must be continuous.

The heart is the source and starting point of vital power, of innate heat. Alfred follows Aristotle in asserting there are three cavities of the heart. The vital heat is concentrated in the left chamber which is the starting point of blood and the veins that channel vital blood, the lifeblood ("horte blod") to all parts of the body. The left ventricle is therefore the seat of the soul: "Thalamus cordis sinister est domicilium animae."[50] Air enters the heart through the lung in the process of breathing and concentrates in the middle chamber which is connected to the left ventricle by "orificia" which open and close. Breathing serves to cool the innate heat and to form the vital spirit which is created in the left ventricle with the help of blood concentrated in the right ventricle and drawn from digested nourishment. Alfred's notion of the whole process is the following: the innate heat of the heart attracts air which streams to it through the lung. Air then helps to change blood into "spiritus vitalis" by exercising its function of cooling. When the inspiration and cooling have been completed, an opening in the left ventricle where the vital spirit is formed conducts the vital lifeblood into the organism. The redundant air not used in the process is expelled. Alfred's theory is one of the first scholastic attempts to explain rhythmically recurring organic processes within the body by means of physics. It is also noteworthy in its effort to explain the observation of Galen that the movements of breathing and the pulsation of the blood stand in a reciprocal relationship.

In *The Owl and the Nightingale*, the nightingale, after some deliberation, knows well "in her thought" that wrath deprives man of common sense. Her rational or deliberative faculty seated in the brain is unimpaired by her mood of anger. This is good Platonic doctrine.

In the Platonic formulation, the "noblest" rational part in the head first becomes aware that an act of wrong is taking place. It sends down a message to "the spirited element," a group of irascible emotions whose seat is in the heart. "Then the blood begins to boil and rush outwards through all the veins, so conveying to all the fleshy parts the impulse to quell the disturbance."[51]

"An sat sumdel & heo bipohte" (l. 940) is made even more convincing by the realization that Aristotle attributed a faculty of sagacity, prudence, and forethought to animals corresponding to intellect in man: "Many animals in their mode of life appear to imitate mankind, and one may observe greater accuracy of intellect in small than in large animals."[52] Aristotle's "De animalibus" was translated from the Arabic by Michael Scot in two stages, the earliest of which, a translation of the *Historia animalium*, at Toledo, dates from 1200 and was used by Alexander Neckam in *De naturis rerum*.[53] Moreover, the faculty of forethought is also attributed to animals in the *Nicomachean Ethics*, which Alfred, in his treatise on the motion of the heart, is the first Latin to cite. His philosophical definition of "violent," in describing the motion which propels the heart, has been shown to be a quotation from book 3, where Aristotle discusses the problems of voluntary and involuntary action, the emotions of lust and anger, self-control and deliberation. Only moral choice, says Aristotle, "is not shared by the irrational animals while Lust and Anger are."54

In the medieval definition of the "internal sense," located in the ventricles of the brain, the nightingale's rationality is the faculty of "estimation," the Arabic *wahm* which in animals is the equivalent of common sense and imagination. According to Avicenna, physicians regarded the two as one faculty from the medical point of view which classified the faculties of the soul according to the bodily organs in which they reside.55 Galen makes a distinction between "errors" of the soul and "passions" of the soul. Errors arise from a false opinion in the head but passions "from an irrational power within us which refuses to obey reason."56

This is how the nightingale sees the physiology of wrath:

> For wrappe meinþ þe horte blod
> Þat hit floweþ so wilde flod
> An al þe heorte ouergeþ,
> Þat heo naueþ no þing bute breþ. . . .

[ll.945–48]

Wrath, a "humorous" distemper, troubles the blood of the heart by mixing itself into it ("meinþ") with the result that the blood flows turbulently, as in fever. The physiological effect of anger on the blood is a commonplace assumption in medieval medicine. The boiling of the blood in the region of the heart as a consequence of anger is described in the *Timaeus*:

> The heart, . . . the knot of the veins and the fountain of the blood which moves impetuously round throughout all the members, they [the members of the body] established in the guardroom, in order that when the spirit should boil with anger at a message from reason that some act of wrong is taking place in the members, whether coming from outside or, it may be, from the desires within, then every sentient part of the body should quickly, through all the narrow channels, be made aware of the commands and threats and hearken with entire obedience, and so suffer the noblest part to be leader among them all.57

Aristotle, in his treatise on respiration, compares the excitement caused by an unnatural change in the blood in the region of the heart to boiling: "for boiling takes place when liquid is aerated by heat: it expands because its bulk increases."58 Galenic physiology assumed as a matter of course that "hot" blood generated vapor, as did the innate heat of the heart.

Because of the idea of vital spirit flowing from the heart to all parts of the body, Galenic medical thought did not envisage the principle of blood circulation. Like Plato and Aristotle, Galen viewed the blood system as a system of irrigation, of the type prevailing in Asia Minor and the Near East: "Numerous canals distributed throughout the various parts of the body bring them blood in the same way as the water is carried along in the garden."[59] The text accompanying an anatomical illustration of the heart, whose date is 1158, relies on "Galenus prudentissimus medicorum" and in describing the arterial system uses the verb *irrigat*.[60] The nightingale's metaphor of "flooding" when the turbulently distempered blood "ouergeþ" the heart at the source is, therefore, medically correct.

In medieval medical usage, the "heart" includes "the arterial system and something more."[61] It is therefore difficult to know exactly what "al þe heorte" means in the poem. In Galenic medicine the heart is the starting point for all the arteries in the body. In the text accompanying the illustration of 1158 the arteries, "which proceed from the heart," are described as "veins which pulsate."[62] The veins of the heart and the flow of blood are described by Galen in the following manner:

> I say that between the diaphragm and the heart no vein is found at all. Upon the heart there is a very large vein indeed which is peculiar to the part named "the heart's ear" [auricle and coronary sinus]. And you will find that the blood which flows through this vein at this spot is in some animals, mankind among them, divided into three portions, but in others, including the ape, into two portions. Most of it goes to the right hand one of the two heart cavities, but the remainder goes to the veins which encircle and wreathe round the whole heart [coronary veins]. There are a few anatomists who have called these veins by this name, that is "those which surround and encircle the heart." Their situation is in the actual substance of the heart near its exterior.[63]

Avicenna speaks of the cardiac cavities as being *emptied* of blood in a state of emotional excess.[64] The description of the nightingale, however, suggests a state of dilation to the extremities in which the "heart" contains nothing but "breath."

"Sages, and those physicians who agree with them," says Avicenna, "are satisfied that joy and sadness, fear and anger, are passions particularly related to the breath of the heart." We also find the following observation in the *Canon of Medicine*: "Anger stirs up the vital power and causes the breath to expand all at once."[65] The Arabic *rūḥ* is translated by "spiritus" in the Latin of Gerard of Cremona[66]—vital breath.

The primary meaning of *breþ* is "breath" or "breathed air."[67] In English, the sense passed through that of "heated air expired from the lungs" or "odor," to "the air in the lungs and mouth."[68] Was the usage of the word in Middle English affected by the ideas of the Latin translators and the variety of meanings, often ambiguous, attached to the term *spiritus*?[69]

If we consider the shift in psychological and physiological concepts which directly affected the circle of Alexander Neckam, the meaning of "breth" as used by the *Owl* poet in conjunction with "heorte" and "horte blod" acquires a peculiar significance. "Breath" in line 948 may indeed be nothing but "passion" (Old French *air*—choler, fury): nothing but passion fills the heart. If "breath" is rendered by "vapor, smoke, or fume," another of its possible Middle English meanings, the *Owl* poet's metaphor of anger would resemble that of Alexander Neckam who describes anger as smoke in the eyes of the soul.

In fact, "vapor" makes perfect medieval medical sense: the boiling of the blood generated vapor which, according to Aristotle, was concentrated in the heart and caused its palpitation in anger.

The most interesting connotation of "breath," however, is that of redundant breathed air in the heart unable to combine with distempered blood in the formation of vital spirit. The substance of breath is "aqueous vapour" when the humors are healthy, and a "fuliginous vapour" if the breath is unhealthy because of superfluities.[70] In the strict sense of breathing, each emotion tends to generate its own type of breath. According to Avicenna, sadness fosters anger and two things follow great depression: the weakening of natural powers and concentration of the breath. Violent condensation and aggregation of the breath obliterates the natural heat and brings about a weakening of the faculties. Avicenna describes the relations between various states of the blood and the several emotions. The effect of "thick, turbid, overhot" blood on breath produces a thickening of breath and a disordering of its proper function, i.e., "to cool properly." When anger and gloom occur simultaneously, says Avicenna, the breath may move in two opposite directions: first there is confinement of the breath in the interior parts. When the power of reason returns and resolution appears, the contracted breath expands again and brings heat to the surface. "The two opposite movements may produce a sense of shame."[71] The nightingale's state seems to correspond to this diagnosis:

> Þe Niȝtingale was igremet,
> An ek heo was sumdel ofchamed. . . .

[ll. 933–34]

Avicenna also discusses the effects of anger on the pulse: "irregularity may also occur if shame is associated, for the intellect warns the person to be silent and not yield to the same evil as did the person who has excited one to anger."[72] It is precisely in the situation of anger mingled with shame that the nightingale finds herself when, obeying the warning of "the intellect," she "ouergan lette hire mod."

According to Alfred, the right ventricle is the seat of the blood, the left ventricle of "spirit," and the middle ventricle is filled with air from the lung. The breathing of the heart is conducted through a vein leading to the lung. When the heart distends it attracts air, when it contracts it expels whatever of "smoky vapors" have been generated in it through humorous superfluities. The most important function of breathing is the formation of vital spirit in the left ventricle of the heart through the association of blood with breathed air. In a state of passion and agitation the heart undergoes adverse effects caused by the unnatural confinement of breathed air which is incapable of exercising its proper function of associating with arterial blood in the formation of vital spirit. Under these conditions, both in Alfred and Avicenna, the heart, as the primary organ of the soul and the principle of all faculties thus "forleost al hire liht."

Whatever their precise meaning, there is a feeling that the lines in *The Owl and the Nightingale* are intended to express some underlying physiological concept of the function of the heart in relation to the faculties of the soul. In the fourteenth century, Chaucer, who "gets quite technical in physiological matters,"[73] unmistakably placed the spirit in the heart. In the *Knight's Tale*, the dying Arcite speaks of "the woful spirit in myn herte" (l. 2765). The use of Galenic medicine by Chaucer is not surprising. But the general assumption that the Aristotelian and Galenic concepts of the heart as the seat of the soul did not affect Western thought until the thirteenth century has been modified in view of the early acquaintance of English scholars like Alexander Neckam with details of zoological and medical material as transmitted by Arab Aristotelians.[74] *The Owl and the Nightingale* is the best possible indication that the Aristotelian view of animals had taken deep literary root. Is the poem also a literary harbinger of the new ideas of the heart which, at the time of its composition, were conveyed to Alexander Neckam by Alfred the Englishman?

The meaning of lines 945–50 would then express contemporary ideas in the following manner: anger mingles with the lifeblood in the heart so that the blood flows like a turbulent torrent and floods all the heart, with the result that in the formation of vital spirit in the left ventricle there is nothing but fuliginous vapor which is unable to combine properly with the distempered blood. As a consequence, the heart loses its light of intellect so that it cannot discern either truth or right.

Scientific Imagery in Chaucer

Chaucer's knowledge of medieval science and philosophy is deeply embedded in his literary work. It is an integral and inseparable part of his poetic vision and expression. Chaucer's "star-wisdom" is crucial to his profound, humorous, and compassionate understanding of the human predicament on "this litel spot of erthe." His use of the contemporary sciences in presenting the physical and spiritual condition of man, medieval and universal, reflects the observations, ideas, and methodology of great Arabian masters whose names occur throughout the body of Chaucer's works: Alkabucius, Alocen, Arsechiel, Averrois, Avycen, Haly, Razis. So do the names of the two most important medieval transmitters: Constantyn (Constantinus Africanus), the earliest translator of medical treatises from the Arabic, and Piers Alfonce (Petrus Alfonsi), the pioneer of Arabic studies on English soil whose interests and gifts, like Chaucer's, encompassed the intellectual discipline of the scientist, the imaginative sweep of the poet, the moral insight of the philosopher, and the accumulated wisdom of folklore. Chaucer's mastery of the medieval sciences, astronomy, astrology, dream-lore, medicine, is a commonplace of Chaucerian scholarship. But the precision with which scientific imagery is used in his works is still a surprising, not fully comprehended factor. The precision is an important aspect of Chaucer's poetic genius and technique. It can only be probed within the rigorous framework of Arabic learning.

Chaucer's use of astronomy and astrology has been a frequent subject of investigation. His expert knowledge of the zodiac is transformed into the thematic content and structural principles of almost all his works. The hold that the Arabic names of the stars had on the poet is perhaps best seen in the unfinished *Squire's Tale*, where the matter of Araby combines rigorously scientific strands with the Arabian romance of the East through its entire texture.

The setting of the *Squire's Tale* in the land of Tartary is riveted in geographical and historical fact:

> At Sarray, in the land of Tartarye,
> Ther dwelte a kyng that werreyed Russye. . . .

Sarai had acquired its fame as a flourishing trading center and the capital of the khanate of the Golden Horde, visited by William of Rubruck, Marco Polo, and Ibn Battuta. The city was founded by Batu Khan in the first half of the thirteenth century and destroyed during Chaucer's lifetime, in 1395, by the famous Tamerlane, lord of Samarkand, in an act of personal vengeance against a rival Kipchak ruler. The town was built around a walled palace, seraglio, from which it derived its name.[75]

> This noble kyng, this Tartre Cambyuskan
> Hadde two sones on Elpheta his wyf,
> Of whiche the eldeste highte Algarsyf,
> That oother sone was cleped Cambalo.
> A doghter hadde this worthy kyng also,
> That yongest was, and highte Canacee.

The names Cambyuskan and Cambalo, like the Byzantine Canacee and Theodora whom Algarsyf was to win for his wife, are recognizable forms. They present no special problems in their correspondence with Mongol or Turkic prototypes. Cambyuskan, it is generally agreed, is a variation of Genghis Khan (1162–1227), founder of the Mongol Empire, "the first sovereign of all the Tartars" according to Marco Polo.[76] Similar forms of the name appear in chronicles and histories (e.g., Friar Ricoldo of Montecroce's "Cambiuscan," or the Armenian Haiton's "Changius Can" in the Latin *History of the Tartars* written at the end of the thirteenth century for his fellow Christians in the West).[77] We may allow the squire sufficient romantic license to ignore the fact that it was Batu Khan who "werreyed Russye" as a victor and established the dominion of the Golden Horde. Cambalo or Cambalus, the name of Cambyuskan's younger son, may be a form of Kambala, one of Kublai Khan's grandsons, rather than "Cambalu" or "Cambaluc" whose meaning, "the King's City" (derived from the Turkish *khanbāliq*), was well known in Chaucer's time.[78]

"As for the names Algarsyf and Elpheta," wrote Pollard in his introduction to the *Squire's Tale*, "no one, as far as I know, has yet suggested an origin for them, but they are certainly not Greek, and do not appear to be Mongol."[79] This is expanded by F. N. Robinson: "*Elpheta* and *Algarsyf* look like oriental forms, and are unlikely to have been invented by Chaucer." Manly suggests that Chaucer took the former from some list of the principal stars. He notes its occurrence in the *Liber Astronomicus, qui dicitur Albion*, ascribed to Richard de Wallingford (MS. Harl. 80, fol. 511).[80]

Elpheta and Algarsyf are, in fact, unmistakably Arabic names. Elpheta, on the face of it, looks like an Arabic word meaning "young woman"—*al-fatā (tu)*. But did Chaucer know that? There is, however, another Arabic Elpheta with which Chaucer was undoubtedly familiar. It leads us to the stars, as Manly surmised, and also, it seems, to Algarsyf, the eldest son of the royal house and the rider of the flying horse, the most wondrous of the four magic gifts bestowed on the Tartar household.

In the prologue to his *Treatise on the Astrolabe* Chaucer told "little Lewis" that he was going to present all that need be known about the astrolabe in English, in the same manner as each people—Greek, Arab, Hebrew, and Latin—forming the chain of transmission of this knowledge acquired it in its own language and style:

> But natheles suffise to the these trewe conclusions in Englissh as wel as sufficith to these noble clerkes Grekes these same conclusions in Grek; and to Arabiens in Arabik, and to Jewes in Ebrew, and to the Latyn folk in Latyn; whiche Latyn folk had hem first out of othere dyverse langages, and writen hem in her owne tunge, that is to seyn, in Latyn.

And God woot that in alle these langages and in many moo han these conclusions ben suffisantly lerned and taught, and yit by diverse reules, right as diverse pathes leden diverse folk the righte way to Rome.[81]

Chaucer's treatise was not a translation. He speaks of himself as "but a lewd compilator of the labour of olde astrologiens."[82] This is not the usual deprecatory statement of Chaucer's personal modesty. One of his main sources, "De compositione et operatione astrolabii" ascribed to Messahala, which accounts for about two-thirds of his treatise, was itself a composite and derivative work, as historians of science have increasingly emphasized. The Latin treatise on the astrolabe generally attributed to Messahala (Māshā'allāh, d. 815), the important Jewish astronomer at the Abbasid court in Baghdad, was a product of the school of Maslama al-Majriti, the eleventh-century Spanish astronomer.[83]

Chaucer's treatise on the astrolabe was composed in 1391. (See figures 6 and 7.) He had planned to divide it into five parts. But he left it unfinished, and we have only two parts—one of which is complete—and some doubtful propositions and conclusions preserved only in late manuscripts with a reference to "Arsechieles tables."[84] The third part, whose content is fully outlined in the prologue, was to contain diverse tables of computation and "diverse tables of longitudes and latitudes of sterres fixe for the Astrelabie." These fixed stars are mentioned in the body of the text: "The riet of thin Astrelabie with thy zodiak, . . . contenith certein nombre of sterres fixes, with her longitudes and latitudes determinat, yf so be errid. The names of the sterres ben writen in the margyn of the riet there that the maker have not as thei sitte, of which sterres the smale point is clepid the centre." Chaucer mentions "Aldeberan and Algomeyse" as well as "the faire white sterre that is clepid Alhabor."[85]

Star catalogues and "tabulae stellarum fixarum quae ponuntur in astrolabio" were an integral part of many astronomical texts from the tenth to the fourteenth century, in particular of treatises on the astrolabe. They stemmed from the seventh and eighth books of Ptolemy's *Syntaxis*, the *Almagest*.

Many examples of such tables circulated in England, attached not only to the treatise ascribed to Masha'allah but in close proximity to Chaucer's treatise as well. The number and variety of these tables make for complicated mathematical and textual problems.

Throughout the Middle Ages many of these tables were detached from their original texts and began a career of wandering from one compiler or scribe to another who arbitrarily attached them to whatever text happened to be at hand. There is a wide variety of nomenclature and an almost anarchical state in the transliteration or transcription of Arabic star names and designations. In many cases the scribe had not the slightest idea of what he was copying, with the result that the manuscripts present a confusion and corruption of the unfamiliar Arabic names.[86]

In considering the Arabic nomenclature in astronomical treatises in the Latin West, one must also remember that the Arabic material derived largely from Spain. The texts and traditions of the Spanish Arab astronomers originated in the East, at the heart of the Islamic Empire, but their transmission and adaptation, including Ptolemy's *Almagest*, stemmed from the Muslim centers in the West to which, as we have seen, English scholars were the first to flock in search of Arabic learning.

One of the most remarkable, "if not the most influential"[87] of these star catalogues in the Middle Ages is found in Alfonso el Sabio's *Libros del saber de astronomía*, a collection of astronomical treatises compiled from Arabic sources and translated into Castilian, mostly by Jewish scholars, under the patronage and immediate supervision of Alfonso the Wise (1252–84), king of Leon and Castile and sponsor of the Alfonsine tables. This detailed description of stars not only gives their Arabic names in Castilian transliteration but also the meaning of each of the names and, in particular, an unusual metaphorical account of the figure formed by each constellation. It is likely that Chaucer, with his special relationship to the kingdom of Leon and Castile through the wife of John of Gaunt, was acquainted with the astronomical writings of the famous Alfonso X, with whom he shared so absorbing an interest.[88]

Chaucer's possible use of the Alfonsine star catalogues is a particularly intriguing question as "there are many outstanding mysteries connected with the transmission of the Alfonsine books to Northern Europe" including "the possibility that they survive in their original form only in English manuscripts."[89] They must have given Western readers a good idea of the meaning of many star names.

Elpheta, veiled in different transliterations, is found on almost any list of astrolabe stars. It is the name of the constellation *corona borealis*, the "northern crown" derived from the Arabic *alfakkah* in the *Almagest*, whose exact meaning and derivation are still unclear. The name appears as Elpheca, Elfeta, Alpheta, and alfeta in the star lists and on the face of the medieval English astrolabes.[90] Gunther, in his edition of Chaucer's and Masha'allah's treatises prints "a table such as Chaucer would have had in his mind," and we can clearly discern the name *alfeta* for corona; it is spelled Alpheta on the illustration of a Chaucerian astrolabe reproduced by Skeat.[91]

The Persian astronomer as-Sufi, whose tenth-century description of fixed stars was also current in medieval Europe, states that the name *alfakkah* designated the constellation of eight stars which form a crown, the first of which, called "al-munīr min al-fakkah" ("the shining one of the crown," is marked on the astrolabe.[92]

We have this description in the "tabula stellarum fixarum que ponuntur in astrolabio" compiled by John of London, the teacher of John of Garland at Oxford, in 1246: "elfeta. et ipsa est clarior in corona."[93]

There are many unsolved problems of nomenclature, in the star list of John of London, for instance, which illuminate the difficulty of finding exact equivalents of the transliteration of all Arabic star names that Chaucer used. The terminology of John of London contains about twenty names and expressions that do not appear in earlier star catalogues at all and whose origin is still undetermined. The form in which these words appear has its closest analogy in the Arabic *Almagest*. The Latin versions of Gerard of Cremona do not reflect these forms either in the manuscripts which have come down to us or in the printed incunabula edition. John of London must have derived them from another version of the *Almagest*, so far unknown, or from the Arabic text itself, through an intermediary.[94]

Aside from its importance as the original source of medieval star names, the Arabic *Almagest* has another characteristic which is not, however, reflected in the version of Gerard of Cremona: it lists the stars of each constellation as a family. We have the stars of *al-fakkah* (Elpheta) listed as "banū al-fakkah" (sons of Elpheta), or the stars of Orion, *al-jabbār* (the Powerful), listed as sons or children of *al-jabbār* (banū al-jabbār).[95] One wonders whether Chaucer was aware of this "family" arrangement of stars in one of his most favorite books. The arrangement is perfect for the structure of the *Squire's Tale*, a family romance. It is unlikely that medieval astronomers were ignorant of this type of classification, though the exact route from the Arabic escapes us for the time being in the maze of problems concerning the transmission of the *Almagest*.

In the Alfonsine books, *elfeca* is described as a figure of great virtue, comprising eight stars in the form of a royal crown or a garland, with its main star, "the shining one of the crown," near the middle.[96] The eight stars that make up the constellation, with the shining main star close to the middle of the crown, are a perfect frame for the household of Cambyuskan and Elpheta, which is the focal point of Chaucer's tale, comprising as it does the royal couple, two sons, and a daughter to be perfected and rounded by the addition of two daughters-in-law and a son-in-law in what was to be, no doubt, a happy ending to the tale. The number of gifts brought to Cambyuskan outlines a fourfold structural scheme, common in Arabian Night stories, which underlies the threefold grouping of a maiden and two brothers.

It is the stars, it seems, which we must scan for Algarsyf as well. The name clearly reveals the Arabic word for sword as one of its elements:

sif (i.e., *saif*) is a common component in names well known to medieval Europe. Sultan Saladin's brother was called Saif ad-Dīn (Sword of the Law). In the *Arabian Nights*, Saif al-Mulūk (Sword of Kings) is an Arabian hero who falls in love with the portrait of a princess, daughter of a demon king, and embarks upon a dangerous sea voyage in order to find and win her. Among four gifts which he receives from the treasury of his father, the king, are a ring and a sword.[97]

In the heavens, *saif* (a sword), is a grouping of stars in the constellation Orion, known as *al-jabbār* (the Powerful or the Giant) in the star catalogues.[98] Saif al-jabbār, the Sword of the Powerful One, is the name of the three central stars in Orion which were considered as forming a sword hanging at the giant's waist. All stars in the constellation are listed as sons or children of *al-jabbār*, which is also called *al-jauzā*, in the Arabic *Almagest*. Among them we find the three stars "joined together on the edge of the sword."[99] Here, too, Chaucer's knowledge of the name is unquestioned. The meaning of "ceyf algebar" is explained in the Alfonsine books,[100] and various stars forming the "anatomy" of *al-jabbār*, in a variety of compounds and transliterations, are common on medieval star lists. Thus we find "Rigel algeuar" for *rijl al-jabbār* as "pes orionis" (the foot of Orion) in a German star list included in Richard of Wallingford's treatise, the "Albion" (1326). It is dated around 1430 and is a translation of a Latin list of astrolabe stars compiled by John of Gmunden.[101] What is particularly important is the transliteration of *al-jabbār* as *algeuar*, clearly showing its Spanish origin on the basis of the Alfonsine *algebar*, and the possibility of simple translation to *algar*. To anyone familiar with the anarchy prevailing in medieval names from the Arabic, the transposition of *saif algeuar* to *algarsyf* presents no insurmountable problem.[102]

Algarsyf is one of two brothers and one of three royal children, two brothers and a sister, whose lives, it would seem, are to be completed by the addition of two maidens and a knight. The structural design of twos and threes in which Algarsyf is a lodestar seems to reflect an astronomical pattern of numbers which Chaucer deliberately wove into the "knotte" of his tale.

The medieval descriptions of Orion were preoccupied with the twofold and threefold grouping of stars as early as the end of the eleventh century. For example, in the account of the constellation by Notker Labeo, abbot of the famous monastery of St. Gall and, like Chaucer, a translator of *The Consolation of Philosophy* of Boethius, there are six stars at Orion's belt: three across his waist and three downward in a row. There are three stars at his head which form a close triangle, a shining red star on his right shoulder, and a shining white star on his left shoulder. There are three stars along the edge of his sword over his left thigh, two at his feet, two at his knees.[103]

Moreover, there is a link between the stars of Orion and Gemini in the medieval star catalogues which listed stars ("nomina stellarum fixarum") under their signs of the zodiac ("nomina signorum").[104] The stars of al-jabbār are listed under Gemini, the two brothers.

In the Alfonsine books Orion is described as a man of strength and bravery with a sword hanging by his side, ready for action. He grips a club in his right hand and holds a raised stick in his left. "And one foot he has placed in front and the other extended as though he wished to run or leap or was awaiting bravely something with which he had to fight." He is called brave and powerful and one promising great, strong, and marvellous deeds.[105]

The *Squire's Tale* is a romance of both brotherly and romantic love. The association of King Cambyuskan's eldest son (born of a celestial Elpheta) with a sword, if we accept a possible derivation from the star name, Saif al-jabbār (alias "Algarsaif") seems particularly appropriate, as a magic sword hanging by the knight messenger's side is one of the four fabulous gifts sent by the King of Araby and Ind. We know from the text that Prince Algarsyf's adventures were to be associated with the magic horse. "The hors that hadde wynges for to flee," we must remember, is also a constellation at whose liveliness the Alfonsine books, like Chaucer's Tartars, express their wonder and delight.[106] Was the magic sword, with its power to wound and heal, to connect Algarsyf's exploits with those of his brother Cambalo "that faught in lystes with the bretheren two"?

The tradition that Chaucer was a master of alchemy as well as astronomy and astrology, was reiterated in 1652 when Elias Ashmole included the *Canon's Yeoman's Tale* in his compendium of English alchemical treatises called *Theatrum Chemicum Britannicum*. Ashmole describes Chaucer as ranking among "the Hermetick Philosophers" and adds that "he that Reads the latter part of the *Canon's Yeoman's Tale*, will easily perceive him to be a Judicious Philosopher, and one that fully knew the *Mistery*."[107] We know that "in portraying the yeoman-narrator, the alchemist-canon, and the canon and priest of *Secunda Pars*, Chaucer made significant use of the alchemical treatises and other writings about alchemy available to him at the end of the fourteenth century."[108]

The use of allegory by medieval alchemists as a strictly defined intellectual system of implicit secrecy is best illustrated in a "code of secrecy" which entered medieval Europe from Arabic sources. Its application reveals itself in two features characteristic of Arabic alchemical literature: the use of "code words" and the "topic" of "secret of secrets."

In the lines that bring the *Canon's Yeoman's Tale* (*CYT*) to an end Chaucer cites some of the source material of his alchemical knowledge: the *Rosarium* of Arnold of Villa Nova (1240–1311) and the "book Senior."

Lo, thus seith Arnold of the Newe Toun,
As his Rosarie maketh mencioun;
He seith right thus, withouten any lye:
"Ther may no man mercurie mortifie
But it be with his brother knowlechyng."
How be that he which that first seyde this thyng
Of philosophres fader was, Hermes—
He seith how that the dragon, doutelees,
Ne dyeth nat, but if that he be slayn
With his brother; and that is for to sayn,
By the dragon, Mercurie, and noon oother
He understood, and brymstoon by his brother,
That out of Sol and Luna were ydrawe.
"And therefore," seyde he,—taak heede to my sawe—
"Lat no man bisye him this art for to seche,
But if that he th'entencioun and speche
Of philosophres understonde kan;
And if he do, he is a lewed man.
For this science and this konnyng," quod he,
"Is of the secree of secrees, pardee."
Also ther was a disciple of Plato,
That on a tyme seyde his maister to,
As his book Senior wol bere witnesse,
And this was his demande in soothfastnesse:
"Telle me the name of the privee stoon?"
And Plato answerde unto hym anoon,
"Take the stoon that Titanos men name."
"Which is that?" quod he. "Magnasia is the same,"
Seyde Plato. "Ye, sire, and is it thus?
This is *ignotum per ignocius*.
What is Magnasia, good sire, I yow preye?"
"It is a water that is maad, I seye,
Of elementes foure," quod Plato.
"Telle me the roote, good sire," quod he tho,
"Of that water, if it be youre wil."
"Nay, nay," quod Plato, "certein, that I nyl.
The philosophres sworn were everychoon
That they sholden discovere it unto noon
Ne in no book it write in no manere."[109]

[ll. 1428–66]

The alchemical teaching which the Canon's Yeoman cites from "Arnold of the Newe Toun" is a classical hermetic passage whose substance,

in a variety of open and hidden forms, is a basic concept of medieval alchemical literature. The core of the matter is an instruction for making the philosopher's stone "Elixer clept" from a compound of mercury and sulphur. In the works of Arnold of Villa Nova, Chaucer's formulation of the alchemical core—"the dragon and his brother"—has been traced to *De lapide philosophorum* and, most recently, to a treatise called *De secretis naturae*: "The discipulus asked: Why have philosophers said that mercury does not die unless it is slain with its brother? The magister replied: The first who said this was Hermes, who said that the dragon never dies unless with his brother it be killed. He means to say that Mercury never dies . . . except with his brother. . . ."[110]

The allegory of alchemy in the works of Latin writers which we have in the above passage reveals their dependence on Arabic treatises in the most direct and dramatic way. The key to an understanding of the mythological symbolism in Chaucer's quotation is the terminology of code words —"Decknamen," Arabic *rumūz* (hints)—in which the secret of alchemical knowledge was transmitted to the initiates of medieval Islam. The symbolic designations (dragon for mercury, the dragon's brother for "brymstoon" [*CYT* ll. 1438–39], sol and luna for gold and silver [*CYT* l. 826]) clearly reveal the astrological pattern which underlies the hermetic tradition of alchemy.[111] Though there is considerable diversity in the attachment of certain "cover-names" to certain metals and minerals, the study of Arabic alchemical works by Ruska, Holmyard, and, most recently, Siggel, has found an essential uniformity of designation, reflected in the alchemical treatises of the Latin West.[112]

The Canon's Yeoman's display of learning which brings his tale to a close represents the most rudimentary elements of alchemical knowledge. Its formulation is properly ascribed to Hermes "that first seyde this thyng." Like Roger Bacon before him, the Canon's Yeoman calls Hermes "the father of philosophers."[113] The authentic touch in using the authority of "the father of alchemy" to teach the properties of mercury may have escaped the Canon's Yeoman's audience if they did not remember that Mercury was the name by which Hermes himself was also known. In its synonymous association with Hermes Mercurius, mercury is therefore the root of alchemical wisdom.

The importance of sulphur in a variety of allied and related forms is also basic in Arabic alchemical writings. Throughout the Middle Ages mercury and sulphur were considered as the primary components in all metals and, at times, as the elixir par excellence.[114] The experimentation to make the elixir was based on a theory of transmutation which derived from the premise that a mixture of mercury and sulphur in various proportions had led to the formation of metals and minerals under planetary influence in the womb of the earth.[115]

The symbolic designation of mercury as "dragon" in Chaucer is only one of over sixty code words for quicksilver by which it was known to Arabic alchemical writers.[116] Many Arabic writers compiled lists of allegorical terms for the benefit of future initiates—e.g., the anonymous author of "The Book of Treasure on the Solution of the Symbol" in which mercury is designated as "serpent-dragon."[117] While the oldest Arabic treatises based themselves on Hellenistic nomenclature, the code names which entered the Latin West are mostly translations of Persian and Arabic designations. They often expressed a quality in the metal or mineral that seemed most apparent. Thus, many code words for mercury express its property of elusiveness or winged flight, e.g., "white bird" (*tair abyad*), "white eagle" (*'uqāb abyad*), "demon" (*ghūl*), "the fleeing one" (*al-farr*), by the side of such images as "foam of the sea" (*raghwrat al-bahr*), "spittle of the moon" (*lu 'āb al-qamar*), "moist pearl" (*lu'lu' ratib*).[118] The term "dragon" (*at-tinnīn*) for mercury is found in an anonymous "Epistle on the Science of Chemistry" which lists twenty-four code words for each substance.[119] "Draco autem est aqua divina," explains the Latin translator in Chaucer's "book Senior," where its original Arabic author, Muhammad ibn Umail, wrote only the Arabic word for dragon—*tinnīn*.[120] The classification of the substances into "bodies" and "spirits" is also as we find it in Chaucer. Mercury is cited as both "body" and "spirit," though its code names are given among "bodies."

> As to quicksilver, we have enumerated its names with the metals. As to its being mentioned among the metals, this is necessary because it is the first of them and the others are derived from it and descend from it. As to its being mentioned among the "spirits," this is because it flees from fire and does not resist it, and thus it is also counted among the "spirits." Accordingly the "bodies" are those which melt in fire and do not flee from it, while the "spirits" flee from fire and cannot bear it.[121]

The "spirits" are mercury, sal ammoniac, realgar, orpiment, "yellow sulphur," "red sulphur," and "white sulphur." The great importance of sulphureous substances is easily apparent to the lay eye in the incipits of medieval Latin alchemical treatises and the chapter headings in Geber's *Summa perfectionis*,[122] Chaucer lists the alchemical trinity: "Arsenyk, sal armonyak, and Brymstoon" (*CYT* l. 799).

The variety of code words for sulphur extends to the designations for *zarnīkh*, termed "arsenicum" in the Latin treatises, which is both realgar and orpiment.[123] Sulphur is most commonly named "scorpion" (*al-'aqrab*), a designation which, for some reason, is not found in the Latin texts.[124] It is also "the winged" (*dhū al-jināhain*), "the golden" (*adh-dhahabī*), and "son of the sun" (*ibn ash-shams*). It is *zarnīkh* which is referred to as "brother" (*akh*) or, to comprise realgar and orpiment as one, "the two brothers" (*al-akhwān*) or "the two friends" (*al-khalīlān*).[125] The sibling relationship which, in Chaucer's passage, links mercury and "brymstoon" is a basic principle of medieval alchemical allegory.

The symbolism of life and death in the transmutation of alchemical substances is explained as follows by a thirteenth-century writer, Abu al-Qasim al-Iraqi:

> By "death" and "life" they [the alchemists] refer to a substance from which it is possible by suitable treatment to remove its lightness, and do away with its movement in the fire, so much so that when it is placed therein it shows no movement. . . . By "life" they mean the opposite of this. . . .[126]

The metaphysical poignancy of the technical term "mortificare" (cf. "this quyksilver I wol mortifye"—*CYT* l. 1126) in its application to quicksilver was fully realized by Arab alchemical writers. Argentum vivum is the "living" ("quick") silver. Its Arabic designation, *zibāq*, is a Persian form which preserves the "living" element of the substance in the Indo-European root, *jiv*.[127] The metaphorical impact in the "killing" of mercury by sulphur, his "brother," which permeates the Chaucerian passage with biblical force, is fully brought home in the opening words of an ordinary instruction contained in al-Razi's alchemical "Book of the Secret of Secrets": "take living quicksilver and kill it."[128]

How closely all alchemists, including Arnold of the Newe Toun and Chaucer, followed conventional Arabic usage in their phrasing of alchemical thought is also clear from the *Turba Philosophorum*, an alchemical classic of the twelfth century which depicts a general debate of philosophers and is a compilation translated from Arabic sources: "Item notificio vobis," says the speaker to the crowd of philosophers, "quod Draco nunquam moritur."[129] An interpolated passage toward the end of the *Turba*, the *Visio Arislei*, is a dream vision of the marriage of sulphur and mercury which explains the "multiplying" family relationships in the idiom of alchemy—"Thogh that he multiplie terme of his lyve" (*CYT* l. 1479)—within a typical allegory of love. The names of the romantic couple are Cabritis, the Arabic word for sulphur (*kibrīt*) and Beua, a corruption of Beida, the Arabic *al-baiḍa* (the white one). The allegorical marriage is incestuous, for Beua is the sister of Cabritis. This immorality, however, is countered by citing the example of Adam, who married his sons to his daughters in order to have them "multiply." The setting in which the marriage takes place is the dream in which Arisleus and his alchemist companions arrive in a region of the sea at the end of the world where nothing "multiplies." They offer the inhabitants and their king to teach them their secret. "If there were a philosopher among you," says Arisleus to the assembled strangers, "your sons could multiply, your trees would not die but your seed would grow and your good things would increase and you would be kings prevailing over your foes."

Arisleus then proceeds to teach the king the facts of life by which a union of male to male, which the natives practice, cannot be fruitful. Nature requires a union of male to female. It is under these circumstances that sulphur and mercury, son and daughter of the king, are to be united in marriage, and the objection of the father—"Heu tibi: Numquid vir suam ducit sororem?"—is overruled on biblical authority. Moreover, the marriage of sister to brother will improve the brother "eo quod ex ipso est." However, at the moment of union, sulphur, Cabritis, "dies." The enraged king puts the alchemists in jail, accusing them of murdering his children. The philosophers promise to resuscitate the son through the daughter if the daughter, quicksilver, is allowed to stay with them in jail for eighty days. At the end of the period, "in the shadows of the waves, the intense heat of summer and the turbulence of the sea," they joyfully announce that the king's son has been resurrected.[130]

The allegorical siblings, sulphur and mercury, change their sex in Arabic alchemical treatises. Sulphur may be mercury's "brother" or "sister," and mercury may be a feminine or masculine "body" allied to sulphur of the opposite sex. Thus we have the following pronouncement by Mercury in an allegorical debate between mercury and gold in a Latin work, *De aluminibus et salibus*, ascribed to Razi by Vincent de Beauvais:[131] "And if anyone unites me with my brother or sister, he will live and rejoice, and I shall be sufficient unto him in all eternity, were he to live a thousand times thousand years."[132]

The descent of mercury and sulphur from the "sun" and the "moon" ("That out of Sol and Luna were ydrawe," *CYT* 1. 1440) is explained in a "Tractatulus Avicennae" in a chapter of "De Natura Corporum: id est, Solis & Lunae, & eorum Sulphure."[133] After pointing out that gold (sol) is the most perfect body, lord and king of all substances, the author states that it has much of the virtue of sulphur and little of its substance, while, conversely, containing much of the substance of mercury and little of its virtue. Silver (luna), on the other hand, has much of the substance of sulphur and little of its virtue, while containing little of the substance of mercury and much of its virtue. Moreover, silver is a feminine body so that the extraction of mercury and sulphur in their perfect relationship and form implies the marriage of Sol and Luna. An Arabic writer explains the allegorical coupling:

They also use the term "marriage" meaning thereby a substance to which this name is necessarily appropriate, since it will join with a substance female in relation to itself, and its lightness is transferred to it as sperm is transferred from the male to the female; they therefore describe it by this characteristic of it. From this thou mayest judge of the rest of the analogies and allegories of the Sages.[134]

The part of the "Tractatulus Avicennae" which deals with Sol and Luna is an excerpt from *De aluminibus et salibus* ascribed to Razi.[135] There is no Arabic original of the treatise among the works of Razi, but a fragmentary Arabic text originating in Spain has been found for parts of the Latin,[136] an illustration of the complex interdependence of Latin tracts and their relation to original Arabic treatises.[137]

The text of the "book Senior" in Chaucer presents no obscure problem of origins. As Ruska was the first to point out,[138] the passage is found in an Arabic alchemical treatise of the tenth century by "Sheikh" Muhammad ibn Umail at-Tamimi as-Sadiq, known to the West as "Senior Zadith filius Hamuel." The work, poetically entitled "The Book of the Silvery Water and the Starry Earth," is a compendium of quotations from ancient philosophers who practiced alchemy. Ibn Umail wrote it as a commentary on an alchemical poem of sixty-seven stanzas, entitled "A Letter from the Sun to the Moon" (*risālah ash-shams ila al-hilāl*). The Latin versions of Ibn Umail's treatise, which constitute the "book Senior," contains large portions of the commentary and part of the risālah under the title "Epistola solis ad lunam crescentem."[139] The Latin "book Senior" and the "Epistola solis ad lunam crescentem" are therefore frequently titles of an identical work.[140]

The learned dialogue between two alchemists with which the Canon's Yeoman impresses the Canterbury pilgrims has the following form in the Arabic original of Ibn Umail:

> Qālimūs said: "Take a stone called Titānūs. And it is a stone, white, red, yellow, black, which has many names and diverse colours, and they are a single spiritual nature hidden in the sand, describe it in its colours which appear from it when it is treated." And Rūnūs said: "Describe it to me, oh sage," he said, "it is the body of the noble magnesia which all philosophers praise." And he said: "And what is magnesia?" He said: "It is congealed composite water which endures the killing through the fire. It is the wide large good sea, whose excellence Hermes described, and he considered as magnesia here the spirit and the soul, and its body is the ashes which are in the core of the ashes." And Plato said: "Everyone is one because every man has a soul."[141]

The teacher Qalimus and his interrogator, Runus, are transformed into Solomon and a sage (sapiens) in the Latin text.[142] In view of Solomon's place in the "wisdom literature" of Jews, Christians, and Muslims, the transformation seems natural. It may, however, have been due to a misreading of the Arabic lettering,[143] one of the most common phenomena in Arabic-Latin translation. The names, transformed from the Greek, are still obscure.[144]

Chaucer's substitution of Plato for Solomon in the dialogue as reported by the Canon's Yeoman may be explained from Ibn Umail's text in which the discussion of magnesia is followed by "and Plato said," both in Arabic and Latin. The association of alchemical teaching with Plato is a common feature of alchemical literature. It is found, in its most representative form, in the *Kitāb muṣaḥḥaḥāt Aflāṭūn* (The Book of Rectifications of Plato) of Jabir, "a very curious compilation" in which Plato initiates his disciple Timaeus into the secrets of alchemy.[145]

In Ibn Umail's text, Plato continues the dialogue on magnesia by affirming the doctrine of the World Soul as One and discussing man's soul in its interdependence with the animate and inanimate world of created beings. He then transfers the Platonic principle of the encompassing soul to the alchemical relation of gold to copper, and of mercury to sulphur and magnesium. The passage ends with the elixir:

> . . . and if they called it a stone, it is one kind which has no equal to it among the stones and no match, and if he collected it, [and] indeed it is the Name, and if it was called water, it is not particles of waters and it has no match, and if he collected it, [and] indeed it is one Name, it is uncompounded, not perfected except from itself and in itself, [and a greeting of peace] and verily this is the secret which is in it and there is none in any outside it.[146]

The Latin "book Senior" has a gloss to replace "the Name" in the Arabic text: "tamen est spiritus, & habet nomen spiritus. Et si dicatur aqua, non est sicut caeterae aquae, nec habet intellectum distinctum."[147] In the Chaucerian version the dialogue ends as follows:

> What is Magnasia, good sire, I yow preye?"
> "It is a water that is maad, I seye,
> Of elementes foure," quod Plato.
> "Telle me the roote, good sire," quod he tho,
> "Of that water, if it be youre wil."
> "Nay, nay," quod Plato, "certein, that I nyl.
> The philosophres sworn were everychoon
> That they sholden discovere it unto noon,
> Ne in no book it write in no manere.
> For unto Crist it is so lief and deere
> That he wol nat that it discovered bee,

> But where it liketh to his deitee
> Men for t'enspire, and eek for to deffende
> Whom that hym liketh; lo, this is the ende."

[ll. 1458–71]

The refusal, in the alchemical Platonic dialogue, to reveal the secret of "the Name," or the "spirit," which is reflected in Chaucer, shows the connection between the idiom of alchemy and the idiom of religious mysticism as transmitted to the Latins from Arabic sources. An additional feature in Chaucer is the elaboration of "the secret" in a Christian admonition about the spiritual hazards of alchemy. In this, as E. H. Duncan has shown, Chaucer was using the "book Senior" as well. He was, in fact, using the literal translation of an Islamic invocation to Allah.

The lines of direct translation are apparent in another passage in Ibn Umail:

> And this is the secret about which they swore that they would not put it into a book and not one of them would reveal it and they referred the matter concerning it to Allah who is great and mighty. His name inspires him whom He wishes to inspire and hinders him whom He wishes to hinder for He is the root without which the art does not avail anyone ever except through Him, and what they concealed is the management of this thing until it becomes firm through the fire so that it becomes a great matter and verily such powers appear from it . . . and if they do not learn it they will not have . . . these powers which this deed makes and Muhammad ibn Umail praises Allah, may His name be sanctified, for what He bestowed on him and that He made him excel in it and inspired him to it with knowledge of this hidden secret and this after the long search and long-lasting wakefulness, and he disclosed what was obscure in their expressions with such praise through which he could attain His pleasure and according to his merits and deserts.[148]

The substitution of Deus for Allah presented no problem to the Latin translator who turned Arabic into Latin for the benefit of his fellow Christians in the West. One of the Latin Geber tracts, composed in the form of a dialogue between Demogorgon and Geber, is opened by hailing Geber as the wisest descendant of "the great Muhammad."[149] The tendency to "translate" from the Arabic whatever ideas presented themselves is an important component in the Christian attitude to alchemy, as it is in the attitude to astrology. The religious view of Islam on the secret art had entered the West as an integral part of the scientific material.

In its immediate context Chaucer's "secree of secrees" expresses the ritual injunction to secrecy from master to pupil and author to reader that characterizes all Arabic alchemical treatises. "Labour not to expose our secret more than we have exposed it unto thee, or thy exposure thereof will expose thyself," says the thirteenth-century Abu'l Qasim al-Iraqi in concluding his "Book of Knowledge Acquired Concerning the Cultivation of Gold."[150] We find the same admonition at the end of Arnold's *Rosarium*, the Canon's Yeoman's acknowledged source: "Et qui habes istum librum in sinu tuo reconde nullique ipsum revelles nec manibus impiorum offeras: quia secretum secretorum omnium philosophorum plenarie comprehendit."[151] Chaucer's own version in the *Canon's Yeoman's Tale*—" 'For this science and this konnyng,' quod he, 'Is of the secree of secrees, pardee' "—is more closely related to a passage in the Arnoldian *De lapide philosophorum* and *De secretis naturae*.[152] However, the medieval rendering of "secretum secretorum" is the usual translation of a common Semitic superlative, the Arabic *sirr al-asrār*, a key designation, widely known in the West, in the literary convention of hermetic writing. It appears in the title of al-Razi's alchemical work "The Book of the Secret of Secrets"[153] and in the pseudo-Aristotelian *Secret of Secrets* whose extraordinary popularity in Western medieval literature in the thirteenth-century version of Philip of Tripoli is attested by 207 Latin manuscripts.[154]

The historical origins of "the secret of secrets" as a figure of speech in the idiom of alchemy take us to the secret fraternities and mystic sects of medieval Islam which were known as the movement of the Isma'iliya and gave rise to the Assassins, the Sufi poets, and the Ikhwan as-Safā (the "Brethren of Purity").[155] The core of their teaching is the belief that the series of revealed prophets who followed Muhammad would stop with the seventh Imam, Isma'il, "the hidden prophet," an incarnation of the divinity. The role of man is to express the need that the universal soul feels to attain perfect knowledge. In the corpus of Jabir ibn Hayyan, the Geber of the Latins, that perfect knowledge is alchemy—the mystic doctrine of "art" by definition.[156]

The authorship of the tenth-century alchemical writings, attributed to the eighth-century mystic Jabir, is one of the most fascinating problems in the history of medieval thought. Jabir was the most famous alchemical authority among the Arabs; Geber was celebrated among the Latins as the author of a Latin alchemical compendium, the "Summa perfectionis," the earliest manuscripts of which date from the thirteenth century. In Arabic, the works of Jabir are a "vast body of literature which comprises all the sciences of the ancients which passed to Islam,"[157] in which, however, alchemy is the science of sciences. The writings cannot be the work of a single author; the scientific terminology, "without exception," is that introduced at the end of the ninth century by Hunain ibn Ishaq, the first translator of "Greek into Arabic."

The Latin Geber tracts have been shown to incorporate Latin translations of al-Razi's *Book of the Secret of Secrets*.[158] According to Ruska, the influence of Razi is most apparent in the methodical classification, for Razi divested alchemy of its superstitions and gave it a strict scientific form.[159] Nevertheless, the title of his alchemical book respects the strict tradition of the "elvysshe craft" in which gold is "the greatest secret" (*sirr aʿzam*); sulphur, "the divine secret" (*sirr ilāhī*); and mercury, "the revealed secret" (*sirr makshūf*).[160]

The reason for the preeminence of alchemy in the writings of Jabir has been explained by Paul Kraus:[161] the empirical "worldly" sciences rank below the religious and metaphysical ones and, in fact, owe their existence to the latter. Alchemy is the most important worldly science, the other sciences having mainly an auxiliary function. Alchemy is the only worldly science to be pursued for its own sake. It is the perfection of empirical knowledge. Its task is the making of the elixir, the completely harmonious substance in which all components are balanced to perfection. This elixir is a third cosmos, linking microcosm and macrocosm. In this way the material sciences are united with the spiritual ones of which they were originally a part, and alchemy is the science which unites them. What is important in the making of the elixir is not the process of transmutation to gold for the sake of its material value but the achievement of perfect religious knowledge, the penetration into the most sublime secret of mystical truth: the hidden Imam.

On the practical level, the injunction to secrecy in the transmission of alchemy may be regarded as the need to guard professional knowledge from outsiders.[162] This "trade" element is discernible in the alchemical portions of the pseudo-Aristotelian *Secret of Secrets* which gave the term *the secret of secrets* wide currency in the West:

> And know, O Alexander, that I am going to impart to thee a secret of divine knowledge which has been strictly guarded and preserved, regarding the secrecy and inviolability of which sages and philosophers have taken mutual promises and oaths, in order that it may not fall into the hands of a weaver, horse-doctor, blacksmith, and carpenter who may cause corruption in the earth, and destroy agriculture and procreation.[163]

The concluding discourse on talismans, astrology, and the virtues of stones is specifically addressed to the practitioners of the "special sciences":

> And know that those who are endowed with clear intellect and good memory for acquiring knowledge, and who can find out the hidden through that which is apparent to them, having reached to

hidden truths of this deep and mysterious science, they observed extreme caution and miserliness in communicating it to others, although it is of such a universal benefit. They did so from the fear that they may come to share this knowledge with those who did not possess sufficient understanding for it, and because God's wisdom has decreed that His gifts should not be equally divided among His creatures. But, thanks to God, thou art not one of those who are debarred from knowing these mysteries, but thou art fully worthy of it.[164]

The importance which Western writers on alchemy attached to the *Secretum Secretorum* is clearly expressed by Petrus Bonus, a "physicus" of Ferrara who in 1330 wrote the alchemical work *Margarita Pretiosa*. He refers to the significance which the Old Philosopher (Aristotle) attributed to the "art": "Et idem scripsit eam Alexand. Regi discipulo suo in lib. de Secretis secretorum, cap. de lapidibus preciosis eodem more, quo antiqui Philosophi alii scripserunt scilicet occulto, figurato, velato sermone. Imo totus ille liber est mysticus, & est de hac arte, sicut de principali proposito."[165] There is also some indication that the *Secretum Secretorum* was regarded as a guide to spiritual mystic knowledge in Europe when the Latin text was translated into the vernacular by a German Cistercian nun.[166] In the works of Jabir, however, the association of alchemy, the dominant subject, with the doctrines of a religious fraternity, the Isma'iliya, is so close as to give the alchemical exposition the character of Isma'ilitic teaching: "For these books, oh brother, are miracles of my master, and nobody—and the Great One may prove it true—may take possession of what is in them of the sciences except our brother."[167]

The Isma'ili content is equally pronounced in the treatises of the "Brethren of Purity" to which the writings of Jabir are closely related.[168] This secret fraternity of Basra, which flourished in the tenth century, produced a compendium of knowledge in the form of fifty-two treatises *rasā'il* ("epistles") addressed to the "faithful brother." The compendium contains the story of the *Magian and the Jew*, which reached Gower from the *Secret of Secrets* and is an analogue of the *Secretum Secretorum* both in content and form.[169] The "secret" is conveyed by the Brethren of Purity in a conventional frame of direct instruction and concealed in the names and actions of a literary plot.[170] "And I think that in this there is an allegory of the allegories and a secret of the secrets," says a king to the head philosopher of the "jinn" in a discourse on the nature of man and beast. "So make known to me what the truth of these sayings is and the allusion of these allegories."[171]

It is the essence of this tradition that is preserved in its original formulation in the writings of the Latin alchemists. Strange as it may seem,

Chaucer's Canon's Yeoman thus expounds the terminology of Isma'ili doctrine in which the outward form (*zāhir*) serves to hide and protect the inward esoteric core (*bāṭin*). The pseudo-Aristotelian *Secret of Secrets* had done most to spread this information among the international elite of learned medieval men:

> The secret means is one peculiar to the saints and sages whom God has chosen from amongst His creatures and endowed with His own knowledge. And I shall impart to thee this secret as well as others in certain chapters of this book, which is outwardly a treasure of wisdom and golden rules, and inwardly the cherished object itself. So when you have studied its contents and understood its secrets you will thereby achieve your highest desires and fulfil your loftiest expectations. Rejoice in it therefore, and may God help you attain this knowledge and to honour the masters thereof.[172]

Part Two: The Literary Heritage

Arabian Source Books

The scientific and philosophical learning transmitted by the Latin translators from the Arabic invigorated medieval literature in specific ways which, as my examples have shown, can be traced to specific sources. There was, however, also a type of moralistic literature with a looser structure which entered the West at the same time and is generally referred to as "wisdom literature." The Latin Middle Ages inherited this "wisdom literature" in the Bible. The Book of Proverbs, Job, Ecclesiastes, Ecclesiasticus, The Wisdom of Solomon, and many sections in other biblical books belong to this type.[1] But the "wisdom literature" of the Old Testament is not original. It represents a long literary tradition stemming from the civilizations of Egypt and Babylonia, which preceded Israel and profoundly affected its moral and literary expression.[2]

The literature of wisdom is a genre whose primary function was didactic and exhortatory. Its various types, moral tales in dialogue from "father" to "son"—or from "master" to "pupil"—like the *Disciplina Clericalis* or the collected sayings of wise men, elders, teachers, and philosophers (like al-Mubashshir ibn Fatik's *Dicts and Sayings*), "are parts of the urgent striving for an order of meaning and values that would illuminate understanding and provide guidance for human behaviour."[3] The diffusion of this literature by the Latin translators in the twelfth and thirteenth centuries was as natural as the spreading of "wisdom," in verse and prose, by the wandering scribes of the ancient Near East.[4]

It is within this context that we have to view what I have called "Arabian source books," that is, secular anthologies of Greco-Arabic wisdom on which the medieval world consciously drew in its literature and thought. Their quintessence seemed to be contained in the treatise known as *The Secret of Secrets*: the art of human conduct and good government conveyed by the greatest of philosophers, Aristotle, to the greatest master in the rule of men, Alexander the Great.

"Disciplina Clericalis"

The *Disciplina Clericalis* of Petrus Alfonsi is a collection of thirty-four tales, meant to serve as exempla in a "rule for clerics": "Huic libello nomen iniugens et est nomen ex re: id est Clericalis Disciplina; reddit enim clericum disciplinatum."[5] The tales are framed by exhortations

from father to son and from teacher to pupil and contain a selection of
sayings attributed to various philosophers, on the model of similar collections by Hunain ibn Ishaq (d. 877) and al-Mubashshir ibn Fatik (b. ca.
1020) which were popular in the Arab world. Among the philosophers
Petrus Alfonsi names Enoch, "qui in lingua arabica cognominatur Edric"
(i.e. Idris, identified with Hermes Trismegistus in some Arabic works),
and Luqman, a legendary figure of the period of Arab paganism who was
adopted into the Koran as a wise maker of proverbs. The sayings of Socrates, Aristotle, and Solomon are introduced in traditional Arab guise.

Petrus Alfonsi's preface explains his purpose in composing the *Disciplina
Clericalis*. It was to serve as a guidebook for practitioners of the Christian
faith. He says that he "translated" the book into Latin, having perhaps
composed it in Hebrew or Arabic. Drawing on Arabic literary patterns,
he tried to make a lasting impression on his readers by inaugurating a new
didactic art: "fragilem etiam hominis esse consideravi complexionem:
quae ne taedium incurrat, quasi provehendo paucis et paucis instruenda
est; duritiae quoque eius recordatus, ut facilius retineat, quodammodo
necessario mollienda et dulcificanda est. . . . " He has "therefore composed this little book partly from the sayings and warnings of philosophers, partly from Arabic proverbs and admonitions both in prose and
verse, and partly from fables about animals and birds [Propterea ergo
libellum compegi partim ex proverbiis philosophorum et suis castigationibus, partim ex proverbiis et castigationibus Arabicis et fabulis et versibus,
partim ex animalium et volucrum similitudinibus]."[6]

In the narrative tradition, both Hebrew and Arabic, on which he was
nurtured, Petrus Alfonsi composed a loose and flexible frame in which the
moralizing intent is subordinated to the fascinating human interest of the
story. The exhortations are distinctly separated. The simple structural
arrangement reflects the clarity of a scientific mind that introduced a
wholly new species of literature to western Europe. Petrus Alfonsi's
"opusculus" is the first link in a Western chain that leads to Chaucer's
narrative art.

The tales of the *Disciplina Clericalis* were drawn from the international
folklore of the East Indian, Byzantine, Persian, Arabian, and Hebrew
storehouse. In recent years, their motifs, sources, and analogues have been
authoritatively described and classified.[7] The singular importance of the
work rests on its character as a bridge by which the literary "matter of
Araby," both in content and form, entered the Western reservoir that
supplied vernacular writers.

Petrus Alfonsi's collection was done into French verse as early as the
twelfth century.[8] Nearly half of its tales may be traced in the most popular
compendium of edifying stories for the use of preachers, the thirteenth-

century *Gesta Romanorum*, in which Petrus Alfonsi is expressly mentioned by name.[9] Between the twelfth and the sixteenth centuries there are sixty-three different manuscripts of Latin versions of the *Disciplina Clericalis*;[10] it is constantly used by a host of writers, including Jacques de Vitry, Albert de Brescia, Odo of Cheriton, Nicholas Bozon, and John of Hoveden. A fifteenth-century Middle English version, carelessly made from the Latin, is extant in a manuscript at Worcester Cathedral. It omits eight of the original tales and adds three tales which were attributed to Petrus Alfonsi in one manuscript of the Latin version (Cambridge University Library MS. Ii. vi. 11).[11] One of them, the tale of the Blind Man and the Fruit Tree, was retold by Chaucer in the *Merchant's Tale*.

In the literature of medieval England, the history of the tales of the *Disciplina Clericalis* is best illustrated by two examples which acquired an independent literary existence in the thirteenth century: the Middle English *Dame Sirith* and *The Fox and the Wolf*. Both poems have been preserved in a single manuscript, Bodleian Digby MS. 86, which also contains the earliest French version of the *Disciplina Clericalis*.[12]

Dame Sirith, the oldest example of a fabliau in Middle English literature, is the story of the Weeping Bitch. It was told by Petrus Alfonsi to illustrate the craft and wiles of women. We also find it in the *Arabian Nights* and the medieval Hebrew *Tales of Sendebar* (Sindbad), a collection representing eight extant Eastern versions of *The Seven Sages of Rome*, in which a series of tales is told by seven sages or viziers, the first of whom is called Sindibad.[13] In the *Arabian Nights* the story of the Weeping Bitch is told by the fourth vizier. The Middle English versions of *The Seven Sages of Rome*, like all other European versions of the *Seven Sages*,[14] have omitted the story, so that *Dame Sirith* has an independent and free-floating existence of its own. In fourteenth-century England its dramatic dialogue is reflected in the *Interludium de Clerico et Puella*.[15]

The plot of the Middle English *Dame Sirith* is identical with that in the *Disciplina Clericalis*. As told by Petrus Alfonsi, a virtuous wife whose husband absents himself on a journey is persuaded by an old woman "religionis habitu decorata" to yield to a lover by means of a trick.

A bitch is fed with mustard bread, after two days of fasting, and is presented to the virtuous woman as an example of what happens when a lover is refused. The bitch sheds tears, and the old procuress gives the following explanation: "Haec quam conspicis canicula mea erat filia casta nimis ac decora. Quam iuvenis adamavit quidam, sed adeo casta erat ut eum omnino sperneret et eius amorem respueret. Unde dolens adeo efficitur ut magna aegritudine stringeretur: pro qua culpa miserabiliter haec supradicta nata mea in caniculam mutata est."[16] The frightening prospect of being turned into a bitch like the old woman's daughter

is sufficient to dispel all marital scruples. The pining lover is brought to
the house and his desire fulfilled.

The extant English versions of the *Gesta Romanorum* do not include the
story, and the compiler of the continental *Gesta* could not tolerate the
sinful but happy ending of the oriental tale and made the husband return
at night and put his wife and her lover to death. "Thus did the wicked
project of an old woman involve many in ruin."[17] Petrus Alfonsi's moralizing epilogue on the wiles of women is turned into an allegory of the
husband as Christ, the wife as the soul exercising her free will and becoming enamored of the flesh, the old procuress as the devil, and the weeping
bitch as the presumptuous belief that one will get away with sin because
of God's mercy.

The ending in the Arabic and Hebrew versions, which are preserved in
the *Arabian Nights* and the *Tales of Sendebar*, differs from Petrus Alfonsi and
seems to have been unknown to medieval writers in the West. On obtain-
ing the virtuous woman's consent by the threatening example of the
weeping bitch, the procuress goes off to call the importunate lover. Not
finding him at his house, she begins to worry about her fee. She goes to
the marketplace to find another customer and happens upon the woman's
husband who has just returned from abroad. She offers to procure him a
beautiful woman. After some hesitation, the husband agrees and follows
her "to see who might be the prostitute in his town." He is led to the door
of his own house where he sees his wife beautifying herself for a lover.
"And she lifted up her eyes and recognized her husband. And with great
cunning she ran towards him and seized his hair and his beard. And she
said to him: 'So this is the covenant that was between us! I knew just what
day you were coming back, so I arranged all this to test you! So that's
how you behaved in foreign lands.' " Having turned the tables on the
embarrassed husband, the clever wife finally allows herself to be molli-
fied.[18] Undoubtedly this dénouement would have thoroughly appealed to
the Wife of Bath.

The significant absence of this ending in Western versions of the Weeping Bitch tends to link *Dame Sirith* with the *Disciplina Clericalis* rather than
with the complicated history of *The Seven Sages of Rome*. The presence of
this ending in the Greek *Syntipas*, the version of *The Seven Sages of Rome* to
which the English tale has been "most closely related," does not support
the view that the English *Dame Sirith* "differs from most other western
versions of the tale in that it is based directly on an oriental version of the
story."[19]

Dame Sirith shows how completely an oriental story was absorbed into
the popular tradition of medieval England within a hundred years of its
first appearance in the West. The characters, unnamed in Petrus Alfonsi
and the original oriental versions, are given thoroughly English features

and names. The setting is clearly marked on native soil and the voices
are as distinctively English as Chaucer's. The opening motif is the love of a
youth, called Willekin, for a wedded woman, called Margery:

> Ich habbe iloued þe moni ʒer,
> Þau Ich nabbe nout ben her
>   Mi loue to schowe.
> Wile þi louerd is in toune,
> Ne mai no mon wiþ þe holden roune
>   Wiþ no þewe.
> ʒurstendai Ich herde saie,
> As Ich wende bi þe waie,
>   Of oure sire:
> Me tolde me þat he was gon
> To þe feire of Botolfston
>   In Lincolneschire.

The tone is that of homely vernacular lyric:

> "Dame, dame, torn þi mod!
> Þi curteisi wes euer god,
>   And ʒet shal be:
> For þe Louerd þat ous haueþ wrout,
> Amend þi mod, and torn þi þout,
>   And rew on me!"

> . . . .
> "Swete lemmon, merci!
> Same ne vilani
>   Ne bede I þe non;
> Bote derne loue I þe bede,
> As mon þat wolde of loue spede,
>   And finde won."

The lady, however, is "wif boþe god and trewe," and the lover departs
"drerimod" to consult "dame Siriz þe hende," and to entreat her help
by "ful riche mede." He promises her

> Moni a pound and moni a mark,
> Warme pilche and warme shon.

The old procuress is also unmistakably "Christian."

> For Ich am old, and sek, and lame—
> Seknesse haueþ maked me ful tame.
> Blesse þe, blesse þe, leue knaue!

. . . .
Ich am on holi wimon;
On wicchecrafft nout I ne con,
Bote wiþ gode men almesdede
Ilke dai mi lif I fede,
And bidde mi paternoster and mi crede,
Þat Goed hem helpe at hore nede
Þat helpen me mi lif to lede,
And leue þat hem mote wel spede

. . . .
"Liჳ me nout, Wilekin, bi þi leute:
Is hit þin hernest þou tellest me?
Louest þou wel dame Margeri?"

Finally the old woman professes to pity Willekin and they make a "fore-ward"—the woman receives twenty shillings to buy sheep and swine. Willekin's scepticism at seeing her feed a bitch with pepper and mustard is quashed by a truly Chaucerian touch: "Be stille, boinard!" Dame Sirith, with the weeping bitch in tow, then gains entry to Margery as a beggar whom the good wife feeds "for loue of Goed." The procuress practices her deceit by lamenting her fate as the mother of a daughter who had refused to commit adultery with "a modi clarc wiþ croune" and was turned by him into a bitch as an act of revenge.

Þis is mi douter þat Ich of speke:
For del of hire min herte brekeþ.
Loke hou hire heien greten;
On hire cheken þe teres meten.

The moral of her tale is not lost on Margery:

A, wose euer is ჳong houssewif,
Ha loueþ ful luitel hire lif,
And eni clerc of loue hire bede,
Bote hoe grante and lete him spede!

Willekin is brought posthaste and Margery is only too delighted to abandon her virtue:

Welcome, Wilekin, swete þing!
Þou art welcomore þen þe king.
Wilekin þe swete,
Mi loue I þe bihete,
To don al þine wille!

Dame Sirith departs with a lusty encouragement and the last word:

And wose is onwis
And for non pris
Ne con geten his leuemon,
I shal, for mi mede,
Garen him to spede,
For ful wel I con.[20]

The homely and localized way in which the story is told shows how thoroughly it has been acclimatized in the native literary tradition. Curiously enough, there is a touch about its ending that recalls Indian versions of the tale. There a married woman is turned into a bitch because, in proudly rejecting a lover, her concern for her own virtue was greater than her consideration for the suffering of a fellow being and her duty to allow the senses their lawful sway.[21] There is something of this in the way the English poet slyly pricks the bubble of virtue in the good wife Margery who proudly declares at the beginning:

And Ich am wif boþe god and trewe.
Trewer womon ne mai no mon cnowe
Þen Ich am

Her tone at the end is rueful and pleading:

Wilekin þe swete,
Mi loue I þe bihete,
    To don al þine wille!
Turnd Ich haue mi þout,
For I ne wolde nout
    Þat þou þe shuldest spille.

Like the fables of the *Disciplina Clericalis*, the tale of the Weeping Bitch originated in India, presupposing a tale of metempsychosis in the transformation of a woman into a dog.[22] By a curious undercurrent of sensibility, the humorous treatment of the English fabliau reflects an original Indian motif which does not appear in any other oriental version of the story. In Syriac, Greek, Arabic, Persian, and Hebrew, a vindication of adultery under any pretext, however ironical, would not only have been utterly immoral but also would have foiled the purpose that it was meant to illustrate: "And you, my lord King, do not be ensnared by the deceit of women."[23] It is this moral that is emphasized in the *Disciplina Clericalis*. It is extended to all sinners in the use of the story by Jacques de Vitry,[24] but completely ignored in the earthy vitality of *Dame Sirith*.

The tale of the Fox and the Wolf in its appearance in Europe is also associated with the *Disciplina Clericalis*. The Middle English poem *The Fox and the Wolf* is generally assumed to be based on an unidentified

French original corresponding to Branch 4 of the *Roman de Renart*.[25] But a relationship of the Middle English poem to the story of the fox and the wolf in the well as told in the *Disciplina Clericalis* is implied in its appearance in Bodleian MS. Digby 86, the only manuscript which has preserved the poem. Its provenance is in the priory of Worcester where the only extant Middle English version of the complete *Disciplina* is also found. The manuscript includes *Dame Sirth*, also uniquely preserved, and a complete French poetical version of the *Disciplina*: "ci comence li romaunz peres aunfour coment il aprist e chaustia dun cher fix belement."[26] What we have in the manuscript are two contemporary versions of the story of the Weeping Bitch, one in Old French and one in Middle English, as well as Petrus Alfonsi's version of the story of the fox and the wolf in Old French by the side of a Middle English variant affected by the *Roman de Renart*.

The names of the *Roman de Renart*, which we find in *The Fox and the Wolf* (Reneuard, Sigrim), are also adopted in an expanded version of the French metrical *Disciplina*,[27] so that by the end of the thirteenth century the parentage of Petrus Alfonsi and the *Roman de Renart* in the fable of the fox and the wolf in the well is inextricably mixed.

The significant element in Petrus Alfonsi's story in relation to *The Fox and the Wolf*, is the trick the fox plays on the wolf by luring him into a well. As told by Petrus Alfonsi, a fox is chosen to arbitrate a dispute between a wolf and a plowman, the plowman having threatened his sluggish oxen with wolves and the wolf having taken him up on the threat and wanting to eat them. The fox agrees to help the plowman in return for two hens and persuades the wolf to accept a cheese as big as a round shield instead of the oxen. The cheese he shows him is the nocturnal reflection of the moon at the bottom of a well. To convince the wolf, the fox lowers himself into the well in one of two buckets which are hanging attached to each other in balance by a rope over the well. He then asks the wolf to come down on the pretext that the cheese is too heavy for him to carry. This the wolf does with alacrity, the fox rising while the wolf descends.[28]

In the Middle English *The Fox and the Wolf*, the event which leads the animals to the well is related to the fable of the fox and the cock in Marie de France[29] and to Chaucer's *Nun's Priest's Tale*, whose precise relationship to versions and analogues of the *Roman de Renart* is an unsolved problem. Driven to the well by thirst after an encounter with a cock and his hens in a barn, the fox does not understand the "ginne" of the buckets and lowers himself into the well. The wolf is induced to replace him there by a vision of paradise which the fox enticingly describes as his abode at the bottom and which is a delightful example of medieval satire on the clerical ideas of afterlife.[30] The core of the matter, the setting of two animals rising and descending in buckets from and into a well, is found before

Petrus Alfonsi in the Hebrew commentaries of Rashi of Troyes (1040–1105) where the actors are also a fox and a wolf and, as in Petrus Alfonsi, the wolf is tempted by the reflection of the moon mistaken for delectable cheese.[31] In the Arabic collection of proverbs by the Persian al-Maidani (d. 1124), contemporary with Petrus Alfonsi, the bucket trick is played by the fox on a hyena which the fox simply invites to join him and drink.[32]

The fables of Marie de France, the oldest collection of fables extant in a European vernacular, do not include the motif of the well and the two buckets. It is also absent in the Hebrew *Fox Fables* of Berachyah Hanakdan (ca. 1190), a contemporary of Marie de France, the translator of Adelard of Bath's *Quaestiones Naturales* into Hebrew. Berachyah's rhymed Hebrew prose reveals, at times, a flavor of English or French. He may have taken his fables from the work of the same "Alfred" whom Marie cites as one of her sources. At any rate, most of the fables are culled from a contemporary Western medieval collection and closely resemble those of Marie de France, though Berachyah, inevitably, also drew on the talmudic and midrashic stock of animal stories.[33] In the context of *The Fox and the Wolf*, this is best represented by Rashi's fable of the fox and the wolf which is the earliest known analogue to the tale as told by Petrus Alfonsi. Rashi tells the fable as a commentary on a talmudic passage in which Rabbi Meir, a teacher of the second century, is credited with a collection of "three hundred fox fables" of which only three were preserved in the speaker's, Rabbi Yochanan's, time. The nature of these fables was explained by Rabbi Hai Gaon (998–1038), the head of a talmudic college: "they were tales of animals containing moral lessons and wise teachings."[34]

Petrus Alfonsi, writing as a newly converted Christian for the benefit of Christians in the Western world, does not mention Hebrew writings among the sources listed in his prologue. But the Jewish source material in the *Disciplina* is an important component of the work. Petrus Alfonsi draws on talmudic sayings and the *Mishlei Sendebar*.[35]

The theme of "ubi sunt qui ante nos fuerunt," the universal theme of the Christian Middle Ages, already found in Old English,[36] is also contained in the *Disciplina Clericalis*. Again, like *Dame Sirith* and *The Fox and the Wolf*, we find it in two versions in Digby MS. 86: the old French metrical version of "the hermit chastening his soul," which is an exemplum of the *Disciplina*, and the hauntingly beautiful Middle English poem beginning "Uere beþ þey þat biforen vs weren." In the *Disciplina* the text is as follows: "Ubi sunt reges, ubi principes, ubi divites qui thesauros congregaverunt et inde superbi fuerunt? Modo sunt sicut qui non fuerunt, modo sunt finiti sicut qui non vixerunt, modo sunt sicut flos qui de arbore cecidit, quo ulterius non redit."[37] This is exquisitely rendered in the French version of Digby 86 which preserves an oriental flavor in the use of the word *Aumacor* (*al-Manṣūr*, "the victorious one"):

> Pren te garde com sont alé
> Cil qui ont devant toi esté:
> Où sont or li Empereor,
> Roi et Contor et Aumacor
> Qui assanblent le grant tresor
> De pierres, et d'argent et d'or?
> Or est si com n'ussent esté,
> Or est tot lor boban alé;
> Ainsi est d'ax com de la flor
> Qui chiet de l'arbre sanz retor.[38]

[Consider how those have gone who were there before you. Where are now the emperors, the kings and counts and emirs who assemble the great treasure of stones, of silver and gold? Now it is as if they had not been, now is all their pomp gone. It is so with them as with the flower which falls from the tree without return.]

The famous theme is treated by Petrus Alfonsi within a speech which a hermit, reflecting on the impermanence of earthly glory, addresses to his soul, reminding it of sin and the day of judgment. The address of the hermit to his soul is preceded by two exempla in a similar vein. They describe the reflections of a philosopher in the cemetery which turn him into a hermit and the ruminations of philosophers surrounding the golden tomb in which the dust of Alexander is enclosed. Both exempla have been shown to reflect Arab tradition, in particular, reflections on once powerful kings, like Shaddad, who built the Earthly Paradise, and the wise sayings of philosophers assembled around the golden bier of Alexander in Hunain ibn Ishaq.[39]

What has not been previously noted is a certain thematic correspondence of the Middle English poem in Digby 86 with the exhortation of the hermit to his soul in the exemplum of Petrus Alfonsi. Like the *Disciplina* exemplum, the Middle English poem is a direct exhortation addressed to man which culminates in a Christian prayer for salvation. The sequence of ideas, from the reflection of "ubi sunt" to exhortation and the culminating prayer, is maintained in both the tale and the poem. Like Petrus Alfonsi, the Middle English poet evokes the transitoriness of whole societies and civilizations rather than of individual figures of history and romance as does the treatment of the theme in Boethius, King Alfred, or in Thomas de Hales's *Love Ron* ("Hwer is Paris and Heleyne").[40]

The *Disciplina* has the following version:

Wherbe now princis, wherbe now Kynges, wherbe now Riche men

that gadreden tresours and therof wern thei prowde? Now bien they as which ne weren; now bien thei as a flour or a blossum whiche that is fallen from the tree whiche no more cometh ageyne. Ne dreede thow nat, my soule, ne drede thow nat to moche the aduersites of the worlde. Dreede the day of thi jugement. Be agast and abasshed of the grete multitude of thi synnes. Have mynde of thi creator and maker whiche shalbe thi juge and thi witnes.[41]

The classical "ubi sunt" reached the *Disciplina Clericalis* from Arabic sources which, in turn, were affected by the treatment of the theme in the literature of the oriental church. In Arabic poetry variations on the theme have been traced to the pre-Islamic period in the work of Adi ibn Zaid (ca. 600).[42] "Ubi sunt reges" with which Petrus Alfonsi begins, is the exact phrasing of a verse on the transitoriness of earthly power which Muslim tradition attributes to Omar al-Khattab, the second caliph, and which appears in a sermon of the first caliph, Abu Bakr.[43] The medieval poets who developed this theme in thirteenth-century England were clearly drawing on a meditation on death which had reached them in almost identical language both from classical sources by way of Boethius and "ex Arabicis" through Petrus Alfonsi and Muslim Spain.

Petrus Alfonsi's prayer which concludes the tale of "The Hermit Chastening His Soul" is the epilogue to the *Disciplina Clericalis* not included in the Middle English version at Worcester Cathedral. It is the most Christian part of the work. The exemplum itself is written in the spirit of Ecclesiastes and has a distinctly Hebraic ring in its use of biblical passages and its emphasis on the fear and judgment of God:

> Memento tui creatoris, qui tuus iudex est et testis, . . . Timete Deum, quia timor Domini clavis est ad omne bonum et ad percipiendam gloriam conductum. De quo Salomon in Ecclesiaste ait: Finem loquendi omnes pariter audiamus: Deum time et mandata eius observa; hoc est enim omnis homo. Et cuncta quae fiunt, adducet Deus in iudicium pro omni errato, sive bonum sive malum sit.[44]

Thirteen tales of the *Disciplina Clericalis* are included in an English version of the *Alphabetum Narrationum*[45] made in the fifteenth century, and thirteen "Fables of Alfonce" were translated from French into English by William Caxton at Westminster in 1483. Caxton's book, of which the thirteen tales are a part, is a translation of Jules de Machault's contemporary *Livre des subtilles Hystoires et Fables de Esope*, itself a version of the German Steinhoewel's *Aesop*, a compilation of fables from the *Disciplina Clericalis* both in Latin and German. The Aesopian material in Petrus Alfonsi's work is in turn related to *Kalila wa Dimna*, the Arabic collection of tales which Petrus Alfonsi is known to have used. The collection was translated in the eighth century from the Pehlevi by Abdallah Ibn al-Muqaffa at the request of the Abbasid caliph al-Mansur.[46]

The Arabic version of Ibn al-Muqaffa was turned into Hebrew about 1250, and thence into Latin, by the converted Jew John of Capua, under the title *Directorium Humanae Vitae* (ca. 1265). The first "englished" version is Thomas North's *Morall Philosophie of Doni* (1570) translated from Anton Francesco Doni's contemporary rendering of the *Directorium* into Italian.

The ramifications of the *Disciplina Clericalis* in Middle English literature illustrate not only the extent to which Arabic subject matter penetrated the vernacular literature of the West but also the interdependence of European literatures in the use of the material. Petrus Alfonsi's "little book," which the author intended as a guide of morals for Christians, became the most important medieval guidebook to international folklore motifs in their passage from East to West. It is intriguing to contemplate that this "rule for clerics" by a Jewish convert molded the shape of Western imagination and Western storytelling. Like the *Secret of Secrets*, it became a key-book for the "amatores litterarum."[47]

The "Secret of Secrets"

The pseudo-Aristotelian *Secretum Secretorum* reached the West through the Arabic *Sirr al-asrār*. The Arabic original claims to be a translation from the Greek by way of the language of *rūmī* (possibly Syriac, though it means *romano*), by the well-known translator Yahya ibn Bitriq, a Nestorian physician of the ninth century.[48] In the tenth century, the treatise is quoted by a Spanish medical writer, Ibn Juljul, who lists it among the works of Aristotle and the translations of Yahya ibn Bitriq. He gives the full title of the work: "The Book of Policy Concerning the Management of Administrations Which Is Known as 'The Secret of Secrets.' "[49] The name Secret of Secrets is therefore secondary and is connected with the complex relationship of the treatise to hermetic literature. In the eleventh century, al-Mubashshir ibn Fatik, author of *The Dicts and Sayings of the Philosophers*, ends his chapter on Aristotle with a metaphorical play on justice ("the world is a garden") which appears in Ibn Juljul and the *Secret of Secrets*.[50] We also hear from al-Mubashshir, in his account of Alexander, that Alexander wrote an epistle to Aristotle in which the king not only reported on the wonders of India, as in the famous "Epistola Alexandri ad Aristotelem"[51] but asked his master to give him his view "on what he should do in administering his power and managing countries and peoples."[52]

There is no request of this sort in the Greek Alexander romance of Pseudo-Callisthenes,[53] the main source of the medieval Alexander, or in the "Indian Tractates"—the most important of which, the letter to Aristotle on the marvels of India, is extant in an Anglo-Saxon translation preserved in the same codex as *Beowulf*.[54] The pseudo-Aristotelian letter to Alexander may be an addition of an Arabic writer. At any rate, the Arabic *Secretum Secretorum* professes to be a genuine letter of Aristotle, written at the request of Alexander the Great. The treatise is believed to have reached something like its present form as an outcome of a gradual process of compilation. It enjoyed great authority among Muslim writers. In the fourteenth century, Ibn Khaldun, the Muslim historian, cites it as "the *Book of Politics* that is ascribed to Aristotle" without mentioning the hermetic subtitle which had spread its fame in the West.[55]

The *Secretum Secretorum* entered Europe in a translation of John of Spain who dedicated his Latin version to a certain Teophina or Tharasia "gracia dei Hispanorum regina," perhaps the mother of the first king of Portugal who was regent for her son from 1112 to 1128.[56] The queen had requested John, her physician, to write a short treatise "de observatione dietarum" or "de continencia corporis," and in his search for material he had come across the book which was called "Cyretesar" (*sirr al-asrār*) in Arabic, "id est Secretum secretorum," and which contained many things useful to a king transmitted by the philosopher Aristotle to King Alexander. John's translation opens with the prologue of Yahya ibn Bitriq and his account of finding the treatise in the temple of Hermes (Aesculapius).[57]

Yahya's *rūmī* into which he claims to have translated the book from the Greek is identified as Chaldean in some manuscripts Whatever the *rūmī*, the pioneers of "Arabic into Latin" were fully aware that "Greek into Arabic" often passed through Syriac as an intermediary stage.

As his preface to the queen indicates, John planned to translate only the medical portions of the treatise. His work, variously entitled as an "Epistola Aristotelis ad Alexandrum Macedonem de conservacione sanitatis," is extant in over sixty manuscripts.[58] It was an excerpt from an Arabic text current in the West also represented in the Hebrew version of al-Kharizi (d. 1218) and a medieval Castilian translation.[59] The complete treatise was rendered into Latin in the first half of the thirteenth century from a longer Arabic version, current in the East. The translator, a certain Philip, cleric of Tripoli, describes the character of his work as a compendium of knowledge: "in quo de omnibus scientiis aliquid utile continetur." Philip states that he found it at Antioch while he was studying with his patron, a certain Guido de Vere of Valencia, on whose urging he undertook to turn this "pretiosissima philosophiae margarita" into Latin. The translation was completed "magno labore et lucido sermone" and dedicated by "the most inferior of his clerics" to "his most excellent lord, most ardent in the cultivation of the Christian religion." Philip says that the Latins do not possess the book and that it "is found with very few

Arabs." He seems to refer to the full Arabic title: "Incipit prohemium in libro Arabum de regimine dominorum et de secreto secretorum ab Aristotele ad Alexandrum."[60]

The earliest quotations from Philip's version appear in Roger Bacon's "Liber (Epistola) de retardatione accidentium senectutis," written between 1243 and 1254.[61] It is unlikely that the scattered passages in Michael Scot's *Physiognomy* reflecting Philip's wording are due to Scot's acquaintance with his text.[62] Michael Scot probably used the original Arabic treatise. Another scholar at the court of Frederick II prepared extracts from the *Sirr al-asrār* for the emperor, drawing on knowledge which he undoubtedly brought from the East. Like his predecessor, Michael Scot, he bore the title of Court Philosopher, having been sent to Frederick II in 1236 perhaps by al-Kamil of Egypt. Master Theodore was said to have studied in Baghdad and Mosul and probably came from Antioch where Philip of Tripoli discovered the work. The importance of the *Secretum Secretorum* at the court of Palermo is clear from a letter he wrote the emperor: "Your Majesty has commanded me to prescribe certain rules for the preservation of your health . . . but you are long since in possession of the most ancient letter from the 'Secrets' of Aristotle, which he sent to the Emperor Alexander when the latter asked to be instructed about the health of the body. All that your Majesty desires to know is completely contained in that letter."[63]

Philip's text had undergone some tampering by the time it reached Roger Bacon in England, for Bacon complains that some fools had deleted parts also missing in four other copies of the work at Oxford. In Paris, however, he had access to complete copies of the work.[64] The result was that "Bacon set himself the task of further rearrangement, dividing it into four parts of approximately equal length instead of the ten of his author, and inserting several paragraphs as well as transforming the chapter headings, without giving any indication of the changes he had made."[65] The four parts deal with the types and characters of kings and kingship; a rule of health according to the four seasons; the uses and properties of nature, public and private manners, justice and morality; the qualities of men and physiognomy.[66]

A variation in the division and arrangement of chapters is also found in Arabic manuscripts of the treatise some of which comprise seven books, while others have eight or, most commonly, ten.[67] The fundamental question is the relationship between the two Arabic forms in which the work was transmitted to Europe, an Arabic manuscript of the Western form having only recently come to light.[68] The Spanish form divides the material into eight discourses as described by Ibn Juljul, while the Eastern has ten: two on the person of the king himself, one on justice, five on ministers, scribes, ambassadors, governors, and military personnel, one on war, and one on "special sciences."[69]

Philip's Latin translation does not vary from the Arabic text in basic content or structure. The most significant modification explains Roger Bacon's complaint. It is the omission of the concluding discourse on "special sciences" which deals with talismans, the secrets of astrology, the special virtues of stones and plants, and "other matter." In the Latin text and the vernacular versions derived from it, this chapter is replaced by the discourse on physiognomy which, in the *Sirr al-asrār*, appears in the second discourse of the treatise. There are no manuscripts of the Latin version in its earliest form but Philip clearly refers to the tenth discourse in describing what he has translated "de Arabico Ydiomate":

> Quem librum peritissimus princeps philosophorum Aristoteles composuit ad peticionem regis Alexandri, discipuli sui. Qui postulavit ab eo, ut ad ipsum veniret, et secretum quarundam artium sibi fideliter revelaret, videlicet, motum, operacionem, et potestatem astrorum in astronomia, et artem alkimie in natura, et artem cognoscendi naturas, et operandi incantaciones, et celimanciam, et geomanciam.[70]

Though the formulas for incantation and talismanic protection were censored from the Latin translation for obvious religious reasons, we find a good deal of the alchemical portions incorporated in the third part of Roger Bacon's text.[71] The material on the properties of stones—fully reinstated in the Achillini edition of 1500[72]—is drawn from a pseudo-Aristotelian Arabic lapidary which may have been used by Hunain ibn Ishaq, the first official translator of Greek into Arabic.[73] It represents one of the oldest components that went into the making of the treatise. A "prophecy" of Hermes, "three-fold in the wisdom of the world," which marks this section both in Arabic and Latin, stems from the Arabic *Tabula Smaragdina*, an alchemical classic with an independent existence in the West.[74] It was translated in the twelfth century and like the *Secretum Secretorum* enjoyed the prestige of Albertus Magnus as one of its readers.[75] Talismans are an important subject in the *Tabula Smaragdina* as they are in the Arabic *Sirr al-asrār*. Apollonius of Tyana, the master craftsman of talismans who appears as Balinas in both, is one of the principal sources in Jabir, the greatest authority of medieval alchemy both East and West. The precise relationship of these texts to each other is still undetermined.[76]

As we have seen in the *Canon's Yeoman's Tale*, the teaching of the *Secretum Secretorum* is conveyed with an injunction to secrecy, the distinguishing mark of the secret fraternities of the Isma'iliyah which used the hermetic tradition for their own doctrinal ends. There are several parallels in the

contents of the epistles of the "Brethren of Purity" and the pseudo-Aristotelian discourses, in particular Gower's story of the *Magian and the Jew*.[77]
The brotherhood also used the story of Barlaam and Josaphat, known
from the *Disciplina Clericalis*—the epistles "being perhaps the earliest
testimony for the existence of this Indian legend in an Arabic translation."[78]

The Brethren of Purity received their name in a singular way. The
designation stems from *Kalila wa Dimna*, the Indian book of fables which
the *Disciplina Clericalis* first brought to the attention of the West. The fable
of the ringdove and its friends illustrates the moral that only a union of
true friends can protect one from the snares of the hunter. The opening of
the tale speaks of "the brethren of purity":

> King Dabshalim said to Bidpai the philosopher: "I have just heard
> an exemplum of two friends: how lies cut between them and what
> was the result of the affair after that. Tell me then if you have seen
> anything concerning brethren of purity (true friendship): how their
> union is begun and how each of them enjoys the support of the
> other."[79]

The role of this passage in naming the fraternity stemmed from the
singular importance attached to the Indian fables in the Neoplatonic
thought of certain groups of Shiite Islam, which were concentrated at
Basra in the tenth century.[80] The method, using animal stories not only as
moral exempla but as allegories of the life of the soul, illumines the use of
popular medieval literature for spiritual purposes, not only by Latin
clerics but also by the type of Muslim hermetic brotherhood which inspired the alchemists of the West.

The *Secretum Secretorum* thus reflects a tradition of Arabic writing closely
allied to Isma'ili religious thought. The influence of the treatise, however,
rested on the conviction that it was a work of Aristotle, and Aristotle,
according to some Arab writers, was a descendant of Aesculapius and had
translated the books of Hermes from Egyptian into Greek.[81] According to
Roger Bacon, some scholars called it "The Book of the Ten Sciences," a
title otherwise unknown.[82] To Roger Bacon it was the book of books, "the
most influential in his whole life, the book which perhaps more than anything else turned him from his life of philosophy to a study of natural
science."[83]

Its importance to all European scholars is borne out by approximately
207 Latin manuscripts and a great variety of medieval versions in verse
and prose: Spanish, French, Italian, Dutch, German, Welsh, and English.[84] Though Gower used parts of the *Secret of Secrets* in Book 7 of *Confessio
Amantis*, there are no Middle English versions of the treatise before the
fifteenth century. The earliest "of known date" is a prose translation, *The*

Gouernaunce of Prynces, prepared for the earl of Ormond, lord deputy of Ireland, by James Yonge in 1422. Lydgate's version in verse, *The Secree of Old Philisoffres*, was completed by Burgh after Lydgate's death, around 1450.[85]

By that time, the prologue of Yahya ibn Bitriq, describing his search in the Temple of the Sun and his encounter with the priest of Hermes from whom he finally obtained the work had become "the prologue of him that translatid this book into latyne." Philip of Tripoli, the Latin translator, appears as "phelip . . . brought forth of parys," in further confusion with ibn Bitriq, i.e., "Parisii" for "Patricci." In the process of westernization, however, both teacher and teaching continued to loom as emblems of the mysterious wisdom of the East: "the secrete of secretis of the makyng of Aristotille, prince of philesofris, sone of Machomete of macedonye."[86]

"THE DICTS AND SAYINGS OF THE PHILOSOPHERS"

Chaucer's Dame Alys, the Wife of Bath, illustrates her expertise in the art of life by quoting two proverbs. They belong to the category of sayings of Arab philosophers which are cited in the *Disciplina Clericalis* and the *Secret of Secrets*. But Dame Alys attributes them to the *Almagest* of Ptolemy:

> Whoso that nyl be war by othere men,
> By hym shul othere men corrected be.
> The same wordes writeth Ptholomee;
> Rede in his Almageste, and take it there.

Her opinion of Ptolemy and the *Almagest* is pronounced with the authority of experience:

> Of alle men yblessed moot he be,
> The wise astrologien, Daun Ptholome,
> That seith this proverbe in his Almageste:
> "Of alle men his wysdom is the hyeste
> That rekketh nevere who hath the world in honde."[87]

Chaucer, in composing these passages, was following the example of the *Roman de la Rose* which gives us an important clue to the exact location of these sayings:

> Langue doit estre refrenee,
> car nous lisons de Tholomee
> une parole mout honeste
> au conmencier de l'*Almageste*,
> que sages est cil qui met peine
> a ce que sa langue refreine,

fors sanz plus quant de Dieu parole.

[The tongue should bridled be, as Ptolemy
Early in his *Almagest* explains
In noble words: "Most wise is he who strives
To hold his tongue save when he speaks of God."][88]

The source "at the beginning of the Almagest," from which Chaucer and Jean de Meun drew different proverbs, is of particular importance as it confirms Chaucer's use of Ptolemy's *Syntaxis* in the translation of Gerard of Cremona from the Arabic.[89] The preface to this version was a biographical note on Ptolemy composed by "Abulguasis." It contained thirty-three sayings attributed to Ptolemy and was taken from an Arabic work, *The Choicest Maxims and Best Sayings*, by Abu al-Wafa' ("Abulguasis") al-Mubashshir ibn Fatik, a Muslim historian and philosopher who lived in Egypt. Al-Mubashshir's work was compiled in 1048–49. It comprises short biographies and descriptions of twenty philosophers, accompanied by a series of sayings under the heading of each, and is related to the widely read compilation of "strange sayings" of Greek philosophers by Hunain ibn Ishaq.[90] However, "contrary to an often repeated assertion, al-Mubashshir's dependence upon Hunain's *Nawādir al-falāsifah* is a minor one."[91] In the twelfth century, al-Mubashshir's compilation was revised by al-Shahrazuri who added sayings of Muslim philosophers.[92]

The Wife of Bath's proverbs are glossed in their original Latin, as they appear in the *Almagest* preface, in two manuscripts of the *Canterbury Tales*. The first is noted on the margin of Cambridge University Library MS. Dd 4. 24: "Qui per alios non corigitur, alii per ipsum corigentur." The second is in the Ellesmere manuscript: "Intra omnes alcior existit, qui non curat in cuius manu sit mundus."[93]

It is obvious that Chaucer chose the proverbs directly from the *Almagest* preface; he did not use the proverbs cited in the *Romance of the Rose*. They are three in number:

1. "Intelligens est qui semper linguam suam refrenat: nisi ad hoc ut de deo loquatur." (See above.)

2. "Cum aliquis sibi placet ad hoc deductus est: ut ira dei sit super ipsum":

> Si s'est en l'ire Dieu boutez,
> hom qui se plest, ja n'an doutez,
> car ausinc le dit Tholomee,
> par cui fu mout sciance amee.

[Doubt not that one who's satisfied with self
Deserves the wrath of God. Thus Ptolemy,

by whom was science greatly loved, has said.]

3. "Quidam rex inuitauit Ptolemeum ad prandium. qui rogans fore se excusatum: dixit Regibus contiguit fere quod contigit considerantibus picturas. que cum a longe videntur placent. propinque vero non dulcescunt."

> Et qui voudroit croire escritures,
> li rai resamblent les paintures,
> don tel example nous apreste
> cil qui nous escrist l'*Almageste,*
> se bien s'i savoit prandre garde
> cil qui les paintures regarde:
> qu'el plesent qui ne s'an apresse,
> mes de pres la plesance cesse;
> de loing semblent trop deliteuses,
> de pres ne sunt point doucereuses.

> [Kings are like pictures, if we may believe
> The Scriptures. He who wrote the *Almagest*
> This illustration gives: he who would view
> A picture best should never stand too near;
> However pleasing it may be afar,
> It loses something when too closely scanned.]

These sayings, too, exactly correspond to their proclaimed source, the *Almagest* preface, and al-Mubashshir's Arabic original.[94]

The translation of Ptolemy's *Almagest* from the Arabic and its Latin version is a problem which has only recently been disentangled.[95] The preface to the Latin *Almagest,* generally considered to be the work of Gerard of Cremona, is extant in two early sixteenth-century printed versions. It explicitly refers to al-Mubashshir's work:

> Quidam princeps nomine Albuguafe [Abu al-Wafa'] in libro suo (quem Scientiarum electionem et verborum nominauit pulchritudinem) dixit: hic Ptolemeus fuit vir in disciplinarum scientia prepotens: preeminens alijs. In duabus artibus subtilis: id est Geometria & Astrologia. Et fecit libros multos. de quorum numero iste est: qui Megasiti dicitur. cuius significatio est Maior perfectus. Quem ad linguam volentes conuertere Arabicam: nominauerunt Almagesti.[96]

The biographical text that follows in the preface, with the exception of one expanded sentence which explains the location of Ptolemy's birthplace, Alexandria, is a literal translation of the Arabic original though the number of sayings has been shortened and the order slightly rearranged.

The Latin wording of the Wife of Bath's sayings is different in the

Liber Philosophorum Moralium Antiquorum,[97] a thirteenth-century translation of an incomplete text of al-Mubashshir's collection made from the Spanish translation of al-Mubashshir's work, the *Bocados de Oro*.[98] This version was composed about 1257, under the sponsorship of Alfonso el Sabio of Castile. The *Liber Philosophorum Moralium* has been regarded as the work of John de Procida, a physician at the court of Frederick II at Palermo who died in 1299.[99]

In the *Liber Philosophorum Moralium Antiquorum*, the two proverbs of the Wife of Bath appear as

1. "qui ab hominibus non corripitur, ab eo homines corrigentur."

2. "Mundi preciosior est homo qui non est perplexus in cuius potestate sit mundus."[100]

The two sayings in Chaucer are the first renderings of al-Mubashshir into English, for the English versions of the whole work were not undertaken until the fifteenth century and were translated from the French *Dits Moraulx* which, in its turn, was "a tolerably close translation of the Latin text" by Guillaume de Tignonville (d. 1414).[101] Tignonville, provost of Paris, addressed his version to Charles VI, king of France, and it is not surprising that he and his worldly English translators omitted the Wife of Bath's Ptolemaic advice to ignore "who has the world in hand."

The earliest use of al-Mubashshir's and Hunain ibn Ishaq's collections of sayings in Latin is found in the *Disciplina Clericalis*,[102] though no systematic study of Petrus Alfonsi's proverbs in relation to his Arabic sources has yet been made. Three sayings of "Piers Alfonce," by way of Albert of Brescia in a French adaptation, are quoted by Chaucer in the *Tale of Melibee*:

1. "Whoso that dooth to thee other good or harm, haste thee nat to quiten it; for in this wise thy freend wole abyde, and thyn enemy shal the lenger lyve in drede."[103]

2. "If thou hast myght to doon a thyng of which thou most repente, it is bettre 'nay' than 'ye.' "[104]

3. "Oon of the gretteste adversitees of this world is / whan a free man by kynde or of burthe is constreyned by poverte to eten the almesse of his enemy."[105]

Petrus Alfonsi and Gerard of Cremona drew on the original Arabic text. But some of al-Mubashshir's sayings are also found in Vincent de Beauvais's *Speculum Historiale*. They present an interesting problem of transmission, as their Latin wording differs from that in the *Liber Philosophorum Moralium Antiquorum* which Vincent's work predates.

Of the three sayings in the *Speculum Historiale* traced to al-Mubashshir, one is from the sayings of Socrates and two from Aristotle. In his chapter on Socrates, Vincent scrupulously mentions his classic and patristic sources,[106] but gives a list of twenty-six sayings which he collected "ex diuersis locis." In this list, there is one saying which closely corresponds to al-Mubashshir's Arabic original. It is translated thus by Scrope: "the bigynnynge of loue is to say wele, and to say evill is the begynnyng of hate."[107] ("Principium amicitiae bene loqui; exordium inimicitiarum, maledicere," *Spec. Hist.* III, cap. 58.) We also find it in the *Liber de vita et moribus philosophorum* of Walter Burley (1275–1345?), an Oxford commentator on Aristotle.[108] His work, containing short lives and sayings of about 120 poets and philosophers, is based on the *Liber Philosophorum*, the Latin version of al-Mubashshir.

The two sayings of Aristotle in Vincent that have been attributed to al-Mubashshir actually stem from Aristotle's *Ethics*, as is stated by Vincent himself and confirmed by a comparison of his wording with that in the *Nicomachean Ethics*.[109] Al-Mubashshir's phrasing, by way of Latin and French, is reflected in the Middle English *Dicts*:

1. "there be many that knowith good dedis and dothe hem not, wherefore thei be like seke peple that askith counsaile of leches and dothe not ther-aftir; and euen liche as for that cause theire bodies beth ferre from helthe, euen so soules be ferre from blissidnes."[110]

2. "for it is fulle light thinge to drawe ferre du bersault *id est* from, and hit is full desceiuable to smyte it."

Or as we find it in the *Nicomachean Ethics*, "easy to miss the mark, but hard to hit it."[111] The English *Dicts and Sayings of the Philosophers* is preserved in thirteen known manuscripts which attest that in the third quarter of the fifteenth century at least six writers were interested in them. Three of the translators, Stephen Scrope, William Worcester, and Earl Rivers, whose version was printed by Caxton, were connected with Sir John Falstaff,[112] a curious coincidence which points to the practical uses of the Polonian wisdom of al-Mubashshir: Earl Rivers had come across the *Dicts* on his way to the shrine of Saint James of Compostela in 1473, when a copy of the French version was lent to him by a fellow traveler. He seems to have been unaware of Scrope's earlier translation:

Thēne I determyned me to take that voyage > shipped from southamptoñ in the moneth of Juyll the said yere, And so sayled from thens till I come in to the Spaynyssh see. . . . Thenne for a recreacoñ > a passyng of tyme I had delyte > axed to rede some good historye And amōg other ther was that season in my cōpanye a

worshipful gentylmañ callid lowys de Bretaylles, . . . that sayd to
me, he hath there a book that he trusted I shuld lyke it right wele,
and brought it to me, whyche book I had neuer seen before, and is
called the saynges or dictis of the Philosophers. . . . Whan I had
heeded and loked upon it as I had tyme and space I gaaf therto a
veray affection. . . . And at the last concluded in my self to trāslate
it in to thenglyssh tonge, wiche in my Jugement was not before.[113]

Thus, the twelfth-century preface to the *Almagest*, which Chaucer consulted, is the earliest known official appearance of al-Mubashshir's anthology in the West, while the English version of Earl Rivers is the latest
medieval translation in a Western vernacular. Both, taking the historical
route from their Arabic source, entered England from Spain.

Figure 1. A list of an early form of Arabic numerals found in England in an inscription at Westley Waterless, Cambridgeshire.

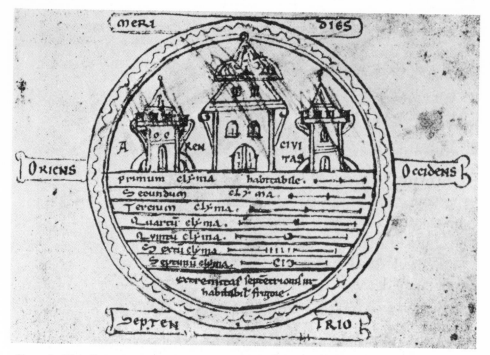

Figure 2. The climate map of Petrus Alfonsi in MS. 1218, Suppl. Lat., Bibliothèque Nationale, Paris.

Figure 3. Caricature of the Prophet Muhammad as a fish, in MS. Arsenal 1162, Bibliothèque Nationale, Paris.

Cum dudum ab anglia
me causa studii excepissem.
& parisii aliquamdiu moram
fecissem: videbam quosdam
bestiales in scolis gravi
auctoritate sedes occupare.
habentes coram se scamna
duo uel tria. 7 desup codices importabiles aurei lit-
teris vlpiani traditiones repsentantes. necn 7 tenen-
tes stilos plumbeos in manib; cu qb; asteriscos 7 obe-
los in libris suis qdam reuentia depingebant. Qui
dum ppt insciciam suam locu statue teneret: tn
uolebant sola taciturnitate uideri sapientes. sz tales
cum aliqd dicere conabant: infantissimos reppie-
bam. C Cum hec inquam in hec modu se hre dephen-
derem. ne & ego simile dampnu incurrere: artes

Figure 4. Daniel of Morley handing his *Philosophia* to John of Oxford, bishop of Norwich, in MS. Lat. 387, Staatsbibliothek, Berlin.

Figure 5. Battle of the Crows and Owls in an early thirteenth-century Arabic manuscript of *Kalila wa Dimna*. MS. Ar. 3465, Bibliothèque Nationale, Paris.

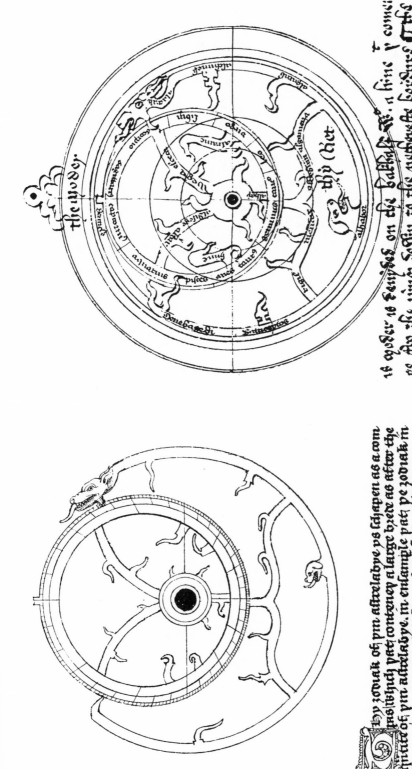

Figure 7. Rete of Chaucer's Astrolabe in MS. Cambridge Dd.3.53, Cambridge University Library, Cambridge.

Figure 6. Rete of Chaucer's Astrolabe in MS. Rawlinson D. 913, Bodleian Library, Oxford.

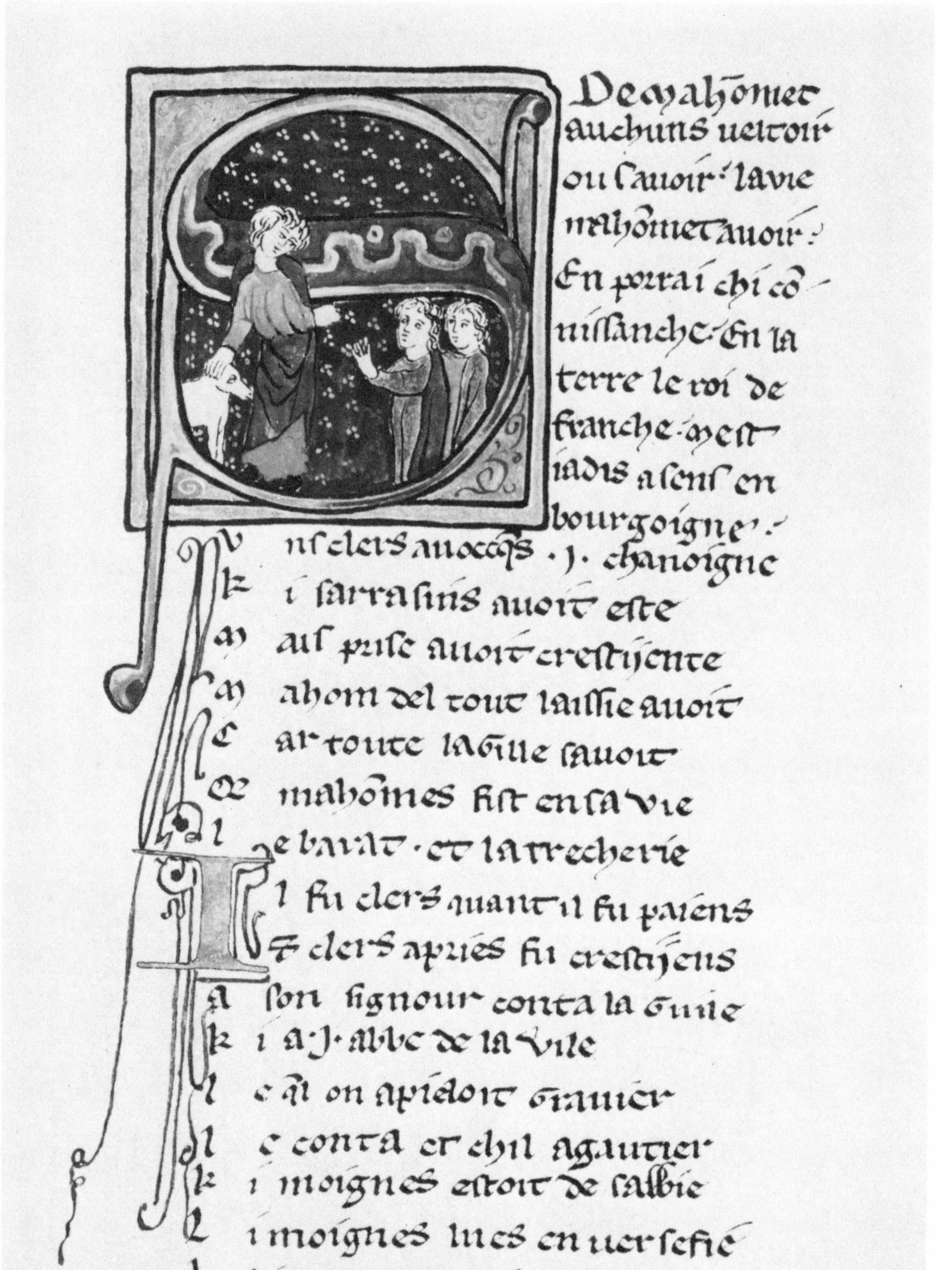

Figure 8. The beginning of Alexandre du Pont's *Roman de Mahomet*, MS. 1553, Bibliothèque Nationale, Paris.

Figure 9. The beginning of the *Liure de leschiele Mahomet* showing Muhammad and his wife in bed, with a cocklike angel. Laud. Misc. 537, Bodleian Library, Oxford.

Figure 10. The Miraj of Muhammad on His Steed in an Islamic painting of 1514 (1974.294.2) at the Metropolitan Museum of Art, New York.

6

History and Romance

The *Song of Roland* is an intellectual and artistic form in which medieval Western civilization rendered account to itself of its supreme effort to cope with the Saracen onslaught from Spain. The epic was regarded as history by the medieval audience—"histoire chantée," a rival of "histoire écrite."[1]

> Charles the King, our great emperor, has stayed seven whole years in Spain and has conquered the haughty country as far as the sea. Not a single castle resists him any longer; not one wall has yet to be broken nor one city taken, except Saragossa, which is on a mountain and is held by King Marsiliun, who does not love God. Marsiliun serves Mahomet and prays to Appolin. But he cannot prevent harm from overtaking him.[2]

Charlemagne's expedition to Spain in 778 is known from the medieval chronicles of both Franks and Arabs, some in poetic versions. It is a historical fact that Charlemagne's rear guard was surprised by an enemy force while crossing the Pyrenees on August 15, 778. We know from the Arab chroniclers who have been consulted in the study of the *Chanson de Roland* that there is historical substance to the epic description of the attackers as Saracens.[3] The Basques (Wascones) whom Charlemagne's biographer, Eginhard, and the official Carolingian annals refer to do not appear in the briefest versions of the annals which Menéndez Pidal considers the most contemporary and reliable Latin report:

> On dit que les annales brèves dérivent des annales royales. Je ne vois aucun trait du récit qui permette d'étayer cette affirmation. . . . En outre, les Annales brèves diffèrent radicalement des Annales étendues. Toutes ces dernières ajoutent à la fin une phrase sur la soumission des Basques et des Navarrais, de telle sorte que le lecteur pense à une conquête de Pampelune sur les Basques seulement. Au contraire, les Annales brèves ne nomment pas les Basques; elles supposent que la conquête de Pampelune est faite contre les Sarrasins.[4]

The Arab chroniclers consider Charlemagne's Spanish campaign solely in the light of his relationship with the Saracen governors of the northern frontier provinces, Barcelona, Huesca, and Saragossa. In the complicated struggle for control between the Eastern (Abbasid) and Western (Umayyad) centers of Muslim power and within the Spanish territories, these men rejected the authority of Abdurrahman I, founder of the Spanish Umayyad Empire, who resided in Cordova in the south. While Latin historiography depicts Charlemagne's incursion into Spain as also prompted by Basque rebellions, not only by the entreaties of Spanish Christendom to liberate it from the Saracen yoke, we learn from Ibn al-Athir that Charles had undertaken the expedition at the request of al-Arabi, governor of Saragossa. We know from Carolingian annals that al-Arabi and other emirs had come to Paderborn to pay homage to Charles. But it is Arab chroniclers who tell us that their purpose was to enlist the help of the Frankish king against Abdurrahman: "In this year Sulaiman ibn Yaqzan al-Kalbi (al-Arabi) made Charles, the king of the Franks, come to the Muslim territory of al-Andalus, and he met him on the way and went with him to Saragossa."[5] One gathers that the real reason for Charles's Spanish campaign was the prospect of ousting the central Saracen power. This indeed is a theme in the Middle English romance of *Otuel and Roland* based on an "eyewitness account," the Latin chronicle of Charlemagne's archbishop Turpin:

> Here bygynneth a batayle grym,
> Off charlys and of Ebrayn,
> That was wonderlyche strong.
> At Cordys how thay fouȝten same,
> All for the loue of cristendom. . . .[6]

According to Ibn al-Athir, the rebels of the northern provinces who were allied with al-Arabi had entrenched themselves at Saragossa to which Abdurrahman had dispatched his general Thalaba to subdue them. Al-Arabi managed to frustrate this attempt by taking Thalaba prisoner and promptly delivering him to Charlemagne. Saragossa, however, did not surrender to Charles, and to ensure himself against treachery Charlemagne took al-Arabi and other Saracen hostages with him when he raised camp to return to France, apparently because of news of a Saxon rebellion in his own kingdom. But on the march homeward, when they were far from Muslim territory and considered themselves secure, the Franks were attacked by two of al-Arabi's sons who freed their father, an incident which, again, is reflected in *Otuel and Roland*: two Saracen *brothers*, Mansur and Beligans, attack Roland's forces in the "forest of rouncyval" and Beligans has his army flee to Saragossa after the battle.[7] It is this raid, probably undertaken with the help of Basque bands to guide them through the mountains, which Menéndez Pidal, like Gaston Paris and

Lévi-Provençal before him, considers to be the historical fabric of the disaster at Roncesvalles. The poetic encounter of Christian and Saracen begins, then, with history and shows that the *Chanson de Roland* is more truthful than the royal historians in the unmitigated clarity of its concentration on Saracen might.

Historians have accepted the value of the *chansons de geste* as social documents as readily as students of fourteenth-century England have accepted *Piers Plowman*. If we disregard the absurd portrayal of Islamic religion—a subject which will be dealt with separately—the general picture of Saracen civilization in the old French epic is substantially correct.

The Saracens are treated seriously in the *chansons de geste*. They are a crucial public theme—political, military, and religious—and what is fanciful in them is made deliberately so for purposes of patriotism, propaganda, and entertainment. In this there is no difference between medieval epic and romance. The Saracens supply the same kind of foil and wonder in both. Before the Crusades the public at larg ewas aware that the Spanish Saracens were allied to the Berbers of North Africa (*Song of Roland*, l. 1236); that the Saracen Empire included Persians (l. 3240), Turks (ll. 3240, 3284), Armenians (l. 3227), Syrians (l. 3131); that the forces of the Saracen world were grouped under the emir of Babylon (i.e., the Fatimid Commander of the Faithful in Cairo to whom the title and power of the caliphate had shifted from Baghdad in the tenth century). The *Song of Roland* is right in crediting the Spanish Saracens with a strong navy (ll. 2630–37). Saragossa was an important depot for merchandise brought from the Orient and transported up the Ebro. Saracen society was rightly seen as resembling the feudal order of medieval Christendom.

We do not know whether the *Song of Roland* was the *cantinela* about Roland which the Norman troops sang while advancing at Hastings.[8] But the Normans had adopted the notion of a holy war against Saracen power *before* the First Crusade. The Norman conquest of England in 1066 and the Norman capture of Palermo from the Saracens in 1072—the most important victory over Islam in the eleventh century—were intimately related, for "Saracen" had become the generic term for all enemies (Laʒamon, a Christian monk writing in the twelfth century in England has the Saxons worshipping "maumets"),[9] and what was happening at Hastings was the subjection of English "Saracens" by men who were brothers and cousins of those who were ousting Islam from its strongholds in Europe and the Byzantine Empire.

The *chansons de geste* sang the heroic virtues of *sapientia* and *fortitudo* in the bold battle of Christian knights against equally brave Saracens: "Deus! quel baron, s'oüst chrestientet!" (l. 3164), says the poet of Emir Baligant in the *Song of Roland*.

Herkneþ boþe ȝinge & olde,
Þat willen heren of batailles bolde,
& ȝe wolle a while duelle,
Of bolde batailles ich wole ȝou telle,
Þat was sumtime bitwene
Cristene men & sarrazines kene.

[*Otuel*, ll. 1–6]

Of the ten metrical romances that survive in Middle English of the
Carolingian tradition three concern themselves with Fierabras and four
with Otinel (Otuel), both Saracen heroes.[10] But there are also Saracens in
the remaining three—a fragmentary Middle English version of the *Song of
Roland; Rouland and Vernagu*, in which Vernagu is a Saracen knight; and a
fifteenth-century Scottish poem, the *Taill of Rauf Coilyear*, in which a
lowly peasant engages in combat with a Saracen giant, a parody of similar
fights against huge Saracens.

When the themes of the Carolingian tradition reached English vernacular literature in the thirteenth and fourteenth centuries, there was no
need to sing the praises of a French national hero. Arthur of Britain had
assumed the central place. We find, therefore, that the main figures the
Middle English romances borrowed from the French national epic and
offered to the English public are not Charlemagne and his *douzeperes* but
Fierabras and Otinel. The surviving Charlemagne romances in English—
ten metrical romances and three prose romances printed by Caxton—
reflect a specific popular interest in the Saracens. *Otinel*, dated at the
beginning of the fourteenth century, is probably the earliest Charlemagne
romance in English. But it is not the earliest Middle English romance to
render a lengthy account of Saracens "so hit is fonde in frensche tale."[11]
This honor belongs to *Sir Beues of Hamtoun* whose links with *King Horn* (the
oldest known romance in the vernacular) and its "Saracens" have not yet
been determined. The date of the English *Sir Beues* is about 1300. By this
time the Saracens are part and parcel of the "romances of prys." *Sir Beues*
tells us what the average Englishman in hall and marketplace knew or
imagined about the Saracens—an account and portrayal that remained
essentially unvaried as late as the Renaissance and Spenser.

The earliest encounter is on home soil. The "Sarazins" in *King Horn*
who ravage the coasts of "Suddene," "Westernesse," and Ireland, slay
Horn's father, and set Horn and his companions adrift in a rudderless
boat, are generally assumed to be Vikings. One wonders, however, whether the poem, so close in spirit to *chansons de geste*, does not preserve an echo
of actual Saracen sea raids from Spain and possible contacts with the
south or west coast of Ireland which can be affirmed from Arabic sources.

There is a curious account of an embassy to "a great island in the

Encircling Ocean, . . . three days' sailing, or 300 miles, from the main-land" across the Atlantic, by Ibn Dihyah who was born in Spain and died in Cairo in 1235. He reports that the Umayyad ruler of Spain, Abdur-rahman II (822–52) sent a mission to "the King of the Norsemen" in a specially built, well-equipped ship which sailed to the country of the *majūs*—"an island of their islands."[12] *Majūs*, the standard designation for Norsemen in western Arabic sources, referred to the infidel northern Europeans as "Magians" in the same generic way in which Laȝamon denounced the heathen Saxons as worshippers of Saracen gods.

The mission was headed by a highly accomplished diplomat known as al-Ghazzal, whose personal account, preserved in a contemporary docu-ment, Ibn Dihyah purports to record. Its purpose was to arrange a peace settlement with the king of the Norsemen in his own country, after the Norsemen had descended on the Atlantic coast of Spain and had been defeated by the Saracens. The first of these raids, in which the Norsemen occupied Cadiz and sacked Seville, took place in 844. It was followed by al-Ghazzal's embassy one year later.

The expedition across the Atlantic, in which the Saracen ship was accompanied by a ship carrying the ambassadors of the king of the Norse-men sent to the Umayyad court to sue for peace, has been viewed as a voyage to Ireland or Jutland. The geographical indications are vague but it is clear that the Saracen ship visited countries within the realm of *King Horn*, the topography of which is equally vague, except for Ireland. "When they passed along the great promontory which enters the sea and which is the boundary of al-Andalus [Muslim Spain] in the extreme West, which is the mountain known as 'Aluwiyah,' the sea assailed them and they were menaced by a violent storm."[13] The name of the mountain, unexplained and otherwise unknown, has been taken to mean Cape St. Vincent or Cape Finisterre, though "Aluya" is the Arabic name for Albion in the earliest geographical account, about 817, which is based on Ptolemy's geography and mentions a number of places in Britain.

The Spanish Saracens first came to one of the islands which made up the country of "al-Majus" where they stayed a few days for repairs and rest, while the native ambassadors sailed on to inform their king of the Saracen arrival. The king of the Norsemen then summoned the Saracen ambassadors to his residence. "This, "says the Arabic account, "is a great island in the encircling sea in which there are flowing waters and gardens, and between it and the mainland are three days which is three hundred miles, and in it are Majus whose number cannot be counted and near this island are many islands, small and big, whose population is all Majus, and some of the mainland belongs to them also. The size of their country is several days' journey. They are Majus and to-day they adhere to the Christian law."[14]

According to the account, the arrival of the Saracen ambassadors caused a stir among the people who came running to stare at them and were stared at in return. The king had been informed in advance that the Saracen envoys would not bow before him. When he tried to outwit them by having them enter his presence through a very low door, al-Ghazzal sat down on the floor and pushing himself with his feet, passed through the door, upon which he rose to face the king of the Norsemen. The remainder of the narrative is occupied with a description of al-Ghazzal's superiority in friendly combat and scholarly disputation among the Norsemen and, above all, with the character of their women and their queen called Thud or Nud. Through an interpreter, she listened to al-Ghazzal's poetry and showed the accomplished Saracen special favors. Indeed, she behaved with a freedom which amazed the Muslims to the point of alarm.[15]

On the return voyage, the Saracen envoys, again accompanied by Majus ambassadors, visited St. James of Compostela in Galicia, evidently under the protection of the northern envoys who carried letters from their king addressed to the people of the town. It was not until 997 that an Arab army, backed by a squadron of the Umayyad fleet, entered Compostela.

At the time of al-Ghazzal's mission, in the ninth century, "everybody had heard of Compostela and its splendid Cathedral, . . . which—to use the phrase of an Arab chronicler—was to Christians what the Ka'aba at Mecca was to Musulmans. Nevertheless, to the Andalusians the holy place was known only by hearsay: to see it, it was necessary to be taken captive by the Galicians, for no Arab prince had yet dreamed of penetrating with an army, this rugged distant region."[16] The account of al-Ghazzal's journey to the Majus therefore stresses that he was greatly honored at Compostela where he stayed two months, proceeding thence to Castile with the Christian pilgrims, and from there to Toledo. He finally reached Cordova after an absence of twenty months.[17]

There is what seems to be another personal experience of Ireland and the surrounding ocean in an account of the Spanish geographer al-'Udhri, written about 1058: "The Norsemen have no base of residence save this island in all the world. Its circumference is a thousand miles. Its people have the customs and dress of the Norsemen. They wear rich mantles, one of which is worth 100 dinars. Their nobles wear mantles ornamented with pearls." The account expressly mentions Ireland (*Irlandah*) "an island which is in the north of the sixth zone (climate) and to the west of it." It gives an elaborate description of whaling along the Irish coast which, however, "reads almost as if it were some whale-boat-man's humorous version of how to catch a whale." Particularly intriguing is the use of garlic which is attributed to Irish whalers: "They prepare much powdered garlic, which they scatter on the water. When the whale smells the garlic, she lets the calf go, and turns backwards in her tracks. Then they cut up the meat of the calf and salt it. Its meat is white like snow, and its skin is black as ink."[18]

We also hear of a certain Khashkhash of Cordova, who as a young man, in the ninth century, "endangered his life" by voyaging with a company of other young men into the Atlantic. They went in a ship which they specially prepared, following the adventurous spirit of previous voyagers "some of whom were saved and some of whom perished," according to the tenth-century historian al-Mas'udi. "Ocean is the name of the Sea of Darkness, and it is called the Green Sea and the Encircling Ocean, whose range cannot be encompassed and whose end and extent are unknown. There is no cultivated land in it and no rational creature lives therein." Nevertheless, Khashkhash and his men "returned with rich booty and their report is famous with the people of Andalusia." To Mas'udi the Atlantic Ocean was the dark unknown bordering on the Mediterranean, the Sea of Rome, in effect, a Muslim lake connecting the centers of civilization. It is clear, however, that Saracen vessels ventured into the Atlantic as far as Britain: "All that is sailed of this sea is near the west and the north, and that is from the farthest point of the land of the Blacks to Britain, which is the great island in the farthest north. And in the Ocean are six islands opposite the land of the Blacks, called the Eternal Islands. Then no one knows what is after that."[19] Britain, perhaps, is also mentioned by an Arab traveler, Abdurrahman ibn Harun al-Maghribi, who related that he sailed the western sea in the year 900 and came to a place called al-Bartun. The account sounds like a typical "traveler's tale," however: "With us was a lad from Sicily, who cast a fish-hook into the sea, and caught a fish, the size of a span. We looked, and saw behind the right ear in writing, 'There is no God but God,' on its head 'Muhammad,' and behind the left ear 'The Apostle of God.' "[20] Al-Bartun, in the ninth century, could be Britain or Brittany. The presence of Saracen raiders on the coast of Brittany is dramatized in an account of a Saracen ship, "as big as a wall," which descended upon the island of Oye at the mouth of the Loire. The islanders were saved from certain attack by a miraculous optical delusion: the Saracens took a congregation of birds on the island for a huge army that was waiting to meet them and "did not dare to approach our island," says the French chronicle.[21] We are not told how the islanders knew this.

In the twelfth century, the Western Muslim geographer, al-Idrisi, who wrote his geographical work, the "Book of Roger," for the Norman King Roger of Sicily about 1154, has a substantial account of the British Isles gathered from a variety of sources, both oral and written. Al-Idrisi's work, written in the West in close touch with the Norman court at Palermo, was apparently unknown among his Christian contemporaries whose general interest in geography was still confined to the rudimentary notions of Latin encyclopedists. The book, however, contains some evidence of Saracen voyaging of the type which would linger in popular romance, perhaps in oral tradition.

There is an account of so-called Adventurers (*mugharrirūn*) who sailed from Lisbon with the purpose of discovering what the Atlantic Ocean contained and where it ended. We do not know when this expedition took place but al-Idrisi tells us that, in his time, there was a street in Lisbon named after these adventurers of the Atlantic.

These were eight sailors who built a ship, provisioned it with food and water for a voyage of several months, and when the east wind began to blow, set forth into "the Ocean of Darkness." Having sailed for about eleven days, they reached "a sea with huge waves and thick clouds, with numerous reefs scarcely illuminated by a feeble light." Fearing for their lives, they changed direction and sailed south for twelve days, when they came to an island where numerous herds of sheep were roaming around without any shepherds. They landed on the island and found a spring of running water and what they took to be wild figs. They caught and killed some sheep but found the meat so bitter as to be inedible. They kept the skin, sailed another twelve days, and finally saw an island which seemed inhabited and cultivated. On approaching it, however, they were surrounded by several boats, taken prisoner, and led to a town which was situated on the coast. They were brought to a house where they saw tall men with weathered red complexions and long hair and women who were of a rare beauty. They remained in that house for three days. On the fourth they were confronted with an interpreter who spoke Arabic and demanded to know who they were, where they were from, and why they had come. After two more days they were conducted to the king of the land who asked them the same questions to which they replied, as before, that they had ventured upon the ocean in order to find out where it ended and what marvelous and curious things it contained. When the king heard this, he laughed and told them through the interpreter that his father had sent some of his slaves on a similar voyage of exploration. They had returned after voyaging for a month until they could see nothing because of dark skies. After mutual assurances of good will, the Saracens were returned to prison to await the rise of a western wind. They were then placed in a boat, with their eyes blindfolded. They floated for three days and three nights until they reached a shore inhabited by Berbers who freed them and told them that they had come to the very limits of the Western world. They were two months' voyage away from their native country. "Whatever the details amount to, the fact of this expedition seems vouched for."[22] The island of sheep, the tall and ruddy-complexioned men, the city on the coast, the exposure in a boat, the Arabic interpreter, the easy but cautious air of the king, suggest that the Adventurers reached some point on the Irish or English coast and a people to whom Saracen sailors along the coasts were not a totally unfamiliar sight.[23]

The memory of Saracen sea raids preserved in the romances has its firmest historical roots along the coast of Provence and the western Mediterranean.

> In the mastery of the sea, the Saracens—like the Scandinavians in the same period—saw above all the means of reaching coasts whence they could carry profitable raids. From 842 they went up the Rhone as far as the approaches of Arles, plundering both banks on their way. . . . At a date not precisely ascertained, probably somewhere about 890, a small Saracen vessel coming from Spain was driven by the winds on to the coast of Provence, on the outskirts of the present town of Saint-Tropez. Its crew hid themselves during the day, then at nightfall emerged and massacred the inhabitants of a neighbouring village.[24]

The Saracen raids from the sea were a counterpart of piratical incursions on the Atlantic coast of Spain by Vikings who not only ravaged the coast but penetrated deep into the interior. Beginning with the ninth century, Western Arab chroniclers speak of a Spanish Saracen fleet whose defensive and offensive strategy was directed both against the Viking peril on the Atlantic and the continuous maritime attacks by the rival Fatimid power from North Africa.

The Saracen pirates who continually raided the coasts of France and Italy came both from Africa and Spain. Between the years 891 and 894 they installed themselves along the gulf of Saint-Tropez and as far inland as the Alps. They have left both historical and archaeological evidence.[25]

Englishmen experienced these raids on land, on the continent of Europe, and at sea as participants in the northern raiding parties on Spain. In the tenth century, we have a record of English pilgrims on their way to Rome being killed in an Alpine ravine by a hail of stones thrown by Saracens hidden in the mountains.[26]

In the eleventh century, most of the northern pirates who descended on the coasts of Spain came from the British Isles and are called "Anglici vel Normanigenae," or simply "Anglici piratae" by contemporary historians.[27] In the Arab accounts, the references at that time point as far as the Orkneys:

> To the north of Cadiz, which is in the Encircling Ocean, are the Fortunate Isles and on them are innumerable towns and villages and from them comes a people which is called Majus and which is Christian. The first of these islands is Britain and it is in the midst of

the Encircling Sea at a great distance to the north from Spain and
they have neither mountains nor springs and their inhabitants drink
rain water and cultivate the land with it.[28]

Considering the strength of the Saracen fleet in the tenth century and
its activities in the Atlantic and Mediterranean until the twelfth, it is not
surprising to have it remembered in the romance of its northern Atlantic
neighbors. Their firsthand experience of Saracens on native grounds,
before the Crusades, was much greater than is generally assumed. By the
twelfth century Saracen was a generic name for any attacker, and we find
Saracens associated with places in the French romances where historical
Saracens never set foot. Nevertheless, in *King Horn* (about 1300), which is
enacted in Viking territory, the historical possibility of Saracen landings
cannot be entirely excluded. The Saracen raiders are given a coloring of
the kind which we have in encounters with real Saracens in the *chansons
de geste* (for example, in *Les Narbonnais* and the literature of the Crusades).
They are led by an *admirad*, a commander bearing an Arabic title whose
earliest recorded occurrence in Middle English is about 1225.[29]

In *King Horn* the title denotes a naval commander. The maritime designation in the poem is particularly intriguing as the title of *"amīr al-baḥr,"*
"amīr al-mā'i" (i.e. "emir of the sea," "emir of the water") was created by
the western Arabs, the Arabs of Spain and Sicily. We have no way of
knowing whether the usage in *King Horn* represents the precise meaning of
the word as simply "any Saracen lord or chieftain" as "admirail" does in
its first occurrence in Middle English in Laȝamon's *Brut* (ca. 1225).[30]
There "on admirail of Babilione" is a commander of troops on land,
while the same title is applied to the prince himself in *Floris and Blancheflur*
(ca. 1250). The word, at any rate, must have suggested the experience of
real Saracens to the audience. In Ireland, on the other hand, Horn fights
with a giant "y-armed from paynim," a stock figure of romance that is
also found in the most historical accounts, like Ambroise's *L'Estoire de la
guerre sainte.*

The Middle English *King Horn* was composed in the first quarter of the
thirteenth century and was preceded by the Anglo-Norman *Horn et Rimen-
hild* of Master Thomas, dated about 1170. The date of the English *Sir
Beues of Hamtoun* is ca. 1300, about a century after the composition of the
original Anglo-Norman romance. While the Saracens in *King Horn* are
raiders, we have Saracen merchants landing on the coast of Britain in
Beues to mark the opening of the story of adventure. This in itself is an
indication that the poem is basically not a Viking saga of the tenth century
as has been maintained by Suchier.[31] The Saracen dromond which lands
on the shores of England in the Anglo-Norman original of *Beues* is indeed
"tut plein de Sarazins felouns."[32] But they are clearly "marchaunz

Sarazin" who buy Beues from the knights of the treacherous queen, willingly paying four times his weight in gold for legitimate and profitable merchandise. Having completed the transaction, they set sail for Egypt through the Mediterranean, the accepted route of Saracen trade. In the Anglo-Norman version they sell Beues at an Egyptian port, presumably to agents of an Egyptian king named Hermyne, who rules over a people called Hermins, presumably the population of Egypt.

The merchant character of the Saracens who transport Beues into exile is made even clearer when we consider that, in the Continental French versions, the merchants are Russians or Egyptians who obtain Beues in Hungary or Russia and sell him to Persia or Armenia. The distinction between Saracen piracy and Saracen commerce is unmistakable in *Beues of Hampton* and is, in fact, emphasized by the role of Armenia whose importance for Western Europe in the twelfth century lay in its Mediterranean ports and its caravan routes used by both merchants and Crusaders.

Saracen merchants coming from the western Mediterranean at the time of the English *Beues* would have landed at Ayas—Chaucer's Lyas[33]—the most important port on the coast of Lesser Armenia which was the point of departure for the caravans that journeyed to Greater Armenia and beyond to Trebizond. It is from Tarsus and Ayas that the ships proceeded to Egypt, Syria, and Palestine. When Beues, having rescued Josian from her nominal husband in "Mombraunt," reaches the sea in the company of the Armenian princess and Ascopart, the Saracen giant whose life he has spared, they find a Saracen vessel bound for "heþene lond" waiting to hire a "mariner." Again, the Saracens, though "stout and fer," are obviously peaceful traders, for Ascopart enters the ship by proclaiming himself a suitable mariner, and then drives the passengers from their ship without much ado. He then carries Beues's horse and Josian's mule aboard and quickly sets sail in the opposite direction, to the port of Cologne on the Rhine.

There is no documentary evidence of English trade with the Saracens of the Levant before the middle of the thirteenth century.[34] Nevertheless, the historical significance of the situation in *Beues*, the manner in which the hero leaves his native England, goes back to an early medieval period when the British Isles provided a supply of slaves who were sold to Saracens in Marseilles and in Danish trading centers as well.[35]

The absence of documentary evidence for early trade between Christians and Saracens, which included the marketing of Christian slaves as an important commodity, is due to the religious preoccupations of Christian chroniclers who were clerics. They were not interested in recording the activities of merchants in the sinful pursuit of worldly goods. Christian missionaries, however, made good use of the trade routes which led from the British Isles to the international trading centers not only along the Mediterranean, but in Scandinavia and Eastern Europe as well. On his famous voyage between 870 and 890, which he reported to King Alfred, Ohthere sailed to an important international trading port in Jutland, Hæthum or Haithabu, where about 950, we find a Jewish merchant by the name of al-Turtushi, who had come from Tortosa, Spain, by ship along the Frankish coast.[36] Al-Turtushi gives us an extensive account of what he had seen on his visit to that very same center where there was a flourishing Saracen trade that included the marketing of Christian slaves from West to East.

In the northern countries, which marked the western limits of Europe, early activities of Saracen trade have been indicated since the eighth century by numismatic evidence in Mercia and Viking Scandinavia.[37] In England, in the eleventh century, there are possibly traces of peaceful Saracen presence under the Normans in Arabic inscriptions on the Isle of Man.[38]

In the thirteenth-century English romance, Beues of Hampton is the son of a young mother, daughter of the king of Scotland, and an old father who is lord of Hampton.[39] Beues's mother wants no interference from her son in the affairs of her body and heart and to protect her lover, the emperor of Almayne, who murders Beues's father and becomes her new husband, Beues is sold into slavery. The queen dispatches four knights with the following order:

> "Wendeþ," ʒhe seide, "to þe stronde:
> Ʒif ʒe seþ schipes of painim londe,
> Selleþ to hem his ilche hyne,
> Þat ʒe for no gode ne fine,
> Whaþer ʒe haue for him mor or lesse,
> Selleþ him riʒt into heþenesse."

[ll. 495–500]

> Forþ þe kniʒtes gonne te,
> Til þat hii come to þe se,
> Schipes hii fonde þer stonde
> Of heþenesse and of fele londe;
> Þe child hii chepeden to sale,
> Marchaundes þai fonde ferli fale
> And solde þat child for mechel auʒte
> And to þe Sarasins him be-tauʒte.

[ll. 501–08]

The ship sails straight to the coast of Armenia:

> Forþ þai wente wiþ þat child,

> Crist of heuene be him mild!
> Þe childes hertte was wel colde,
> For þat he was so fer isolde;
> Napeles, þouȝ him pouȝte eile,
> Toward painim a moste saile.
> Whan hii riuede out of þat strond,
> Þe king hiȝte Ermin of þat londe. . . .

[ll. 509–16]

The setting reflects a situation that encompasses both Greater and Lesser Armenia and stresses the historical significance of the Christian province nearest the Muslim frontier. In the complicated historical geography of the Crusades, it was Christian Armenia that fired the imagination of the Western public as a bridge between Christians and Saracens. Greater Armenia, though mostly inhabited by Christians, was brought under Muslim rule at an early period. In 1064, Alp Arslan, sultan of the Seljuk Turks, overran Christian Armenia, an event that broke up the older Armenian kingdom and led to the founding of the kingdom of Lesser Armenia in the Taurus region, situated like a wedge between the Ayyubid and later Mameluke, sultanate of Syria and the Seljuk sultanate of Iconium. It was Lesser Armenia that lay at the heart of the sea and caravan routes of medieval warfare and trade. Between the eleventh and twelfth centuries, this province was traversed three times by the armies of the Western Crusaders.

In the first half of the thirteenth century, when the Tartars overran Asia Minor, Greater Armenia became a tributary of the Persian Mongol Empire, while the kings of Lesser Armenia attempted to form a solid alliance with the Tartars against the Muslim powers of Seljuk Turkey, Syria, and Egypt by which it was engulfed. At the time of Ghazan, the Tartar ruler of Persia who was the last of the Ilchans to maintain Western hopes of Tartar conversion to Christianity, Lesser Armenia suffered repeated attacks by Egyptian sultans. The sultan of Babylon, who consistently appears in early medieval romances, represents a realistic awareness of the Egyptian dynasty as the center of Saracen power which, throughout the thirteenth century in Asia Minor, tried to contain both Christians and Tartars.[40]

The topographical indications in the Middle English *Sir Beues* link the port of Southampton with Armenia and Syria. Saracen merchants, unequivocally professing Islam and trading with Asia Minor, are the means by which the setting of the romance is shifted to the Near East. The kingdom of Armenia to which Beues is transported is explicitly Muslim in the romance. Josian is the conventional Muslim princess in love with the Christian knight, Beues. She is wooed by the neighboring

Syrian emir of Damascus and later by Yuor, king of Mombraunt, a city
to the north of Armenia and one of the "noblest" cities "in all þe lond of
Sarsine" (l. 2046). Yuor is a Muslim emir allied to the sultan of Babylon,
that is, Egypt. In a conventional happy ending, Josian is baptized by the
bishop of Cologne and becomes Beues's wife and the mother of his twin
sons. The crown of Armenia is lawfully passed into the hands of one of
Beues's sons, the declared heir of Josian's father, King Ermin. Beues
himself replaces the slain Muslim Yuor as "king of Mombraunt." Beues's
other son marries the only daughter of the king of England and becomes
his rightful heir. What the hero of the romance has accomplished is the
union of England, Armenia, and "Mombraunt."

The alliance of England and the kingdom of Armenia against Muslim
power, which is celebrated in the romantic theme, faithfully expresses the
needs of a serious political reality. English kings both in the thirteenth and
fourteenth centuries took an active part in the efforts of popes and
emperors to stem the tide of Islam by pacts with Armenia, the Christian
outpost on the Muslim frontier. The steady pursuit of this policy is seen in
Edward I (1272–1307), in Haithon, the Armenian prince who fled to the
West and composed the well-known, propagandistic history of the Tartars,[41] and, in the time of Chaucer, in the diplomatic activities of Leo V,
king of Lesser Armenia, at the court of Richard II.[42]

The author of the English *Sir Beues of Hampton* refers to his original: "so
hit is fonde in frensche tale" (ll. 888, 1566, 1782). However, like other
English poets who rendered French romances into their own vernacular,
he did not merely translate but adapted his narrative to contemporary
conditions which had topical interest. When Beues, disguised as a palmer,
is questioned by his rival, King Yuor of Mombraunt, the Middle English
version presents a significant shift and expansion of the range of countries
which Beues has visited in the French tale. In the earlier versions, most of
these countries are clearly imagined as lying in the traditional territory of
Alexander the Great and in the western realm of Saracen power in Africa:

> "Sire," ceo dist Boeves, "jeo ai esté a Nubie
> e en Cartage e en Esclavie
> e a l'Arbre Sek e en Barbarie
> e a Macedoyne, par tut en Paenie,
> mes a chastel de Abilent, la ne fu ge mie."[43]

["Sir," said Boeuve, "I was in Nubia and in Carthage and in the land
of the Slavs and at the Dry Tree and in Barbary and in Macedonia,
throughout all the lands of the Paynim but at the castle of Abilent,
there I was never at all."]

In the Middle English romance, about 1300, there is a distinct shift to the territory of the Crusades, the Saracen East, as the scene of romantic action.

The question which is asked about distant lands in the English Beues probes to the core of medieval reality and gives us a realistic sense of what preoccupied "the medieval mind":

> Palmer, þou comst fro ferre:
> Whar is pes and whar is werre?
>
> [l. 2257–58]

The state of affairs on which Beues, in the guise of a palmer, reports is surprisingly peaceful. It suggests the period of relatively peaceful coexistence that marked the era of Saladin, after the battle of Hattin in 1187, once the triumph of Islam in the Holy Land had been assured.

> "Sire, ich come from Iurisalem
> Fro Nazareþ & fro Bedlem,
> Emavns castel & Synaie;
> Ynde, Erop and Asie,
> Egippte, Grese and Babiloine,
> Tars, Sesile and Sesaoine,
> In Fris, in Sodeine & in Tire,
> In Aufrik and in mani empire,
> Ac al is pes þar ichaue went,
> Saue in þe lond of Dabilent. . . . "
>
> [ll. 2261–70]

The enumeration of the places and countries Beues claims to have visited is typical of a wide range of medieval romances in the age of the Crusades. With minor variations, it is one of the conventional *summae* both of romantic and real travel. The question is what, concretely, these countries and their inhabitants suggested to the medieval audience and how their presentation in romance compares with the historical knowledge transmitted about them at the same time.

Before he meets the palmer with whom he exchanges clothes on the outskirts of Mombraunt, Beues's itinerary is as follows: he escapes from Damascus where he was imprisoned for seven years, by the emir of Syria to whom he had been treacherously sent from Armenia by King Ermin, the father of his lady, Josian. On his way from Damascus to Armenia he goes to Jerusalem to visit the patriarch. Before reaching Jerusalem, Beues has swum on his horse across a sea, which may be the Sea of Galilee, leaving the pursuing Syrian Saracens behind on the shore. He reaches a Saracen castle in Palestine, apparently in the region of Tiberias, where he obtains food by killing the giant who is lord of the castle. He then continues his journey to Jerusalem along a "strem," evidently the Jordan.

From Jerusalem he turns toward Armenia. He meets a Saracen knight who "had borne him good company in Armenia" and who informs him that Josian has been taken to Mombraunt. Beues has obviously not heard of Mombraunt, though it is one of the most splendid cities in Saracen land, for he asks the knight where it is situated and is told to go north.

Beues's sojourn in the cities of Palestine, Jerusalem, Bethlehem, Nazareth, and at Emmaus castle, in the region of Tiberias, is implied in his actual route within the plot of the romance. To reach Armenia he would have had to travel along the coast to Tyre and Sidon and on to Antioch. It would have weakened his claim as a palmer not to have visited Sinai, the seat of the famous monastery of St. Catherine founded by the Byzantine emperor Justinian, at the foot of which, as Benjamin of Tudela reports in the twelfth century, there was a flourishing city.[44] India, Europe, Asia, and Africa are thrown in for bravado; Egypt and its capital, Cairo, would have been visited on the way to Sinai; Frisia suggests the long and arduous distance a medieval palmer traversed, from the northwestern extremes of Europe to the ports of Sicily, Greece, and, finally, Tarsus. If "Dabilent" is Dabil, the capital of Muslim Greater Armenia, the geographical setting of the romance is sufficiently exact to locate Mombraunt as one of the northern Seljuk emirates. We learn from Josian's chamberlain that the location of Dabilent is a four-day journey from Mombraunt and that Dabilent is governed by Yuor's brother. It is by making a false report about Dabilent being under siege that Beues gets Yuor and fifteen vassals to leave Mombraunt and Josian. The fact that Beues himself, at the end of the romance, becomes the ruler of Mombraunt while his son, also a Christian knight, becomes the king of Armenia suggests the outline of a definite historical period that lasted over two centuries, from 1077 to 1300, when the establishment of the Seljuk Turks in Asia Minor coincided with the rise of the Christian kingdom of Lesser Armenia. In the middle of the thirteenth century the Seljuks gave way to the Tartars of the Levant, as the Mongols of Persia were called, but the Christian rule of Lesser Armenia, skillfully coping with the Mongol invasion by alliances and trading pacts with the Christians of Western Europe and the religiously tolerant Tartars themselves, only came to an end in 1342.[45]

The composite picture of Mombraunt that emerges from the French versions is that of an important port with a flourishing trade in luxurious oriental products, wine, and especially spices (pepper and cumin are expressly named). Mombraunt exudes the flavor of merchant cities described by William of Rubruck and Marco Polo, of Trebizond and Samarkand. In the Middle English poem we hear that

> Mombraunt is a riche cite,
> In al þe londe of Sarsine

> Nis þer non þer to iliche
> Ne be fele parti so riche.

[ll. 2045–48]

We are told that it is situated to the north of Armenia in Asia Minor. Moreover, its character as a brilliant and rich city makes it clear that it is situated along the most important commercial tracks connecting it with Lesser Armenia and the sea. In the English poem the impression is given that the town is some distance from the sea. Beues and Josian hide in a cave for two days, Beues slays two lions and fights with the giant Ascopart and only then

> Forþ þai wenten alle þre,
> Til þat hii come to þe se;
> A dromond hii fonde þer stonde,
> Þat wolde in to heþene londe,
> Wiþ Sarasines stout & fer. . . .

[ll. 2551–55]

The place and function of palmers in medieval society is made very clear in the romance. Beues disguises himself as a palmer on learning that Josian welcomes palmers. Her purpose is to obtain information:

> Herde euer eni of ȝow telle
> In eni lede or eni spelle,
> Or in feld oþer in toun,
> Of a kniȝt, Beues of Hamtoun?

[ll. 2129–32]

The disguised Beues reports to the king on war and peace in foreign lands.

We know that pilgrims and palmers were often confidential agents when they traveled to the Holy Land. Wilbrand of Oldenburg, later bishop of Paderborn, who went to Palestine and Asia Minor in 1211, points this out in the preface to his *Peregrinatio*: he was not an ordinary pilgrim but "bent on and engaged in some business which was not to be considered as blameworthy." His purpose was to describe the conditions and fortifications of the places he visited as he found them at the time. His mission was obviously to survey the territory. We hear from Wilbrand of Oldenburg that he and his companions were reviled when they tried to bathe in the holy waters of the Jordan. A group of Arabs threw dirt at them. On the other hand, Wilbrand is hardly grateful to "the sons of Mammon" for being allowed to visit the Church of the Holy Sepulchre, unmolested and secure.[46]

If a palmer made his journey after 1187, when the Muslim victory at Hattin had finally doomed the Latin kingdom of Jerusalem,[47] he went there in violation of the edicts of several popes who forbade ordinary pilgrimages beyond Cyprus in order to prevent the Saracens from enriching themselves by the tax which they had instituted for Christians and other non-Muslims.[48] Jerusalem, Nazareth, and Bethlehem were, however, easily accessible to Christians after the fall of Jerusalem, for Saladin's political wisdom had extended full rights to the Orthodox Christians and had made them guardians of the Church of the Holy Sepulchre and other shrines in Palestine. When Saladin entered Jerusalem, the Church of the Holy Sepulchre was closed for only three days. When he was urged to destroy it, he pointed out that it was the site, not the building, which the Christians considered holy and that Christian pilgrims might as well be admitted on payment of a fee.[49]

The chivalry of Saladin in his attitude to Christian pilgrims is clearly impressed upon the audience of L'Estoire de la guerre sainte, a poem which was recorded in England at the end of the thirteenth century but appears to have been composed about the same time as the French Boeuve de Hamtoun. The "estoire" is an eyewitness account of Ambrose, a Norman poet and jongleur who was present at the coronation of Richard in London and accompanied him to the Holy Land.[50] Ambrose was also one of the crusader-pilgrims who visited Jerusalem after the truce with Saladin in September 1192. He describes their reception in the holy city: the pilgrims set out in three groups, one of which was guided by Hubert Walter, bishop of Salisbury (later archbishop of Canterbury). They were unarmed and were carrying a letter from Richard. Through negligence, however, they had failed to obtain a safe-conduct from Saladin in advance. On approaching Jerusalem at sunset, they were terrified at the sight of ferocious Muslim troops encamped outside the city wall and expected to be massacred. They had good reason for their fear, for the Christians had massacred 2,500 Muslim prisoners at Acre by Richard's orders.[51]

But contrary to their expectations, the advisers of Saladin counseled moderation. Not only did Saladin allow them to visit the Church of the Holy Sepulchre unscathed, but he received the bishop of Salisbury with special honors granting him protection and showering him with gifts. The bishop even secured the special favor of having two Latin priests and two deacons permanently conduct regular Latin services in addition to the Syrian custodians of the Holy Sepulchre. This permission was also extended to services in Bethlehem and Nazareth. The identical account is given in the Itinerarium Regis Ricardi whose relationship to the Estoire is not quite clear.[52] The events recounted are historical, however, and the medieval audience was given a true impression of Muslim tolerance of pilgrims from the West.

We see this clearly in Matthew of Westminster's Flores Historiarum, A.D. 1230:

The same year, the city of Jerusalem was restored to the emperor
Frederic, and to the Christian population, with the crown of the
kingdom of Jerusalem; and the emperor was crowned in that city.
And of the manner and time of his coronation, he, with a view to give
them pleasure, certified the king of England and the other princes by
elegant letters, sealed with seals of gold, which contained the statement of which I will here give the heads:

"The soldan of Babylon, as had been before settled, has restored
the city of Jerusalem to the Christian population and form of worship; and the whole country is free in every direction, so that free
access to the holy places is open to the Christian pilgrims. Moreover,
the city of Bethlehem is restored, and likewise all the territory which
lies between Acre and that city, and the whole district of Tyre, which
is very fruitful, and very desirable for the Christians. So too is the city
of Sidon, which is commonly called Sacra, with the whole of its plain,
and all its belongings, which was of great use to the Saracens especially, as it has a desirable harbour, and as the adjacent land is very
fertile, and as arms and provisions, and many necessaries used to be
conveyed from thence to the city of Damascus, and from Damascus
to Babylon. . . . we are permitted to rebuild the city of Jerusalem
better than it was ever built before, according to the agreement, and
also the castle of Joppa, the castle of Caesarea, the castle of Sidon."[53]

Latin Christian officialdom felt imposed upon, however. Albert, abbot
of St. Mary's Stade who lived in the first half of the thirteenth century,
records with some resentment that the Syrian Christians had to "buy"
the Church of the Holy Sepulchre back from the Muslims at a rent of
40,000 gold pieces a year. He also tells us that Pope Clement forbade
Christians to go to Jerusalem to pray and that the Christians who did so
exposed themselves to vilification and scorn in Muslim Jerusalem.[54]

The fact of the matter is that Alberic de Trois-Fontaines, a Cistercian
monk writing in 1234, was deeply impressed by the respect in which the
Saracens held Christian sites in the Holy Land. He speaks of an emir of
Damascus who recovered his sight at the shrine of Our Lady of Sardenay,
in the hills of the Anti-Lebanon, a quarter hour's journey from Damascus. The emir presented the sanctuary with sixty measures of oil—an
endowment continued by his successors. Alberic mentions three sanctu-
aries in Muslim territory whose unmolested existence he considered
"miraculous": Sardenay, Bethlehem, and Saint Catherine on Mount
Sinai.[55]

A palmer would have visited Emmaus castle near Jerusalem as a matter
of course. Sinai, which in the days of King Baldwin depended on the protection of the fortress of Karak (Petra Deserti), was visited by Thietmar
in 1217.[56]

Thietmar's chronicle gives us the oldest account of its state after the fall of Jerusalem. We learn of the mosque on the site of the church, the destination of Muslim pilgrims as well. It was from Karak in Transjordan that Reynald of Châtillon, its Crusader lord, attacked the caravans of pilgrims to Mecca thus breaking the truce with Saladin. The sultan of Babylon used to visit Mount Sinai, says Thietmar, and when he did so, he took off his shoes.[57] Though the monastery and the Christian pilgrims were often attacked and plundered by the Bedouins, this was not for religious reasons. For the monks stood under the protection of the sultans from whom they exhibited a long series of firmans going back to an alleged letter from the Prophet Muhammad himself. The traffic of pilgrims was clearly uninterrupted even in times of hostility.

The factual knowledge of countries and cultures did not, however, supplant traditions and conventions associated with them in literary treatment or give reality to Babylon or Tars. Another striking example of this is the literary treatment of India, which is on Beues's itinerary as well.

Western ignorance about India as late as the time of Chaucer strikes one as unnecessarily prolonged. A good deal of factual knowledge was available to merchants, pilgrims, and Crusaders in their movements between Spain, Sicily, Constantinople, and Syria. The first Arab traveler to India and China to write an account dates from the time of King Alfred.[58] In fact, the Saxon king himself is said to have sent alms to St. Thomas the Apostle in India and to have received many precious gems from his returning emissary.[59]

In the first half of the eleventh century we have al-Biruni's great work on India, an account of its religion, philosophy, literature, chronology, astronomy, laws, and astrology.[60] In Europe, the earliest notions of that mysterious continent stem from descriptions of the wonders of the East and the legend of Alexander. In England, we have an Old English translation of the letter of Alexander to Aristotle in which the wonders of India are described.[61] In spite of the myth, however, an impression of Indian reality is also received from these pages. We sense a country of innumerable reptiles, lions, leopards, tigers, elephants, and hippopotami; naked men immersing themselves in rivers; gold and gems—diamonds, smaragds, and pearls; the southern part of the continent unbearably hot, the northern cold and frosty. But even Mandeville's India does not extend beyond the connection with St. Thomas and Alexander's letter. The geographical indications are vague. In *Beues* and Chaucer it is at the other end of Denmark or Thule, a topos for the extreme limits of the medieval world.

THE MARRIAGE THEME AS A PORTRAYAL OF CHRISTIAN-MUSLIM RELATIONS

The exploits of Beues of Hampton, Méliacin, the hero of Girard d'Amiens, and Chaucer's Arcite, the faithless lover of *Anelida and Arcite*, are all enacted on territory in which Armenia is the focal point. Beues is sold into slavery to the king of Armenia and marries an Armenian princess; Méliacin is a prince of Armenia; Anelida, the heroine of *Anelida and Arcite*, is queen of Armenia. Between the twelfth and fourteenth centuries Armenia, as we have seen, had a special significance in the image of the Saracen and Christian East and its importance in the location of Western medieval romances is readily apparent to every reader.

The theme of the *King of Tars and the Soudan of Damas* is the marriage of a Tartar khan and an Armenian princess. As in the tale of Constance, daughter of the emperor of Rome—a tale retold by Trivet, Gower, and Chaucer—the marriage between Christian and Saracen has the approval of the pope and is the hope of peace between two opposing creeds and cultures. In Chaucer's *Squire's Tale* the alliance is foreshadowed in the marriage of Algarsif and Theodora, possibly, like the original Constance, a Byzantine princess. Wherever we find it in medieval romance, the marriage of Christian and Saracen as a literary theme seems to be Arabo-Byzantine in origin, and relates in particular to events in Asia Minor, the location of Christian provinces nearest to the Muslim frontier.

The story of the *King of Tars* is as follows:

> To spare her people from war, a self-sacrificing Christian princess marries a heathen sultan. When their offspring is born a formless lump of flesh, the father accuses her of having merely pretended to believe in his gods. His pleas to the heathen deities fail to restore the child; at the mother's request the infant is baptized, and immediately becomes a handsome boy. Induced by this miracle to adopt the Christian faith, the father himself changes in the baptismal water from black to white. He then joins his wife's father to convert or kill those of his vassals who do not accept Christianity.[62]

The plot of *The King of Tars and the Soudan of Damas* has been related to analogues in England, France, Germany, Italy, and Spain, which parallel a brief account in Thomas of Walsingham's *Historia Anglicana* and one attributed to Matthew of Westminster in the *Flores Historiarum*.[63] The account, under the year 1299, reports the marriage of an Armenian princess to the brother of Ghazan, the Tartar khan, who expelled the Saracens from Jerusalem. The historical background of the *King of Tars* is therefore suggested by this event,[64] the appearance of the Tartars, under the leadership of Ghazan, before Damascus, and the general hope of Christendom to convert the victorious hordes that were containing the tide of Islam. The chroniclers, moreover, reflect the poem in the treatment of the most crucial point in such intermarriages, that is, the offspring that is to unite Christianity and Islam: a shaggy masculine creature is born to the couple (Frater hujus regis Tartarorum ex filia Regis Armeniae genuit filium hispidum et pilosum).[65] Once he is baptized, all hairiness disappears, and the child becomes smooth-skinned and beautiful. The miracle converts the Tartar prince and all his house.

Another event recorded concerns a king of the Tartars who falls in love with one of his concubines, a Christian. The Christian woman bears him a son who is white on his right side and black on his left. The mother entreats him to have the child baptized. This is done, the blackness disappears and the miracle makes such an impression on the heathen king that he sends emissaries to the pope to request that he and his people be instructed in the Christian faith and baptized.[66]

In the *King of Tars*, it takes a miracle *after* marriage to convert the Muslim to Christianity. The Syrian emir becomes a Christian *before* the marriage, however, in the tale of Constance and in the *Digenes Akrites*, a famous Byzantine epic of the tenth century.[67]

Related to the Christian-Muslim marriage motif are the role of the sultan's mother in the story of Constance, and, in the *King of Tars*, the change of color from black to white in the sultan's face after conversion. In *The Man of Law's Tale*, Chaucer's tale of Constance, the mother of the sultan is the "well of vice" and, as in Trivet, pretends to adopt Christianity in order to lure her Christian victims, including her son, to destruction. She arouses her son's subjects against him and his marriage by her religious fervor:

> The mooder of the Sowdan, welle of vices,
> Espied hath hir sones pleyn entente,
> How he wol lete his olde sacrifices;
> And right anon she for his conseil sente,
>
> . . . .
>
> "Lordes," quod she, "ye knowen everichon,
> How that my sone in point is for to lete
> The hooly lawes of our Alkaron,
> Yeven by Goddes message Makomete.
> But oon avow to grete God I heete,
> The lyf shal rather out of my body sterte
> Or Makometes lawe out of myn herte!
>
> [ll. 323–36]

In the third book of the *Digenes Akrites*, the emir, having married his Christian wife in "Rome," receives a letter from his mother requesting his return to Syria:

> Thus happening that wonderful Emir,
> Despising fame and great authority,
> Forgot his kin, his parents, and his country,
> Even denied his faith for a girl's love,

One indeed truly fair and very noble.
The one-time foe was seen the slave of love;
For his beloved he dwelled in Romany;
From Syria had a letter from his mother,
Resolved to go away fearing her curse—
(For it is righteous not to anger parents).

[ll. 646–55]

Leaving his wife and young son in her native land, the emir and his retainers set out for their own country to see his mother.

The meeting on Syrian ground, though joyous, has elements of tension:

And thus began to speak the Emir's mother:
"O sweetest child of mine, light of my eyes,
And consolation of my soul in age,
Pleasant delight and gladness of my heart,
Say why you tarried, child, in Romania;

. . . .

Do strange wonders happen in Romania
Such as are done, child, at the Prophet's tomb,
Where you went with me going to my prayers?

. . . .

How did you come, child, to transgress all this,
And power did despise and greatest fame?
They all believed that you would conquer Egypt,
But you turned obstacle of your own fortune,
And gave up everything for a Roman girl."

[ll. 768–72, 775–77, 790–94][68]

The emir then expounds his new faith to his mother, and such is his fervor for his new religion and the virtuous beauty of his Christian wife that his mother and his kinsmen adopt Christianity and return with him to "Romania." It is not unlikely that the pretended conversion to Christianity of the sultan's mother, which we find in the story of Constance, is a trace of an actual conversion as related by the Byzantine narrator of the Saracen-Christian marriage theme.

In *The King of Tars and the Soudan of Damas* the following happens after the sultan has received baptism:

The preste hihte sire Cleophas,
And nempnede so the soudan of Damas,
After his owne name;
His colour that lodlich and blak was,

Hit bi com feir thorw godes gras,
And cler withoute blame.[69]

The description of the Syrian emir about to marry a Christian princess in
the *Digenes Akrites* emphasizes his "fairness":

Was an Emir of breed, exceeding rich,
Of wisdom seized and bravery to the top,
Not black as Aethiops are, but fair and lovely,
Already bloomed with comely curly beard.

[ll. 30–33]

The implications of this in the context of a Christian poem are in no way
surprising. What is interesting is the appearance of this color scheme in
the offspring of a Tartar-Christian marriage which has also been found in
two Franco-Latin chronicles,[70] representing a significant variation in the
account of the monstrous birth in the *King of Tars*.

In spite of the differences in treatment, the core of the Christian-Muslim
marriage theme in the *King of Tars* and the story of Constance is the same
as in the *Digenes Akrites* and in the Arabian story of Omar an-Nuʿman:
the importance of the interreligious and binational marriage. The child
of such a marriage, of biracial origin, is a "di genes," often symbolically
half black and half white. It is he who will bring about the harmonious
union of two warring peoples. The dream of oriental romance throughout
the Middle Ages is the union of Christian and Saracen.

Greet was the prees, and riche was th' array
Of Surryens and Romayns met yfeere
[*Man of Law's Tale*, 1. 393–94]

The literary expression of Arabo-Byzantine contact on the Christian-
Muslim frontier in Asia Minor is first found in the *Arabian Nights* and the
Digenes Akrites, and poses interesting questions about the pattern of literary interrelationships. In the *Arabian Nights*, Sophia, a Byzantine princess,
becomes the wife of Omar an-Nuʿman, a Muslim ruler, and is the mother
of the ensuing dynastic offspring. It is this tale of *King Omar Bin al-
Nuʿuman and His Sons Sharrkan and Zau al-Makan and His Daughter Nushat
az-Zaman*[71] which brings us to the channels of Arabo-Byzantine material
that lead from the Eastern Empire to the West. Its English prototype is
the *Squire's Tale*. As an oriental romance, the *Squire's Tale*, both in theme
and genre, represents a Western version of the compilation of interde-
pendent stories in a loose framework that have come down to us in the
Arabian Nights. The *Squire's Tale* was to weave a narrative tapestry befit-
ting a noble romantic youth by joining several strands of Eastern romance,
of Tartary, Byzantium, India, and Araby in which the four gifts brought

by a knightly messenger of the king of Araby and Ind—the magic horse, the mirror, the ring, and the sword—would form the links of connection.

The tale of the flying horse from the *Arabian Nights*, as we have it in the French romances of *Méliacin* and *Cléomadès* and in Chaucer's *Squire's Tale*, presents a complicated problem of transmission which has led to Spanish sources of the Arabian tale. There is the evidence of miniatures in manuscripts of both *Méliacin* and *Cléomadès*.[72] One illustration in *Cléomadès* displays the coat of arms of Castile and shows Blanche of Castile, the king of France's sister and, after 1275, widow of Ferdinand of Cerda, infanta of Castile, narrating the tale of the poet.[73] The conclusion is that the poems are independent versions of the tale of the Ebony Horse which the widow of the infanta of Castile brought back to France after a sojourn of nine years at the Spanish court.

Another tale from the *Arabian Nights*, the story of Taj al-Muluk and the Lady Dunya, has been recognized as an analogue to the episode of Canacee and the lovelorn falcon in the *Squire's Tale*.[74] It depicts the distinction between true and false love in the example of faithless male birds, an important element in the *Squire's Tale* which Chaucer most probably intended to affect the heroine's own romance.

The story of Taj al-Muluk and his princess has a significance for the Chaucerian material of which students of the *Squire's Tale* have not been aware: it is an integral part of the largest and most important group of interlinked stories in the *Arabian Nights* which together form a "family romance," namely, the tale of King Omar ibn an-Nu'man, his two sons Sharkan and Dhu al-Makan, and his daughter Nuzhat az-Zaman.

Like the tale of the learned maiden Tawaddud,[75] whose bearing on Chaucerian material will be discussed later, this romance was originally an independent narrative; it was later incorporated in the *Arabian Nights*. It forms the longest tale in the collection, in the estimation of Burton, about one eighth of the whole.[76] Like the *Squire's Tale*, it is a tale of knight-errantry set in a royal household comprising two sons and one daughter, and evolves against the background of complicated warfare between Islam, Byzantium, and Frankish Christendom. Within the knot of the royal court we have a long series of intertwined exploits in war and love of the type which Chaucer clearly intended to develop on an Arabian model.

An indication of this lies in the French *Méliacin*. Both Girard d'Amiens's *Méliacin* and Adenès le Rois's *Cléomadès* are thirteenth-century versions of the tale of the Ebony Horse whose common source is assumed to have been an early Spanish version of the oriental story.[77] The setting, however, differs in the two romances. Like Chaucer's *Squire's Tale*, the *Méliacin* opens with the feast of the king's nativity and the scene is laid in Asia. *Cléomadès*, the better-known version of the two, is located in Spain. The names in the two French romances are not the same in a single instance, and there are many divergencies in the incidents. *Cléomadès* is mentioned in Froissart's *L'Espinette amoureuse* and "it seems almost certain that Chaucer knew the romance of Adenes."[78] Yet he laid his scene in Tartary, in Asia.

Méliacin, the hero of the French poem that bears his name, is the son of the king of Greater Armenia. The name of the poem has also appeared as *Meliadius*, a form not found in the four extant manuscripts, but recorded in the sixteenth-century entries of Claude Fauchet and Croix du Maine.[79] Méliacin's sister, the eldest princess, is named Melide or Meliade which, as a typical cognate form in family names, seems to confirm the etymological association of Méliacin and Meliadius. There is a fascinating suggestion in the name and the setting of the poem. For it leads us to a famous Armenian hero named Mleh or Melias in Greek, a historical ruler of medieval Armenian Melitene (Malatya) whose name appears in an Armenian form as Melemendzis in the *Digenes Akrites*.[80]

The heroic exploits of knightly warfare in the Byzantine epic are enacted on specific territories of Asia Minor in which Armenia is a focal point. We find the same exploits and territories in the family tale of Omar an-Nu'man and his sons in the *Arabian Nights*. They contain historical traces of the relationship between Christianity and Islam and are reflected in the subject matter of both Eastern and Western romance.

The importance of Melitene in the Arabo-Byzantine cycle of epics reflects the campaigns of Byzantines and Muslims in the Muslim conquest of Asia Minor. Under the emperors Trajan and Justinian, Melitene was the capital of the province of Armenia. Its strategic location on the upper Euphrates, at the crossing of important trade routes, made it one of the crucial points of contention between the Byzantine and Muslim empires. It was one of the most important strongholds of the Muslim-Byzantine frontier.

The Arab historian Istakhri describes it as a large town surrounded by hills on which grew vines, almonds and other nut trees, for its lands produced the crops of both the hot and cold regions.[81] Abu-'l-Fida, the historian of the Crusades, says that Christians and Muslims lived in the city on the best of terms.[82] Throughout the Middle Ages Melitene was an important seat of Armenian, Byzantine, Saracen, and Tartar power, being taken and retaken as the tides of war ebbed and flowed.

In the ninth century a famous Emir Omar of Melitene fought off Byzantine attacks until he was defeated and killed in 863. His son and then his grandson, Emir Abu Hafs, established a modus vivendi with the Byzantines. But in 934, the Greeks, led by an Armenian general and an Armenian prince Mleh, or Melias, succeeded in retaking the city from the Muslims.[83]

It is the cycle of popular narratives in Greek and Arabic connected with

Omar, the emir of Melitene, and the Armenian hero Melias or Mleh which Grégoire has dubbed the "geste of Omar" or the "geste of Melitene." According to Grégoire, this material entered Byzantine folklore from Arabian sources.[84] Grégoire follows the traces of Omar of Melitene in Arabian tales of chivalry: the fourteenth-century Turkish "Sayyid-Battal" and the Arabian romance called "Dhat-ul-Himmat" on which the Turkish story is based.

Although Melitene is not mentioned in the tale of Omar an-Nu'man and his two sons, the narrative is clearly part of the "geste of Omar":

> Certes, alors que dans le Sayyid Battâl Mélitène est d'un bout à l'autre la capitale de l'émir et le centre de l'action, le nom même de la glorieuse citadelle euphratésienne de l'Islam a disparu des *Mille et une Nuits*. Mais le patronymique de Nééman, qui est donné à Omar dans le Sayyid Battâl, lui a été gardé dans les *Mille et une Nuits* comme surnom traditionnel, et ce détail, comme cent autres, nous prouve qu'il s'agit du même personnage, et permet de restituer à Mélitène le vaste épisode du *Conte d'Omar al Néman et de ses deux fils merveilleux Sharkân et Daou'lmakân*.[85]

Goossens discusses the composite figure of the *Arabian Nights* Omar in detail:

> Si Omar, dans lequel nous n'hésitons pas à reconnaître l'émir historique de Malatia, est devenu "roi" de Bagdad, c'est peut-être qu'on l'a confondu avec ses homonymes les khalifes, tantôt avec le grand Omar, le second khalife, le conquérant de la Syrie et de l'Égypte, tantôt avec Omar II: c'est ainsi qu'il y a dans notre roman, un siège de Constantinople, qui naturellement n'est pas prise: sans doute le siège historique, qui fut levé en 717, sous Omar II.
>
> Les principaux héros du conte sont naturellement le Roi Omar et ses fils: Scharkân, Daoul'makan (Dū'lmakān). Son troisième fils, Rumzān, n'apparaîtra guère que dans la dernière partie du récit, qui constitue à vrai dire un second conte, annexé au premier, et dont le héros est "un petit-fils d'Omar."
>
> Omar-al-Némān, le héros de la geste, est un personnage presque aussi exclusivement "décoratif" qu'il le sera dans le roman turc, quelque chose comme le Charlemagne des dernières épopées françaises: ce grand conquérant ne se bat jamais, ne quitte pas sa capitale: mais il est déjà l'ancêtre glorieux dont ses descendants se réclament fièrement, comme l'émir de Digénis: "nous sommes les fils d'Omar, les héros aux grands desseins" chante l'un d'eux.[86]

Omar, then, is the ancestral hero in the epic material of both Greeks and

Arabs, and his role is comparable to that of the aged Charlemagne in the matter of France.

The relevance of the *Digenes Akrites*, which in its written form dates from the eleventh century, for the study of Chaucer's raw material in the *Squire's Tale* has so far been completely ignored.

Like the *Squire's Tale* and the tale of Omar an-Nu'man, the *Digenes Akrites* is a "family romance." The frame of its action is a royal household, comprising warrior father, mother, one sister, and two brothers in various patterns of interrelation and of repeated and interwoven motifs.

The epic is preserved in several manuscripts, the oldest of which dates from the fourteenth century. There are, however, fragments of a thirteenth-century version preserved in Russian, which contains episodes that have not yet been discovered in the original Greek.[87]

The setting of the poem is the historical background of the tenth-century conflict between Byzantines and Muslims in Asia Minor and the Armenian frontier. However, the poem gives no history but a composite arrangement in which fragments of many actual events are rearranged to give a universalized image of conflict between faiths and empires. In its composition the poem combined features of Chaucerian romance:

> the poem of *Digenes* is in fact a romance, and a romance destitute of theological or political propaganda. . . . It is marked by a complete absence of fanaticism or political urgency because it is based on floating folktale; and it is of learned execution because it is written by a monk or scribe with enough education to want to make out of floating folk-story something permanent. . . .[88]

The hero, Digenes Akrites, is the son of an emir of Syria who is converted to Christianity in order to marry Digenes' mother, daughter of a Byzantine strategos or general. He is called Digenes (*dio genes*) because he was "born of two people," Arab and Byzantine, and Akrites, from the Greek word for "border," a defender of the outermost borders of the empire.

Digenes is introduced in the fourth book of the epic in which the story of his father, the subject of the first three books, is recapitulated:

> Called also Twyborn as from his parents,
> A pagan father and a Roman mother;
> Grown formidable, as the tale shall show,
> The borders quelled, is surnamed Borderer.
>
> [ll. 1030–33]

We are given a portrait of Digenes as a young squire:

> Indeed the young man had a comely stature,
> And fair hair, curling a little, and large eyes,
> A white and rosy face, a brow all black,
> His breast like crystal was a fathom broad.
> Looking on him his father was most glad. . . .
>
> [ll. 1076–80]

The name *Akrites* is the Byzantine designation of knights who were defenders against Muslim incursions. The word was known as the name of a popular national hero in the twelfth century and, in the early Middle Ages, occurs as a place name as well.[89] For generation after generation the tide of strife between Byzantine Christianity and Islam

> flowed backward and forward over the mountain barriers, and was the great imminent fact for the Christian population of Asia Minor. This perennial war and all it meant entered into their very soul. To hold the mountain passes—everything depended on that; and the commanders of frontier fortresses, Greek and Saracen, maintained continually a wild irregular warfare, full of surprises and adventurous incidents. These circumstances developed a new type of warrior, a *kavallarios*, whose heart was set on adventure and who was accustomed to act independently of orders from the emperor or a military superior. These watchers of the frontier were popularly called *akritai* or hillsmen, and in the tenth century many of them possessed large domains and resembled feudal barons rather than Roman officers.[90]

It is from the cycle of tales gathered around the figure of an ideal *akrites* that the epic of *Digenes Akrites* was formed.

The poem opens on a situation that brings its family structure into full play: in one of his raids into Byzantine territory the Syrian emir, Digenes' father, captures the daughter of the strategos:

> And captive took a very lovely girl,
> The general's daughter, and she was a virgin.
> The general himself was then in exile;
> The girl's brothers happened to be on the borders.
> Her mother, having escaped the pagans' hands,
> Forthwith wrote all had happened to her sons,
> The pagans' coming, the Rape of the Girl,
> The parting from her dearest, crowds of woes;
> And this she added writing with lament:
>
> "O children dear, have pity on your mother,
> Her soul in wretchedness and soon to die.
> Be mindful of the love you bear your sister.

> Hasten to free your sister, and your mother,
> Her from captivity, and me from death."

[ll. 61–74]

   Though there are five brothers in this part of the tale, only two, the eldest and the youngest, are singled out in the narrative. Only one, young Constantine, twin brother of the captured girl—Dhu al-Makan is twin brother of Nuzhat az-Zaman in the tale of Omar an-Nu'man in the *Arabian Nights*—is mentioned by name. It is he on whom the lot falls to accept the emir's challenge to fight him in single combat for the release of his sister. The combat is brought to an end when the emir yields to the young Christian. He cannot bear to lose the Byzantine girl. He becomes a Christian and marries her with the consent of her family.

   The thematic pattern of brotherly combat for a captured maiden is repeated in the story of the emir's son, the hero Digenes. In the fourth book of the poem we hear of Digenes' winning of Evdokia, daughter of the Byzantine general Doukas, a personage who appears as Loukas in the tale of Omar an-Nu'man in the *Arabian Nights*.[91]

   The hero arrives at the chamber of the maid, all gold and mosaic, beholds the lovely girl at the window, and is inflamed by unquenchable passion:

> In truth the girl was like a picture painted;
> A bright and charming eye, hair blond and curly,
> A brow she had all black, unmixed the sable
> A face like snow, and tinctured in the middle,
> As with the chosen purple kings do prize.
> So gazing there the wonderful young man
> His soul was straightway wounded, hurt his heart,
> Boundless his pain, and there distressed he stood.

[ll. 1431–38]

   His love is returned and the maiden gives him her ring. Though he has been warned of the dangers that lie in wait for him from the maiden's father and brothers, Digenes sets out on his favorite horse to elope with the girl by the light of the moon. After some trepidation regarding her honor and safety, the maiden consents but she warns the youth:

> But if you misguide me, and I come with you,
> And if my brothers know it and my kin,
> My father with a crowd should overtake you,
> How could you get me out and save your life?

[ll. 1531–34]

Digenes reassures her and swears undying love:

> Having well bound each other by their vows,

> The maiden leaned out of the golden casement,
> The boy upstanding on his horse received her,
> The partridge flew out and the falcon caught her.
> Sweetly they kissed each other as was right.
>
> [ll. 1663–67]

We then come to the pursuit of the lovers by the whole household of the strategos and a parallelism with one strand of the narrative pattern as outlined by Chaucer in the *Squire's Tale*. For Digenes' Byzantine bride has *two* brothers, as the story explicitly states, and it is these "brethren two" that Digenes engages in combat to win her. The maiden, watching the pursuers from the safety of a tree to which the horse that carried her and her lover has been tied, is filled with anxiety for her brothers:

"Harm not, my soul, those own brothers of mine," she says to Digenes. Our hero obeys the request of his lady to spare them:

> The brothers then rushing madly on him,
> He circled so and threw them from their horses
> As strictly not to harm or wound at all.
>
> [ll. 1733, 1749–51]

In the *Digenes Akrites*, the motif of the two brothers is an integral part of the hero's elopement with their sister. Needless to say, there is a reconciliation in which the Byzantine general offers the hero a splendid dowry. There is a royal feast when Digenes brings his bride and her family in triumph to his father's house. The wedding celebrations last three months, first at the house of the emir and then at the house of the general. The two houses, the Syrian and Byzantine, are united in a pattern of family relationships which are doubly knit in the second generation and center around a captured maiden who is to harmonize warring nations of different faiths.

The interwoven story of two generations and of a ruling house and its relation to neighboring nations is also the pattern of Chaucer in the *Squire's Tale*:

> First wol I telle you of Cambyuskan,
> That in his time many a citee wan;
> And after wol I spek of Algarsif,
> How that he wan Theodora to his wif,
> For whom ful ofte in greet peril he was,
> Ne hadde he ben holpe by the steede of bras:
> And after wol I speke of Cambalo,
> That faught in lystes with the bretheren two
> For Canacee, er that he myghte hire wynne;
> And ther I lefte I wol ageyn bigynne.
>
> [ll. 661–70]

The tale of the Ebony Horse is regarded by Grégoire as an integral element of the *Digenes Akrites* in the treatment of Digenes' abduction of Evdokia.

> Et nous y trouvons dans tout son éclat un développement auquel les versions grecques ont presque entièrement renoncé (et qui est à peine mieux conservé dans la version russe) celui du cheval merveilleux que monte le héros, la nuit où il enlève sa bien-aimée.[92]

The horse is "rationalized" in the epic into a noble black living horse. But Grégoire points out that the marvellous qualities of a magic horse on which the hero makes his escape are preserved in popular ballads of the "acritic cycle" and, most important, that the Arabian tale of the Ebony Horse explains one version of the *Digenes Akrites* which would otherwise be totally unintelligible from the Greek point of view.[93] The version, preserved in the Trebizond manuscript, differs in the treatment of the elopement and the subsequent reconciliation of Digenes and his father- and brothers-in-law. As has already been mentioned, the reconciliation takes place after the fight with the two brothers *before* the wedding. In the Trebizond version, however, Digenes brings his abducted bride home, and only then, three months *after* the consummation of the marriage, receives his father-in-law's forgiveness and blessing.

This, says Grégoire, is the only trace of a version alien to the spirit of Greek Christian romance.[94] The surprising marriage component is found in only one other source: the tale of the Ebony Horse. After Prince Qamar al-Aqmar's safe return to his father's palace with his princess on the ebony horse

> they held high festival a whole month, at the end of which time he went in to the Princess and they took their joy of each other with exceeding joy. But his father brake the ebony horse in pieces and destroyed its mechanism for flight; moreover the Prince wrote a letter to the Princess's father, advising him of all that had befallen her and informing him how she was now married to him and in all health and happiness, and sent it by a messenger, together with costly presents and curious rarities. And when the messenger arrived at the city which was Sana 'a and delivered the letter and the presents to the King, he read the missive and rejoiced greatly thereat and accepted the presents, honouring and rewarding the bearer handsomely. Moreover, he forwarded rich gifts to his son-in-law by the same messenger, who returned to his master and acquainted him with what had passed; whereat he was much cheered.[95]

The extraordinary treatment of consummated love before the official marriage arrangement with the bride's father is a valuable guideline to the second part of the *Digenes Akrites* which describes his married life and an act of adultery by our hero that deeply shocked W. P. Ker.[96]

The fifth book of the *Digenes Akrites* tells of Digenes' rescue of a betrayed maiden (with whom he falls in love). Digenes comes upon this maiden, the daughter of an emir, in an oasis in the Arabian desert where she has been abandoned by a false lover, a Byzantine nobleman whom, with the consent of her mother, she freed from her father's captivity. The episode is a striking analogue to the narrative of the piteous falcon that arouses Canacee's compassion in the *Squire's Tale* and is, in the end, restored to her repentant lover:

> . . . as the storie telleth us,
> By mediacioun of Cambalus,
> The kynges sone. . . .
>
> [ll. 655–57]

Digenes hears a piteous voice near a tree, the sound of "lamentations with weeping and much tears." He approaches and asks for the cause of the moaning. The betrayed girl tells her unhappy story, "tearing her locks, with beating of her face," like Canacee's falcon:

> I loved a Roman to my own despite,
> One whom my father held captive three years;
> He said he was a famous general's son;
> I loosed his chains, delivered him from prison,
> Gave him horses, my father's champions,
> Made him an eminent chief in Syria,
> With my mother's consent, my father absent,
> Who always used to be engaged in wars.
> Then he appeared to have much love for me,
> Would die if he chanced not see me for a while;
> But he was false as the event did show.
> For on a day, having planned to run away,
> And wishing to depart to Romania,
> His will he told me, and the fear he had
> Because of my father in case he should return.
> He tried to force me to set out with him,
> Promising and with the most dreadful vows,
> Never to deny me but make me his spouse,
> Which I trusting agreed to fly with him.
> . . . .
> We had our fill of sleep and took our food;

The secrets of our loves I blush to tell,
And the affection toward me shown by him;
His soul he would name me, call me his eyes' light,
And soon he said I was his wife, his dearest,
Unfilled with kissing held me in his arms.
      Thus all the way rejoicing in each other,
We arrived at this fountain which you see;
For three days here reposing and three nights,
Love's changes celebrating without fill,
His inner purpose craftily concealed
The dire transgressor now began to show.
For while we slept together the third night,
He rose up secretly, saddled the horses,

. . . .

I am bereft of all, without all hopes;
For to my parents I dare not return,
I am ashamed of neighbours, and companions.
Where to find my traitor I know not at all.
I beg you give a knife into my hands,
And I will kill myself for folly done.
It boots me not to live now all is lost.
O my misfortunes and most great disasters!
From kin I am estranged, from parents parted
To win a lover, and have been robbed of him.

[ll. 2241–59, 2276–89, 2312–21]

As the girl's tale unfolds, Digenes realizes that the faithless lover is a youth whom he rescued from Bedouin Arabs only a few days before. The youth is found, "much admonished," and publicly bidden to make the girl his lawful wife.

There is an extraordinary occurrence in this episode which combines the tale of the false lover with the theme of adulterous love. In the *Squire's Tale* the falcon's false lover, the tercelet, leaves her for "newfangelnesse" in pursuit of a kite:

Thogh he were gentil born, and fressh and gay,
And goodlich for to seen, humble and free,
He saugh upon a tyme a kyte flee,
And sodynly he loved this kyte so
That al his love is clene fro me ago;
And hath his trouthe falsed in this wyse.

[ll. 622–27]

In Chaucer's *Anelida and Arcite*

> This Theban knyght [Arcite] eke, soth to seyn,
> Was yong, and therwithal a lusty knyght,
> But he was double in love and no thing pleyn,
> And subtil in that craft over any wyght,
> And with his kunnyng wan this lady bryght;
> For so ferforth he gan her trouthe assure
> That she him trusted over any creature.
> What shuld I seyn? she loved Arcite so
> That when that he was absent any throwe,
> Anon her thoghte her herte brast a-two.
> For in her sight to her he bar hym lowe,
> So that she wende have al his herte yknowe;
> But he was fals. . . .

[ll. 85–97]

In the episode of the betrayed damsel in the Byzantine epic, it is Akrites himself who commits adultery. He falls in love with his charge, the betrayed girl, and makes love to her on the journey to find her false lover! The incident is glossed over by the restoration of the girl to the youth and Digenes' repentant return to his wife, both unsuspecting agents in a happy ending. The situation, it seems, is another indication of mores that originated in the households of Muslims as depicted in the *Arabian Nights*. What concerns us here is that Akrites, like Cambalo, restores the betrayed lover to her false partner.

The source of the plot of *Anelida and Arcite* is unknown, and so is the reason for Chaucer's choice of Armenia as the dominion of Anelida. The name of Arcite was taken over from Boccaccio's *Teseida* which Chaucer reworked in the *Knight's Tale*, first entitled "Palamon and Arcite." The origin of the name Arcite is unknown.

Chaucer tells us that he found "this olde storie" of the Armenian queen and the false Arcite in Latin and that Arcite is a Theban knight.[97] Did Arcite (Boccaccio's Arcita) derive his origins from Byzantine material which Boccaccio acquired through his studies of Greek?[98] Arcite, or Akrite, at any rate, is the name of Akrites the Borderer, the Byzantine hero whose association with Armenia, as Grégoire has shown, is at the core of the "acritic" cycle of poems.

Grégoire's researches have also shown that Akrites is sometimes paired with another hero, an investigation which leads to historical and eponymous personages in the Persian *Shah-Nameh* and the *Arabian Nights*.[99] In the ballads of the "acritic" cycle, says a translator of the Byzantine epic, "we might expect to find, distorted perhaps by oral tradition but still easily recognizable, many of the episodes of *Digenes*. We are surprised to discover an entirely different world: a world of supernatural feats, magic weapons, and talking birds, in which Digenes is only one of a number of heroes."[100]

What the *Digenes Akrites* reveals are motifs that we also find at the core of the *Squire's Tale*: a royal or noble household consisting of a famous father, a mother who is actively present in the narrative, a sister and two brothers; an elopement on a specially distinguished horse; a knightly fight against two brothers for a captured maiden. In the Byzantine poem the motif of the two brothers is an integral part of the hero's elopement with their sister. It is a mirror image of the combat of brothers in the first generation, in which the hero's father is challenged by a brother to free his captive sister who then becomes the emir's wife and mother of Digenes Akrites.

The literary history of the tale of Omar an-Nu'man is still obscure, but the relationship between the Arabic romance and the Byzantine epic, established in the studies of Grégoire and Goossens, has revealed elements which bring this tale, too, into the Western orbit of the *Squire's Tale*.

King Omar, the head of the household, is a valiant warrior like Cambyuskan. The Tartar king is associated with Aries, "the colerik hoote signe." When Omar was angry, "there came forth from his nostrils sparks of flame."

We gain an impression of the festive stateliness of Omar's court:

> One day, as King Omar was sitting in his palace, his Chamberlains came in to him, and kissing the ground before him, said, "O King there be come Ambassadors from the King of Roum, Lord of Constantinople the Great, and they desire admission to thee and submission to thy decree: if the King commands us to introduce them we will do so; and, if not, there is no disputing his behest." He bade them enter and, when they came in, he turned to them and, courteously receiving them, asked them of their case, and what was the cause of their coming. They kissed the ground before him and said, "O King, glorious and strong! O lord of the arm that is long! Know that he who despatched us to thee is King Afridun, Lord of Ionia-Land and of the Nazarene armies, the sovereign who is firmly established in the empery of Constantinople, to acquaint thee that he is now waging fierce war and fell with a tyrant and a rebel, the Prince of Caesarea."[101]

Though King Omar, like a good Muslim, has four wives "legally married" and three hundred and sixty concubines, "after the number of days in the Coptic year," there is, in fact, only one woman who is singled out by name in the king's harem, a Byzantine Greek by the name of Sophia who turns out to be daughter of the king of Constantinople, brought in captivity as a slave girl to the court of Omar. It is Sophia who bears the king a son, Dhu al-Makan, and a daughter, Nuzhat az-Zaman. An elder son, Sharkan, whom the king had begotten on one of his nameless wives, is at first jealous of his younger brother whom he regards as a threat to his right of succession. But after many knightly exploits in his father's campaigns and in affairs of the heart, Sharkan's enmity towards his brother resolves into harmony and brotherly devotion.

The motif of incestuous love between brother and sister is also worked into the relationship of the royal family in the Arabic tale. Sharkan marries Nuzhat az-Zaman without knowing her true identity, for she is brought to him when he is ruler of Damascus by a merchant who offers her for sale.

The intricate family relationships are carried over into a third generation in the love story between Qudiya Fakan, daughter of Sharkan and Nuzhat az-Zaman, and Kanmakan, son of Dhu al-Makan, in which a noble stallion, named al-Qatul (the slayer) and surnamed al-Majnun (the mad one) plays a significant role. Al-Qatul is not a magic horse but it plays a vital part in ensuring the hero's victory, which is obviously the function of Chaucer's flying steed in the exploits of Algarsif. We have a scene which Chaucer might well have painted of Algarsif setting out on his adventures:

> Then Kanmakan, having fixed a day for departure, went in to his mother and took leave of her, after which he came down from his palace and threw the baldrick of his sword over his shoulder and donned turband and face-veil; and mounting his horse, al-Qatul, and looking like the moon at its full, he threaded the streets of Baghdad, till he reached the city gate.[102]

In sum, the Arabic tale is a "family novel." There is no magic machinery beyond the gift of three talismanic jewels that enable the children of the royal family to recognize each other and serve to protect them from illness. The traces of parallelism with the *Squire's Tale* lie in the structure and core motifs.

The threads which lead from the *Squire's Tale* to the *Man of Law's Tale* are visible in the oriental and Byzantine origin of both tales. The story of Constance, as told by the Man of Law, is in the main enacted in the setting of Syria and Rome, "Rome" originally being Constantinople, as known by its Arabic designation of *rūm*. The name of the heroine, Constance, first found in Trivet,[103] reveals its Byzantine origins. Trivet seems to have synchronized a historical Aella of Northumbria (d. 580), the second husband of Constance, with the reign of the sixth-century Eastern Emperor, Tiberius Constantinus, father of a daughter named Constantina.

The introduction to the *Man of Law's Tale* has suggested the assumption that the unfinished state of the *Squire's Tale* is explained by Chaucer's reluctance to pursue what seems to be an incestuous theme. In the *Squire's Tale*, Cambalo, Canacee's brother, is to fight

> the bretheren two
> For Canacee er that he might hire wynne.
>
> [ll. 668–69]

This has been connected with the reference to Canacee in the Man of Law's introduction. Chaucer, says the Man of Law, does not write

> Of thilke wikke ensample of Canacee
> That loved hir owene brother synfully
> (Of swiche cursed stories I sey fy!)
>
> [ll. 78–80]

The theme is indicated in the *Legend of Good Women* and was, in fact, fully treated by Gower.

The relation between the story of Canacee in the unfinished *Squire's Tale* and the reference of Canacee by the Man of Law has remained problematic. But the story which the Man of Law finally tells stems from a familiar and certain source. The tale of Constance, also found in book two of Gower's *Confessio Amantis*, was drawn from the Anglo-Norman version of Nicholas Trivet. There is an important feature in Trivet's characterization of the heroine which leads us to a figure of a good woman in the *Arabian Nights*. In medieval Spain, she was known by the name of Theodor.

Trivet describes the careful education of Constance at her father's court. Before she was thirteen, the age when her extraordinary beauty and virtue impressed themselves on the Saracen merchants who carried her reputation home to their sultan, Constance was instructed by special tutors in the seven sciences: logic, natural science, moral science, astronomy, geometry, music, and "perspective." She was carefully taught Christian doctrine and various foreign languages. When the Syrian merchants arrived in Constantine Rome she conversed with them, seeking information about their religion and country. On hearing that they were pagans, she preached the Christian faith, making such an impression that they had themselves baptized and, in turn, became so knowledgeable about Christianity as to defend their new faith in successful argument on their return to their own land.

Gower's tale of Constance preserves some traces of the intellectual accomplishment of his heroine:

> And over that in such a wise
> Sche hath hem with hire wordes wise
> Of Cristes feith so full enformed,
> That thei therto ben al conformed,
> So that baptesme thei receiuen
> And alle here false goddes weyeuen.
>
> [*Confessio Amantis* II, 605–10]

Chaucer omitted the detailed characterization of the young Constance and all material which was not strictly relevant to the dramatic interest of the main plot. His heroine is the perfect woman of Christian saintly tradition: obedient, intensely religious, and innocently accused.[104]

In the *Man of Law's Tale*, the marriage of Constance, daughter of the emperor of Rome, to the sultan of Syria is justified by the missionary zeal of Christianity against Islam in which Constance is decreed by the pope to be the tool of salvation:

> That in destruccioun of mawmettrie,
> And in encrees of Cristes lawe deere,
> They been acorded, so as ye shal heere.
>
> [ll. 236–38]

It is for love of Constance that the sultan and his entourage are converted to Christianity, only to be cruelly slaughtered in the name of the holy laws of Islam by the treachery of the sultan's mother. There is no need for Constance to show her intellectual abilities in her brief sojourn in Syria for the sultan's conversion is the prerequisite for the marriage in strict accordance with canon law. When, however, cast adrift in the Mediterranean, her ship tossed through the Straits of Gibraltar into the Atlantic and on to the coast of Northumberland where her cruel fate is to be reenacted, she nevertheless survives; she is seen as a woman whose force of persuasion succeeds in converting her heathen rescuer and his wife:

> And so ferforth she gan oure lay declare
> That she the constable, er that it was eve
> Converted, and on Crist made hym bileve.
>
> [ll. 572–74]

The hint of her theological gifts is reserved for the conversion of the Northumbrians, evidently of more immediate interest to Canterbury pilgrims who, like the audience of *Piers Plowman*, had to be reminded that: "Al was hethenesse some tyme Ingelond and Wales" (B xv, 435).

Constance's intelligence and learning, like the intellectual side of Criseyde, are apparent in the story of her fate and survival, but Chaucer does not stress them in retelling the story. They are just there as an integral part of the character and her womanhood. Trivet, as has already been mentioned, goes into greater detail. Constance's father, Emperor Tiberius Constantine, "la fist enseigner la fey Cristien, e endoctriner par mestres sachaunz en lez sept sciences, que sount logicience, naturel, morale, astronomie, geometrie, musique, perspectiue, que sount philosophies seculeres apelez, e la fist endoctriner en diuerses langages."[105] Trivet's description is of particular interest as it represents a medieval topos, the literary figure of the beautiful and learned good woman whose shining virtue comprises both heart and head. There are several such women in the *Arabian Nights*, Sheherezade herself and particularly Nuzhat az-Zaman, daughter of King Omar an-Nu'man. The prototype of such women in Arabic literature is Tawaddud, a slave who was known as Theodor (Tūdūr, Teodor, Teodora, Theodora) in medieval Spanish versions of the tale from the *Arabian Nights* of which she is the heroine.[106]

The tale of Tawaddud, also preserved in a form independent of the *Arabian Nights*, reached Spain as the "Historia dela doncella Teodor" of which the oldest version probably dates from the thirteenth century. The tale has "all the characteristics of the style of the fourteenth century, if indeed it does not go back to the end of the thirteenth century, at which time so many analogous works were translated."[107] The text, in substance, agrees with the Arabic original of the *Arabian Nights*. A comparison of three different versions which are extant in five fifteenth-century manuscripts shows that the Spanish text must have derived from a very long tradition going back to the middle of the thirteenth century. A printed edition, dated 1642 at Seville attributes the tale of Teodor to "Mossen Alfonso Arragones." Is this perhaps an attribution to Moshe Sephardi, known by his Christian name of Petrus Alfonsi after his godfather Alfonso I of Aragon?

The tale of Theodor is related to the didactic literature of dialogues, debates, and theological and scientific treatises in the form of questions and answers. There are traces of such questions in the *Squire's Tale*:

> As soore wondren somme on cause of thonder,
> On ebbe, on flood, on gossamer, and on myst,
> And alle thyng, til that the cause is wyst.

[ll. 258–60]

In the Arabic story Tawaddud—the personal name is not otherwise found in Arabic literature—is the beautiful and accomplished slave of a young merchant who has squandered his father's inheritance. The virtuous Tawaddud, whom he has inherited without realizing her exceptional worth, advises him to offer her for sale to the caliph in order to make himself solvent. The advice is taken and Tawaddud is offered to Harun al-Rashid. The caliph is ready to pay the high price of ten thousand dinars on condition that she passes the test of knowledge she is claimed to possess. A number of learned men, representing all branches of learning, among them a physician and an astronomer, as well as the famous philosopher al-Nazzam (d. 845), conduct the examination at the caliph's request. Tawaddud surpasses herself, answering all questions put to her in the fields of theology, medicine, astronomy, mathematics, rhetoric, philosophy, and music. Her answers comprise a compendium of medieval learning. She also amazes them with her skill in singing and playing the lute and in various games which require mental agility, like backgammon and chess. She, in turn, tests her examiners with questions they are unable to answer.

The learning of Tawaddud left traces in the characterization of various heroines of medieval romance. It is emphasized by the age of the heroines. Constance has mastered the seven liberal arts before the age of thirteen when she questions the Syrian merchants. Tawaddud's age is fourteen when she undergoes her examination. Though the age is conventional in the *Arabian Nights*, it is constantly stressed in the tale, for the caliph marvels that one so young should be so skilled in the arts and sciences. Moreover, the Arabic tale seems to have been modeled on a Byzantine original found in another story actually translated from the Greek: the book of the philosopher who was examined by the maiden Qitar.[108] The chain of oriental and Byzantine interrelationships in the motif of the learned and virtuous maiden is also linked to the saints' legends. It is found in the disputation of St. Catherine.[109] The extreme complexity of these interrelationships has not yet been disentangled, but there is a clear outline in Trivet's story of Constance which joins it to the oriental prototype.

What then of the Western Tawaddud, Theodora? The evidence is that the "Historia de la doncella Teodor" was a popular tale in the Middle Ages.[110] It was reworked by Lope de Vega and continued to be widely known until the end of the nineteenth century, the name of the learned slave Theodora having become proverbial. The specifically Christian elements introduced into the later Spanish versions are taken from the collection of stories known as *L'Enfant sage*, the dialogue of the Emperor Hadrian with the child Epitus, also preserved in a fourteenth-century Middle English version.[111] In the printed versions the merchant owner of Teodor is a native of Hungary who resides in Tunis, where he first beholds the heroine,

> . . . a Christian girl who was from the parts of Spain being sold
> by a Moor. And recognizing from her genteel disposition and up-

bringing that she must be noble, he had her taught to read and write and all the sciences that she could learn. She applied herself so much to virtue and study that she surpassed all the men and women who lived at that time, in science as well as in music and in other infinite varieties of arts.[112]

The merchant, having fallen on evil days, accepts the advice of the maiden and offers her to the king Miramamolin (Amīr al Mu'minīn) Almancor (Almanṣūr). At the royal palace the king was much amazed by the merchant because of the high price (ten thousand *doblas* of good red gold) that he asked for the maiden.

And the merchant answered the king saying: "Lord, be not amazed because I demand of you such a great price for this maiden; for you must know that she knows so many kinds of science that I believe that there is no wise man who can vanquish her, man or woman. For I, Lord, have spent a great fortune on her to teach her what she has learned; and she has studied well in all kinds of sciences that can be written and that learned men of letters can know in the whole world, men as well as women." And the king, when he heard this, looked much at the maiden and ordered that she remove the veil that she wore over her eyes, and that she raise the shawl and place it on her head. And the maiden immediately took it off and did everything the king commanded her. And there the king saw the great beauty and loveliness that the maiden possessed. And she seemed the most beautiful that he had seen in his entire life, and he was greatly pleased by the sight of her, and asked her that she tell him what her name was. And the maiden answered him with very great modesty and humbly, saying thus: "Very illustrious lord King, Your Highness will know that they call me Teodor." And the king said to her: "Theodor, please tell me what is the knowledge that you learned of all the sciences of this world."

And the maiden answered him and said to him: "Lord king, you ought to know that the first science that I learned is the law of God and his commandments, and I learned besides the art of the stars and the planets and the courses and movements of them and the houses in which each one of them dwells, and I know the names of the stars, which God, Our Lord, created in his high heavens; and I learned besides the language of animals; and I learned besides the seventy-two languages that exist in the whole world, those of Christians as well as of Jews and Moors, and of all the laws and ceremonies; and I learned besides medicine and surgery, and I have studied it well and tried it all out; and I learned besides subtle geometry and grammar and logic and the nature of it; and I learned besides the art of poetry and music. . . ."[113]

The catalogue of accomplishments continues, to include the crafts of weaving and embroidery and the recognition of all kinds of precious stones. The king then calls the wise men together to conduct the examination. In the questions and answers there are references to biblical matter, the matter of Troy, and Alexander. In the oldest versions Teodor knows the language of birds and beasts, like Canacee in the *Squire's Tale* who acquires this talent with the help of a magic ring. In one of the manuscript versions Teodor speaks of making a pilgrimage to the Christian holy places: Jerusalem, Rome, and Saint James of Compostela.[114] As in the Arabic original, the maiden's knowledge of medicine and astronomy is particularly extensive. It represents a complete survey of the medieval sciences. It is safe to assume that the reputation of the learned maiden of Arabian romance was not confined to medieval Spain. The tale of *Theodor* was so popular and well known that it may have reached Chaucer—and even reached him directly from Spain. The safe-conduct granted to Geoffrey Chaucer and three companions by the king of Navarre leads us to assume that Chaucer was in Spain in 1366.[115] Constance, daughter of Don Pedro, king of Castile, became the wife of John of Gaunt in 1372 and was attended by Chaucer's wife, Philippa. We know that the *Chronique* into which Trivet introduced the story of Constance was written for Princess Marie, daughter of Edward I. "The long and romantic digression . . . may have been inserted to interest the royal patroness. . . ."[116] Skeat's view that the tale of Constance is a piece of Chaucer's early workmanship, and was revised for insertion among the *Canterbury Tales*, would support the conjecture that Chaucer found in Trivet what he was looking for between 1369 and 1379.[117] "Of Constance is my tale especially," is evidently a theme of the matter of Araby.

In the *Squire's Tale* Algarsif's bride, Theodora, has a Byzantine name in a setting partly drawn from the *Arabian Nights*. There is the emphasis that was noted by Pollard:

> This is the only mention of Theodora, and without pressing the point unduly, it may certainly be said that she is introduced as if the readers or hearers of the story would know who she was. If we suppose Chaucer to be retelling in his own way a story or stories which others beside himself might have heared at the English court, the familiarity of this reference would be explained.[118]

Was Theodora to be a Byzantine princess with the learning of Tawaddud-Theodora? The extraordinary feature of the *Squire's Tale* is that it fastens on material of the *Arabian Nights* as the essence of romance. The teller is the young squire, Chaucer's embodiment of the spirit of romance: "embrouded was he, as it were a meede / al ful of fresshe floures, whyte and reede." It is striking to find a description of the *Arabian Nights* by Littmann, one of the foremost authorities on their character and composition:

"they resemble in a way an Oriental meadow with many different beautiful flowers intermingled with a few weeds."[119]

The Treatment of the Saracens in the English Medieval Romances

In her characterization of the English medieval romances, Everett
speaks of "the unromantic nature of the majority of these poems."[120]
The Middle English romances that depict the military confrontation of
Christians and Saracens—for example *Beues of Hamtoun* or *The Sowdone
of Babylone*—barely fit a definition of romance. They are unromantic
because, though embodying the adventures of some hero of chivalry,
Christian knight or converted Saracen, and belonging both in matter and
form to the ages of knighthood, they are essentially vehicles of fanatical
propaganda in which the moral ideal of chivalry is subservient to the
requirements of religion, politics, and ideology. Pagans are wrong and
Christians are right whatever they do.[121] The ideal held up to the audience
is not courtly love or perfect knighthood. It is the triumph of Christianity
over Islam.

Like the chansons de geste on which they are modeled, these romances
revel in "actions accomplished" and the heroic figures of "those who
accomplished the deeds."[122] But the question of conduct, of *how* the game
is played—the crucial problem in *Gawain and the Green Knight* with which
these romances are contemporary—does not arise in these poems. The
utter humiliation of the hated enemy is an end that justifies every perversion of decency in the "chivalric" hero. Thus appalling filial disloyalty
is presented as a virtue in Ferumbras and a Goneril virago like Floripas
is celebrated as an honored Christian princess.

It may be maintained by the defenders of Christian ideals in medieval
romance that Ferumbras and Floripas are, after all, Saracens by birth
whose fundamental nature is determined by non-Christian upbringing.
Their conversion to Christianity, moreover, must imply the rejection of
their father the sultan who, in his defeat and his refusal to be baptized,
embodies unregenerate Saracen might. The brutality of the hero and
heroine as depicted in the treatment of the sultan, however, goes far beyond any necessity in the plot. It is a vital element in a "heightened"
characterization obviously relished by narrator and audience. It expresses
a genuinely unromantic conception of a triumphant hero which, in the
romances, was usually sublimated into a high chivalric ideal.

The *Chanson de Roland* has been described, however unjustly, as never for
a moment ringing true on the psychological level—that of character,
motive, and conflict.[123] The Middle English Saracen romances fall into
this category. They are primarily concerned with one basic theme: the
war of Christianity against Islam. In a wider sense, they depict a brutal

political struggle as it is invested with glamor and sanctified as "religion" and "history" in popular literature.

The assemblage of myth, legend, fact, and propaganda that reflects the image of reality in the literary encounter between Christians and Saracens enables us, in the English medieval romances, to discern specific patterns and themes that dominated and shaped public opinion.

It is easier to detect these patterns in the type of literature of the second rank which these romances represent. Their artistic and psychological crudeness lays bare the general tendencies of a whole culture. There is no trace of Chaucerian irony or the moral refinement of the author of *Sir Gawain and the Green Knight*.

Within the general notions of topography and Saracen peoples derived from knowledge and experience, the popular image of the medieval Saracen comprised four stock figures of medieval romance: the enamored Muslim princess; the converted Saracen; the defeated emir or sultan; and the archetypal Saracen giant whom the Christian hero overpowers and kills.

Like the converted Saracen, the figure of the enamored Muslim princess did not only embody romantic wish fulfillment but passed into romance from a historical situation of Saracen-Christian propinquity in war and peace. This state of affairs lasted for centuries. It was marked by a complex of constantly shifting alliances between frontier principalities in the East and the West in which intermarriage and conversion were not infrequent. Thus, in the twelfth century, the figure of the enamored Muslim princess is firmly established in the French epic and the chronicle accounts of the First Crusade.

An early merging of history and romance with the help of this figure is found in the *Historia Ecclesiastica* of the Anglo-Norman chronicler Orderic Vital. This work describes the captivity of Bohemond, prince of Antioch by the Danishmand emir.[124] Bohemond's imprisonment lasted from 1100 to 1103; Orderic was writing about 1130. He was thus narrating events that had taken place in his own lifetime and concerned one of the most famous leaders of the First Crusade.

The historical facts are known from both Christian and Arab chroniclers: in the continuous struggle of Byzantines and Franks against the Seljuk Turks in Asia Minor, Bohemond, prince of Antioch, son of the Norman ruler of Sicily, Robert Guiscard, answered an appeal from the Armenians of Melitene. But he fell into an ambush in the hills near Melitene and was captured by Malik Ghazi, the Danishmand emir. His army, comprising three hundred knights and some infantry, was annihilated, and "Bohemond, so long the terror of the infidel, was dragged off into an ignominious captivity" to the castle of Niksar in northeastern Anatolia. His imprisonment lasted three years. After some intrigue by the Byzantine

emperor, he was finally ransomed by the Franks of Syria. We know from
the description of Anna Comnena who saw him at the court of Constantinople that Bohemond was a tall, handsome, glamorous man in whom the
ladies of any household were bound to take an interest.[125]

Orderic, the "Angligena" among the contemporary chroniclers, attributes Bohemond's liberation to the favors of the Danishmand emir's
daughter. She becomes a Christian, is promised to Bohemond in marriage,
and finally marries Bohemond's nephew, Roger. In the account of the
miracles of Saint Leonard of Aquitaine, Bohemond's patron saint, it is
the emir's wife, a secret *Christian*, who provides Bohemond with food,
clothing, and other comforts and sees to it that the noble captive is treated
gently by his jailers. Thus Danishmand, the heathen, is saved from the
infamy of having imprisoned a Christian knight by the grace of his Christian wife. The story illustrates the Apostle's text: "Salvabitur vir infidelis
per mulierem fidelem."[126]

There are no ladies to help Bohemond in Albert of Aix or Fulcher of
Chartres whom Orderic mentions as one of his sources.[127] Kamal ad-Din
and Ibn al-Qalanisi are equally unromantic. In particular, the account
of Bohemond by the Arab side constitutes an excellent example of the
high standard of Arab historiography as compared to the West:

> In Rajab of this year (May-June, 1100), Bohemond, King of the
> Franks and lord of Antioch, marched out to the fortress of Afamiya
> (Apamea), and besieged it. He remained there for some days and laid
> waste its crops, when he received news of the arrival at Malatiya of
> al-Danishmand. . . . On learning of this, Bohemond returned to
> Antioch, and having collected his forces, marched against the Muslim
> army. But God Most High succoured the Muslims against him, and
> they killed a great host of his party and he himself was taken captive
> together with a few of his companions. Messengers were dispatched
> to his lieutenants at Antioch, demanding the surrender of the city,
> in the second decade of the month of Safar in the year 494 (Decem-
> ber, 1100).[128]

The account of Orderic is a perfect and typical symbiosis of history and
romance: after Bohemond and his companion, Richard of Salerno, have
been captured, the Turkish emir (called Daliman by Orderic) decrees
that Bohemond, "whom the Turks called the little God of the Christians,"
should be kept in fetters at all times. The Frankish knights are visited in
their dungeon in the emir's fortress by the emir's daughter, Melaz, who
is a paragon of beauty and wisdom. Orderic stresses her power in her
father's household, her great riches, and her many slaves. She bribes the
guards, descends to the prisoners and converses with them about the
Christian faith. She also supplies them with food and clothing. "Her

father, intent on much other business, either did not know this, or perhaps was not concerned about it because of the proved frugality of his beloved child."

After two years, a civil war breaks out between the emir and his brother, Soliman. To secure victory for her father, the emir's daughter mobilizes the help of the Frankish prisoners. She arms them, unhesitatingly putting her trust in their reputed military prowess and the professed ethics of the Christian faith. She makes them promise on their faith as Christians that they would follow her counsel and, having put her father's enemy to flight, return to the castle and to her. She, in the meantime, would have all watchmen descend from the citadel and post themselves at the lower doors. On their return from battle, she would give orders to bind the prisoners again. But Bohemond and his knights should overpower their jailers and seize the palace and the sultan's treasury. "If my angry father should want to punish me for my deeds," says Orderic's scheming Saracen maiden, "I beg of you, oh friends whom I love as I love my own heart: help me quickly!"

As foreseen, Daliman's victorious return bodes no good to the emir's daughter. He upbraids her for her treachery in arming the Frankish prisoners and swears "by the divine crown of Muhammad" to burn her and her Frankish knights. Melaz is duly rescued by Bohemond who has witnessed the scene from a window in the tower. The Frankish knights surround the emir and his men on all sides. Melaz, "presiding among the Franks like a 'domina,'" reads her father a lesson on Christian loyalty, considering that the Franks chose to return when they might have escaped. She then comes to the crucial theme which, in the literary presentation of the encounter of Christians and Saracens is persistently embodied in the figure of the enamored Muslim princess: "Make peace with the Christians, and let there be an inviolable alliance between you as long as you live." This plea is followed by a profession of faith in the superiority of Christianity which is the only condition of peace to be envisaged: "I am a Christian, and wish to be baptized according to the sacrament of Christian law," declares the enamored Muslim princess. It is not enough to have the princess abandon her father and convert to Christianity. She must also become the enemy of her people and belittle her own religion. "The law of the Christians is holy and true," she says to the emir, "but your law is full of vanities and polluted with all kinds of filth."

The Turks, speechless with outrage—according to Orderic, "prevented by God" from uttering the profane malice which is in their hearts —are locked up as prisoners in their own palace. Their wives, female servants, and unarmed eunuchs are permitted to see them in order to minister to their needs. The emir finally acts the part inevitably assigned to him in medieval romance: his indignation expresses itself in curses against Muhammad, "his God," and his faithless retinue. In the end, he has no choice but to agree to peace with the Christians. Melaz is promised in marriage to Bohemond. The prudent Saracen princess, however, counsels Bohemond to summon armed help from Antioch so as to ensure his safe return and to frustrate any possible treachery. This is done, and Tancred, the ruler of Antioch during Bohemond's absence, appears in person to conduct his uncle home. In his train, he brings Muslim prisoners who have been freed from Christian captivity by agreement, among them the daughter of the former Muslim emir of Antioch. This Muslim lady is much upset at leaving her Christian imprisonment because she has developed a fondness for pork. "For though the Turks and most other Saracen people greedily devour the flesh of dogs and wolves," says our knowledgeable author, "they abhor pork." Moreover, "they thus prove that they are without all the law of Moses and Christ, and belong neither to the Jews or the Christians."

In the meantime, Bohemond engages the Turkish emir in long and friendly talk which results in violent denunciations of "the execrable Muhammad, our God" by the Muslims. After mutual assurances of "perpetual peace," the Christians depart, followed by the emir's daughter, complete with waiting women and eunuchs. She is baptized into the Latin church, and, after a long speech by Bohemond in which he excuses himself from marrying her because of his arduous and uncertain life and his pledge to make a pilgrimage to Saint Leonard in Aquitaine, Melaz consents to being married to Roger, son of Richard of Salerno.[129] Roger is the future prince of Antioch. Thus the threat to Antioch from the Turks has been eliminated by marriage to the enamored Muslim princess.

Orderic's *historia* is grounded in two solid facts: Bohemond's imprisonment and release in 1101, and a dispute that broke out in 1103 between the Seljuk emir of Anatolia and the lord of Melitene, Bohemond's captor.

In the account of Albert of Aix, the falling out between the Seljuk emir and Bohemond's captor, whom he calls Donomannus (cf. Orderic's Daliman), leads to Bohemond's release after Donomannus has sought his prisoner's advice on how to deal with the situation.[130] In Orderic, as we have seen, Bohemond rushes to Daliman's support in battle at the instigation of Melaz. This part of the story seems to reflect the negotiations about Bohemond's release that went on between the Byzantine emperor Alexius and the Danishmand emir. They are described by Steven Runciman:

> The emir had already been offered the large sum of 260,000 besants from the Emperor Alexius in return for Bohemond's person, and would have accepted, had not the Seljuk Sultan, Kilij Arslan, come to hear of it. Kilij Arslan, as official overlord of the Anatolian Turks, demanded half of any ransom that the Danishmend might receive.

The resultant quarrel between the two Turkish princes prevented the immediate acceptance of the Emperor's offer, but it served the useful purpose of breaking their alliance. Bohemond, in his captivity, was aware of these negotiations.[131]

The introduction of Tancred in Orderic's story is a propagandistic distortion to convey the impression of Christian unity. Actually, Tancred took no part in Bohemond's release; he did not even contribute to the ransom money. As to Bohemond himself, he was far from keeping the assurances of "perpetual peace" of such concern in Orderic's story. As soon as he was released, he led the Christians in a raid to exact large tribute from the Muslims of Aleppo in order to repay those who had lent money for his ransom.

Roger, prince of Antioch, was properly married to a Christian, Baldwin of Edessa's sister. However, according to Fulcher of Chartres, Roger's death in battle against the Turcoman emir Ilghazi was due to the wrath of God against Roger's adulterous practices.[132] His reputation as a ladies' man may have helped the idea of linking him with a Muslim princess, though such links in the romances are never purely amorous intrigues. They serve to consolidate a Christian-Muslim alliance.

Bohemond died in 1111, Orderic in 1143. Within those thirty-odd years, the theme of the emir's daughter and the Christian knight, which had been deliberately introduced by a monkish chronicler to heighten the interest and political significance of his narrative, was embedded in the popular idea of a famous historical hero of the First Crusade.

The reflection cast by the enamored Muslim princess on the record of Western chroniclers is mirrored in the enamored Christian princess of the *Arabian Nights*. The closest parallel to Orderic's Bohemond story is "The Tale of the Muslim Hero and the Christian Lady"[133] set in the days of the second caliph, Omar ibn al-Khattab, and the battle for the capture of Damascus from the control of the Eastern Roman Empire. A Muslim warrior whose brother is killed in battle is taken captive in the siege of a Christian stronghold outside the city and imprisoned in the fortress of the Christian commander. The valor and nobility of the Muslim make such an impression on the Christian captain of the fort that he wishes his prisoner were one of them: "Verily to kill this man were a pity indeed; but his return to the Moslems would be a calamity. Oh that he might be brought to embrace the Nazarene Faith and be to us an aid and an arm!"

Convinced that Arabs have a passionate love for beautiful women, one of the Christian knights offers his daughter to tempt the Muslim to abjure his faith. The Christian maiden, splendidly attired, is brought face to face with the prisoner in all her beauty and grace. The Muslim sees "the evil sent down upon him," commends himself to Allah, closes his eyes, and applies himself to reciting the Koran. "Now he had a pleasant voice and a piercing wit; and the Nazarene damsel presently loved him with passionate love and pined for him with extreme repine." This lasted seven days, at the end of which she said to herself, "Would to Heaven he would admit me into the Faith of Al-Islam!"

In the end, the maiden can stand it no longer. She throws herself at the feet of the knight begging him to tell her about his religion. On his instruction, she goes through the necessary ritual and prayer and accepts his faith. However, there is no pretense at a "true" conversion: "O my brother, I did but embrace Al-Islam for thy sake and to win thy favours."

The knight promises not to take an additional wife—an important concession in a Muslim—on condition that she contrive to bring him out of captivity so that they can escape. The maiden then practices a ruse upon her parents by telling them that "indeed this Moslem's heart is softened and he longeth to enter the faith." She persuades them to let her go with him to another town to be married on the pretext that her lover cannot convert in the town where his brother has fallen in holy war for Islam. The captive is given his freedom and the lovers escape. They arrive in Medina, are joyously welcomed, and a wedding feast is prepared at the caliph's command. "Then the young Moslem went in unto his bride and Almighty Allah vouchsafed him children, who fought in the Lord's way and preserved genealogies, for they gloried therein. . . . And they ceased not to be in all solace and delight of life, till there came to them the Destroyer of delights and the Sunderer of societies."[134]

What is remarkable about the *Arabian Nights* tale is the absence of the ferocious intolerance and vindictiveness found in the crusading romances of the West. Though it deals with the subject of conversion with theological conviction, the sophisticated narrative art of the Arabian tale conveys the themes of love and war independent of ideology. In spite of the lie she tells her parents, there is a sweet dignity in the portrayal of the converted Christian maiden which sharply contrasts with the characterization of Muslim princesses who follow Christian knights in the romances of the West. The scheming that brings the lovers together is done by the maiden's father, not the maiden. Her frank avowal that it is only for the love of the stranger that she becomes a convert rings psychologically true, giving a moving depth to the feeling between hero and heroine. The Christian parents are lied to as parents everywhere in elopement. But though they are abandoned, they are not mocked, and neither is their faith. We have a sense of a secure, though officially antagonistic relationship between two stable civilizations whose differences may be bridged in war by the power of love.

This mature encounter between Christianity and Islam is also seen in the Byzantine epic where conversion is honestly depicted as the means of a lover to gain the object of his love. There is no belittling of Islam in the *Digenes Akrites*, and the deeply human situation between the Syrian emir and his Byzantine bride, individuals caught between cultures, is moving, convincing, and dignified. In the Arabian tales and the Byzantine epic the psychological refinement in the portrayal of converts is due to the profound understanding of two oriental civilizations that stemmed from a natural intermingling of peoples and languages in war and peace, within a defined Byzantine-Muslim frontier. In the West, there was no such general and far-reaching intermingling, only clash and withdrawal. The isolation of Britain from the scene of the actual encounter with the Saracens of Western Europe must have accentuated the design of a propagandistic stereotype in Middle English literature. In no other realm in medieval England is the distinction between the "lered" and the "lewed" more marked. For the crude caricature of the medieval Saracen flourished in the popular imagination at the very time when the superiority of Arabian learning was taken for granted.

The manner in which Josian, in the Middle English *Sir Beues of Hamtoun* (ca. 1300), is introduced to the audience is designed to direct it to the basic attitude with which they are to view the Saracen world. They are to be impressed by its opulence, while constantly bearing in mind that it is non-Christian and therefore out of bounds. The distinguishing features in the portrait of Josian are her golden shoes. The immediate reservation about her, in spite of her beauty and learning, is that she is not Christian:

> Iosiane þat maide het,
> Hire schon wer gold upon hire fet;
> So faire ȝhe was & briȝt of mod,
> Ase snow upon þe rede blod;
> Whar to scholde þat may discriue?
> Men wiste no fairer þing aliue,
> So hende ne wel itauȝt;
> Boute of cristene lawe ȝhe kouþe nauȝt.[135]

The physical appearance of the Muslim lady of Armenia does not differ from the ideal of beauty in the West. In Orderic, the dark complexion of the emir's daughter is suggested by her Greek name, Melaz, meaning black or swarthy. Josian's beauty is like "snow upon the red blood." She is meant to be both familiar and unfamiliar, a psychological preparation for her standing as the "good" infidel to be "saved" as the wife of a Christian knight.

Like the father of the Christian maiden in the *Arabian Nights*, King Ermin is so impressed with Beues that he at once offers his daughter in marriage, provided Beues abandons his faith. In spite of Beues's curt refusal to believe in false gods, the Saracen king of Armenia duly assumes the role of the inept father which is assigned to Muslim emirs in medieval Western romances.

King Ermin's liking for Beues and his carelessness about his daughter are such that he himself encourages Josian to heal Beues's wounds, though Beues has slain fifty of his knights in a quarrel on Christmas Day. The princess completely restores Beues to the king's good graces and is given the task to serve the Christian knight food after Beues has subdued Brademond, king of Syria, a suitor of Josian's, who has invaded Armenia.[136]

The Muslim princess characteristically pursues her own ends with cool deliberation. She is entirely unaffected by Beues's unchivalrous conduct when she summons him to her presence and is told he has called her a "heþene hound" (l. 699). The Muslim princess par excellence is the wooing lady of medieval temptation scenes: she walks unbidden into her hero's chamber, kisses him, and professes her love. She takes the hero into her own chamber and, with Beues sitting on the maiden's bed,

> "Merci," ȝhe seide, "ȝet wiþ þan
> Ichauede þe leuer to me lemman,
> Þe bodi in þe scherte naked,
> Þan al þe gold, þat Crist haþ maked,
> And þow wost wiþ me do þe wille!"
>
> [ll. 1105–09]

When Beues virtuously refuses, the Saracen lady surrenders to a fit of temper and despair:

> Ȝhe fel adoun and wep riȝt sore:
> "Þow seidest soþ her be-fore:
> In al þis world nis þer man,
> Prinse ne king ne soudan,
> Þat me to wiue haue nolde,
> And he me hadde ones be-holde,
> And þow, cherl, me hauest for-sake:
> Mahoun þe ȝeue tene and wrake!
> Beter be-come þe iliche,
> For to fowen an olde diche,
> Þanne for to be dobbed kniȝt,
> Te gon among maidenes briȝt;
> To oþer contre þow miȝt fare;
> Mahoun þe ȝeue tene & care!"
>
> [ll. 1111–24]

What is to be noted is the transition from Christ to Mahoun to mark her reversal from humble entreaty to furious anger.

The convincing features in the characterization of Josian are her passion for Beues and her keen and alert intelligence. What is stereotyped in the romance is the relation of the heroine to her kindred and her religion in which denigration is the essential element. Only once, in a fit of nostalgic despair at the court of Mombraunt, is Josian allowed an outburst against Beues's foreign god:

> "O allas," ȝhe seide, "Beuoun,
> Hende kniȝt of Soup-hamtoun,
> Now ichaue bide pat day,
> Pat to þe treste i ne may:
> Pat ilche god, þat þow of speke,
> He is fals & þow ert eke!"
>
> [ll. 2103–08]

Josian's christening by the bishop of Cologne is a routine procedure in which the limelight is taken by her companion, the giant Ascopart, who *refuses* to be "drowned" by the priest—"Icham to meche to be cristine" (l. 2596). Josian's role in the scene of her conversion is entirely passive. The passivity of the heroine in presumably so crucial a point is stressed by the almost fatuous complacency of Beues—a marked contrast to the genuine trepidation which we sense in the Arabian tale of the Christian lady and the Muslim knight.

> "Who is þis leuedi schene?" asks the bishop of Beues.
> "Sire, of heþenesse a quene,
> And ȝhe wile, for me sake,
> Cristendome at þe take."
>
> [ll. 2581–84]

A mechanical compliance is all that is required in the conversion of a Muslim princess.

Floripas, a Saracen "burde briȝt," is the heroine of the most popular "Saracen" romance in medieval England, *The Romaunce of the Sowdone of Babylone and of Ferumbras his Sone who conquered Rome*. It incorporates the story of *Sir Ferumbras* and is a Middle English translation of a French original which combined two Charlemagne poems, *La Destruction de Rome* and *Fierabras*.[137]

The character has been said to represent the stereotyped features of a heathen princess in the *decadent* chansons de geste. Nevertheless the appeal of this type is instructive, not only as the popular image of a "good" Muslim princess but also in conjunction with the theory that the aggressive and masterful nature of such heroines was foreign to the feminine ideal of the West.

The authenticity of the setting in which Floripas holds sway lends the figure authority as a representative type of an alien civilization envisaged

in a historical framework. The main action takes place at Aigremour, the
Saracen capital, a port on the Spanish coast of the Mediterranean from
which Sultan Laban, father of Ferumbras and Floripas, undertakes a raid
on Rome because of its interference with Saracen shipping. The Christian
prisoners in the Saracen castle who seize the tower with the help of the
emir's daughter are Roland, Oliver, Guy of Burgundy (Floripas's lover),
and the other nine of Charlemagne's twelve peers. It is Roland and
Oliver who are first taken captive in the attack of Charlemagne's forces to
avenge the Saracen sack of Rome and recapture the holy relics which the
Saracens have abducted.

As the character is revealed in the romance there is not one redeeming
feature in Floripas. She commits perfidy and murder, is a Goneril to her
father, and the reader is entirely on the side of the sultan when he curses
her and calls her "hore serpentyne."[138] Yet, in the Christian context,

> Dame Florip was Baptysed than
> And here maydyns alle,
> And to Sir Gye I -maryed.
> The Barons honoured hir alle.

[ll. 3191–94]

There is no lack of skill in the characterization. The sultan dotes on her
and her brother, Ferumbras. Both accompany him on his expedition to
Rome.

> Sire Ferumbras, my sone so dere,
> Ye muste me comforte in this case;
> My ioye is alle in the nowe here
> And in my Doghter Dame Florypas.

[ll. 93–96]

The strong personality of the Muslim princess is impressed on the audience from the beginning. The sultan promises her hand to one of his
vassals, Lukafere, king of Baldas, who boasts that he will bring him Charlemagne and his twelve peers. Floripas dismisses this with contempt:

> Tho sayde Floripe "sire, noon haste,
> He hath note done as he hath saide.
> I trowe, he speketh these wordes in waste,
> He wole make bute an easy brayde.
> Whan he bryngith home Charles the kinge
> And the xij dosipers alle,
> I graunte to be his derlynge
> What so evere therof by-falle."

[ll. 244–51]

When Roland and Oliver, the first of the *dozepers* to be captured, are brought to the sultan as prisoners while Ferumbras has been taken by the other side, Floripas shows her quick intelligence in preventing the execution of the two peers for the sake of her brother:

> Tho saide maide Florepas:
> "My fader so dereworth and der',
> Ye shulle be avysed of this cas,
> How and in what manere
> My brothir, þat is to prison take,
> May be delyuered by hem nowe,
> By cause of these two knightes sake,
> That bene in warde here with you.
> Wherefore I counsaile you, my fader dere,
> To have mynde of Sir Ferumbras.
> Pute hem in youre prison here,
> Tille ye haue better space.
> So that ye haue my brother agayn
> For hem, þat ye haue here;
> And certeyn elles wole he be slayn,
> That is to you so lefe and dere."
>
> [ll. 1511–26]

The sultan's reply is a moving testimony to fatherly love, not to be taken for granted in what is meant to be an unsympathetic figure:

> "A, Floripp, I-blessed thou bee,
> Thy counsaile is goode at nede,
> I wolde not leve my sone so free,
> So Mahounde moost me spede,
> For al the Realme of hethen Spayne,
> That is so brode and large."
>
> [ll. 1527–32]

There is nothing at all in the scene to prepare us for the outrage to be perpetrated on him by his two children in the name of love and Christianity.

We are still within the bounds of conventional literary expectations when we see Floripas, like Chaucer's Emily in the *Knight's Tale*, gathering flowers in her garden "in morne colde" (l. 1553). However, she dismisses her maidens when she hears the sound of lamentation from "the Prison, that was ther nye" (l. 1556), and displays an iron determination to get to the prisoners. When her duenna, Maragounde, refuses to comply with her wish to flout the sultan's command and bring the prisoners food, she murders her by pushing her out of a window into the sea. It has been

pointed out that this episode occurs in all the different versions of
Fierabras but that "the English author treats it with evident relish":[139]

> Floripe by-thought hir on a gyle
> And cleped Maragounde anoon right,
> To the wyndowe to come a while
> And se ther a wonder syght:
> "Loke oute" she saide "and see a ferr
> The Porpais pley as thay were wode."
> Maragounde lokede oute, Floripe come ner
> And shofed hire oute in to the flode.

[ll. 1571–78]

Moreover, Floripas's reflection on her deed serves to point to a Christian
moral:

> "Go there" she saide "the devel the spede!
> My counsail shaltowe never biwry.
> Who so wole not helpe a man at nede,
> On evel deth mote he dye!"

[ll. 1579–82]

In the Middle English *Sir Ferumbras*, the murder of the duenna is motivated by fear and is made more genuinely oriental by the role of the
princess's chamberlain in a situation not uncommon in tales of the
Arabian Nights, for Maragounde discovers the prisoners in Floripas's
chamber where the sultan's daughter had secretly led them. When
Floripas hears her threaten to inform her father, "chaunged was al hure
blee" (l. 1360). In this version, the scene of the duenna's murder has the
authentic coloring of oriental despotism, servility, and intrigue. Floripas
goes to a window

>   þat lay out to þe see;
> & atte wondowe sche lynede out: hure angre sche poȝte
>   awreke.
> Hure maistresse þanne sche clipede aloud: & bad hur with
>   hure to speke.
> Marigounde compþ til hure renne: & hure hed til hire gan
>   layn,
> Flo[rippe] stod up & preynte þenne: to-ward hure
>   Chamberlayn,
> & aȝen sche laid hur there: & fur out sche bent hure þo,
> & to whyte what hure wille were: hure maistrasse dude al-so.
> Þyderward þe Chamberlayn hym faste ran: þat hur cast y-knew
>   ful wel,

& By þe legges lifte he þe schrewe þan: & schef hur out ech
   del.

[ll. 1361–69]

The hapless old creature falls "in-to þe salte see" and drowns. Her
mistress and murderess blesses "Maumecet my mate" (l. 1372)—it is not
clear whether she addresses her chamberlain or the prophet—for preventing harm to the Christian knights.

The murder of the duenna in *Sir Ferumbras* is preceded by the murder
of the jailer, Brytamon, which enables Floripas to lead the prisoners
"pryuiliche & stille" (l. 1320) out of the dungeon into her private apartment, built in splendid isolation on a rock overlooking the sea. We have
the following sequence of events: the maiden "fair & swet" hears the
lament of the prisoners in her chamber and, prompted by curiosity,
descends with her ladies to speak with the foreign knights. When the
keeper of the jail does his duty and refuses to open the door, Floripas
"fair and gent" calls him "harlot gadelyng" (l. 1234) and berates him for
being rude to a gentlewoman. She then gives a sign to one of her attendants—also a maid "boþe wys and sleзe" (l. 1235)—who, knowing her
mistress well, brings a strong staff with which the gentle maiden herself
first tries to break the prison door. When the jailer tries to prevent this,
she clubs him to death "þat out sterte al is brayne" (l. 1251). Her callous-
ness and willfulness are truly amazing:

"Rest," quaþ sche, "þow sory wyзt: god зyue yuele chaunce!
now schal y speke my fille riзt: with þes knyзtes of fraunce."

[ll. 1252–53]

In the *Sowdone of Babylone*, Floripas murders the jailer after she has
killed her duenna. Her bloodiness is matched by a ruthless capacity for
deceit.

> To hire Fader forth she goth
> And saide "Sire, I telle you here,
> I saugh a sight, that was me loth,
> Howe the fals Iailour fedde your prisoner,
> And how the covenaunte made was,
> Whan thai shulde delyuered be;
> Wherefore I slough him with a mace.
> Dere Fadir, forgif it me!"

[ll. 1607–14]

The sultan promptly gives the prisoners into the guard of his "doghtir
dere" and "Floripe, that was bothe gente and fre" (l. 1628) is celebrated
as the deliverer of the Christian knights whom she, in the best harem

tradition, pulls up by ropes into her chamber where they become permanent guests "withouten wetinge of the Sowden" (l. 1660).

The description of the hospitality extended to Charlemagne's knights in Floripas's chamber is used by the poet to convey a touch of voluptuousness—intensified when Guy of Burgundy, whom Floripas has decided to marry before she set eyes on him, joins the prisoners in the lady's chambers. Guy and the other Carolingian peers have come to Aigremour with a defiant message from Charlemagne and are put in Floripas's charge by the unsuspecting sultan:

> "Gramercy, doghter, thou saieste welle,
> Take hem alle into thy warde.
> Do feter hem faste in Iren and stele
> And set hem in stray3te garde."
>
> [ll. 1847–50]

In her bower, Floripas blackmails the knight. She has loved Guy of Burgundy many a day in her dreams, she wants him, and she is prepared to be baptized and leave "Mahoundes laye" for his sake. But woe to them all if he refuses to take her to wife:

> "And but he wole graunte me his loue,
> Of you askape shalle none here.
> By him, þat is almyghty aboue,
> Ye shalle abye it ellis ful dere."
>
> [ll. 1899–1902]

Guy goes through the motion of honorably refusing to take anyone to wife who has not been chosen for him by his liege lord, Charlemagne. But he yields to the entreaties of Roland and Oliver to save them all, and there is much carousing and kissing to mark the betrothal.

A fierce sensuousness, emanating from the Muslim princess, is worked into a night scene in Floripas's apartment before the knights make their final defensive stand:

> "Truste ye welle alle to me," says Floripas.

> "Therefore go we soupe and make merye,
> And takith ye alle your ease;
> And XXX^{ti} maydens lo here of Assyne,
> The fayrest of hem ye chese.
> Take your sporte, and kith you knyghtes,
> Whan ye shalle haue to done;
> For to morowe, when the day is light,
> Ye mooste to the wallis goon
> And defende this place with caste of stoon

> And with shotte of quarelles and darte.
> My maydyns and I shall bringe goode wone,
> So eueryche of us shalle bere hir parte."
>
> [ll. 2082–94]

In the *Sowdone of Babylone* the drama within the sultan's castle reaches its climax after the goings-on in Floripas's chamber have been discovered by Lukafer of Baldas, the legitimate suitor of the princess. But Lukafer is cast into a fire and roasted to death in the lady's bower in a manner thoroughly approved by the heroine. The knights break out of Floripas's tower, surprise the sultan and his men at table, and massacre all. The sultan himself leaps through a window and escapes along the seashore to summon help. He returns with a host to besiege his own castle which has been endangered by the perfidy of his own child.

Thus the story of Floripas is enacted according to a standard scenario in which noble Christian prisoners overpower their Saracen captors with the help of the emir's daughter or wife. The Saracen castle, which they seize from within, is well provisioned and contains the sultan's treasure. The Christian knights are thus well equipped to withstand a long siege. The sultan, alarmed for his treasure, gives up the assault from outside. What seems important in this framework is not the military defeat of the Saracen forces but a sadistic pleasure at the degradation of the sultan or emir through the enmity and treachery of his own kin.

We find the identical setting in Orderic's account of the captivity of Baldwin, count of Edessa, later king of Jerusalem, who was taken prisoner by the Turks in 1104 at the disaster of the battle of Harran.[140]

Orderic's account of the incident proceeds as follows: during a Frankish attack organized to free the prisoners, which necessitates the emir's absence from his castle, Baldwin and his companions break out from their prison and seize the tower. There they find the emir's three wives, of whom only one is mentioned by name. She is Fatima, daughter of the Persian king Ali, "pulchritudine praecellebat ac potentia." Another wife, daughter of Ridwan, lord of Aleppo, sends a message by carrier pigeon from the tower to inform the emir of what has occurred. The emir returns. He is called Balad by Orderic, probably in confusion with a historical Balak who took part in the campaigns against Baldwin. After a fruitless siege of eight months, which the Christians can easily withstand because of the ample provisions in the castle, the emir offers Baldwin an armistice. He appeals to the chivalry of the knights as well as to the ethics of their faith:

> For shame; You afflict the noble matrons and oppress them in-
> decently; which does not accord with either royal magnificence nor
> with Christian religion. I entreat you, soften your iron breast, have

pity on my old age, spare feminine fragility. . . . Return my wives
to me, I ask, and I shall give you and yours security under oath.
. . . You will have free trade throughout all my province and you
may have from my treasury what you wish.[141]

A council is called in the tower to decide whether to accept the emir's
terms. It is at this point that Orderic gives us a most surprising speech of
Fatima, the emir's wife, without taking the trouble to explain her motive.
Fatima tells the "strenuissimi viri" not to give a straw for her husband's
words because they contain nothing but lies. The emir cannot do anything
as long as they hold the impregnable tower and keep her and the other
wives with them as hostages.

Her advice is that they should stay where they are and use their
superiority in arms and provisions. In her exhortation, Fatima recalls the
siege of Troy to the knights reminding them of the cantilena which will
be sung about them in both the West and the East if they persevere. The
emir's wife would rather be enclosed with them "quam daemonicam cum
idolatris observare culturam."[142] Her most ardent wish is to receive the
sacraments of Christianity. Baldwin's sense of propriety, however, gains
the upper hand, and he restores the wives against their wishes to Balad
who promptly takes their escort of five knights into captivity.

What is interesting in Orderic's account is an element that is probably
coincidental. There is a trace of a Muslim princess who was actually
connected with the historical events surrounding Baldwin's captivity: in
the battle around Edessa that followed the Frankish defeat at Harran,
when Baldwin was taken prisoner, a highborn Seljuk princess from the
Turkish emir's household fell into Tancred's hands. So highly did the
emir, called Jekermish, value this lady

> that he at once offered either to pay 15,000 besants to ransom her or
> else to exchange Count Baldwin himself for her. News of the offer
> reached Jerusalem; and King Baldwin hastened to write to Bohe-
> mond to beg him not to lose this opportunity for obtaining the
> Count's release. But Bohemond and Tancred needed money, while
> Baldwin's return would have thrown Tancred out of his present
> post back on his uncle's hands. They answered that it would be
> undiplomatic to appear too eager to accept the offer; Jekermish
> might raise his price if they hesitated. But meanwhile they arranged
> with the emir to have the money payment; and Baldwin remained
> in captivity.[143]

When considering Orderic's account, we must remember that we are
reading the story of events as part of the events themselves. The problem
of the relation between "romance" and "history" did not arise in medieval historical writing.[144] We find Isidore of Seville following the classics

in making the distinction between *fabula* and *historia*, *res fictae* and *res factae*. Both "fabula" and "historia," however, were branches of "poesis."[145] Their relationship to "reality" was determined by the way they depicted not only factual "truth" but an ideal and allegorical "truth" at a deeper level which served not merely for entertainment—the province of romance, but presented exemplary situations for exhortation and moral enlightenment—the task of history.[146]

Medieval historiography did not have the problem of distinguishing events from their legends and their reflection in the imagination of men because historical reality was what was experienced as reality—the living existence of men in which the stuff of romance (the alien, exotic, and miraculous)—was an integral part of the divine scheme of things that history depicted. In their portrayal of the alien Saracens, medieval history and romance reinforce and reflect each other so as to give the modern reader a sense of an integrated and unified "historical" experience.

The Converted Saracen

On his way to Armenia to find his Muslim princess after his imprisonment in Damascus, Beues of Hamtoun meets a Saracen knight who "had borne him good company in Armenia."

> He þouȝte, þat he wolde an hie
> In to þe londe of Ermonie,
> To Ermonie, þat was is bane,
> To his lemman Iosiane.
> And also a wente þeder riȝt,
> A mette wiþ a gentil kniȝt,
> Þat in þe londe of Ermonie
> Hadde bore him gode companie;
> Þai kiste hem anon wiþ þat
> And aþer askede of oþeres stat.
>
> [ll. 1981–90]

Beues learns that Josian has been married to Yuor and has accompanied her husband to Mombraunt. Beues has not heard of Mombraunt, though it is one of the most splendid cities in "all the land of Sarsyne," for he asks the knight where it is situated and is told to turn back and go north. It is only then that Beues's friend is identified as a Saracen, for he swears by one of the conventional Saracen gods:

> "Sere," a sede, "be Teruagaunt,
> Þow miȝt nouȝt þus wende forþ,
> Þow most terne al aȝen norþ!"
>
> [ll. 2038–40]

The Saracen of this encounter is nameless. He drops out of the narrative as soon as he has served his purpose of directing the hero to Mombraunt. Yet there is a genuine quality about this episode which lingers in the mind because of its disinterested and unselfconscious presentation of a "good" Saracen to play a minor role in the requirement of the plot, while the "official" Saracen knight in medieval romance can only be turned into an acceptable figure with the fanfare of conversion.

There is only one case in which an unbaptized Saracen, prominently endowed with a significant role, is treated with respect for his moral qualities. He is Clarel, one of four Saracen kings who go out in search of battle in the *Otinel* romances of the Charlemagne cycle. The hero, Otinel or Otuel, is a converted Saracen whose "historical" traces in the Charlemagne legend have been followed to the *Cronica* of Jacopo d'Acqui.[147] His counterpart is the Saracen king Clarel who engages him in a decisive combat after his conversion.

The climax in the Otuel story is not a battle between Christian and Saracen but a confrontation between Saracen and Saracen in which, in spite of the official theme, there is a double evaluation that reveals the tension between dogma and psychological reality.

> Here by-gynnyth A batayll felle
> Off kynk Clarell and Otuel,
> And wondurlyche strong,
> How they fouten for the lawe.
> Lystenyth to my sawe,
> And thynkyth nouȝt to long![148]

Otuel kills Clarel in accordance with conventional requirements, but not before Clarel's chivalry is revealed in protecting Ogier the Dane, one of the *dozepers*, who had spared him before, and sending the wounded Ogier to Enfamy, Clarel's "owyn lemman" who nurses him back to health. Clarel even slays one of his own party, a Saracen emir, who refuses to respect the protection granted to the Christian knight. Clarel's integrity is given its proper Muslim framework:

> "Come to me," Clarel seyde,
> "off nothyng ne schaltou drede,
> Ne off no sarsins tresoun!
> ffor-sothe there schal no man the drede,
> Whyles my body may the were,—
> By my god Mahoun!"

[ll. 971–76]

Slain by Otuel, Clarel dies the death of a noble opponent, and the reader's sympathy is fully engaged with the Saracens who mourn him:

> kyng Garcy and hys knytys
> to the temple ȝede anon ryȝtys,
> And kneleden elde & ȝong,
> And cryed on Mahoun, and Appolyn,
> Termagaunt, and Iouyn:
> "why suffur ȝe all thys thyng,—
> that Clarel hath lore the swete?

[ll. 1529–35]

We are made to understand that the inevitability of his death is determined not by the Saracen's personal wickedness but by the need to demonstrate a higher cause:

> kyng Clarell fyl tho a-down.
> tho men myȝt se that ys god Mahoun
> was but of lytyl myȝt.

[ll. 1520–22]

The unbaptized state of an exemplary "good" Saracen is not a psychological or cultural concession. It is a deliberate design in the interest of a religious function whose purpose is made clear in the effect of Clarel's death on his liege lord, King Garcy of Spain. At the beginning of the romance it is Garcy who sends Otuel, his trusted knight and cousin (*Otuel*, 1. 340), with a challenge to Charlemagne. From Garcy's point of view, Otuel, our converted Saracen hero, is a renegade and a traitor. This cannot be tolerated by the narrator, for it questions the hero's moral authority at the most vital and vulnerable point of the chivalric code: loyalty to his liege lord in battle. It is here that the death of "swete" Clarel serves the crucial purpose of presenting Otuel's abandonment of the Saracen cause as morally justified. For Clarel's death undermines King Garcy's own faith in his god *before* his battle against the Christians:

> All thouȝ y make to the my mone,
> ȝe stondyn stylle as ony stone,
> No word nyl ȝe mynne.
> y wene that ȝe ben domne & def,
> On ȝow was all my bylef
> More thanne to alle my kynne.

[ll. 1541–46]

The gods are broken and thrown into the fire, in the traditional manner, by a defiant Garcy who prepares for battle to beat not only Charles but his own god as well:

> and thus we schulle bete oure mametrye,
> ffor þat thay nolde nouȝt ous socurye,
> Thus we schulle hem dyȝt.
>
> [ll. 1568–70]

Nevertheless, when the Saracen host is defeated and Garcy is taken captive by Oliver, the Saracen king's motive in accepting Christianity is still only to save his life rather than his soul:

> þenne bede he Olyuer pur charite,
> þat he ne schulde hym nouȝt sle,
> hys hondys he gan wryngge,
> And he wolde cristen be.
>
> [ll. 1668–71]

The concern about Garcy's salvation is left to Archbishop Turpin:

> The erchebyschop, syre turpyn,
> A swythe good clerk off dyuyn,
> Crystened hum that day,
> The soule of that sarsin
> ffor to saue fro helle pyn.
> he lered hym goddys lawe.
>
> [ll. 1680–85]

There is, moreover, a special touch which reveals an underlying ambivalence in the general feeling about the converted Saracen hero. Though the fleeing Garcy is pursued and confronted by his former vassal Otuel, who lustily invokes "hym þat for ous bledde" (l. 1657), it is Oliver who takes him prisoner. In the social framework of medieval romance, the humiliation of a former liege lord by a renegade vassal would demean the hero's character and degrade the feudal code embracing both Christian and Saracen. But there must also have been some hesitation to bring about the "official" surrender of Islam through a Christian made not born. After Garcy's surrender and baptism, Otuel drops out of sight in the romance.

The dramatic and psychological climax in *Otuel* is the confrontation of the converted Saracen hero with his unconverted alter ego in the person of Clarel. It enables the hero, miraculously turned Christian by the grace of the Holy Ghost, to slay his unredeemed self and transfer his innate nobility to the cause of the Christians where, in the conception of medieval romance, it properly belongs.

Otuel is the hero of three Middle English *Otuel* romances.[149] In *Otuel and Roland* he is introduced as a potential Christian from the very beginning:

> And ther Rouland, the gode knyght,
> Ouer-come Otuell in fyȝt,
> Nowe ye schulle y-huyre.
> . . . .
> and was cristenyd with-oute fayle
> and helpe Charlys in many a batayle
> and was hym lef & dere.
>
> [ll. 24–29]

Once his ultimate salvation has been assured, he is allowed to be himself as a Saracen knight. He threatens Charles as a trusted messenger of his lord, Garcy of Spain, demanding adherence to his faith:

> And otuel gan to carpe yvylle
> To syre charlemayne,
> And sayde, "Garcy sent me the tylle,
> And sayde, that he wyl thy body spylle,
> ffor the wynnyng off Spayne.
> By-leue on hys god mahoun,
> Iubiter, & syre platoun!"
>
> [ll. 115–21]

Otuel is also permitted to sneer at Roland, who calls him "Schrew sarsin" (ll. 73), and to challenge him to a fight "by Mahoun swete name." But it is clear from the first that Otuel is a "worthy" opponent, for Charles bids his daughter Belisent to arm him well in her chamber, and he is treated throughout with honor and respect. Belisent even prays for Otuel while he is still unbaptized. When the combat with Roland proves inconclusive, Charles himself falls on his knees and prays to god in heaven "that he sende pes hem by-[t]wene, / and the sarisin to be cristene" (ll. 506–07). Roland adds the offer that Otuel should have Charles's daughter to wife and the friendship of himself and Oliver, if he abandons his faith. This is nobly rejected by Otuel:

> Quod Otuel, "so mote y the,
> that ne schalt-ou neuer se
> to for-sake Mahoun,
> ne turmegaunt, that ys so fre,
> ne Iouyn, the goddys thre,
> that beth goodys of grete renown."
>
> [ll. 521–26]

The fight is resumed, and Roland is on the point of losing his life in defeat— "at lyte they knewe that hethyn knyȝt" (l. 548). It is only then that we have the miracle of Otuel's conversion in answer to the Christian prayers to Jesus for help.

The hero's conversion itself is handled rather mechanically. It is brought about by a miracle from outside, as if there were a sense that a sudden and unmotivated change from within would affect the hero's stature. In the *Sowdone of Babylone*, Ferumbras, the hero, consents to be christened after he has been wounded by Oliver and has despaired of his gods:

> His bare guttis men myght see;
> The blode faste down ranne.
> "Hoo, Olyvere, I yelde me to the,
> And here I become thy man.
> I am so hurte, I may not stonde,
> I put me alle in thy grace.
> My goddis ben false by water and londe,
> I reneye hem alle here in this place,
> Baptised now wole I be."
>
> [ll. 1351–59]

In the *Otuel* romances, the only way to cope with the hero's super-human "maystrye" is to bring in the Holy Ghost:

> the holy gost thoruȝ here alder prayer
> a-lyȝt apon that sarisin there
> thoruȝ goddys holy myȝt.
> tho sayd the messanger,
> "leue Roulond, come me ner,
> y haue for-lorne my fyȝt.
> Mahoun & Iouyn, y wyl for-sake,
> and to Ihesu crist ye wyl me take,
> to bene hys knyȝt."
>
> [*Otuel and Roland*, ll. 569–80]

Ferumbras and Otuel are the two main heroes whom the Middle English romancers borrowed from the French national epic. Evidently among all the exploits of Charlemagne and his twelve peers, the conversion of the two Saracens was the topic that aroused popular interest most. Of the ten metrical romances, three concern themselves with Ferumbras, and four with Otuel.[150] But Ferumbras, as is shown by the reference in Barbour's *Bruce*,[151] was the more popular of the two.

The whole fantastic might of the Saracens is conjured up in the figure of Ferumbras as he appears before the Carolingian host in *Sir Ferumbras*:

> Erlich on þe morrwenyng þe kyng aras: & al his chiluelarie,
> & hurd is masse wan hit was: & so to þe mete gan hye,
> & al on murȝþe was he y-sete: wiþ a fair baronye;
> Ac or he hadde þane half y-ȝete: on herte him ȝan to nuye,
> Wan cam þer a Sarsyn [werreour] þere: by-fore is host al-one:

Of such anoþer herde ȝe nere: nowar þar ȝe han gone,
Of Strengþe, of schap, of hugenys: of dedes of armes bolde.
Þe kyngdom of Alysandre was al his: & fro babyloyne, þat
   holde,
Riȝt in to þe rede see: lord was he and syre.
To ma[r]tyre cristen men & slee: þat was his desyre.[152]

Not only does Ferumbras, in the manner of an *Arabian Nights* potentate, slay all Christian women with whom he lies but he is even allowed to slay the pope before his conversion, not to speak of

Cardynals, Abbotes & Pryours: monekys & frerys eke,
& alle clerkes of honours: boþe pore & reke,
Saue nunnes: sloȝ he sykerly: þe relygous þat þar war.
                      [ll. 60–62]

Having destroyed Rome and carried away the holy relics, he has come to challenge Charles himself. But he is defeated by Oliver in a duel and rapidly converted to Christianity—without, in the English version, even having to listen to Oliver's proselytizing prayer, which occupies forty-three lines in the French original.

The relish in the account of his previous atrocities against the pope and the clergy may indicate a secret wish of poet and audience, in the century of *Piers Plowman,* to have the representatives of Rome soundly abused. At any rate, it does not complicate the conversion of Ferumbras. On the contrary, the scene of the combat with Oliver makes Ferumbras a thoroughly likable figure, a noble Saracen knight full of largesse towards his enemy in the best tradition of Christian chivalry. The highest compliment is paid him by the author before his conversion:

Wiþ þat þe Sarsyn þat was þor: wax wroþ on his herte
& bente hym brymly as a bor: & up hym gan to sterte;
& wan he stod appon þe ground: huge was he of lengþe,
Fifteuene fet hol & sound: & wonderliche muche of strengþe.
Had he ben in cryst be-leued: & y-vollid on þe haly fant,
A bettre knyȝt þan he was preued: þo was þer non lyuand.
                      [ll. 544–49]

There is an understanding of Christianity in the Saracen Ferumbras which is totally absent in the characterization of Otuel, who is scornful before his conversion. Ferumbras offers Oliver an ointment for his wound, contained in a bottle hanging at his saddle.

hwych ys ful of þat bame cler: þat precious ys & fre,
þat ȝoure god was wiþ anoynt: wan he was ded & graued,
y wan hym wyþ my swerdes poynt: many man haþ he saued.
                      [ll. 511–13]

When Oliver's courage and prowess have shown Ferumbras that his opponent has hidden his true identity, his appeal to his adversary's religious beliefs is polite and respectful.

> He drew him þanne apart & sayde: "y pray þe, iantaile
>   kniȝt,
> As þov louest þat ilke mayde: þat baar þy god almyȝt,—
> Wel y wot þou art ful gret of fame: a bettere kniȝt wot y
>   non,—
> Tel me þer-for þy riȝte name: Wat calleþ me þe at
>   hom.

[ll. 636–39]

Even Ferumbras's invocations to Mahoun and Appolyn lack the ferocity of Otuel before his conversion. The most genuinely "Saracen" characteristic is conveyed in his wrath when Oliver cuts off some of his beard.[153]

Ferumbras does not protest too much about his gods because, unlike Otuel's Saracen liege lord, King Garcy, he has never had reason to doubt them. Before his encounter with Oliver, they have never let him down:

> Siþþe þe tyme þat he was bore: on batail ne com he non,
> In-to þe day þat he com þore: þat he ne ouercom his fon;
> ne a-ȝen no man ne tok querel: by-for þat in no lond
> þat he ne hadde þe betere deel: & eke þe heȝere hond.

[ll. 666–69]

Now he has found his peer in a Christian knight and the issue is formulated as between god and god: "by Mahoun, my god al-one; / þy god ne may þe helpe noȝt" (ll. 688–89).

When Ferumbras is mortally wounded, his inevitable conversion is graceful and moving. The fierce stereotyped Saracen of the opening has been turned into a Christian knight who, unlike his sister Floripas, the converted Muslim princess, maintains the vestiges of humanity even in the atrocious final scene with his father, the sultan.

In *The Romaunce of the Sowdone of Babylone and of Ferumbras his Sone who conquered Rome*, Ferumbras from the beginning is presented as a noble knight of human proportions, though in the final scene his humanity is less pronounced than in *Ferumbras*. His last words in the *Sowdone of Babylone* are a good indication of what poet and audience expected of a converted Saracen. Ferumbras is a prig who, with a touch of expediency, sacrifices his father to his newly found faith:

> Ferumbras saide to the kinge,
> "Sir, ye see, it wole not be,

> Lete him take his endynge,
> For he loueth not Cristyante."
>
> [ll. 3179–82]

The most interesting feature of the characterization in the *Sowdone of Babylone* is the introduction of the hero in the battle of Rome in which he is shown as sparing the pope when he recognizes him as a priest:

> Tho come the Pope with grete aray,
> His baner to-fore him wente.
> Ferumbras than gan to assaye,
> If he myght that praye entente,
> Supposynge in this though[t]e,
> Ther was the souerayne;
> He spared him therfore right noght,
> But bare him down ther in þe playn.
> Anoon he sterte on him all ane
> His Ventayle for to onlace,
> And saugh his crown newe shafe,
> A-shamed thanne he was.
> "Fye, preest, god gyfe the sorowe!
> What doist thou armede in the feelde,
> That sholdest saie thi matyns on morwe,
> What doist thou with spere and shelde?
> I hoped, thou hadiste ben an Emperoure,
> Or a Cheftayne of this Ooste here,
> Or some worthy conqueroure,
> Go home and kepe thy Qwer.
> Shame it were to me certayne
> To sle the in this bataile,
> Therfore turne the home agayn!"
> The Pope was gladde þer-of certayne. . . .
>
> [ll. 547–70]

Ferumbras's worth as a potential convert is thus demonstrated from the very beginning, whereas in *Sir Ferumbras,* we are faced with the hero as a Saracen giant who slays pope and cardinals. We must wait for the encounter with Oliver to appreciate the qualities of knighthood which mark him as a potential Christian.

It is clear from the *Sowdone of Babylone* and *Sir Ferumbras* that the converted Saracen knight was expected to conform more fully to the Christian ideal than his female counterpart. The Saracen lady served to embody erotic longings and aristocratic eccentricities which could not be given expression in the conventional heroines of Christian romance.

The final scene of *Sir Ferumbras* is the glorification of the converted Muslim princess as the dark lady of unbridled desire who is the real heroine of romantic longing beneath the veneer of Christian womanhood. After her father has been beheaded, "Florippe com forþ & was wel fawe." She claims Guy of Burgundy who "gladlych" takes "þys lady fair & briȝt." The Muslim princess then undresses before the assembled court to be baptized:

> þe Damesele dispoilled hure þanne anon, Hyr skyn was as whyt so
> þe melkis fom,   fairer was non on molde:
> Wyþ eȝene graye, and browes bent, And ȝealwe traces, & fayre y-trent,
>   Ech her semede of gold.
> Hure vysage was fair & tretys, Hure body iantil and pure fetys,
>   & semblych of stature.
> In al þe werld ne miȝt be non fayrer wymman of flesch & bon,
>   þan was þat creature.
> Wan þys lordes had seyȝen hur naked, In alle manere wyse weel
> y-maked,   On hure þay toke lekynge.
> Was non of hem þat ys flechs ne-raas, Noþer kyng, ne barou:ı, ne non
> þat was,   Sche was so fair a þynge.
>
> [ll. 5879–5900]

The christianized Saracen knight had no such sexual glamour in the unconscious. He was a purely propagandistic figure in which well-established notions could, however, be given an exotic and therefore dramatically more exciting form.

In the attempt to dramatize the familiar conflict between Christian good and Saracen evil, the Middle English romances are not concerned with psychologically convincing characterization but with the drama of the religious issue enacted in a fast-moving narrative. The primary feature which distinguishes Christians from Saracens is their adherence to their respective faiths. The focus of the differentiation is in the portrayal of the sultans and their rages against their gods when success eludes them. They are ready to burn or break Mahound at every moment of frustration and rage. Their unregenerate nature is also asserted in their obstinate refusal to accept baptism. Yet, whatever the intended effect, it is this refusal that asserts their individual being and lends the narrative a vestige of psychological truth.

By any objective standard the stereotyped scenario of Christian-Saracen encounter in the romance of the *Sowdone of Babylone* has potentially tragic dimensions. Ferumbras, the sultan's son and the hero, is chivalrous to his enemies but is the willing cause of unmitigated disaster to his own father. One cannot help feeling that he fully deserves the characterization of "fals cursed Ferumbras" which is hurled at him by the sultan. As to Floripas, she is a destroyer of man, a woman of iron will and unbridled passion. One wonders how anyone can make a point of accepting her proudly into Christianity.

In *Sir Ferumbras*, the hero at least implores his father to accept the true faith and save his life.

þan Fyrum[bras] ys sonne cryede aȝen—	hym sette on knen By-fore ys fader: & "Mercy, fader," he sayde,
"Swete fader, do hys lykyng,	And ne make þer-of no more taryying, for gode loue y pray þe."

[ll. 5775–78]

This touching scene is repeated three times. Its intended effect is to emphasize the sultan's hopeless recalcitrance. But it does achieve the psychological reality of a humanized Ferumbras who "wep & syȝte sore" at his father's plight and is, in this instance, acceptable as a hero without violating the reader's sensibilities. Floripas, on the other hand, is even more repulsive in *Sir Ferumbras* than in the *Sowdone of Babylone*. Her stony-hearted coldness is meant to personify the rectitude of a true believer. While Ferumbras tries to bring his father "out of his error into a better way," Floripas, without ado, urges Charlemagne to slay him:

þanne spak Florippe, þat burde bryȝt noȝt aryȝt,	—"Syr Emperour, þov dost To tarye þus: for ys sake.
ȝe hadde don wel, by god almyȝt,	Had ȝe do slen him ȝesternyȝt, Wan þat he was take."

[ll. 5763–66]

The peak of the reader's outrage is reached when Floripas's conduct surpasses even what her brother can tolerate. She has spoken of her father as "þat man" (l. 58) to the emperor. Ferumbras finally says to her what the reader has felt throughout the romance:

	"Sustre ne ys he þy fader;
alas!	Take of hym pytee:
He þe gat & forþ þe broȝte,	Thar-for ert þow mys-byþoȝte, To procury hym to slee."

[ll. 5823–26]

The Defeated Sultan

A recent student of the *Chanson de Roland* has noted "the author's skill and—perhaps first-hand—knowledge of the pagans he describes" in his clear differentiation "between the somewhat decadent type of Saracen to be found in Spain in the eleventh century, when the gentler arts had partially replaced the pursuit of arms, and the more virile types that accompanied the Sultan of Cairo on his expedition from North Africa in answer to their request for aid."154

There is no such clear differentiation in the Middle English Saracen romances, though the *Sowdone of Babylone*, which is situated in Spain, depicts the amenities of courtly civilization as practiced by Sultan Laban. Whatever they are named or wherever they come from, the romantic Saracens of the military encounters are stereotypes petrified in a literary convention which served as a vehicle of propaganda and psychological warfare. They are cast from a shallow mold and mechanically grouped around the preposterous figure of the sultan of Babylon, an emotionally satisfying caricature of an exotic and fundamentally incomprehensible enemy alien whose defeat and humiliation is the fervently desired happy ending of the tale.

This is not to say that the characters of the Christian side are invariably idealized in the Charlemagne romances. On the contrary, Charles is presented as an old and autocratic king who insults his knights, and Roland even refuses to fight Ferumbras when bidden to do so. But while the Christians are individualized and humanized in such incidents and soon transcend them in the triumph of their cause, the failings of the Saracen sultan are not personal characteristics but typological guidelines. The worldly power of the sultan is depicted rationally enough. It is, in fact, exalted in order to make his degradation more enjoyable. The sultan of Babylon, Laban, is introduced as "the kinge of hie degre, / And syr and Sowdon of hie Babilon" who was born in Ascalon and "conquerede grete parte of Christiante."

> And in the Cite of Agremare
> Vppon the Rivere of Flagote
> At þat tyme he soiorned ther
> Fulle roially, wel I wote,
> With kinges xij and Admyralles xiiij,
> With many a Baron & Kniȝtis ful boold,
> That roialle were and semly to sene;
> Here worþynesse al may not be told.

[ll. 33–40]

In the *Sowdone of Babylone*, the destruction of Rome is not a wilful act of Saracen savagery, as might have been expected, but a deed of reprisal which provides the poet with the opportunity to enlarge on the genuine splendors of Saracen trade along the Mediterranean. The narrator, unselfconsciously, gives a plausible reason for the Saracen expedition to conquer Rome. The sultan, whose castle in Andalusia overlooks the sea, observes

A Dromonde com sailyng in þe see
Anone he charged to bekyn him with honde
To here of him tidinges newe.
The maister sende a man to londe,
Of diuers langages was gode and trewe,
And saide, "lorde, this Dromonde
Fro Babyloyne comen is,
That was worþe thousande poundis,
As it mete with shrewes I-wis,
Charged with perle and precious stones
And riche pelure and spicerye,
With oyle and bras qweynte for the nones
To presente yow my lorde worthy.
A drift of wedir vs droffe to Rome,
The Romaynes robbed vs anone;
Of vs thai slowgh ful many one.

[ll. 63–78]

After hastily summoning his forces from Asia and Africa, Sultan Laban, accompanied by his son, Sir Ferumbras of Alexandria, and his daughter, Floripas, as well as numerous Saracen "kings," among them Lukafer of Baldac (Baghdad), sets sail for Rome in a dromond of characteristic oriental splendor:

The sailes were of rede Sendelle,
Embrowdred with riche araye,
With beestes and breddes every dele,
That was right curious and gaye;
The Armes displaied of Laban
Of Asure and foure lions of goolde.
Of Babiloyne the riche Sowdon,
Moost myghty man he was of moolde,
He made a vowe to Termagaunte,
Whan Rome were distroied & hade myschaunce,
He woolde turne ayen erraunte
And distroye Charles the kinge of Fraunce.

[ll. 129–40]

Any genuine coloring found in the external setting, however, is deliberately and crudely destroyed by the introduction of the main feature that distorts all characterization of Saracen leaders in the romances: the idol worship they practice as religious leaders and their wild and grotesque relation to their faith and kin. But the most persistent characteristic of these sultans is their instant readiness to be "woode" and to "renay" their "gods" at the slightest intimation of defeat or failure. This leads to the

anticipated climax: the breaking and burning of the Saracen gods and, in
the final scene, the sultan's enforced baptism or his "liquidation." Sultan
Laban is a typical example in cursing his gods:

> O ye goddes, ye faile at nede,
> That I have honoured so longe,
> I shalle you bren, so mote I spede,
> In a fayre fyre ful stronge;
> Shalle I neuer more on you bileve,
> But renaye you playnly alle.
> Ye shalle be brente this day er eve,
> That foule mote you befalle!
>
> [ll. 2431–38]

He is restrained by his counselors, who fear the vengeance of the gods.
His fury is temporarily superseded by anxiety for his treasure, which is
flung from the castle at the behest of Floripas to confuse her father's
assaulting army for the benefit of her Christian lover and his knights.
However, as things continue to go wrong, the sultan storms at his gods
again:

> In Ire he smote Mahounde,
> That was of goolde fulle rede,
> That he fille down to the grounde,
> As he hade bene dede.
>
> [ll. 2507–10]

Again, he is induced by the priests' "howlynge and wepynge sore" to
propitiate his gods and ask their forgiveness. The ritual of alternating
blasphemy and appeasement is repeated three times and must have
proved a high point of entertainment to medieval readers. Psychologically, however, the sultan's finest hour comes when he hurls a curse at his
unnatural children and contemptuously defies Christianity in the face of
death:

> Turpyn toke him by the honde
> And ladde him to the fonte.
> He smote the bisshope with a bronde
> And gaf him an evel bronte.
> He spitted in the water cler
> And cryed oute on hem alle,
> And defied alle þat cristen wer.
> That foule mote him by-falle!
> "Ye and thou, hore serpentyne,

And that fals cursed Ferumbras,
Mahounde gyfe hem both evel endyng,
And almyghty Sathanas!
By you came all my sorowe,
And al my tresure for-lorne.
Honged be ye both er tomorowe!
In cursed tyme were ye born."

[ll. 3163–78]

In the Arabian tales of conversion, the Christian god is never insulted. In Western romance, on the other hand, whenever a Christian knight in Saracen captivity refuses to convert to Islam, he throws insults at the other religion.

I nolde for-sake in none manere
Iesu, þat bouȝte me so dere:
Al mote þai be doum and deue,
Þat on þe false godes b-leue!

[*Sir Beues of Hamtoun*, ll. 565–68]

The lines are spoken by Beues to the Saracen king of Armenia called Ermin, to whom he has been sold as a slave. An unconscious compliment to Saracen tolerance is paid by the poet in the very next line: "Þe king him louede wel þe more. . . ."

In *Floris and Blancheflur*, a genuine oriental romance transplanted to the West probably by way of Byzantium,[155] the emir of Babylon's fairness and moderation contrast with the habitual rashness and temperamental excesses which characterize the stereotyped sultans of the romances composed in the West. Lukafer of Baldac, in the *Sowdone of Babylone*, has rounded up "ten thousande maidyns faire of face" in the sack of Rome. But instead of distributing them among the harems of his vassals, as might have been expected, Sultan Laban commands that they should all be slain.

. . . "my peple nowe ne shalle
With hem noughte defouled be,
But I wole distroie ouer all
The sede over alle Cristiante."

[ll. 232–35]

The emir of Babylon, on the other hand, having discovered Blancheflur and Floris in his harem in bed together, deals with a situation which would justify punishment by death under any medieval code, with compassion and humanity. Floris is knighted, and the tolerant and generous emir has the lovers married in church:

And efte he made him stonde upright
And dubbed him there knight
And bade he shulde with him be
The furthermast of his meiné.
Floris falleth doun to his feet
And prayeth geve him his sweet.
The Amiral gaf him his leman;
All that there were thankid him thanne.
To a chirche he let hem bring
And dede let wed hem with a ring.
Both these two swete thinges, y-wis,
Fell his feet for to kisse; . . .[156]

At the end of the *Sowdone of Babylone* the sultan's head is smitten off and "his soule was fet to helle, / To daunse in þat sory lande / With develes, þat wer ful felle" (ll. 3188 ff.). In most of these romances the reader cannot help posing the question of Shylock: Hath not a sultan eyes? hath not a sultan hands, organs, dimensions, senses, affections, passions? If you wrong him, shall he not revenge?

THE SARACEN GIANT

The figure of the giant is a mythical archetype which has dominated the human imagination from times immemorial. In medieval literature it often appears as Green Knight or Wild Man who embodies in himself supernatural powers and an organic strength which threatens and terrifies the precarious order of civilized man.[157] The composers of "Saracen" romances drew on this tradition to heighten the fearsomeness of the Muslim adversary whom their Christian heroes had to face and overcome. It has been noted, however, that while the features ascribed to gigantic Christian warriors in the chansons de geste tend to stem from mythology and folklore, Saracen giants have distinctly realistic aspects of their own.[158] The feeling of reality conveyed by the huge, exotic Saracen champions in the romances derives, in the first place, from their relation to the Eastern giants of biblical tradition, so vital in the medieval concept of "gigantes" in which giants incarnated primordial evil in the history of the Holy Land.[159] The fight of David against Goliath was the classic historical example of the grace of God and the victory of the true faith against the fearsome might of unbelievers.

The Saracen giant Vernagu, the earliest representative of the species engaged in a Christian-Saracen duel, is explicitly derived from Goliath in the pseudo-Turpin chronicle of Charlemagne, the source of the Middle English (early fourteenth century) *Rouland and Vernagu*[160] by way of a French version: "gygas quidam Ferracutus nomine de genere Goliath advenerat de horis Syrie, quem cum .c.xx. milibus Turcorum Babylonis

ammiraldus ad bellum contra Karolum regem miserat."¹⁶¹ He is thus
described to the English audience:

> Stout he was & fers,
>   Vernagu he hiȝt;
> Of babiloun þe soudan
> Þider him sende gan,
>   Wiþ king charls to fiȝt,
> So hard he was to fond,
> Þat no dint of brond,
>   No greued him apliȝt.
>
> He hadde tventi men strengþe,
> & fourti fet of lengþe,
>   Þilke panim hede,
> & four fet in þe face,
> Y-meten in þe place,
>   & fiften in brede,
> His nose was a fot & more,
> His browe as brestles wore,
>   He þat it seiȝe it sede,
> He loked loþeliche,
> & was swart as piche,
>   Of him men miȝt adrede.
>   [*Rouland and Vernagu*, ll. 465–86]

Unlike Alagolafre, the Ethiopian giant in the *Sowdone of Babylone*,
Vernagu is a true Brobdingnagian, sharply defined by his huge proportions, differing from the Frankish knights in color and size, but not in
kind. He is depicted as exactly double the height of Charlemagne, whom
the poet describes as twenty feet tall:

> Tventi fete he was o lengþe,
> & al so of gret strengþe,
>   & of a stern sight,
> Blac of here & rede of face,
> Whare he com in ani place,
>   He was a douhti kniȝt.
>   [*Rouland and Vernagu*, ll. 431–36]

Charlemagne royally towers over his *dozepers* who are skilfully turned
into Lilliputians by the poet to give us an accurate perspective of monstrous inequality in the Christian-Saracen fight. One by one, Vernagu
carries the king's renowned champions off under his arm, and Roland,
who finally does succeed in slaying the giant in a duel, is first picked out

of his saddle like a puppet. The only special feature to mark Vernagu's strength besides his size is his hard skin "fram þe nauel vp ward."

The two heathen giants in the *Sowdone of Babylone*, on the other hand, distinctly belong to the species of animal-headed and devilish Wild Man. We first meet the giant Estragot, accompanying the Saracen raid on Rome "With bores hede, blake and donne. / For as a bore an hede hadde / And a grete mace stronge as stele" (ll. 347–49).

> This Astrogot of Ethiop,
> He was a kinge of grete strength;
> Ther was none suche in Europe
> So stronge and so longe in length.
> I trowe, he were a develes sone,
> Of Belsabubbis lyne,
> For ever he was thereto I-wone,
> To do Cristen men grete pyne.
>
> [*Sowdone of Babylone*, ll. 352–59]

Estragot has a wife, the giantess Barrok who, armed with a deadly scythe, "grenned like a develle of helle." Her function is to assist Alagolafre, the giant who guards the bridge which leads to the sultan of Babylon's castle. Alagolafre has an animal head:

> This geaunte hade a body longe
> And hede, like an libarde.
> Ther-to he was devely stronge,
> His skynne was blake and harde.
> Of Ethiope he was bore,
> Of the kinde of Ascopartes.
> He hade tuskes, like a bore,
> An hede, like a liberde.
>
> [*Sowdone of Babylone*, ll. 2191–98]

In *Ferumbras*, however, in both the Ashmole and Fillingham versions,[162] the animal features are absent. Gulfagor is a faithful bridge warden of huge proportions. Like Gawain's Green Knight he carries a huge ax; he is "like a devil broken out of hell." But he is a recognizably human figure, in spite of his frighteningly dark complexion and black teeth:

> The porter ys a geaunt; the sothe to telle,
> he ys lyche a deuyl that were broke out of helle.
> Ten thousand sarsins wel armed & dyȝt,
> whenne he wyl blowe hys horn, [ben] al redy to fyȝt.
> . . . .
> Whenne þe geaunt sey al the knyȝtes come,

he went it hadde byn a pray þat sarisins hadde y-nome.
ffor to wete what it was, he dude ys entent.
A-ȝens hem swythe, he toke þe gate and went.
he sette hym with-oute on a marbel ston.
A fowler deuyl þan he was, sey þey neuer none.
he held an ax in hys hond, muche and vnryde,
þe byt y-grounde scharp,—to fot it was of brede.
he was brod and thykke in bale and in bak.

· ·

Brod were hys eyȝen, hys browes euyl y-schape,
hys nose Brod and Croked, hys schyn as a nape,
hys schulders, wonder thyk,—a gloten to fede.
To large elne, y wot, he was of Brede.
Swart teþ: and blo and ȝolw was hys swyre:
Bothe blak, and lothely, and grysly of chere.
In alle maner wyse, euyl was he schaped:
he semed a deuyl of helle þat out was a-schaped.
Constable was he, and hadde in kepyng
þe Brygge of mautreble vnder balam þe kyng,
þat no man schulde passe, neyþer loude ne stylle,
But it were at hys grace and hys wylle.

        [The Fillingham MS of *Ferumbras*, ll. 1217–61]

Ascopart in *Beues of Hamtoun*, presumably like Alagolafre, "of the kinde of Ascopartes" as his name shows, is also an ordinary giant in his physical appearance: Beues and his Saracen lady Josian meet Ascopart in their flight from her husband's kingdom Mombraunt:

And metten wiþ a geaunt
Wiþ a loþeliche semlaunt.
He was wonderliche strong,
Rome pretti fote long;
His berd was boþe gret & rowe;
A space of a fot be-twene is browe;
His clob was, to ȝeue a strok,
A lite bodi of an ok.

        [ll. 2505–12]

Wondering about his huge size, Beues asks him whether all the inhabitants of his native land are as big as he. The curious reply is that Ascopart was despised as a dwarf before he took refuge in King Yvor's land and became its champion, under the vice-regency of Garcy:

"Me name," a sede, "is Ascopard;
Garci me sente hideward,

> For to bringe his quene aȝen
> And þe, Beues, her of-slen.
> Icham Garci is chaumpioun
> And was idriue out of me toun;
> Al for þat ich was so lite,
> Eueri man me wolde smite;
> Ich was so lite & so meruȝ,
> Eueri man me clepede dweruȝ,
> And now icham in þis londe,
> I-woxe mor, ich vnderstonde,
> And strengere þan oþer tene,
> And þat schel on vs be sene;

[ll. 2517–30]

Ascopart's mission is to fetch back Josian to her rightful husband, Yvor, and kill Beues. A fight ensues in which Beues, predictably, is the victor. The giant's life, however, is spared at the request of Josian, and Ascopart becomes Beues's page and their means of escape from the lands of the Saracens. For when the three travelers reach the Mediterranean, he carries hero, heroine, as well as their horse and mule, to a Saracen merchant ship whose crew he has single-handedly driven off. He thus enables them to reach Cologne and baptism. While Josian, "of heþenesse a queen" is duly baptized, Ascopart endears himself to the reader in a comic scene: he categorically refuses to enter the baptismal font that has been especially built to contain his size, for fear of drowning:

> Þe nexste dai after þan
> Þe beschop cristnede Iosian.
> For Ascopard was mad a koue;
> Whan þe beschop him scholde in schoue,
> A lep anon vpon þe benche
> And seide: "Prest, wiltow me drenche?
> Þe deuel ȝeue þe helle pine,
> Icham to meche te be cristine."

[ll. 2589–96]

What is more, Ascopart gets away with it. He is subsequently entrusted by Beues with the protection of Josian in Europe, helps the hero to his rightful heritage in England, but in the end remains a faithful Muslim and loyal to his Saracen lord, Josian's legal husband, King Yvor of Mombraunt. His last oath, before he is cut to pieces, in his native Asia, by Beues's liege men, is "be Mahoun" (l. 3880). Ascopart is not an ignoble figure, and rather likable.

According to the *Sowdone of Babylone*, "the kind of Ascopart"[163] came from Ethiopia, which is also given as the provenance of Amiraunt, the Saracen giant who engages Guy of Warwick in a judicial combat, in the version of the romance printed by Copland.[164] The Auchinleck manuscript, which is the earliest of the five Middle English versions of the poem, describes the giant as coming from Egypt,[165] while in the fifteenth-century version "comyn he ys fro the lande of Ynde."[166]

The humanization of the gigantic Saracen goes so far as to turn him into "Sir Amoraunt" in the Auchinleck manuscript, which heightens the impression of worth in Sir Guy of Warwick's imposing opponent, and to make him the lover of the sultan's daughter, a touch that conveys a whiff of authentic harem intrigue from the *Arabian Nights*.[167]

The most striking characteristic, however, is, again, the absence of specifically "supernatural" features, particularly as he, too, like Algolafre, is compared to the devil of hell. It is Amiraunt's outsized body, his dark complexion and enlarged features that are frightening, but he is only two or four feet taller than other men.[168]

Thus, in a general way, the portrayal of Saracen giants in medieval literature differs from the purely folkloristic tradition in a particularly important aspect: it reflects accounts of indigenous or hostile tribes in exotic countries as we find them, for instance, in *Mandeville's Travels* where the giants under the rule of Prester John are said to be twenty-eight to fifty feet tall.[169] We must remember that to medieval anthropology Eastern "giants" were verifiable phenomena, like black-skinned men, described by geographers, naturalists, and travelers, and realistically associated with tall Africans in Saracen armies. Unlike the mythical giants of fairy tales, the Saracen giant in the romances has a footing in contemporary reality. His exoticism is mitigated by his truly representative function as a "counter-knight," i.e., a most concrete and powerful embodiment of a profoundly alien and terrifying *real* enemy that *actually* threatened Christian survival.

"Makomet and Mede": The Treatment of Islam

William Langland attributed the misshaping of his and future times to "Makomet and Mede."[170] But his view of Islam and its Prophet represented the most liberal opinion in the medieval outlook on the religion of the Saracens:

> For Sarasenes han somwhat · semynge to owre bileue,
> For thei loue and bileue · in o persone almiȝty;
> And we, lered and lewede · in on god bileueth.
>
> [B xv, 386–88]

The core of tolerance in these lines is the acceptance of Islam as a

monotheistic faith "seeming to our belief." This is particularly pronounced in the later version of the poem:

> Iewes, Gentiles, and Sarrasines · Iugen hem-selue
> That leeliche thei by-leyuen · and ȝut here lawe dyuerseth;
> And on god that al by-gan · with goode herte thei honoureth,
> And either loueth, and bileuith · in on lord al-myȝti.
>
> [C xviii, 132–35]

When the dreamer questions Free Will about Charity, and whether
Saracens have a part of it, he receives the following answer:

> "Hit may be that Sarrasyns hauen · a suche manere charite,
> Louye, as by lawe of kynde · oure lord god al-myghty."
>
> [C xviii, 151–52]

The conclusion is that Saracens, like Jews, may aspire to salvation:

> For sutthe that thes Sarasyns · scribes, and thes Iewes
> Hauen a lippe of oure by leyue · the lightloker, me thynketh,
> Thei sholde turne, who so trauayle wolde · and of the Trinite
> techen hem.
> For alle paynymes preyen · and parfitliche by leyuen
> In the grete heye god · and hus grace asken,
> And maken here mone to Makamede · here message to shewe.
>
> [C xviii, 252–57]

The treatment of Islam in *Piers Plowman* reflects a tradition of Christian
polemical scholarship which drew on original Muslim sources and
represented the most serious medieval attempt to grapple with the
spiritual problem of Islam.

The crux of the matter resided in the figure of Muhammad:

> Ac one Makometh, a man · in mysbileue
> Brouȝte Sarasenes of Surre · and se in what manere.
> This Makometh was a Crystene man · and for he moste nouȝte
> be a pope,
> In-to Surre he souȝte · and thorw his sotil wittes
> Daunted a dowue · and day and nyȝte hir fedde;
> The corne that she cropped · he caste it in his ere.
> And if he amonge the people preched · or in places come,
> Thanne wolde the coluer come · to the clerkes ere,
> Menynge as after meet · thus Makometh hir enchaunted,
> And dide folke thanne falle on knees · for he swore in his
> prechynge,
> That the coluer that come so · come fram god of heuene

As messager to Makometh · men forto teche
And thus thorw wyles of his witte · and a whyte dowue,
Makometh in mysbileue · men and wommen brouʒte,
That lered there and lewed ʒit · lyuen on his lawes.
And sitth owre saueoure suffred · the Sarasenes so bigiled,
Thorw a crystene clerke · acursed in his soule;

[B xv, 389–405]

The information which Langland, in the second half of the fourteenth century, conveyed to his audience was that the founder of Islam, whom Muslims considered their Messiah ("A man that hihte Makamede · for Messye thei hym heolde," C xviii, 159) was a Christian clerk thwarted in his ambition to become pope. This "Crystene man" converted the people of Syria by a trick in which he pretended that a dove on his shoulder, which he had trained to pick a corn from his ear, was a divine messenger, attesting to the truth of what he preached.

Islam, then, was a Christian heresy perpetrated by a heretical cardinal:

Men fyndeth that Makamede · was a man ycrystned,
And a cardinal of court · a gret clerk with-alle,
And porsuede to haue be pope · pryns of holychurche;

[C xviii, 165–67]

It is the name of Muhammad, this "fals Crystine" (C xviii, 183), which is synonymous with the root of all evil—Mede:

Ac for drede of the deth · I dar nouʒt telle treuthe,
How Englissh clerkes a coluer feden · that Coueityse hatte,
And ben manered after Makometh · that no man vseth treuth.

[B xv, 406–08]

Allas, that men so longe · on Makometh shulde byleue . . .

[B xv, 484]

The comparatively sophisticated view of Islam as we find it in Langland, and the primitive literary conception of Saracen idolatry in the Middle English romances, both reflect a polemical method arising from an authoritative doctrinal approach. The medieval Saracen of literary convention was not merely the concoction of ignorant and fanatical propaganda. The portrayal of Islam as paganism, which we find in the popular romances, was rooted in ideas sanctioned in the twelfth century by no less an "Orientalist" than Peter the Venerable, abbot of Cluny.[171] At the same time, the translation of the Koran and other Islamic treatises in 1143, which Peter initiated, is the first evidence, on the territory of "Gaul," of a serious preoccupation with the nature of Saracen religion. Even before that, about 1106, we have the *Dialogus* of Petrus Alfonsi which, as we have seen, for the first time in the language of Western Christendom, gives some authoritative information about Islam. What is important about these works and the influence they exerted on Western Europe is "that what is contained in them, however heterodox or fabulous, has at least some basis in Islamic scripture, theology, law, history, or legend."[172]

In the East, in the wake of the Crusades, this can only be said of William of Tripoli, writing in his convent at Acre in 1273. Ricoldo of Montecroce's later account "does not represent any advance on William of Tripoli's work."[173]

Langland's view of Islam as a Christian heresy is eloquently expounded by Peter the Venerable in his letter to Bernard of Clairvaux reporting on the circumstances surrounding his project of translation. "I cannot clearly decide," writes the abbot of Cluny in a preface to a treatise based on the Koranic corpus,

> whether the Mohammedan error must be called a heresy and its followers heretics, or whether they are to be called pagans. For I see them, now in the manner of heretics, take certain things from the Christian faith and reject other things; then—a thing which no heresy is described as ever having done—acting as well as teaching according to pagan custom. For in the company with certain heretics (Mohammed writes so in his wicked Koran), they preach that Christ was indeed born of a virgin, and they say that he is greater than every other man, not excluding Mohammed; they affirm that he lived a sinless life, preached truths, and worked miracles. They acknowledge that he was the Spirit of God, the Word—but not the Spirit of God or the Word as we either know or expound. They insanely hold that the passion and death of Christ were not mere fantasies (as the Manichaeans [had held]), but did not actually happen. They hold these and similar things, indeed, in company with heretics. With pagans, however, they reject baptism, do not accept the Christian sacrifice [of the Man, and], deride penance and all the rest of the sacraments of the Church. . . . Choose, therefore, whichever you prefer; either call [the Moslems] heretics on account of the heretical opinion by which they agree with the Church in part and disagree in part, or call them pagans on account of the surpassing wickedness by which they subdue every heresy of error in evil profession. . . . If you call them heretics, it has been proven that they are to be opposed beyond all other . . . heresies; if you call them pagans, I shall demonstrate, by the authority of the Fathers, that they are to be resisted nonetheless.[174]

In the Islamic sources that came into view in the twelfth century, the essential connection of Islam with Christianity was suggested by the Bahira legend and the arguments of Muslim polemicists. In Muslim traditions there are two parallel legends according to which the boy Muhammad, accompanying the trade caravan from Mecca to Syria, met a Christian monk called Bahira (Aramaic "the elect") who reveals the youth's prophetic destiny.[175] Bahira had found the announcement of the Prophet's coming in Christian books, the property of those uncorrupted Christians whom the faithful will find "the nearest in friendship," according to the Koran: "this is because there are priests and monks among them and because they do not behave proudly" (Sura V, 82). A Christian monk who was a historical personage to Muslims of the ninth century was thus the witness of the mission of Islam which the corrupted Christianity of the official Church tried to deny. Inevitably, in the Byzantine polemic against Islam—the earliest of which is represented by Theophanes (d. 818)—Bahira became a heretical Christian monk. He is variously called Sergius or Nestorius and is depicted as the inspirer and accomplice of the "false prophet" who, in the West, by a natural development, himself became "a crystene clerke acursed in his soule."

In his account of the story of Bahira, William of Tripoli, author of "de statu saracenorum," is closest to Islamic sources.[176] He describes Muhammad as "puer videlicet orphanus, egrotativus, pauper et vilis, custos cameli, natione Arabs de genere Ysmaelis," but quotes Genesis 16:12, "And he will be a wild man; his hand will be against every man, and every man's hand against him; and he shall dwell in the presence of all his brethren." However, the Dominican friar of Acre does not condemn Bahira as a heretical monk. On the contrary, it was from Bahira that the boy learned "to flee the cult of idols and to worship one God and to invoke Jesus, the son of the Virgin Mary with all his heart."[177]

In the West, even before the material of Petrus Alfonsi and Peter the Venerable, we have a poem called *Vita Mahumeti* which has been attributed to Hildebert, Bishop of Mayence (1057–1134), and may have been composed even earlier, around 1040.[178]

There a "magus" called Mahumet is forced to flee from Jerusalem at the time of Emperor Theodosius, that is, at the end of the fourth century. He comes to Libya and begins to wield his influence on "Mamucius," a slave of the consul. Mamucius's master is strangled, and Mamucius, "ille magi socius,"[179] marries the consul's widow whose infatuation with him has been aroused by magic art. Eventually Mamucius becomes the ruler of Libya and the tool by which the magician Mahumet is able to introduce the corrupting religion that threatens the Church.

The most forceful element in the poem is the suggestion of a dual persona for the Muslim prophet: he is both demoniac magician and slave. The correspondence of the two names, Mahumet and Mamucius, points to

the origin of both characters in free-floating scraps of biographical information in which Muhammad's humble beginnings and his marriage to the
rich widow Khadija were prominent elements. The *Vita Mahumeti* clearly
connects Muhammad as "magus" with the early history of Christian
heresy in the Holy Land. Over three hundred years later, the popular
image of the Muslim prophet as an "enchanter" still dominates one of the
most rational discussions of Islam in medieval literature.

Langland, however, does not condemn Muhammad's "magic" without
marveling at its success in converting men's souls. On the contrary, by a
twist of unconscious irony, the Muslim Prophet in *Piers Plowman* is held
up as an example to the Christian Pope:

> And take hede hou Makamede · thorwe a mylde doue,
> He hald al Surrye as hym-self wolde · and Sarasyns in quyete;
> Nouht thorw manslauht and mannes strengthe · Makamede hadd
>   the mastrie,
> Bote thorw pacience and pryuy gyle · he was prynce ouer hem
>   alle.
> In suche manere, me thynketh · moste the pope,
> Prelates, and preestes · prayen and by-seche
> Deuowtliche day and ny3t · and with-drawe hem fro synne,
> And crye to Crist that he wolde · hus coluere sende,
> The whiche is the holy gost · that out of heuene descendede,
> To make a perpetuel pees · by-twyne the prynce of heuene
> And alle manere of men · that on this molde lybbeth.
>
> [C xviii, 239–49]

The idea of Muhammad embodying the exemplary virtue of Christian
patience is found only in the C-version of the poem. It is remarkable not,
as Skeat would have it, "for its wide deviation from the truth"[180] but for
the significant change in the attitude to Islam which it manifests. Muhammad the evil enchanter has become Muhammad the political sage and
has been accepted on an equal footing:

> Eueriche busshope, by the lawe · sholde buxumliche wende,
> And pacientliche, thorgh hus prouynce · and to hus peple hym shewe,
> . . . .
> And enchaunte hem to charite · or holychurche to be-leyue.
>
> [C xviii, 283–88]

The first voice of true authority on the Saracens in the Christian West
is that of the converted Jew Petrus Alfonsi—one who "had read their
books and knew their language."[181]

He gives us an excellent reason for expounding the doctrines of the
Saracens: "When you relinquished the faith of your fathers," says Moses,

his Jewish self, to his alter ego, the Christian Peter, "I wonder why you chose the faith of the Christians rather than that of the Saracens with whom you have always conversed and among whom you have been reared."[182] Moses is kinder to Islam than is Peter, the convert. Moses enumerates the good points of the faith, the scrupulousness of required ablutions, the proclamation of one God, the abstention from wine, the fasting of Ramadan.[183] Peter's Christian refutation of the tolerance advanced by Moses centers on three aspects: the effect of pre-Islamic idolatry on the Muhammadan faith, the fraudulence of Muhammad's claim to prophecy, and the carnality of Islamic practice and belief. Islam is a heresy derived from Nestorians and Jacobites as well as Samaritan Jews. Petrus does not mention Bahira by name. His Christian culprit is a Jacobite archdeacon of Antioch, "vinde ad Concilium vocatus est, & damnatus." The heretic, "damnationis pudore contristatus," seeks refuge with his friend Muhammad and, together with two native Arabian Jews, inspires the heresy of Islam which is first propagated among the heretical Jews and heretical Christians in Arabia.[184]

An account of Muhammad's Christian teacher was contained in the most famous Christian apology current in the Arab world: the *Apology of al-Kindi*. This "epistle" (risālah) in defense of Christianity against Islam was reputed to have been written by a Nestorian at the court of the Caliph al-Ma'mun in the ninth century. In the twelfth century, it was fully known to the Christian world—it was the final part of the Koranic corpus sponsored by Peter the Venerable.[185]

Thus Vincent de Beauvais (d. 1264) expressly refers to the epistle as "the pamphlet of disputation of a Christian and a Muslim."[186] It was translated by Peter of Toledo, a Mozarab expert in Arabic, with the help of another Peter, the abbot's secretary who scrupulously watched over the Latin.[187]

Al-Kindi's account of the monk Bahira Sergius was included by Peter the Venerable in his own compositions against the "nefarious" heresy of the Saracens. It was widely used, in various excerpted forms, by a great number of medieval writers who were delighted to buttress their zeal against Islam with apparently historical facts.

In vernacular literature, a century before Langland, the story of Bahira is accurately reported in the *Roman de Mahomet*, a metrical composition based on a twelfth-century Latin poem by a French monk. (See figure 8.) The poet, Alexandre du Pont, takes pains to give us the exact place and date of his work—Laon, 1258—and, most interestingly, follows his source in tracing his material to a converted Muslim, resident of Sens in Burgundy.[188] The attribution must have been most convincing to the poet's audience, for in 1253, according to Matthew Paris, some converted Saracens had arrived in France from the East.[189] Thus, by the time of the *Golden*

Legend (1273), one of Langland's important sources, we have a striving
for authenticity which begins to distinguish myth from historical truth.

The legend of Muhammad as a Roman cardinal who founded a new
religion out of spite has been traced to the work of French grammarians in
the eleventh and twelfth centuries.[190] In the age of Dante, it is particularly
evident in northern Italy, where it is told by Brunetto Latini, who names
the cardinal Pelagio, called "malchonmetto" after his fall.[191] The idea of
the "pseudopropheta" as a Christian renegade, developed from a natural
confusion of the person of Muhammad with that of his traditional teacher,
has taken hold of the Christian imagination. But the heart of the matter is
Dante's own view of Muhammad as a divisive force, "seminator di
scandalo e di scisma" (*Inferno* xxviii, 63).

"Before the gross ignorance displayed in . . . crude misrepresenta-
tions," writes Asín Palacios, "the sober picture drawn by Dante stands
as a silent rebuke to his contemporaries. One is tempted to think that
Dante was content to depict Mahomet as a mere conqueror, not because
he was unaware of the other sides to his character, but because the portrayal of these would have been incompatible with the absurd image
stereotyped on the minds of his readers."[192] In the *Divine Comedy*, the
horribly mutilated figure of Muhammed towers over the anonymous mass
of deformed corpses on the battlefield, speaking its warning against heresy
and schism.[193] Like the rest of his contemporaries, Dante did not consider
Muhammad as the founder of a religion but as an instigator of heretical
strife. The matter was pursued by the early commentators of Dante who
added the two ingredients we find in Langland: the legend of the cardinal
and the miracle of the dove.

At the time of Langland, the popularity of Muhammad as a Roman
cardinal is exemplified in France by the "life" of Muhammad which is
included in the *Roman de Renart le Contrefait*, a satirical work composed in
the first half of the fourteenth century by Jean le Clerc of Troyes.[194]

In a version extant in Champagne, Muhammad was the wisest and
most learned of cardinals. His reputation as a preacher was such that he
was urged by the sacred college to convert the Saracens in the East. He
first refused to undertake this mission but was met by the promise that he
should be pope. Muhammad left Rome on that condition. He attracted
great crowds of Saracens wherever he preached and converted them to
Christianity. However, upon the death of the ruling pontiff, the cardinals
broke their promise and elected another. Muhammad's revenge was to
divert the people from the path he had shown them and to preach the
contrary of Christian truth.[195]

A special touch is provided by an account of Muhammad's death in
another variant of the poem in which Renart recounts universal history
in prose. The account clearly draws the baptismal scenes of Saracens in

medieval romance into the fabric of the clerical view that baptized Saracens were essentially prodigal sons returning to the Christian fold:

> Toutteffois quant il deüst morir, il fist aporter de l'eaue et le fist jetter sur sa teste, et ce fu en signifiance que nul ne pooit estre sauvé sans baptesme, et oncquez puis mot ne parla. Et pour ce, ilz ne leur peüst exposer la cause pour quoy il se fist jetter de l'eaue sur la teste. Maint dient qu'il se repenti qu'il avoit si mal preschiet. Et a la cause ditte, les Sarrasins se font jeter de l'eaue sur leur testes, quant ilz doivent morir, et si ne scevent pour quoy, car oncquez Mahonmet ne leur exprima la cause.[196]

> [When he was about to die, he had water brought to him and had it poured on his head and that had the significance that nobody could be saved without baptism, and he never after said a word. And because of that, he could not explain the reason to them why he had water poured on his head. Many say that he repented having preached such evil things. And because of that the Saracens have water poured on their heads when they are about to die and they do not know why, for Muhammad never explained the reason to them.]

Langland's account of the Muslim prophet, though liberal to "Sarasenes and scismatikes" (B xi, 115) by medieval standards, followed the literary tradition which Dante shunned. The tale of Muhammad in the C-version is associated with the *Golden Legend*:

> Ac meny manere men ther beoth · as Sarrasyns and Iewes,
> Louyeth nat that lorde a-ryght · as by the Legende Sanctorum,
> And lyuen oute of leel by-leyue · for their leyue in a mene.
> A man that hihte Makamede · for Messye thei hym heolde,
> And after hus lerynge thei lyuen · and by lawe of kynde.
>   [C xviii, 156–60]

However, Jacob de Voragine, its author, was aware of the mythic elements in the literary tradition as distinct from what was "truer history." Thus the matter of Muhammad as a Christian clerk and the miracle of the dove are known to be the "table-talk" of romance, while the Bahira legend, the teaching of the heretical Christian monk, is history: "Thus it is sayd comynlye, but thys that shal here folowe is had fro more trewer hystorye," runs Caxton's translation in the account of Muhammad in the *Golden Legend*.[197] Among Langland's contemporaries Ranulf Higden took care to paraphrase this statement in his own account of the "pseudo-propheta" in the *Polychronicon*: "Ista praetacta vulgariter traduntur, sed quod sequitur magis communiter approbatur."[198]

Langland, however, chose to follow an account of Muhammad which

the *Golden Legend* and Higden expressly called popular ("vulgariter"). In
Trevisa's translation, contemporary with the C-version, the story is
chronicled as follows:

> Þanne þe fifte pope Bonefas his tyme, while Heraclius regnede,
> aboute þe ȝere of oure Lord sixe hondred and twenty, Machometis
> þe false prophete þe whiche bygiled þe Ismaelitis [and] Agarenes in
> þis manere. A famous clerk was at the court of Rome and myȝt nouȝt
> spede at his wille, and passede [þe see, and plesede meny] men, and
> hadde hem at his assent. Among þe whiche he byhet Machometis
> þat he wolde make hym prince of his peple ȝif he wolde doo as he
> seide. Þanne þis clerk fedde up a colver and made hym fecche his
> mete in Machometis ere, for þere he dede þe corn þat the colver
> schulde ete, and þerof þe colver ofte schulde fede hym self. Þanne in
> a day þis clerk gadrede þe peple to geders, and byheet þat he wolde
> make hym here prince whom þe Holy Goost wolde schewe in colveres
> liche, and lete fle his colver anon, and þe colver, as he was i-woned,
> satte uppon Machometus his schuldres, and putte his bele in
> Machometus his eres; þerfore Machometus was i-chose prince and
> ledere of þe peple. *Þis þat is i-seide in þe comyn table but what now foloweþ*
> *is more alowed and apreved.* A monk þat heet Sergius was i-put out of þe
> companye of þe monkes þat he was among for he was i-falle into
> Nistorius his errour. He com into Arabia, and putte hym self to
> Machometus, and enformed hym; þeiȝ it be i-rad þat þis Sergius
> were archedecon of Antiochia oþer patriark of Ierusalem. Þanne
> Machometus faderles [and moderless] was in his emes kepynge in
> his childhode; he worschipped mawmetrie somwhat of tyme wiþ his
> contrey men of Arabia, and he ȝaf hym specialiche to worschippe
> Venus, and þerfore it is þat ȝit the Saracens holdeþ þe Fridy holy as þe
> Iewes dooþ þe Satirday and we þe Soneday. After þat Machometus
> com to age, and was scharp of witte, and wente into meny londes
> by cause of marchaundise, and ofte was in companye of Iewes and
> of Cristen men, and lernede þe maneres and usages and customs of
> boþe lawes of Cristen men and of Iewes, and kouþe boþe wicchecraft
> and nigromancie, and was a wonderfel man and fer castynge, and
> hadde nobil ffacounde and faire speche.[199]

Like the Middle English romances, Higden takes note of pre-Islamic
paganism by describing Muhammad in his childhood as worshipping
"mawmetrie" (idolorum cultui deservivit) with his countrymen of
Arabia. However, when he became their leader, "he forbeed þe paynims
mametrie," translates Trevisa.[200] The association of Islam with classical
pagan gods, so persistent in the romances, is explained in a logical way:
the Saracens worship Venus, as they observe Friday, the day of Venus—

an assertion which, throughout the Middle Ages, was supported by the celebrated carnality of Muhammad's life and tales of the Muhammadan paradise.[201]

All this is ignored in Langland's account of Muhammad. Its purpose in *Piers Plowman* is single-minded: the portrayal of Muhammad as a corrupted Christian abusing the power of the Holy Ghost—the dove, like the Christians of Langland's own age. The moral of this was so important that Langland deliberately ignored the doubts about the veracity of his version in the *Golden Legend*, which he knew. In this he resembles Vincent de Beauvais who, in *Speculum Historiale*, gave the legend of Muhammad and the dove widespread respectability. The tale of the dove is the first of the "signs and prodigies" which Muhammad, says Vincent, wishing to attract the people to his side by mitigating the severe laws of Jews and Christians, fraudulently used to land his claim to prophecy miraculous support.[202]

Al-Kindi's *Apology*, which Vincent knew, made short shrift of the miracles claimed for Muhammad by Arab tradition in which his power over animals was involved. It pointed out that the Prophet himself disclaimed miracles as proof of his mission. Indeed, says al-Kindi, "do we not see that multitudes of these same Arabs did accept his ministry, although they saw no miracles, neither heard of any wonderful work?"[203] Vincent's source for the tale of the dove is an unknown work which he calls "libellus in partibus transmarinis de Machometi fallaciis."[204] A contemporary of Vincent, Matthew Paris, cites a "narratio" of Muhammad which, he says, Gregory IX received from the Orient in 1236. The account was written for the use of preachers, "specialiter in partes Orientales destinatus."[205] There Muhammad's own refutation of miracles is clearly reported. The author lays stress on Muhammad's respect for the Old and New Testaments, his abomination of idolatry, and his adoption of circumcision and "baptism." There is no trace of the fantasies of the Muslim prophet as a Roman cardinal or of a spurious Holy Ghost as a dove in Muhammad's ear.

Vincent's use of the material about Muhammad which he collected illuminates a method that also distinguishes Langland's approach. It is clearly distinct from the "lewed" missionary zeal of the Middle English romances but also from the refreshingly sober reservations of "lered" medieval clerks. Langland, like Vincent, sought "facts rather than arguments, but facts useful for polemic."[206]

The second coming, in the vision of *Piers Plowman*, is preceded by a time deformed by "Makomet and Mede." This formulaic coupling of the prophet Muhammad with the root of Antichristian evil, *cupiditas*, is a reflection of a propagandistic idea, generally prevalent in medieval literary works: Muhammad was an idol made of gold—the golden calf of the biblical desert. Throughout the Middle Ages and late into the Renaissance, "mahimet," "maumet," "mahum" was the generic word for a false god or an idolatrous image: "Here he prophecies of þe destruction of Beel, þat was principal maumet of þe Babilonies," runs a Middle English biblical commentary on Isaiah 46.[207]

It is hard to determine what the audience of the romances really believed about Islam and its prophet, but traces of serious religious debate were incorporated in the romances as well. The fight of Roland and the Saracen giant, Vernagu, for example, is marked by religious questions and answers between the champions that raise the most important doctrinal issues in the medieval polemics between Christianity, Judaism, and Islam: the divinity of Jesus, the virgin birth, and the concept of the Trinity.[208]

Though Saracens, in the romances, like Vernagu, mostly accept the Christian assumption that victory in battle is an indication of the superiority of the winner's religion and, like the sultan of Babylon, berate their god in defeat, they also exemplify whatever religious tolerance there is. "Honour thy god as I shall mine," says Ermin to Beues of Hamtoun, reminding his disoriented Christian prisoner of Christmas:

> Þe Sarasin be-held and louȝ:
> "Þis dai," a seide, "i knowe well inouȝ:
> Þis is þe ferste dai of ȝoul,
> Þe god was boren wiþ outen doul;
> For þi men maken þer mor blisse
> Þan men do her in heþenesse:
> Anoure þe god, so i schel myn,
> Boþe Mahoun and Apolyn."
>
> [*Beues of Hamtoun*, ll. 599–606]

While Christian knights in Saracen lands are invariably characterized by a fierce missionary spirit, the striking lack of religious fanaticism in their Saracen opponents is not due to the poet's sophistication. It is the result of his unwillingness to put vilifying statements about Christianity into anyone's mouth. The Christian knight conducts a *jihād*, a holy war with fire and sword:

> Þanne sire Beues and sire Gii,
> Al þe londe of Ermony
> Hii made cristen wiþ dent of swerd,
> ȝong and elde, lewed and lered.
>
> [ll. 4017–20]

All a Muslim can do is break and insult his impotent gods in defeated frustration:

> "O fals goddis, that ye beth,
> I have trustid to longe youre mode.
> We were lever to suffr dede,
> Than lif this life here lenger nowe.
> I haue almoste loste the breth,
> xij fals traytours me overe-lede,
> And stroyen alle þat I haue.
> Ye fals goddis, the devel youe spede!
> Ye make me nowe for to rave;
> Ye do fayle me at my nede."
> In Ire he smote Mahounde,
> That was of goolde fulle rede,
> That he fille down to the grounde,
> As he had bene dede.
>
> [*Sowdone of Babylone*, ll. 2497–2510]

There could not have been a psychologically more satisfying way of disposing of an "enemy alien." As Norman Daniel has put it: "In the Middle Ages the evident harm caused by Islam—in medieval eyes—was too great and too effective to allow scope for generosity of attitude," even in the face of better knowledge. However, "there is little that is similarly absurd outside the poetic field."[209]

The greatest absurdity consistently perpetrated "in the poetic field" was the idea that Muhammad, Apollo, and "Termagant" constituted a pagan counter-trinity. How this idea got into the chansons de geste, which propagated it throughout Western Europe, is a matter for analysts of war propaganda. To the proclaimers of the Reconquest of Spain and the First Crusade facts were irrelevant. We know from modern experience that Grégoire's explanation is undoubtedly closest to the truth:

> Je crois pouvoir montrer qu'il y a eu une intention, et une intention très particulière et très perfide, et que l'accusation de polythéisme formulée contre les musulmans, à la veille même de la Première Croisade, n'est pas absolument gratuite, je veux dire inventée de toutes pièces. . . . Par définition, l'inventeur du thème doit être un clerc, un théologien et un "humaniste."[210]

There are indications, in the textual history of the *Song of Roland*, that the linking of Islam with classical pagan gods and an assortment of mythical deities of obscure origin may have been the work of a redactor at the end of the eleventh century or the beginning of the twelfth.[211] The chroniclers of the First Crusade consistently speak of Saracen "gods."[212] The conclusion is that "wherever it was possible to insinuate that those who reproached Christianity with a polytheist tendency were themselves inclined to the same crime, this was done."[213] The assumption, in the romances, that an image of Muhammad was worshipped, may have a rational explanation in stories about the Black Stone of the Kaaba.[214] The idea of the Muslim prophet as god may have derived from such garbled versions of the Muslim profession of faith as "non est Deus nisi Machimetus."[215] But the propagation of a pagan Saracen trinity in the romances appears to be the invention of a zealous medieval clerk who saracenized the classical pantheon for the purpose and may have fished "trivigant" out of a Latin reference to "trivia," an invocation of the moon by three of its names.[216] Laȝamon, in whose *Brut* "Teruagant" makes his first appearance in Middle English, turns the tables in considering him a Roman rather than a Saracen god.[217] In the century of Chaucer and Langland, however, when the knowledge of Islam as a monotheistic religion was widespread, we still have a Muslim sultan regaling the populace by invoking "Termagaunte" and defying "Mahounde and Apolyne, / Iubiter, Ascarot," though, mercifully, "and Alcaron [the Koran] also" (*Sowdone of Babylone*, ll. 137, 2761–62).

The Muslim Paradise as the Land of Cockayne

The standard medieval notion of the Muslim paradise in Western Europe derived from no less an authority than Petrus Alfonsi:

> Promisit itaque Deus sibi & Mahometh suo fideli prophetae credentibus, legisque eius mandata complentibus, paradisum, id est, hortum deliciarum, praeter fluentibus aquis irriguum, in quo sedes habebunt perpetuas. Proteget eos arborum umbra, nec frigore affligentur, neque calore. Omnium fructuum, omnium ciborum vescentur generibus. Quicquid appetitus cuique suggeret coram se confestim inveniet. Sericis induentur vestibus omnicoloribus. Accubabunt in deliciis, & angeli pincernarum ministerio inter eos cum vasis aureis & argenteis deambulabunt, in aureis lac, in argenteis vinum offerentes, & dicentes. Comedite & bibite in omni laetitia, & quod vobis Deus promisit ecce completum est. Iungentur virginibus, quas nec humanus, nec daemoniacus violauit contactus, hiacinthi coraliique splendore forma praestantioribus.[218]

The "garden of delights" (*hortus deliciarum*) that Petrus Alfonsi depicts follows the description in the Koran, centering on Sura 69:

> So he shall be in a life of pleasure, in a lofty garden, the fruit of which are near at hand: "Eat and drink pleasantly for what you did beforehand in the days gone by."[219]

Thus the earliest account in Latin, around 1106, reaching France and England from Spain, from one who was nurtured among Muslims and knew their language, presented the Muslim paradise as a perfect reali-zation of "this-worldliness"[220] in religious thought. Paradise is a dream-land of earthly desire: whatever one's appetite suggests is at once fulfilled.

The idea was impressed on the Western imagination by Peter the Venerable who, leaning heavily on the translation of the Koran which he sponsored in 1143, depicts a paradise of sensual earthly delights that undermines every notion of Christian spirituality:

> Paradysum non societatis angelicae, nec uisionis diuinae, nec summi illius boni quod "nec oculus uidit, nec auris audiuit, nec in cor hominis ascendit," [Isaiah 64:4; 1 Cor. 2:9] sed uere talem, qualem caro et sanguis, immo fex carnis et sanguinis concupiscebat, qualem-que sibi parari optabat, depinxit. Ibi carnium et omnigenorum fructuum esum, ibi lactis et mellis riuulos, et aquarum splendentium, ibi pulcherrimarum mulierum et uirginum amplexus et luxus, in quibus tota eius paradysus finitur, sectatoribus suis promittit.[221]

Encompassed by warnings but stirring the senses, the Muslim paradise dramatically made its entrance into Western literature as a land of Cock-ayne.

The first description of a Western paradise of the senses called "Coca-gne" is found in a French poem of the thirteenth century. A medieval Dutch version follows the French fairly closely, while the Middle English poem, *The Land of Cockayne*, preserved in a manuscript of the first quarter of the fourteenth century, is a more freely conceived composition that culminates in a satire against monks and nuns.[222]

The English land of Cockayne is an island region which, above all, abounds in excellent food and drink. Even the walls of buildings are made of "rich met, / þe likfullist þat man mai et." Everyone may eat his fill to his heart's content. Rivers flow with oil, milk, honey, and wine. Luscious fruit trees include a tree of rare spices which gives out sweet odors. Birds sing. Four wells, gushing with healing waters, overflow into streams that drench the whole landscape in precious stones and gold. There are pillars of crystal, green jasper, and red coral. Glass windows turn into translu-cent crystal. There is no death in the land, life is eternal, and there is perpetual light of day. Last but not least, each vigorous male may have twelve wives every year.

While the flying roast geese, baked larks, pies, and puddings of the land of Cockayne give it the earthy flavor of a peasants' utopia with deep sociological roots in the reality of *Piers Plowman* and the Peasants' Re-volt,[223] the stock motifs of the land of delights—rivers of balm, streams and riverbeds of precious stones, an abundance of fruit, sweet odors, and singing birds—are strictly literary features. They were particularly prominent in depictions of the earthly paradise which the Middle English

poet is careful to distinguish from Cockayne. Both are "under heuen."
But while Cockayne is a place bursting with the good things of life and
fellowship, the earthly paradise, in the poem, is a deserted land inhabited
by only two patriarchs, Elias and Enoch. Its description by the medieval
poet resembles the pastoral New World in the quizzical view of Henry
James. There is no hall, no bower, no bench; all we have is grass, flowers,
green trees, and water:

> What is þer in Paradis
> Bot grasse and flure and grene ris?
> Þoȝ þer be ioi and gret dute,
> Þer nis met bote frute;
>
> Þer nis halle, bure, no bench,
> Bot watir manis þurst to quench.
> Beþ þer no men bot two—
> Hely and Enok also.[224]

The splendors of light, color, and music of the traditional earthly paradise
have been transferred to Cockayne—the dreamland of true human
desire. The heavenly paradise is completely ignored in the poem. Perhaps
the goliardic spirit stopped short of blasphemy. It is abundantly clear that
a disembodied existence in heaven, even in perpetuity, was felt by poet
and audience to be no compensation for an ideal life of well-being here on
earth. Paradise, says the fox to the wolf, calling from the pit in *The Fox
and the Wolf*, is an absence of hunger and woe:

> Her is þe blisse of Paradiis—
> Her Ich mai euere wel fare,
> Wiþouten pine, wiþouten kare.
> Her is mete, her is drinke;
> Her is blisse wiþouten swinke.
> Her nis hounger neuermo,
> Ne non oþer kunnes wo—.
> Of alle gode her is inou![225]

The comic juxtaposition of "paradise" and "the land of Cockayne"
suggests the paradoxical effect of precisely the type of admonition which
Peter the Venerable directed to his fellow Christians in warning them
against the Saracen "heresy." The contrast between the "angelic society"
of the Christian paradise and the carnal delights of eternal bliss envisaged
by Muslims as a serious religious concept must have presented an almost
irresistible temptation to the imagination of the most pious and other-
worldly. Given the goliardic character of the comic antitype of paradise, it
is generally assumed that the parody was inspired by classical authors,

especially by the "Isle of the Blest" of Lucian.[226] It stands to reason, however, that the clerical indictments of Muslim delights also served to propagate the Muslim paradise in alluring detail. The involuntary but inevitable result was to implant a "counter-paradise" in the popular mind which gave comic and thoroughly human relief to the strain of Christian ideals. The land of Cockayne, says the English poet, is "fur in see, bi west Spayngne."[227] The direction is that of "land's end" Finisterre,[228] diametrically opposed to the biblical Eden. To a medieval audience in France and England its location was bound to suggest the vicinity of the western lands of Islam.

The etymology of "cocagne" is still uncertain. The word has been derived from *coco*, Provençal for "cake," and connected with the goliardic "abbas Cucaniensis" who appears as king of the revelers in an early thirteenth-century drinking song.[229] Whatever its derivation, the word is clearly a place-name modeled on familiar countries (e.g., Espagne, Allemagne):

> Li païs a a non Cocaingne;
> Qui plus i dort, plus i gaaigne.

> Sach ye man beter lant
> Dan dat land van Cockaengen?
> Die helft is beter dan al Spaengen,
> Dander helft is beter dan Betouwen.
> Men hefter vil van schonen vrouwen.

> Fur in see, bi west Spayngne,
> is a lond ihote Cokaygne.

There is, however, the obvious suggestiveness of the name as "the land of the cock" and the strange coincidence, never noticed, by which a cock is the guardian of paradise in the most popular account of Islamic paradisial abodes in medieval Europe—the *Liber Scalae* (see figure 9).

The story of the Miraj, the ascension of Muhammad to Paradise, was translated from the Arabic at the court of Alfonso the Wise and forms an integral part of the corpus of Arabic works that entered the ken of medieval Europe in the twelfth and thirteenth centuries. (See figure 10.) The Arabic original, by an anonymous author, as well as the Spanish translation by the royal physician, Abraham of Toledo, are lost. What we have is a French version, dated May 1264 and preserved in a unique manuscript, presumably of English origin, at Oxford, and a Latin version in two manuscripts.[230] Both translations, into French and Latin, were done by Bonaventura de Siena of Seville, notary and scribe of Alfonso the Wise:

> Hic incipit liber, qui arabice uocatur Halmahereig, quod latine interpretatur in altum ascendere. Hunc autem librum fecit Macho-

metus et imposuit ei hoc nomen; et ideo sic a gentibus appellatur. Denotat quidem liber ascensum Machometi, quomodo ipse per scalam ascendit in celum. . . . et uidit omnia mirabilia, que sibi Deus ostendit. . . .[231]

The "Book of the Ladder" comprises eighty-five chapters in which the prophet himself, in the first person ("ego Machometus, filius Abdillehe, oriundus de Arabia, de ciuitate Mecke"),[232] guided by the angel Gabriel, and ascending through seven heavens to the eighth heaven, describes how he reached the sight of the heavenly throne and saw several paradisial abodes.

The account of the paradisial regions begins at chapter xxx and is introduced, at chapter xxix, by a curious sight: the prophet Muhammad is shown a cock whose crest reaches to the heavenly throne and whose feet to the extremes of the earth, while his wings, when opened, encompass the whole world from Orient to Occident. This cock is an angel of God—"Et ce ange estoit en figure de coc." (The prophet first sees him earlier, at chapter ix, after meeting the angel of death and before entering the first heaven.) When this cock praises God, "toz les cocs dient autretel; et issinc font tottes les foies, quil chante." The description of the cock is rather elaborate:

> Et apres ce ie regardei la facon de ce coc, et ui quil auoit les pennes grosses par dessus, totes blanches si merueilleusement que nul porroit conter la blanquour delles; et la menue plume par de soz estoit si tresuerd qua la lor uerdour nul ne la porroit dire ne penser. Et certes ie nauoie molt grant delit et grant sollas en lui regarder, si que ie ne men pooie saoller.[233]

> [And after that I looked at the appearance of the cock, and saw that he had big feathers on top, so marvelously white that nobody could describe their whiteness, and the down underneath was so green that nobody could imagine or speak of its greenness. And certainly I had great delight and great comfort in looking at it so that I could not get enough of it.]

In the legends of Muslim tradition (*ḥadīth*) on which the account in the *Liber Scalae* is based the cock appears as follows:

> Praise be to God: There is a white cock, whose two wings are set with emeralds and pearls, one of the wings being in the East and the other in the West, whose head is under the Throne (of God), and whose legs are in the air; it calls to prayer every morning at dawn, and the people of the heavens and the earth, excepting the two classes of heavy beings, men and genii, hear that crowing, and the

cocks of the earth respond to it at that time. When the Day of Judgment will draw near, God will say to it, "Fold thy wings and lower thy voice," upon which the people of the heavens and the earth, excepting the two classes of heavy beings, men and genii, will know that the Hour of Judgment has approached.[234]

The gateway to the seven paradisial abodes of Islam is thus in the guardianship of a gigantic cock.

In his investigation of the influence of the *Liber Scalae* on Dante's vision of Paradise, Asín Palacios has specifically related Dante's image of the eagle in the heaven of Jupiter to the Muslim angel in the form of a cock.[235] Whatever the historical relation of the Muslim cock to Christian eschatology, the French and Latin versions of the *Liber Scalae* are sufficient evidence on one point. In the thirteenth century, the Muslim association of paradise with a cock was known in Spain, Italy, France, and England.

The seven distinct paradisial abodes of Muslim tradition are fully described in the *Liber Scalae*:

> . . . ego Machometus ivi per omnes Paradisos. Et, dum per illos modo hic modo illuc respiciendo sic irem, ecce vidi quod Paradisi facti erant maneriebus diversis et quod unus melior erat aliis. Hoc autem fecit Deus ut plus gracie plusque honoris conferat eis quos dilexerat ipse magis. Didici quoque Paradisorum nomina, et dicam vobis prout ipsorum quilibet nominatur. Sciatis quod primus ubi factus est Adam, de quo locutus sum vobis, nominatur "Heden," secundus "Daralgelel," tercius "Daralzelem," quartus "Genet halmaulz," quintus "Genet halkode," sextus "Genet halfardauz," et septimus "Genet hanaym." Hic autem septimus est velut castrum Paradisorum; nam ipse alcior est aliis, et de ipso potest homo cunctos alios respicere Paradisos. Ad hunc eciam venit Deus quando vult Paradisos videre. Et hic est, cum illuc venit, proprie domus ejus.[236]

The enumeration begins with the Garden of Eden, "where Adam was made" and leads through various other gardens to the "castle of paradises," the most elevated point, from which "man can see all other paradises" and which is the proper house of God.

It must be noted that in the legend of the prophet's ascension the earthly paradise has been bodily transferred into the heavenly regions.[237] It is separated from the highest Garden of Delight (*jannat an-naʿīm*) "to which God Himself comes when he wishes to view the other paradises" by five other paradisial enclosures, each of which is "better than the others": they are the abode of glory (*dār al-jalāl*); the abode of peace (*dār as-salām*); the garden of refuge (*jannat al-maʾwa*); the garden of eternity (*jannat al-khuld*); and the garden of paradise (*jannat al-firdaus*).

The reason for the variety is explained by the angel Gabriel: what is called Paradise is nothing but delight. But God distributes this delight in various ways and gives it to each of the believers according to merit.[238] We have therefore intermediary stages of pleasure, experienced in different enclosures and gardens of well-being that abound in the kind of sensuous imagery which in medieval vernacular literature typifies descriptions of the earthly paradise and the land of Cockayne.

In chapter xxix, Muhammad, having reached the highest point of ascent in heaven, sees the paradisial cock in a backward glance which encompasses all the celestial regions: "ecce spiritus Dei me duxit per omnes celos; et omnia, que primo per more spacium videram, fecit me in momento unico revidere."[239] In this vision Gabriel first guides him to the great Wall of Adam's Paradise. The wall is built of precious stones. They are square in shape but arranged in a mosaic of gold, ruby, and silver which radiates a blinding light. The mortar holding the stones together is musk and amber moistened with rose water—a combination of odors so sweet to the senses as to defy description. Once inside, the Prophet finds himself in a region "que ce estoit la plus bele chose, qu'om poust penser." All is bathed in pure light, there is neither day nor night, neither sun, nor moon, nor stars—"la clarte qu'i est si est tresgrant que la clarte du soleil est autele ver celle clarte com est la clarte d'une estoille ver celui du soleil."[240]

The garden, "towards the part of the East whence the sun comes," is full of shade-giving trees and is traversed by four biblical rivers flowing with honey, milk, wine, and fragrant water in such a way as to change the honey, milk, and wine into water when they leave paradisial territory. The entrance gate is marked by two columns; one of emerald and one of ruby, which between them encompass the distance between Orient and Occident. All paradisial abodes Muhammad sees in the heavens radiate the luminousness of the biblical visionary books. There are cities and castles, walls and towers, palaces, mansions, halls, chambers, and pavilions all transfigured by a blinding profusion of light. An infinite variety of trees grows in these gardens. Their sweet-smelling fruit is more magnificent than rubies and emeralds. The rivers that flow glitter with manifold colors. In the "Garden of Delight," there is a riverbed of precious stones in a landscape of sapphire mountains that contain mines of silver, gold, and a multitude of gems. The imagery is often cumulative and repetitious. Musk and amber provide the redolent formula in almost all the gardens that the prophet sees, and there are gardens within gardens behind walled enclosures which blur the distinction between the various kinds of paradise. There are also unique touches which characterize Paradise as a specifically Islamic domain; for example, the faithful are transported from bliss to bliss in a caravan of spotless white camels.[241]

Most important is the detailed description of the ultimate "Garden of Delight" (*jannat an na'ïm*) "qui est propre la maison de Diex en Paradis et plus ault de toz les autres." It is a garden "compliement habundant de tottes delices que cueor d'ome puisse penser." Its walls are of rubies, so are the towers and mansions within. Their interiors contain opulent couches and coverlets and, in particular, doors made of pearls. Amorous maidens of indescribable beauty and gaiety await the faithful to dispense unspeakable bliss. Pavilions are made of rubies, emeralds, pearls, and a variety of precious stones more beautiful and wonderful than the heart of man can imagine. The pavilions are set over fountains of water and wine of manifold colors and taste. The air is filled with the sweet song of maidens sitting under trees of precious stones, their fruit tastier and sweeter than anything else in the world. Below this garden are two other gardens, one of which is completely encircled inside and outside by precious stones; the other is made of the purest red gold. The Garden of Delight itself is constructed of one hundred steps, each of them so high and wide that it would take a man two hundred and fifty years to traverse them in either direction; "and of these steps one was of gold, another of silver, another of ruby, another of emerald, another of pearl, and thus were in this manner all hundred." As in all other gardens, the mortar that holds the steps together consists of musk and amber "que fleroit ad merveille bien."[242]

The presence of the *Liber Scalae* at Oxford, in a French manuscript of the first quarter of the fourteenth century, most probably of English provenance, has suggested a relationship to fourteenth-century Middle English works which use an analogous pattern of imagery.[243] On the model of Asín Palacios, an attempt has been made to link the *Liber Scalae* even to so strictly biblical a poem as *Pearl*, a profusion of pearl imagery, pearl-maidens, and a luminousness transcending the light of sun and moon being as characteristic of the paradise which the Prophet sees as of the Heavenly City of *Revelation*.[244] A more likely example of the possible influence of non-Christian paradisial abodes is "the proud court of paradise" in *Sir Orfeo*. Orfeo's passage through a cave leads him to an Other World meadow of Celtic mythology and what he sees there also reflects the type of paradisial imagery we find in the *Liber Scalae*:

> Amidde þe lond a castel he siȝe,
> Riche & real & wonder heiȝe:
> Al þe vt-mast wal
> Was clere & schine as cristal;
> An hundred tours þer were about,
> Degiselich & bataild stout;
> Þe butras com out of þe diche
> Of rede gold y-arched riche;

Þe vousour was auowed al
Of ich maner diuers aumal.
Wiþ-in þer wer wide wones,
Al of precious stones;
Þer werst piler on to biholde
Was al of burnist gold.
Al þat lond was euer liȝt,
For when it schuld be þerk & niȝt
Þe riche stones liȝt gonne
As briȝt as doþ at none þe sonne.
No man may telle, no þenche in þouȝt,
Þe riche werk þat þer was wrouȝt:
Bi al þing him þink þat it is
Þe proude court of Paradis.[245]

The serious representation of paradise in medieval Christian literature undoubtedly relied on the visionary books of the Bible and their exegetical tradition. But the role of Muslim eschatology in inspiring the *comic* idea of paradise does not seem to be farfetched. To the Western public the Muslim garden of delight was the antitype par excellence of the Christian paradise. The fantasy of eating savory dishes to one's heart's content without the effort of preparation is central in Muhammad's vision of "the Paradise of Eternity" in the *Liber Scalae*. There the faithful finds a set table ("une table mise devant soi") which gives him all the food and drink he wants. The dishes are not described in detail. We simply learn that as soon as the faithful put their hands on the table they are as easily satisfied as if they had eaten all the food in the world ("si tost com il metront lor mayns sor la table, il seront si saollez com s'il eussent mangies tottes le viandes du monde"). There is, however, a tree which gives seventy thousand salvers of prepared viands comprising all manner of meat and fowl.

> Et sachez que ces oiseaux n'ont point de plumes ne de pennes ne nul os; et si ne sunt cuiz ne en aive ne ad feu rostiz. Et sunt ausinc savoreus ad mangier com bur et miel mesleez ensenble. Et si flerent ad musc et ad ambre. Et de ces mangiers mangerunt il tant com il voudrunt, deus foiz li iour au disner et au supper; et li derreain morsel de ces viandes le serra ausinc savoreus com le primier.[246]

> [And know that these birds have no feathers nor pinions nor any bone; and they are not cooked in water nor roasted in any fire. And they are as tasty to eat as butter and honey mixed together. And so they smell of musk and ambergris. And of these they will eat as much as they want twice a day for dinner and for supper; and the last morsel of these viands will be as tasty as the first.]

The *Liber Scalae* contains a significant number of features which formed the literary landscape of both paradise and counter-paradise in Western literature. It is, at the least, a valuable analogue of the descriptions of the earthly paradise in Europe. The fact that it was translated into the vernacular as early as 1264 shows that it was known in France and, on the evidence of the Bodleian manuscript, in England. It must be stressed, however, that there is no evidence of direct borrowing; and specific details, like the jeweled "tube" tree, for instance,[247] are conspicuously absent in the best-known poetic depictions of the paradisial abodes. The presence of the book at Oxford at a crucial time for the impact of works from the Arabic suggests a possible current of influence, however submerged. Its most natural direction would take us to the idea of a paradise of the senses and its crystallization in luscious and voluptuous imagery.

7

The Voyages and Travels of Sir John Mandeville

"And whoso that wole may leve me yif he wille.
And who wille not may leue also."

Chapter XXIII

When Herman Melville, almost two decades after his Near Eastern journey, published his extraordinary poem *Clarel*, he was giving the public some account of his actual experience as a traveler. There were, however, a number of standard books on the Bible Lands which he purchased and used while composing *Clarel*. Their influence is clearly discernible in the poem, not only in the description of scenes and sites but in the structure of the poem itself.[1] It is with the story of *Clarel* in mind that we best approach the most popular travel book of the Middle Ages, *Mandeville's Travels*. Its most recent editor, M. C. Seymour, casts strong doubt on the proclaimed author and on the authenticity of the work as a personal account of genuine travel by one "Mandeville":

> It is perhaps ironical that this exotic book should overshadow the popularity of Marco Polo's *Divisament dou Monde*, and that the genuine and truthful traveller should be dubbed *Il Milione*, a liar who described everything in millions, while the fictitious "Mandeville" should be believed by all. For *Mandeville's Travels* is a compilation at second-hand of other men's travels and contains a sufficient number of inaccuracies and inconsistencies to make it extremely improbable that its author ever left his native Europe.[2]

If we look at the genuine and truthful traveler, Marco Polo, we find in him several features of Mandeville. Marco Polo, says Leonardo Olschki,

> dictated the *Milione* not so much for the information of travellers, traders and cosmographs, as mainly for the enjoyment of his contemporaries who eagerly yearned for this kind of pleasant instruction in an epoch of prevailing didactic interests in culture and literature. Thus all the positive and practical information offered by this book on the basis of personal experience and observation appears in a tidy and elaborated frame of tales of wonders of Hellenistic, biblical and Islamic origin. . . . the literary image of Asia was so deeply rooted in the medieval culture that it determined the character and the structure of Marco Polo's book.[3]

John Mandeville the traveler must therefore still be given some benefit of doubt. He cannot be altogether dismissed as a Baron Münchhausen because the attempts to pierce his anonymity have so far failed. After centuries of effort, for that matter, we still have no clue to the author of *Pearl* and *Gawain and the Green Knight*, contemporary and acquainted with *Mandeville's Travels*.[4] In the book the fourteenth-century author purports to speak for himself:

> And for als moche as it is longe tyme passed that ther was no gen-eralle passage ne vyage ouer the see, and many men desiren for to here speke of the Holy Lond and han thereof gret solace and comfort, I John Maundevylle knyght, alle be it I be not worthi, that was born in Englond in the town of Seynt Albones, and passed the see in the yeer of oure lord Ihesu Crist m.ccc. and xxii. in the day of Seynt Michelle; and hiderto haue ben long tyme ouer the see and haue seyn and gon thorgh manye dyuerse londes and many prouynces and kyngdomes and iles; and haue passed thorghout Turkye, Ermonye the Litylle and the Grete, thorgh Tartarye, Percye, Surrye, Arabye, Egypt the High and the Lowe, thorgh Lybye, Caldee, and a gret partie of Ethiope, thorgh Amazoyne, Inde the Lasse and the More a gret partie, and thorghout many othere iles that ben abouten Inde where dwellen many dyuerse folk and of dyuerse maneres and lawes and of dyuerse schappes of men; of whiche londes and iles I schalle speke more pleynly hereafter. And I schalle devise you sum partie of things that there ben, whan tyme schalle ben after it may best come to my mynde, and specyally for hem that wille and are in purpos for to visite the holy citee of Ierusalem and the holy places that are thereaboute. And I schalle telle the weye that thei schulle holden thider, for I haue often tymes passed and ryden that way with gode companye of many lordes, God be thonked.[5]

The importance of *Mandeville's Travels* as a true mirror of medieval knowl-edge and fantasy of the East is revealed in almost all European languages. The book, first written in French about 1357, incorporates the reports of several great medieval travelers whose itineraries, in French translation, were compiled by a monk of St. Omer, near Liège, Jean le Long.[6] The major works in this compilation are the account of the Holy Land by William of Boldensele (1336), the journal of Odoric of Pordenone, the Franciscan missionary to the Mongols (1330), and the Tartar Prince Haiton's *Fleurs des Histoires d'Orient* (1308). Mandeville's debt to Marco Polo and William of Rubruck is less certain, but another of Marco Polo's precursors, Friar John de Plano Carpini, entered *Mandeville's Travels* by way of Vincent of Beauvais.[7] On the basis of his sources, "it seems certain that the library to which 'Mandeville' had access was Continental;

many of his sources are not known to have been in England in 1357."[8] What the author tells us himself is that he had written the book in French "because more people understand French than Latin" and translated it out of French into English, "that every man of my nation may understand it." As to the inaccuracies and inconsistencies in his book, the author may be charitably taken to offer his own explanation:

> But lordes and knyghtes and othere noble and worthi men that conne not Latyn but litylle and han ben beyonde the see knowen and vnderstonden yif I seye trouthe or non. And yif I erre in de-visynge for forgetynge or elles, that thei mowe redresse it and amende it. For thinges passed out of longe tyme from a mannes mynde or from his syght turnen sone into forgetynge, because that mynde of man ne may not ben comprehended ne withholden for the freeltee of mankynde.[9]

To the medieval world, Jerusalem was the center of the earth. All roads of medieval travelers, including Mandeville's fascinating con-temporary, Margery Kemp, led first and foremost to the Holy Land and Jerusalem.

Mandeville's Travels is therefore primarily a guide to the Holy Land, as its author says, "to teche you the weye out of Englond to Constantynoble" and then, by way of Cyprus, to Jerusalem.[10] Like Western guidebooks throughout the ages, it covers the "Bible Lands," Egypt and Syria, as well as the manners and customs of their "mysbeleuynge" inhabitants, the Saracens. Its character as a medieval handbook, however, is parti-cularly brought out by its preoccupation with the Tartars and the inclu-sion of fabulous material on the Wonders of the East from the legends of Alexander, some of which had been circulating in England in literary form since A.D. 1000.[11]

Mandeville wrote his book with the knowledge that "many men had gret likyng to here speke of straunge thinges of dyuerse contreyes." In his book these strange things comprise material that was thoroughly familiar, but also puzzling descriptive details which, in the West, are found only in Mandeville. The book is divided into thirty-four sections, beginning with a description of Constantinople and ending with an account of the region of Prester John, the legendary Christian prince of the East. Uniquely in Middle English, the historical stronghold of the Assassins is associated by Mandeville not only with the Earthly Paradise but with the lordship of Prester John.[12]

By 1356, when Mandeville composed his book, fairly accurate informa-tion about the Assassins had been available to the West for almost two centuries. The Old Man of the Mountain and his brotherhood appear as a figure of speech in troubadour poetry; the word *assassino* was used by

Dante.[13] Most strikingly, the oldest literary appearance of the fanatical Isma'ili sect is in five Provençal poems where it is an image for the unswerving loyalty of the feudal relationship between the lover and the beloved: the lover is the lady's Assassin liege man. He is the Assassin who hopes to win paradise through her commands. "Just as the Assassins serve their master unfailingly, so I have served Love with unswerving loyalty," proclaims one troubadour. Another says to his lady: "You have me more fully in your power than the Old Man his Assassins, who go to kill his mortal enemies, even if they were beyond France."[14] The audience of the poets clearly understood the allusion without explanation. Raymond of Tripoli, the first Frankish victim of the Assassins, was killed in 1152. The murder of Conrad of Montferrat by an Assassin, in the streets of Tyre in 1192, directed the attention of the West to the Syrian branch of the sect in the most dramatic way. As a result of this assassination, moreover, the French Crusader king, Philip Augustus, in fear for his life, announced that Richard the Lion-Hearted had induced the Old Man of the Mountain to send assassins to France.[15]

The Western public got its first knowledge of the Assassins from the Crusaders. One of the earliest written accounts by a Western traveler, written in Hebrew between 1164 and 1173, is that of Benjamin of Tudela who set out from Spain to visit Jewish communities in the East. In the neighborhood of Gabala, in the Lebanese mountains, he found

> a people called Al-Hashishim. They do not believe in the religion of Islam, but follow one of their own folk, whom they regard as their prophet, and all that he tells them to do they carry out, whether for death or life. They call him the Sheik Al Hashishim, and he is known as their Elder. At his word these mountaineers go out and come in. . . . They are faithful to each other, but a source of terror to their neighbors, killing even kings at the cost of their own lives. The extent of their land is eight days' journey. And they are at war with the sons of Edom who are called the Franks. . . .[16]

About the same time, in 1175, Emperor Frederick Barbarossa sent an envoy to Egypt and Syria whose report included a description of the Assassins. It is cited in the chronicle of Arnold of Luebeck (d. 1212):

> On the confines of Damascus, Antioch and Aleppo there is a certain race of Saracens in the mountains, who in their own vernacular are called Heissessim. This breed of men live without law; they eat swine's flesh against the law of the Saracens, and make use of all women without distinction, including their mothers and sisters. They live in the mountains and are well-nigh impregnable, for they withdraw into well-fortified castles. They have among them a Master,

who strikes the greatest fear into all the Saracen princes both far and near, as well as the neighbouring Christian lords. For he has the habit of killing them in an astonishing way. The method by which this is done is as follows: this prince possesses in the mountains numerous and most beautiful palaces, surrounded by very high walls, so that none can enter except by a small and very well-guarded door. In these palaces he has many of the sons of his peasants brought up from early childhood. He has them taught various languages, as Latin, Greek, Roman, Saracen, as well as many others. These young men are taught by their teachers from their earliest youth to their full manhood, that they must obey the lord of their land in his words and commands; and that if they do so, he, who has power over all living gods, will give them the joys of paradise. They are also taught that they cannot be saved if they resist his will in anything. Note that, from the time when they are taken in as children, they see no one but their teachers and masters and receive no other instruction until they are summoned to the presence of the Prince to kill someone. When they are in the presence of the Prince, he asks them if they are willing to obey his commands, so that he may bestow paradise upon them. Whereupon, as they have been instructed, and without any objection or doubt, they throw themselves at his feet and reply with fervour, that they will obey him in all things that he may command. Thereupon the Prince gives each one of them a golden dagger and sends them out to kill whichever prince he has marked down.[17]

William of Tyre (d. ca. 1190), the main contemporary historian of the Crusader states, describes an incident in which an envoy of the Assassins was treacherously slain by some brothers of the Knights Templars who thus prevented the Assassins from embracing the faith of Christ. William was aware that the Assassins, an Isma‘ili sect, were heretics in the eyes of traditional Muslims. But he attributed their fanatical hatred of Sunni Islam to the influence of "the gentle and noble doctrine of Christ and His followers." He gives, however, important historical details about the number of their members ("sixty thousand or possibly more") and fortresses (ten) and, most importantly, acknowledges the ignorance of both Christians and Saracens, concerning the origin and meaning of their name. It is also clear from William of Tyre that the designation "Old Man" is simply a translation of *shaikh*—elder (sheik).[18]

The English chronicler Matthew Paris closely follows William's account but he also relies on the chronicle of St. Albans to inform the reader of the detestable Assassins' fury and superstition and their destruction by the less detestable Tartars.[19] It is striking to find Muslim historians expressing their abhorrence of the heretical sect in almost identical language. To them the "detestable doctrine" of the Assassins was prompted by nothing but malice. Its deceitful and treacherous adherents had to be punished and destroyed.[20]

The method of the Assassins in dealing with their enemies is described from the actual experience of Muslims and Christians. In April 1103, writes Ibn al-Qalanisi,

> news was received from Hims that its lord, . . . on descending from the citadel to the mosque for the Friday prayer, surrounded by his principal officers with full armour, and occupying his place of prayer, according to custom, was set upon by three Persians belonging to the Batiniya [i.e., the Isma'ili Assassins]. They were accompanied by a shaikh, to whom they owed allegiance and obedience, and all of them were dressed in the garb of ascetics. When the shaikh gave the signal they attacked the amir with their knives and killed both him and a number of his officers.[21]

The assassination of Conrad of Montferrat, in April 1192, is related by Roger of Hoveden (d. 1201?). Roger ends his account by recording the rumor among the Franks that the deed was perpetrated on the instigation of the king of England—a propagandistic charge spread throughout Europe during Richard's imprisonment in Austria and never fully cleared up.[22]

The liveliest historical account of the castles and valleys of the Assassins from the literary point of view is that of Jacques de Vitry (d. 1240), bishop of Acre. Unlike William of Tyre whom his description closely resembles, Jacques de Vitry mentions the important fact that the sect was not only represented in Syria—to most of the Crusaders the Syrian Assassins were *the* Assassins par excellence—but was also found near Baghdad and in Persia where it came into being. In particular, Jacques de Vitry speaks of the two motifs found in troubadour poetry: the absolute loyalty of all members of the order to the Old Man, their master, and the promise of paradise if they fulfilled his commands—a feature that does not appear in William of Tyre.[23]

With Jacques de Vitry, the parent sect of the Persian Assassins begins to enter Latin accounts until we have a full-fledged description of Alamut (eagle's nest) in northwestern Persia by Marco Polo and his precursors. Both William of Rubruck, in 1253–55, and Marco Polo, passing through Persia in 1273, correctly refer to the Persian Assassins as Muliech or Mulihet, explaining that the word, from Arabic *mulḥid* (plural *malāḥida*, "deviators") signified holders of heretical tenets.[24]

When we compare Mandeville's account of the Assassins with that of Marco Polo we are struck by several features in Mandeville's narration.

Like Marco Polo and Odoric of Pordenone, Mandeville describes the stratagem by which the chief of the Assassins, by means of hashish, induced in his followers the illusion of paradise. Marco Polo's knowledge clearly derived from Muslim sources:

> For the Old Man desired to make his people believe that this was actually Paradise. So he had fashioned it after the description that Mahommet gave of his Paradise, to wit, that it should be a beautiful garden running with conduits of wine and milk and honey and water, and full of lovely women for the delectation of all its inmates. . . . So when the Old Man would have any Prince slain, he would say to such a youth: Go thou and slay So and So; and when thou returnest my angels shall bear thee into Paradise. And should'st thou die, nevertheless even so will I send my Angels to carry thee back into Paradise. So he caused them to believe; and thus there was no order of his that they would not affront any peril to execute, for the great desire they had to get back into that Paradise of his.[25]

Mandeville, like Friar Odoric, gives the reader a vivid sense of the abundance of flowing water in the Old Man's garden. But Mandeville is the only one to mention a subterranean channel and the ministrations of young striplings, as well as fair maidens, to entice the Old Man's followers. The two elements are significant because they appear in the only extant literary and "romantic" account of the chief of the Assassins by a Muslim author. They do not appear in Marco Polo, Friar Odoric, or any of the most popular Western chroniclers.

The legendary Assassin garden is thus portrayed in an Arabic tale related by Ibn Khallikan (d. 1282):

The Assassin Chief Isma'il entered Masyaf in Syria, and stayed there for a time to recruit men into his service who would be his Fedawis ("devotees") in heart and in body. He built a large garden, which he watered with sinuous rills, and a pavilion in the middle of the garden which had four stories. In the upmost story he set a dormer window which he ornamented and gilded, into each of the four sides. He then "took some of the slaves that had come with him and some of the protégées whom he had brought from the coastal region, ten young females, who had not yet reached the age of puberty, and clothed them in silk and in fine linen and put ringlets of gold and silver on their hands and perfumed the corners of the place with musk and ambergris."

The pavilion served as a retreat to the youths and the surrounding garden is worth describing as an example of Muslim ideas of an earthly paradise:

> he divided the extreme ends of the garden into four parts, in the first there was a quince and pears and apples and figs and grapes and

mulberry and prunes and crab-apple and jujube and cherries and apricots and sycamore-figs and carobs. And in the second part citrons and oranges, and lemons and sour pomegranates and sweet fruit and mastic, and in the third part watermelon and four sorts of cucumber and cabbage of all kinds, and in the fourth part there were roses and jasmin and privet and palm-trees and narcissus and aromatic plants and violets and lilies and anemones and eglantine and camomiles. And rills of water meandered through the whole of the garden, and he laid around the pavilion meadows and pools, and he planted on its sides all kinds of trees where he placed gazelle and ostriches and wild asses and wild cows and oxen, and wandering at random from the pools were geese and ducks and Ethiopian pheasants and quails and partridges and there were also hares.

The Assassin chief then built a high enclosure around the pavilion and erected a mansion for himself with a chamber below and a chamber above. He also dug a subterranean passage from the garden to the mansion leading to a private room which was turned into a place of assembly for his men. The procedure was then as follows: he placed a couch before the door and seated his men on it; he then gave them helpings of food and drink the whole day long.

When night came he looked around at the men and saw which of them possessed a steadiness that aroused admiration and then said to him: "Oh So-and-So, come here and sit by my side," and he sat by the side of the Chief Isma'il and he was not able to disobey him . . . and he bestowed the cup on him and he gave him to drink and he told of the virtues of the Imam 'Ali may God be pleased with him and what courage and chivalry and manliness he had, and the Chief Isma'il did not complete his narration until the one sitting by his side fell asleep and after a quarter of an hour, the drug began to work in the man and he fell down, and when he lay prostrate the Chief Isma'il . . . carried him on his shoulders and put him in the subterranean passage leading to the garden, and . . . brought him to the pavilion in which he was received by the youths and young slavegirls. . . . When the young man awoke the youths who were at his service said: "And we are only awaiting your death and this is the place which is yours and this is the palace of the palaces of Paradise and we are the houris and the children of paradise and if you were dead you would be with us, but you are sleeping and the hour has come for your awakening."

When the youth looked around he saw youths and slave girls of extreme beauty adorned with ornaments, and he smelt the odor of musk and frankincense, and in the garden he saw beasts, birds, running water, and trees. And he glanced at the beauty of the pavilion and the vessels of gold and silver while the maidens and the youths conversed with him, and the man was utterly bewildered.

> But the Chief Isma'il said to him: "Oh So-and-So beware of disclosing this dream to anyone otherwise you will be forbidden this place and know that your lord 'Ali has shown you your place in Paradise." Then the Chief Isma'il ordered food to be brought and they set before him vessels of gold and silver and on them was meat and fowl, roasted and boiled, and other foods beside, and the man ate it. Then the Chief Isma'il took a goblet and put in it hashish and gave it him to drink, and when he fell asleep he took him up and carried him through the subterranean passage into the rooms in the mansion, and when he awoke he saw himself among the same companions in the place where he was before.

The Chief of the Assassins then said to him: " 'Oh So-and-So the dream which you saw some time ago is not a dream but one of the miracles of the Imam and know that your name has been written with the beloved and if you conceal your secret you will have mastered your affair and if you disclose your word you will anger the Imam and if you die you will be a martyr so beware lest you tell anyone.' "26

In Mandeville, the "conduyt vnder erthe" is connected with the paradisaical springs of milk, wine, and honey and is not mentioned as a tunnel leading to the chief's house.27 It is significant, however, that there is a subterranean conduit at all and that Mandeville, like the Arab sources, never mentions the word Assassin. Like the Arabic narrator, he makes, quite a point of the tender age of the fair damsels and striplings, and, like orthodox Sunni Muslims, is full of abhorrence for the chief's "sotylle disceytes." Mandeville places his domain of the Assassins, Malasgird in Armenia, beside the land of Prester John, a characteristic that is also distinctive:

> Besyde the yle of Pentexoire, that is the lond of Prestre Iohn, is a gret yle long and brode that men clepen Milstorak, and it is in the lordschipe of Prestre Iohn. In that yle is gret plentee of godes.
>
> There was dwellynge somtyme a riche man—and it is not longe sithe—and men clept him Gatholonabes. And he was fulle of cauteles and of sotylle disceytes. And he hadde a fulle fair castelle and a strong in a mountayne, so strong and so noble that no man cowde devise a fairere ne a strengere. And he had let muren alle the mountayne aboute with a strong walle and a fair. And withinne tho walles he had the fairest gardyn that ony man myghte beholde, and therein were trees berynge alle maner of frutes that ony man cowde

deuyse. And therein were also alle maner vertuous herbes of gode smelle and alle other herbes also that beren faire floures. And he had also in that gardyn many faire welles.

And beside tho welles he had lete make faire halles and faire chambres depeynted alle with gold and azure. And there weren in that place many dyuerse thinges and manye dyuerse storyes and of bestes and of bryddes that songen fulle delectabely and meveden be craft, that it semede that thei weren quyke.

And he had also in his gardyn alle maner of foules and of bestes that ony man myghte thenke on for to haue pley or desport to beholde hem.

And he had also in that place the faireste damyseles that myghte ben founde vnder the age of xv. yeer and the faireste yonge strip-lynges that men myghte gete of that same age. And alle thei weren clothed in clothes of gold fulle richely, and he seyde that tho weren aungeles.

And he had also let make iii. welles faire and noble and alle envyround with ston of iaspre, of cristalle, dyapred with gold and sett with precious stones and grete orient perles. And he had made a conduyt vnder erthe so that the iii. welles at his list, on scholde renne mylk, another wyn, and another hony. And that place he clept "paradys."

And whan that ony gode knyght that was hardy and noble cam to see this rialtee, he wolde lede him into his paradys and schewen him theise wonderfulle thinges to his desport and the merueyllous and delicious song of dyuerse briddes and the faire damyseles and the faire welles of mylk, of wyn, and of hony plentevous rennynge. And he wolde let make dyuerse instrumentes of musik to sownen in an high tour so merily that it was ioye for to here, and no man scholde see the craft thereof. And tho he seyde weren aungeles of God, and that place was Paradys that God had behight to His frendes seyenge, *Dabo vobis terram fluentem lacte et melle.*

And thanne wolde he maken hem to drynken of a certeyn drynk whereof anon thei scholden be dronken, and thanne wolde hem thinken gretter delyt than thei hadden before. And than wolde he seye to hem that yif they wolde dyen for him and for his loue, that after hire deth thei scholde come to his paradys, and thei scholden ben of the age of tho damyselles and thei scholde pleyen with hem and yit ben maydenes. And after that yit scholde he putten hem in a fayrere paradys where that thei scholde see God of Nature visibely in His magestee and in His blisse.

And than wolde he schewe hem his entent and seye hem that yif thei wolde go sle such a lord or such a man that was his enemye or contrarious to his list, that thei scholde not drede to don it and for to be slayn therfore hemself. For after hire deth he wolde putten him into another paradys that was a c. fold fairere than ony of the tothere, and there scholde thei dwellen with the most fairest damyselles that myghte be and pley with hem eueremore.

And thus wenten many dyuerse lusty bacheleres for to sle grete lordes in dyuerse contrees that weren his enemyes and made hemself to ben slayn in hope to haue that paradys. And thus often tyme he was revenged of his enemyes be his sotylle disceytes and false cawteles.

And whan the worthi men of the contree hadden perceyued this sotylle falshod of this Gatholonabes, thei assembled hem with force and assayleden his castelle and slowen him and destroyeden alle the faire places and alle the nobletees of that paradys. The place of the welles and of the walles and of many other thinges ben yit apertly sene, but the ricchesse is voyded clene. And it is not longe gon sith that place was destroyed.[28]

A careful reading of the legend of the Assassin garden as we find it in Mandeville disposes of the assumption that Mandeville obtained his material from Odoric of Pordenone. There are, it is true, some striking resemblances in phrasing and sequence but they are few and insignificant compared to important variations. Most important of all, the usual designation of "senex de monte," which we also find in Odoric, is conspicuously absent in Mandeville. He speaks of the Assassin chief as "a riche man" by name of Gatholonabes. This "puzzling name"[29] has been most recently equated with Hasan ibn Sabbah, the well-known founder of the sect, and first lord of Alamut, who died in 1124.[30] This equation seems puzzling in its turn because Mandeville explicitly speaks of the destruction of the Assassin castle under Gatholonabes by "the worthi men of the countree," adding that "it is not longe gon sith that place was destroyed." The fall of Alamut, the stronghold of the Persian Assassins, and the destruction of its famous library by the Mongols took place in 1258, as we know from the eyewitness account of the Persian historian Juvaini.[31] Even then, for a brief period, the Isma'ilis were able to recapture Alamut in 1275. However, the power of the Assassins was broken not only by the Mongols but also by the assault of Baybars, the Mamluk sultan of Egypt. As one would expect,

> In Syria, the Assassins joined with the other Muslims in repelling the Mongol threat, and sought to win the good graces of Baybars by sending him embassies and gifts. . . . But Baybars, whose life-work was the liberation of the Muslim Near East from the double threat of the Christian Franks and the heathen Mongols, could not be expected to tolerate the continued independence of a dangerous pocket of heretics and murderers in the very heart of Syria.[32]

By 1273 the castles of the Syrian Assassins were all occupied.

Whatever his sources, Mandeville's skill as an author and his sense of affairs are amply attested. He would not lightly tell his public that the Assassin stronghold was destroyed "not long ago" by "the worthy inhabitants of the country," not the Tartars, unless he was thinking of a specific event and was deliberately departing from the customary way of other chroniclers. His supposed source, Odoric of Pordenone, fully informs his hearers and readers of the role of the Tartars in destroying the Assassin paradise:

> And when the Tartars had subdued a great part of the world, they came unto the said old man, and took from him the custody of his paradise: who being incensed thereat, sent abroad divers desperate and resolute persons out of his forenamed paradise, and caused many of the Tartarian nobles to be slain. The Tartars seeing this, went and besieged the city wherein the said old man was, took him, and put him to a most cruel and ignominious death.[33]

Mandeville, on the other hand, does not mention the Tartars as destroyers of the Assassin castle, though he devotes several chapters to them in his book. Moreover, the name he gives to the chief of the Assassins, Gatholonabes, is not found in any other writer. This, surely, must be a sign that he was not simply following the customary Western form of the legend. His account, as has already been mentioned, strikingly reflects the Muslim legend of the garden in mentioning both female and male adolescent slaves. He is also the only Western author to give the pleasure building in the garden several stories.[34] The name of the chief, Gatholonabes, or Catolonabes as in the Egerton manuscript, could simply be a Latinization of a name picked up from local Syrian usage.[35] The various designations of the Assassins in local Syrian parlance are still an interesting problem. Even de Sacy's famous explanation of the term *Assassin* as Hashishiyyun or Hashishiyyin, the users of hashish or hemp, rests on popular local usage in Syria rather than on written Muslim accounts which commonly refer to these particular Isma'ili heretics as Nizaris. In the Near East, at the time of the Crusaders as it is today, hashish was no secret monopoly. The use of the name for the Nizaris by the local population points "more to the fact that, already despised as a minority, they had special opportunities to become associated with the prevailing vices."[36] The name Catolonabes, like Mandeville's account of Egypt and his list of Mamluk sultans, is another indication that *Mandeville's Travels* cannot be brushed aside as a compilation and nothing more.

Mandeville's wise choice of authorities in his description of Muslim manners and customs is known by his reliance on William of Tripoli, one of the most knowledgeable and least prejudiced Latin authorities on Islam, whose work was largely unknown or ignored by other writers.

William's "Tractatus de statu Saracenorum," written at Acre in 1273, stands apart from other writers of his time because of its use of Arabic material. The version of the Bahira legend (the tradition of Muhammad's Nestorian tutor) in William's biography of Muhammad, is close to its Arabic form—see above, chapter 6. Only Mandeville among Western writers follows William of Tripoli in the story of Muhammad's hermit:[37]

And yee schulle vnderstonde that Machamote was born in Arabye, that was first a pore knaue that kepte cameles that wenten with marchantes for marchandise. And so befelle that he wente with the marchandes into Egipt, and thei weren thanne Cristene in tho partyes. And at the desertes of Arabye he wente into a chapelle where a eremyte duelte. And whan he entred into the chapelle that was but a lytille and a low thing and had but a lityl dore and a low, than the entree began to wexe so gret and so large and so high as though it had ben of a gret mynstre or the gate of a paleys. And this was the firste myracle the Sarazins seyn that Machomete dide in his youthe.

After began he for to wexe wyse and riche. And he was a gret astronomer, and after he was gouernour and prince of the lond of Corrodane [Quraish—the Prophet's tribe]. And he gouerned it fulle wisely in such manere that whan the prince was ded he toke the lady to wyfe, that highte Gadrige. And Machomete felle often in the grete sikeness that men callen the fallynge euylle, wherefore the lady was fulle sory that euere sche toke him to husbonde. But Machomete made hire to beleeue that alle tymes whan he felle so, Gabriel the angel cam for to speke with him and for the gret light and brightness of the angelle he myghte not susteyne him fro fallynge. And therefore the Sarazines seyn that Gabriel cam often to speke with him.

And also Machomete loued well a gode heremyte that duelled in the desertes a myle fro Mount Synay in the weye that men gon fro Arabye toward Caldee and toward Ynde, o day iourney fro the see, where the marchauntes of Venyse comen often for marchandise. And so often wente Machomete to this heremyte that alle his men weren wrothe, for he wolde gladly here this heremyte preche and make his men wake alle nyght. And therefore his men thoughten to putte the heremyte to deth. And so befelle vpon a nyght that Machomete was dronken of gode wyn and he felle on slepe. And his men toke Machometes swerd out of his schethe whils he slepte, and therewith thei slowgh this heremyte and putten his swerd al blody in his schethe ayen. And at morwe whan he fond the heremyte ded, he was fulle sory and wroth and wolde haue done his men to deth. But thei alle with on accord [and oon assent seide] that he himself had slayn him whan he was dronken, and schewed him his swerd alle blody. And he trowed that thei hadden seyd soth. And than he cursed the wyn and alle tho that drynken it.

Also it befalleth sumtyme that Cristene men becomen Sarazines outher for pouertee or for sympleness or elles for here owne wykked-ness. And therfore the Archiflamyn or the Flamyn,as oure e[r]che-bisshopp or bisshopp, whan he resceyueth hem seyth thus, *La ellec olla syla Machomet rores alla*, [*la allahu illa lah wa Muhammad rasūl llah*], that is to seye, There is no god but on and Machomete his messager.[38]

What Mandeville took from William of Tripoli in the above passage are two distinctive details of which there is no trace in Vincent of Beau-vais's *Speculum Historiale*, the most complete medieval collection of truth and legend relating to the Prophet's life. The enlargement of the desert chapel and its door on Muhammad's entry is a specific feature that may have inspired the changing architectural dimensions of Milton's Pande-monium by way of Mandeville. The explanation of the Koranic proscrip-tion of wine, illustrated in the killing of the hermit by Muhammad's jealous companions and their gulling of the inebriated Prophet, is unique in the Latin of William of Tripoli as it is in the vernacular of *Mandeville's Travels*.

Mandeville's account of the Saracens is most important to those readers who see in the *Travels* a combination of fact and fiction narrated by a genuine traveler. The chapters on Egypt and the Saracens contain traces of evidence to show that the author was there. Mandeville is most em-phatic in his insistence that he knew Mamluk Egypt from personal ex-perience. Speaking of the "Sultan of Babylon" in his "Calahelyk," he says: "I ought right well to know it; for I dwelled with him as soldier in his wars a great while against the Bedouins. And he would have married me full highly to a great prince's daughter, if I would have forsaken my law and my belief."[39] He also gives a correct list of sultans, beginning with Saladin's "father," (actually his uncle) Shirkuh, and continuing up to his own time in 1341. A similar enumeration appears in the Armenian Hai-ton's *Oriental History* but Mandeville adds two successors to an-Nasir Nasir ad-Din Muhammad that have mystified the source-hunters. His eldest son, called "Melech Mader," says Mandeville, was succeeded by his brother "Melech Madabron"—"and he was sultan when I departed from those countries." The identification of the two immediate successors of an-Nasir is thus crucial to those who believe that the author of *Man-deville's Travels* actually visited Egypt.

Mandeville gives the names of the sultans as follows:

And the firste soudan was Zarocon that was of Mede and was fader to Sahaladyn, that toke the Califfee of Egipt and slough him

and was made soudan be strengthe. After that was soudan Sahaladyn, in whoos tyme the kyng of Englond Richard the Firste [cam]
with manye othere that kepten the passage that Sahaladyn ne myghte
not passen. After Sahaladyn regned his sone Boradyn, and after him
his nevewe.

After that the Comaynz that weren in seruage in Egipt felten
hemse[l]f that thei weren of gret power. Thei chesen hem a soudan
amonges hem, the whiche made him to ben cleped Melech Salan.
And in his tyme entred into the contree of the kynges of France
Seynt Lowyzs, and faught with him and toke him and enprisound
him. And this was slayn of his owne seruantes. And after thei chosen
another to be soudan that thei cleped Tympieman, and he let delyu-
eren Seynt Lowys out of prisoun for certeyn raunsoun.

And after on of theise Comaynz regned that highte Cachas and
slough Turqueman for to be soudan and made him ben cleped
Melech Emes. And after another that hadde to name Bendochdare
that slough Melech Emes for to be soudan and cleped himself Melech
Dare. In his tyme entred the gode kyng Edward of Englond in Syrye
and dide gret harm to the Sarrazines. And after was this soudan
enpoysound at Damasce. And his sone thoughte to regnen after him
be heritage and made him to ben clept Melesch Sach. But another
that had to name Elphy chaced him out of the countree and made
him soudan. This man toke the cytee of Tripollee and destroyede
manye of the Cristene men the yeer of grace m.cc.iiii. score and ix.
And after was he enprisound of another that wolde be soudan, but he
was anon slayn. After that was the sone of Elphy chosen to ben soudan and cleped him Melech Asseraf, and he toke the citee of Akour
and chaced out the Cristene men, and this was also enpoysond. And
than was his brother ymade soudan and was cleped Melech Nasser.
And after on that was clept Guytoga toke him and put him in prisoun
in the castelle of Mount Ryualle, and made him soudan be strengthe
and cleped him Melech Cadelle and he was [a] Tartaryne. But the
Comaynz chaced him out of the contree and diden hym meche sorwe
and maden on of hemself soudan that hadde to name Lachyn, and
he made him to ben clept Melech Manser; the whiche on a day
pleyed at the chess and his swerd lay besyde him, and so befelle that
on wratthed him and with his owne propre swerd he was slayn.

And after that thei weren at gret discord for to make a soudan,
and fynally thei accordeden to Melech Nasser that Guytoga had put
in prisoun at Mount Rivalle. And this regnede longe and gouerned
wisely so that his eldest sone was chosen after him Melech Mader;
the whiche his brother leet sle priuyly for to haue the lordschipe,
and made him to ben clept Melech Madabron. And he was soudan
whan I departed fro tho contrees.[40]

As with Mandeville's debt to Odoric of Pordenone in the matter of the Assassin paradise, the derivation of the above passage from Haiton has been taken for granted. But, again, the similarities with Haiton's text are offset by variations and differences that suggest an independent, discriminating approach.

Both Odoric of Pordenone and Haiton were Mandeville's contemporaries, Friar Odoric writing his journal in 1330. Haiton, of the royal house of Armenia, having found refuge from the Tartars at Poitiers with the help of Pope Clement V, dictated his history in 1307, assuring his readers of the truth of what he had to tell and of the events to which he had borne personal witness.[41] Both Odoric and Haiton, as well as Mandeville, were included, with Marco Polo, the German traveler von Boldensele, and Friar Ricoldo of Monte-Croce, in Jean le Long's anthology of fourteenth-century Eastern travelogues, most of them translated into French from the Latin. Jean le Long died in 1383. In 1399 his book was bought by the Duc de Bourgogne. Whether the narrations of Haiton, Ricoldo, and Mandeville were contained in the original manuscript is not clear but they appear in an early fifteenth-century copy.

Haiton left Egypt before 1307, that is to say before an-Nasir Nasir ad-Din Muhammad became sultan for the third time. Mandeville, completing his book in 1356, most probably drew on Haiton's list of sultans for reinforcement as he drew on Odoric and Boldensele. However, there is also need to account for striking omissions. Here again, Mandeville's chapter on the Assassins renders a clue. Haiton mentions the Assassins in all historical sobriety. Most significantly, in a chapter on the sultan's domain in Syria preceding the names of the sultans, Haiton states that the sultan maintains foot-archers in the territory of the Assassins around the Lebanon.[42] The name "Assassins" does not occur in Mandeville at all, nor, as we have seen, does the designation "Old Man of the Mountain." There is also Haiton's statement within the chapter on the chronology of the sultans that in the time of "Melecdaer" (Zahir Rukn ad-din Baybars-Bundukdari, 1260–77), the king of England (Edward I) had come to Syria. The sultan, says Haiton, had planned his murder by a certain Assassin but he only managed to wound the king with a poisoned sword.[43] There is no trace of this incident in Mandeville, though he, too, recounts that at the time of "Melech Dare" Edward of England entered Syria. Why should Mandeville, so obviously aware of the political role of "Gatholonabes" studiously avoid the most common terms used by all other Western writers if all the knowledge he had came from his reading?

The historically accurate circumstances are that, in 1309, an-Nasir, who had been deposed by one of his emirs, Ketbogha, in 1294, became sultan for the third time, remaining in power until 1341 when he was seized with a serious illness. Being jealous of his own sons, he nominated none to succeed him until a dangerous crisis forced the dying monarch to invest, not his eldest son whom he hated, but Abu Bakr, who, like "Lachyn" (al-Mansur Husam-ad-Din Lajin al-Mansuri became sultan in 1296) whom Mandeville mentions, was also "Melech Manser," his full name being al-Mansur Saif-ad-Din Abu Bakr. While an-Nasir was still on his deathbed, however, a deadly struggle for power began between his two leading ministers, Beshtak and Qawsun, both married to daughters of the sultan and, therefore, in a sense, his "sons" as well. Using Abu Bakr, a cruel and overbearing tyrant of twenty, Qawsun had Beshtak carried off to Alexandria and put to death. Qawsun, now supreme, deposed Abu Bakr and raised another son of Nasir, six years of age, to the throne, living, however, in dread of Ahmad, the eldest son who had been bypassed by his father. Ahmad, with the help of the emirs of Syria, finally gained ascendancy, becoming sultan in 1342 as an-Nasir Shihab-ad-Din Ahmad. It is these events that Mandeville's account seems to reflect. "Melech Mader," the eldest son, is probably a garbled rendering of an-Nasir Ahmad, distinguishing him from Melech Nasser, his famous father. The form of the name is closest in the Egerton manuscript whose "Melechinader" clearly reflects the correct pronunciation of the Arabic article, Malik-an-Nasir (Melech in-nasir).44

Melech Madabron may then be the name of the brother-in-law, Qawsun, whom an-Nasir Ahmad had put to death. The chaotic state in the Latin transliteration of Arabic lettering is a commonplace of medieval scholarship. The confusion in the relationships and breathtaking sequence of events would be most natural in the mind of a Western foreign observer. Even a modern historian has a great deal of trouble disentangling the maze of succession at the Egyptian court under the house of Nasir—"from first to last a miserable tale." Nasir's sons and grandsons

> rose and fell at the will of the Mameluke leaders of the day, some mere children; the younger, indeed, the better, for so soon as the puppet Prince began to show a will of his own he was summarily deposed, or he was made away with, few of such as reached maturity dying a natural death. The Emirs rose and fell; each had his short day of power; then deposed and plundered, exiled or strangled, others succeeded but to share their fate. There were short intervals of able rule; but for the most part, murders, torture, execution, crime, and rebellion were rife throughout the period. The tale is sad and unattractive. . . .45

Mandeville, then, to mention the eldest son of an-Nasir as sultan must have left Egypt in the winter of 1342 shortly after Qawsun's power had come to a dismal end. Under the best of conditions, as an outsider, he could hardly be expected to follow the web of intrigues and secret murders between brothers, brothers-in-law, and titular "brothers" among the emirs in the struggle for power. That he mentions a "Melech Mader" and a "Melech Madabron" at all, however, indicates special knowledge of an exceptional kind. These two names, or anything resembling them among Nasir's immediate successors, are not found in Mandeville's presumable sources and, considering the evidence of Haiton, a writer of Mandeville's sophistication would destroy his own credibility as a traveler by making them up.

A matter that has been somewhat neglected in assessing Mandeville's familiarity with Naserite Egypt, beyond his sources, is a letter from the sultan to the pope which, in a corrupt text, is found in two Latin and two French manuscripts of *Mandeville's Travels*.[46] The letter is supposed to be from Melechmasser, identified in the manuscripts as Melechmandabron's son which, aside from the nature of the letter itself, is an interesting and genuine reflection of the confusing kinships in the chaos of successions after Nasir's death. The attribution of this interpolated letter makes Melechmasser (or Melechmader, Melechinnader in the spelling of other manuscripts) the successor of Melechmandabron[47]—an important point if we take this Melechmasser to be an-Nasir Ahmad, the eldest son of the great an-Nasir. The letter warns the pope and King Philip of France that they underestimate the might of

> the soudan of the Babylonians, Assyrians, Egyptians, Amaricans, Medes, Alexandrinians, Parthians and Ethiopians . . . provost of the Earthly Paradise and guardian of the Sepulchre of the Crucified, king of Jerusalem, of Africa and Asia, lord of Barbary from East to West, king of kings and prince of princes, offspring of the gods, standard of Mohamet, lord from the Dry Tree to the river of Paradise and to the high hill of Ararath, terror and threat to the enemies, killer of Christians, comfort of paynim, piercer of harnesses. . . .[48]

Editors of Mandeville have come to the conclusion that "the Philip of the mock-heroic epistle can only be Philippe Auguste, who fought Saladin in the third Crusade."[49] The letter, of course, is spurious, like the letter of Prester John to Pope Alexander III.[50] But like much spurious material throughout the ages it was woven from threads of reality. In 1327, the great an-Nasir was asked by the pope to treat his Christian subjects kindly, with the promise that the same should be done for Muslims in the West. Philip VI of France sent an embassy in 1330 demanding that Nasir should give the Christians Jerusalem and part of the coast of Palestine.[51] The "philippus francorum rex" of the Mandeville letter is therefore a King Philip of France who had indeed dealings with an-Nasir, not Saladin, as did the pope, probably Pope John XXII, who sent an envoy to Cairo. The confusion between the famous an-Nasir Muhammad and his eldest son an-Nasir Ahmad is a plausible explanation for the fanciful reply to the pope and King Philip of France by Melech-masser, "filius senior" of Melechmadabron, that is to say, one who followed "Melechmadabron," most probably Qawsun, in the assumption of power.

Mandeville tells his reader that he was, for a time, attached to the sultan's court in his "Calahelyk" and was employed as a soldier against the Bedouins.[52] Here again, the Turkish suffix in the name of the Mamluk citadel al-Qal'ah, rings of authenticity. Warfare against the Bedouins who kept Upper Egypt in a constant state of alarm was a perpetual task in Naserite Egypt, while Nasir himself was most tolerant toward Christians. Indeed, what Mandeville says about the sultan's court is not only found in Haiton, who spoke from personal experience, but also in Arabic histories. There is no reason to assume that our traveler had not actually "dwelled with him as soldier in his wars a great while against the Bed-ouins." We learn from Haiton, correctly, that the soldiers of Nasir's army were assembled from various nations because the natives did not distinguish themselves in the bearing of arms: in the translation of Jean le Long, "L'ost de la chevalerie d'Egypte sont gens de diverses parties et d'estranges terres. Car la gent du pays ne valent riens en fait d'armes, ne a pie, ne a cheval, ne par mer, ne par terre."[53] "Unde oportet," says the Latin text, "quod de alienis gentibus ejus potentia roboretur."[54] As to Mandeville's claim that the sultan "would have married me full highly to a great prince's daughter, if I would have forsaken my law and my belief," there is ample evidence of Christians turning Muslim to become full-fledged members of the court. The marriage of Christian converts to daughters of Muslim princes was a theme that entered romance from actual history. Oriental potentates, with their harems of wives and con-cubines, steadily populated their court with their offspring. It was accepted policy to marry their daughters to those of their followers whose loyalty they thus hoped to ensure. We know of eleven emirs at Nasir's court, most of them Christian converts, who were sons-in-law of the sultan.[55] The most powerful one was Qawsun who seized power after Nasir's death and is probably Mandeville's "Melechmadabron."

Robert Fazy, the first and only modern scholar to have investigated Mandeville's itinerary to Syria and his purported sojourn in Egypt in detail, comes to the conclusion that "il n'y a pas de raison plausible de douter que Jehan de Mandeville ait bien vécu en Egypte, dans l'entourage du sultan Melik Nâçir."[56] The concrete landmarks of veracity that Fazy discerns are the following: Mandeville's description of an equestrian statue of Justinian in front of the Hagia Sophia in Constantinople is amazingly accurate, for at the time of Mandeville's arrival there, in 1322 or 1323, the statue had lost an orb ("a round appelle of gold") in its hand, just as Mandeville describes it. The orb was restored by 1333 when Boldensele saw it, and Mandeville is the only one to relate the incident of its falling off.[57] The observation of a curious custom in Cyprus, corroborated by a later sixteenth-century traveler, is also peculiar to Mandeville. He remarks on the manner "of lordes and all othere men . . . to eten on the erthe" and is the only one to be precise in mentioning the organization of the Cypriote ecclesiastical hierarchy (an archbishop at Nicosia and four other bishops).[58] In his accurate description of Egypt Mandeville is the first European to remark on the circuit traced by the Blue Nile in Ethiopia and extraordinary in his knowledge that Damietta was razed and rebuilt by the Saracens who called it "the newe Damyete."[59] In addition, there are Mandeville's versions of legend, myth, and miracle in Cos, Acre, and Jaffa which would be "presqu'impossibles à expliquer si Mandeville n'a pas été sur les lieux."[60]

8

The Matter of Araby and the Making of Romance

When Gibbon, in the *Decline and Fall of the Roman Empire* (chapter LII), wrote with relief of Oxford as saved from the fate of having the Koran taught in its schools and the revelation of Muhammad proclaimed in its pulpits, he touched upon the crucial reason for the importance of the matter of Araby in the medieval world: historical reality. The making of romance, in other words, like all human experience both of reality and imagination is deeply rooted in the dignity of historical events from which it takes its stuff, yet it also serves history by expressing deep-seated dreams and ideas which enlarge the horizon of existence, both private and public, and, in their turn, shape the course of events.

At the heart of romance there is man's tragic yearning for an ideal state of peace and stability in which reality and dream become one. The perilous journey of life, the crucial combat against nature and enemies, is transcended in an exaltation of individual man, the knightly hero, who through love and adventure pursues a pure ideal of personal, inner worth, thus ennobling his native ground, the society that contains and sustains him.

The intense preoccupation with the Orient as theme, image, and metaphor in the romantic literature of the Western world derives from roots that are deeply embedded in the unconscious. An archetypal longing for "a vision unique," an illusion of "the very life of life awaiting one at some point within the unknown" was "magnetized" by the very name of the East,[1] the distant region of the rising sun and the birth of moral civilization. The apostles of the Age of Reason felt this "emotive compulsion" as well. Hayy ibn Yaqzan ("Alive, son of Awake"), the hero and perfect man of a Neoplatonic romance by Ibn Tufail (d. 1184–85), became fashionable after he had reached England in Pocock's translation in 1671. It is this tale of two islands, one corrupted by a materialistic civilization, the other in a state of nature on which Hayy leads a pure existence, that is considered to have inspired the idea of Robinson Crusoe.[2] Samuel Johnson, who despised the "fantastical," chose an oriental setting for *Rasselas* (1759), his didactic romance of the human condition.[3] Beckford's *Vathek*, published in 1786 as a rendering from the Arabic, was an oriental fantasy that marked the breakup of eighteenth-century classical forms. The whole phenomenon of oriental settings, images, themes, and motifs is a distinctive feature of romanticism as a literary trend and movement. The question of the origin of romance greatly preoccupied the savants of the eighteenth century. They saw "romantic" medieval literature as presenting a contrast to the literary heritage of classical antiquity and explained it as an import from the Arabs. "That peculiar and arbitrary species of Fiction which we commonly call Romantic," writes Thomas Warton (1728–90) in his essay *Of the Origin of Romantic Fiction in Europe*, "was entirely unknown to the writers of Greece and Rome. It appears to have been imported into Europe by a people, whose modes of thinking, and habits of invention, are not natural to that country. It is generally supposed to have been borrowed from the Arabians."[4] Warton rightly considered Spain as the main transmitter of Arabic subject matter. Dismissing the "established maxim of modern criticism, that the fictions of Arabian imagination were communicated to the western world by means of the Crusades," he points out "that these fancies were introduced at a much earlier period. The Saracens, or Arabians, having been for some time seated on the northern coasts of Africa, entered Spain about the beginning of the eighth century."[5]

That oriental fiction was received with some ambivalence is apparent in the remarks of James Beattie (1735–1803), a critic of Galland, the French translator of the *Arabian Nights* (1704). Beattie had this to say of oriental romance:

> But, first, it may be proper to observe, that the Oriental nations have long been famous for fabulous narrative. The indolence peculiar to the genial climates of Asia, and the luxurious life which the kings and other great men, of those countries, lead in their seraglios, have made them seek for this sort of amusement, and set a high value upon it. When an Eastern prince happens to be idle, as he commonly is, and at a loss for expedients to kill the time, he commands his Grand Visir, or his favourite, to tell him stories. Being ignorant, and consequently credulous; having no passion for moral improvement, and little knowledge of nature; he does not desire, that they should be probable, or of an instructive tendency: it is enough if they be astonishing. And hence it is, no doubt, that those oriental tales are so extravagant. Every thing is carried on by enchantment and prodigy; by fairies, genii, and demons, and wooden horses, which, on turning a peg, fly through the air with inconceivable swiftness.
>
> Another thing remarkable in these eastern tales is that their authors expatiate, with peculiar delight, in the description of magnificence; rich robes, gaudy furniture, sumptuous entertainments, and palaces shining in gold, or sparkling with diamonds. This too is conformable to the character and circumstances of the people. Their

great men, whose taste has never been improved by studying the *simplicity* of nature and art, pique themselves chiefly on the *splendour* of their equipage, and the vast quantities of gold, jewels, and curious things, which they can heap together in their repositories.[6]

It is amusing to contemplate that Beattie suspected the tales of the *Arabian Nights* to have been invented by Galland. At any rate, he considers the imitation of the oriental by English and other European authors as deplorable in "figurative style, and wild invention of the Asiaticks."[7]

Unlike the eighteenth-century conception of the extravagant oriental tale, medieval romance is a serious literary form. Its appearance and popularity in medieval Europe stand in some relation to Arabian tales, though the precise nature of this relation is still elusive. The matter is complicated by the relation between the classical heritage of Greece and medieval Islam in which "the more obvious borrowings, such as the plot of an action or a major part of it, are far outnumbered by the more subtle imprints left by Hellenistic ideas of life and love on the responsive minds of the Arab public."[8]

What then is a medieval romance? The primary meaning of "romance" denoting the language of France is illustrated in the chronicle of Robert Mannyng of Brunne (ca. 1338), a translation of the chronicle of Peter Langtoft who wrote it in French:

> Ffrankysche speche ys cald Romaunce,
> So sey þis clerkes & men of ffraunce.
> Peres of Langtofte, a chanoun
> Schauen y þe hous of Brydlyngtoun,
> On Romaunce al þys story he wrot
> Of Englische kynges, as we wel wot,
> He wrot þer dedes alle þat þey wrought;
> After hym in Englische y hit brought.[9]

In *Guy of Warwick* we find "Romans" extended to the language of Africa in the sense of any "Romantic" language. Russian merchants, having kidnapped Guy of Warwick's son, are stranded in Africa and decide to offer the boy to the king in order to obtain his favor. The emissaries are "wele ydyght of Romans"—a phrase which translates "Qui corteis furent a bien parlant" in the French original.[10] A list of Middle English works which call themselves "romance" in the sense that they are fictitious narratives "of which the scene and incidents are very remote from those of ordinary life"[11] includes *Sir Beues of Hamtoun, The Romance of Duke Rowland and Sir Otuell of Spayne* and *The Sowdone of Babylone*.[12] "Romance" as used in these works in Middle English designates a narrative poem—not a "historie" in prose—which exhibits "a certain set of

literary and social conventions"[13] regarding love, adventure, and chivalry. It is this set of conventions concerning strange adventures in distant
lands which the eighteenth century regarded as the "progeny" of an alien
"Arabian fancy"[14] and which modern scholarship is still engaged in
tracking down and defining. What is certain is that a considerable portion
of the subject matter and some structural elements of romantic medieval
literature passed through Muslim hands before reaching the West and
were due to Christian contact with Muslim spheres of culture.

The most obvious example is the romance of *Floris and Blancheflur*, a
truly international tale preserved in over a dozen languages and frequently cited in other medieval poems.[15] The romance appeared in England
about the middle of the thirteenth century, in a Middle English version of
a twelfth-century French original which is considered the oldest European
form of the tale.[16] The core of the story is formed by an oriental, specifically Arabian, theme and is permeated by Arabian motifs.

The children, Floris, son of the king of Spain, and Blancheflur, a captive
maiden, are brought up together and love each other. Fearing Floris's
future marriage to Blancheflur, his parents send him away and sell the
maiden to Babylonian merchants. The merchants in turn sell her to the
emir, in whose harem she is kept as his prospective queen. When Floris
returns and sees a tomb (erected by his parents) bearing Blancheflur's
name, he attempts suicide. They reveal the truth; so, disguised as a
merchant he goes in quest of the girl. At Babylon (Cairo) he learns from a
conversation at an inn that she is held in an inaccessible tower. He bribes
the porter and is carried in a basket of flowers to the tower. The lovers are
united. Found sleeping together, they are condemned to be killed. Neither
is willing to survive the other with the aid of a magic ring that can preserve
one of them from death. The rivalry as to which shall die first and their
pathetic story win their pardon. Floris and Blancheflur are married and
leave to rule their own country. The emir marries Clarice, a friend of
Blancheflur.[17]

What is remarkable in the romance is not only the Saracen setting in
which "we are introduced into the home life of the East"[18] but the sym-
pathetic treatment of the emir ("Now the Amiral-woll him tide! / Floris
setteth next his side"—l. 1054–55), which has a ring of genuineness.

There is no Arabic analogue to *Floris and Blancheflur* in the sense in
which the tale of the ebony horse is analogous to Adenet le Roi's *Cléomadès*,
Girard d'Amiens's *Méliacin*, and Chaucer's *Squire's Tale*. But the Arabian
motifs in the story are incontestable and have many parallels in the
Arabian Nights. Most of the parallels have been analyzed by Huet and are
apparent in any classification of themes and motifs in Arabian stories.[19]

The central motifs are the tower of maidens, a harem customarily
guarded by eunuchs, and the habit of oriental merchants to deliver a

particularly beautiful slave to the king. Blancheflur, sold by oriental
merchants, is placed in such a harem where a separate room is allocated to
each concubine.[20] Like Blancheflur and her friend, Clarice, concubines
are present at the caliph's awakening.[21] A breach of the harem and the
possession of one of the ruler's favorites is an unforgivable offense punished
by death. There is, however, a tale in the *Arabian Nights* in which the
caliph pardons the lovers in circumstances much like *Floris and Blancheflur.*

In "Ardashir and Hayat al-Nufus"—the tale of a prince disguised as a
merchant and a king's daughter—a eunuch, sent by the king to fetch his
daughter, surprises the lovers in bed. He informs the king. "When the
King heard these words he started up and taking a sword in his hand,
cried out to the Rais [chief] of the eunuchs, saying 'Take thy lads and go
to the Princess's chamber and bring me her and him who is with her as
they twain lie on the bed; but cover them both up.' " The scene before the
king shows the selflessness of the lovers as it does in *Floris and Blancheflur.*
The lovers vie with each other to be killed first. The king is quite prepared
to kill his daughter: "He looked at her and would have smitten her neck:
but the Prince threw himself on the father's breast, saying 'The fault was
not hers but mine only: kill me before thou killest her.' The King made at
him, to cut him down, but Hayat al-Nufus cast herself on her father and
said: 'Kill me, not him; for he is the son of a great King, lord of all the
land in its length and breadth.' " What finally saves the lovers is the intervention of the prince's father and his troops. The marriage is celebrated
and the lovers, like Floris and Blancheflur, "abode in all comfort and
solace and joyance of life."[22] In the same story, we have a warder of the
palace garden bribed by the lover to gain access to the garden and the
description of the garden itself. Like the orchard in *Floris and Blancheflur,*
the garden is "compassed about with high walls and strong, rich in trees
and rill-full leas and goodly fruiteries. And indeed its flowers breathed
perfume and its birds warbled amid the bloom as it were a garden of
Paradise."[23]

Other parallels have been pointed out by Huet: a boy and a girl are
brought up together and love each other;[24] a false tomb is erected to
deceive the lover—in this case the caliph Harun al-Rashid;[25] a prince
disguises himself as a merchant;[26] a prince goes in search of his beloved,
alights at a khan, and hears of the whereabouts of his beloved from a
company of merchants sitting at talk;[27] a lover is hidden in a chest and
introduced into the harem.[28]

Whatever the origin of *Floris and Blancheflur,*[29] it is so genuine a reflection of life in an Islamic environment that even a biographical account of
the seventh-century Arab poet 'Urwah, which describes young love, has
been cited as one of its analogues.[30] There is a similar motif of young love
in the Old French "cantefable" *Aucassin and Nicolette,* which betrays its

Arab inspiration in the name of the hero, al-Qasim, as well as in its pro-
simetric form, characteristic of Arab narrative style. Wolfram of Eschenbach's Provençal poet Kyot, who, according to Wolfram, took the story
of Parzival from an Arabic account in Toledo, continues to mystify scholars.[31] What is significant, however, is that Wolfram, who also wrote the
very Saracenic *Willehalm*, attributes the romance to an Arabic source. One
gains the impression that the literary matter of Araby was as intriguing to
medieval poets as Arabic science and philosophy were to Dante, Chaucer,
and medieval clerks.

In the eyes of most Arabists, "there can be little doubt as to the influence of Arabic poetry on the songs of the troubadours."[32] Their argument runs as follows: the first examples of Provençal poetry that have
come down to us exhibit a strictly conventional pattern both in structure
and theme, thus representing not a beginning but an established system.
No evolution in the direction of troubadour lyric has been traced in the
earlier literature of the West.[33] But there are convincing analogues in
theme, imagery, and verse form in the poetry of Spain and Sicily preceding the troubadours, and what seems to be the closest parallel to the new
poetic system is found with Hispano-Arabic poets.[34]

The verse form of William of Poitiers has been found to show remarkable analogies with the versification of Ibn Quzman, an Andalusian court
minstrel (d. 1160) who was responsible for the introduction of a new
poetic form into the art of Arabic poetry.[35] In tenth-century Spain the
formal tradition of classical Arab poetry was broken by a new *rhymed*
popular verse form which, both in language and meter, departed from
accepted literary usage. The new poetry was called *muwashshah*, that is, a
"chain belt" of rhymed verse. The strictly quantitative classical stanza
which permitted only one rhyme at the end and demanded grammatically
correct language was superseded by the rise of a popular lyric which
achieved its earliest literary representation in the *zajal* or "song" of Ibn
Quzman.[36] According to Ibn Khaldun, the fourteenth-century historian,
the *zajal* was a popular copy of the artistic *muwashshah*:

> *Muwashshah* poetry spread among the Spaniards. . . . They made
> poems of the *muwashshah* type in their sedentary dialect, without
> employing vowel endings. They thus invented a new form, which
> they called *zajal*. They have continued to compose poems of this
> type down to this time. They achieved remarkable things in it. The
> *zajal* opened a wide field for eloquent poetry in the Spanish-Arabic
> dialect, which is influenced by non-Arab speech habits.[37]

The popularity of the *muwashshah* is reflected in the Hebrew poetry of
medieval Spain. Beginning with the first half of the eleventh century, we
find the verse form in the work of almost all Hebrew poets. Ibn Gabirol,

Yehuda Halevi, Moshe ibn Ezra, Abraham ibn Ezra.[38] The poetics of
the *muwashshaḥ*, explained by an Egyptian poet, Ibn Sana al-Mulk, have
been of particular significance to the students of the troubadour lyric.[39]
For the last part of the verse form comprises a *kharja* ("envoi") of two to
four lines written in the dialect of the speaker, colloquial Arabic, or
Spanish, or a mixture of both.[40] These *kharjas* of the Arab Andalusian
poets have been considered "the first spring of the European lyric" and
the prototype of the *cantigas de amor*.[41] Comparative metrical studies have
led to the conclusion that the correspondence of Arabian and Romance
forms is not an isolated phenomenon in certain lyrical poems but comprises a whole "morphological family."[42] The structure of the *zajal*, which
in its simplest form consists of a three-line rhymed stanza (*a a a*) concluded with a rhyming tag that serves as a refrain, is the nucleus of this
family which Menéndez Pidal has classified and described in seven
types.[43] The structural elements are also reinforced by the appearance
of Arabic words in Provençal poetry and by images and motifs which are
common to medieval lyric and romance in Arabic, medieval Latin, and
the European vernaculars.[44]

As to the theme of the troubadours, the art of "fin amour," attempts
have been made to link it with *The Ring of the Dove* (Tauq al-Hamamah)
of Ibn Hazm (994–1064), an Andalusian poet, historian, jurist, philosopher, and theologian.[45] However, the anatomy of love that Ibn Hazm's
treatise unfolds is very different in kind from that of Andreas Capellanus.[46]
The theme of love, which includes homosexual love, is discussed by Ibn
Hazm as a revelation of human character in a general sense. Unlike the
De Arte Honeste Amandi of Andreas, an entertaining and ironical literary
exercise, Ibn Hazm's work is a profoundly philosophical and psychological analysis of the spiritual and carnal sides of man and their place in a
moral order. Thus, "among the laudable instincts, noble characteristics
and virtuous habits by which men may be adorned, whether they are
engaged in love-making or any other activity, Fidelity ranks high. It is
one of the strongest proofs and clearest demonstrations of sound stock
and pure breed; it differs in degree of excellence according to that vari-
ability which is inherent in all created beings." There are many valuable
observations on the nature of human intercourse in general: "A wise man
of old has said, 'Make friends with whom you will, but avoid three sorts
of men—the fool, who desiring to help you only harms you; the weary,
because in the hour when you rely upon him most, on account of the long
and firm friendship between you, in that very hour he lets you down;
and the liar, since the more you believe in him the more surely he will
do you a dirty trick, when you least expect it.' "[47]

Ibn Hazm's view of women was determined in childhood and there is a special, though not ungrudging tribute to women whose place in the society of Muslim Spain was an exalted one.

> I have myself observed women, and got to know their secrets to an extent almost unparalleled; for I was reared in their bosoms, and brought up among them, not knowing any other society. I never sat with men until I was already a youth, and my beard had begun to sprout. Women taught me the Koran, they recited to me much poetry, they trained me in calligraphy; my only care and mental exercise, since first I began to understand anything, even from the days of earliest childhood, has been to study the affairs of females, to investigate their histories, and to acquire all the knowledge I could about them.[48]

The typical figures that frequent the medieval traffic of what Ibn Hazm calls "the love-business" are classified in his treatise as the messenger and go-between, the spy, the slanderer, and "the helpful brother," a cross between Pandarus and Polonius: "In such a friend the lover may truly find his greatest repose. But where is such a man to be found? If you are able to lay your hands upon him, grapple him to you as a miser hugs his gold, and grasp him tightly as a niggard grips his silver."[49]

What is most significant, however, is that the setting and theme of a medieval romance like *Floris and Blancheflur* are reiterated in the reality of Ibn Hazm's Spain. Ibn Hazm himself had fallen in love with a young girl with whom he had been brought up. He also relates an incident of "union" relating to "a most trustworthy man who comes from one of the best families" who "was smitten when a boy with a violent passion for a slave-girl attached to a house belonging to his people. He was strictly barred from coming to her, and was at the same time quite crazy for her." There are innumerable parallels of lovesickness such as Floris experienced in the life that Ibn Hazm describes, in particular in his chapter "Of Wasting Away."[50] But the feature that binds Ibn Hazm most closely to the feudal society in which the literary conventions of amour courtois flourished is his emphasis on loyalty, "a mark of true nobility of character,"[51] and the ennobling power of love.

The making of medieval romance falls into a period when there was not only the most intimate personal contact with Islam that Europe has ever experienced but when there was considerable knowledge about Islam in spite of the propaganda of literary stereotypes. Thus the author of the *Chançun de Willame*, on which Wolfram of Eschenbach's *Willehalm* is based, does not mention Apollin or Tervagant, the usual "godheads" which, by the side of Muhammad, make up the mythical Islamic trinity, but puts the Muslim prophet in his proper place. "Deus est el ceil e Mahomet en terre."[52] The "romances of prys" that Chaucer satirized contain much of the matter of Araby that Chaucer used himself. As the *Squire's Tale* shows, he too considered the matter of Araby as the quintessence of "romance" which, in the relation of teller and tale, was to express the "romantic" young Squire as much as the youth's association with love and the month of May. The theme of *Sir Beues*, which Chaucer parodies in *Sir Thopas*, nevertheless reflects the most vital and fateful subject of its time—the meeting of Islam and Christianity. What has happened is that romance has moved from the strictly confined territory of Arthurian legend into the historical and geographical frame of the whole known contemporary world, from the British Isles to Egypt and Damascus. The making of medieval romance was thus a historical enterprise which developed side by side with intellectual pursuits of the highest sophistication and political events of the highest complexity, all centered on the assimilation of the legacy of Islam.

In its preoccupation with the matter of Araby the romantic imagination throughout the Middle Ages invaded the realm of contemporary reality on its most solid ground—that of physical and cultural survival. In the matter of Araby, the quest of the mythical Arthurian hero battling against the evil forces unleashed by a Merlin or a Morgan la Fay, is translated into the reality of both actual experience and its imaginative interpretation in "a confirmed literary habit of the race."[53] In assessing the role of Arabic material in medieval romance, we must remember, again and again, that we are not merely dealing with "the exotic" or the "esoteric"—fashionable eccentricities of a later "orientalizing" age—but with an aspect of the most concrete reality of medieval existence. The caricature of the Saracen presence in the popular medieval romances was a way of coping emotionally with a real threat:

> Til that ther cam a greet geaunt,
> His name was sire Olifaunt,
> A perilous man of dede.
> He seyde, "Child, by Termagaunt!
> But if thou prike out of myn haunt,
> Anon I sle thy steede
>   With mace."[54]

At the same time, Chaucer's treatise on the astrolabe tells the other side of the story. In dealing with its Saracen subject matter, medieval romance shared the lucid apprehension of reality which characterized the best intellectual effort of the age. What medieval popular romance did was to absorb and assimilate this reality in a psychologically viable form for the general public. Like other factors in medieval civilization, including allegory, even the crudest "Saracen" romance represents the intuitional assimilation of an experience that was organically rooted in the visible world and the visible events of the day.

It is Alain of Lille, a medieval poet, who shows us the significance of medieval romance as a striving for the enhancement of the real: "Sometimes poets combine historical events and imaginative fancies, as it were in a splendid structure, to the end that from the harmonious joining of diversities a finer picture of the story may result."[55] He is echoed by the late Marc Bloch: "The material is in part authentic, in part imaginary; and no attempt at interpretation can be acceptable which fails to give equal consideration to both elements."[56]

What has been attempted in the preceding pages is to discern "the matter of Araby" in the making of the Middle Ages through its presence in the literature and thought of medieval England. "The matter of Troy" and "the matter of Britain" are deeply rooted in the myth of British national origin. But "the matter of Araby" and the process of its absorption and assimilation are an extraordinary phenomenon because extraneous to the tradition of Latin Europe. On the rational level, in science and philosophy, the assimilation of Arabic material proceeded deliberately and systematically because it was the work of individual scholars who recognized the Arabs as mediators of Greek philosophy and science. In this process, the Arabs did not only transmit and interpret the knowledge and ideas of classical antiquity, but became the teachers and inspirers of the West at the very heart of its cultural life: its attitude to reason and faith. The migration of literary works, as well as concepts, images, themes, and motifs, was a natural by-product in this work of transmission. The literary material brought Islamic modes of thought within the reach of a far wider circle of readers than the intellectual élite, for it was widely translated into the vernacular.

The "romantic" component in "the matter of Araby" is more elusive, because it lies in the fantasies of medieval romance and in the relation of romance to reality. It is perhaps true that "the average, plodding, medieval English romance writer, quite ignorant of the classics, took his material ready-made from the French and knew little and cared less about the superior ethics, learning, and civilization of Islam."[57] But even if he did, he created a fantasy which found a ready response in his audience and reflected the spirit of the age. At the lowest level of the Christian encounter with the Saracens, the spirit of the age was religious bigotry and hate, though even here we may recall Spitzer's caveat: the medieval mind "knew hatred only on dogmatic, not on racial, grounds."[58] At the highest level, as in *Floris and Blancheflur*, the Arabian theme is perfectly fused into an original work which reveals the striving for harmony from dissonance at the core of the medieval concept of order, in music, science, philosophy, and canon law.[59] The romance of *Floris and Blancheflur* aspires to the highest human ideal, perfect love, which is romantic in its essence because it sublimely disregards the experience of reality. The marriage of Floris the Saracen, and Blancheflur the Christian, ennobles and harmonizes the two opposite cultures. It is a literary "concordia discordantium," a "consonantia dissimilium"[60] on the territory of the alien culture itself. In this romance there is a fulfilment which the tragic Saracen marriage of Chaucer's Constance is not destined to bring about: a perfect integration of the romantic theme in the medieval idea of world harmony and universal order.

Notes

CHAPTER 1

1 "Saraceni dicti, vel quia ex Sarra genitos se praedicent, vel sicut gentiles aiunt, quod ex origine Syrorum sint, quasi Syriginae." *Isidori Hispalensis Episcopi Etymologiarum sive Originum Libri XX*, ed. W. M. Lindsay (Oxford, 1911), lib. IX, I, ii, 57.

2 H. A. R. Gibb, *Arabic Literature* (London, 1926), p. 5.

3 K. Erdmann, *Die Entstehung des Kreuzzugsgedankens* (Stuttgart, 1935), p. 27. For a summary of various theories of origin, see P. Rousset, *Les Origines et les caractères de la première croisade* (Neuchâtel, 1945), pp. 13–22.

4 H. Prutz, *Kulturgeschichte der Kreuzzuege* (Berlin, 1883), pp. 396–415.

5 J. G. von Herder, *Ideen zur Geschichte der Menschheit*, ed. Julian Schmidt (Leipzig, 1869), book XX, p. 217.

6 Steven Runciman, *A History of the Crusades* (New York, 1964), III, 469.

7 A. H. L. Heeren, *Essai sur l'influence des croisades* (Paris, 1808), p. 405.

8 Runciman, III, 492.

9 *Die Quaestiones Naturales des Adelardus von Bath*, ed. M. Mueller in *Beitraege zur Geschichte der Philosophie und Theologie des Mittelalters* 31 (Munster, 1934), p. 49, lines 25–29. Stephen of Pisa, trained in Salerno, translated, in Antioch, the *Royal Book* of Haly Abbas, a medical source well known to Chaucer. See Max Meyerhof, "Science and Medicine," *The Legacy of Islam*, ed. Sir Thomas Arnold and A. Guillaume (Oxford, 1931), pp. 311–55, 329. On the importance of Antioch as a seat of learning after the Arab conquest (A.D. 638) see Meyerhof, "Von Alexandrien nach Bagdad," *Sitzungsberichte der Preussischen Akademie der Wissenschaften, philos.-hist. Klasse* (Berlin, 1930), pp. 389–429, 410; and "On the Transmission of Greek and Indian Science to the Arabs," *Islamic Culture* 11 (1937), 19. The Arabs merely followed a tradition of learning which prevailed in Antioch from ancient days. On a "building of learning" in ancient Antioch and the custom of bringing a boy "slow of understanding" to an image before him so that he "straightway acquires knowledge," see W. F. Stinespring, "The Description of Antioch in Codex Vaticanus Arabicus," Ph.D. dissertation, Yale University, 1932, pp. 13–14.

10 C. H. Haskins, *Studies in the History of Medieval Science* (Cambridge, Massachusetts, 1924), p. 130; idem, *The Renaissance of the Twelfth Century* (New York, 1960), p. 282.

11 See the discussion of William of Tripoli in N. Daniel, *Islam and the West* (Edinburgh, 1962), p. 237.

12 H. S. Gehman, "The Arabic Bible in Spain," *Speculum* 1 (April, 1926), 220.

13 *Alvari Cordubensis Indiculus Luminosus* in Migne, *Patrologia Latina* 121, cols. 555–56. Quotation in English from R. Dozy, *Spanish Islam: A History of the Moslems in Spain*, trans. F. G. Stokes (London, 1913), p. 268.

14 J. Kritzeck, *Peter the Venerable and Islam* (Princeton, 1964), pp. 62–65. See

Peter the Venerable's letter to Bernard of Clairvaux ("Epistola de translatione sua") in Migne, *P.L.* 189, cols. 649D–650C; cf. "tam prece quam
pretio," col. 671C; in Kritzeck, pp. 212–14. The crucial work on the
translation of the Koran under the sponsorship of Peter the Venerable was
done by Marie-Thérèse d'Alverny who rediscovered and studied the
original manuscript, MS. 1162 of the Bibliothèque de l'Arsenal in Paris.
See d'Alverny, "Deux traductions du Coran au Moyen âge," *Archives
d'histoire doctrinale et littéraire du Moyen âge* 22–23 (1947–48), 69–131.

15 Peter the Venerable, *Contra Sectam Saracenorum*, lib. I, 1: "Aggredior,
inquam, vos, non, ut nostri saepe faciunt armis, sed verbis, non vi, sed
ratione, non odio, sed amore." Migne, *P.L.* 189, col. 673B; Kritzeck, p. 231.
Cf. *Sancti Raymundi de Pennafort Ordinis Praedicatorum Summa* (Verona, 1744),
Titulus IV, 1, p. 24: "Quia coacta servitia non placent Deo"; Oliver of
Paderborn, *Epistola salutaris regi Babilonis:* "Si gens tua doctrinam Christi
et predicatores eius publice admitteret, ecclesia Dei gladium verbi Dei
ibenter ei mitteret et ad consortium fidei catholice gaudens invitaret" in
Die Schriften des Koelner Domscholasters . . . Olivers, ed. H. Hoogeweg
(Tübingen, 1894), pp. 299–300; see Daniel, pp. 116–17.

16 Marie-Thérèse d'Alverny and G. Vajda, "Marc de Tolède, traducteur
d'Ibn Tumart," *Al-Andalus* 16 (1951), 99–140, 259–308; 17 (1952), 1–56;
see preface to the translation of Galen's "De tactu pulsus," *Al-Andalus* 16
(1951), 260.

17 O. Hartwig, "Die Uebersetzungsliteratur Unteritaliens in der mohamme-
danisch-staufischen Epoche," *Centralblatt fuer Bibliothekswesen* 3 (1886),
161–90, 223–25, 505 ff.; see p. 167.

18 M. Amari, *Storia dei Musulmani di Sicilia* (Florence, 1854–68), III, 365.

19 *The Travels of Ibn Jubair*, ed. W. Wright and M. J. de Goeje (Leyden, 1907),
pp. 325 ff.

20 E. Kantorowicz, *Frederick the Second, 1194–1250* (London, 1931), p. 355.

21 Ibid., p. 27.

22 C. H. Haskins, *The Normans in European History* (New York, 1966), p. 229.

23 *Ioannis Saresberiensis . . . Policratici Libri VIII*, ed. C. C. I. Webb (Oxford,
1909), II, lib. VII-XIX, 682a–682b, pp. 173–74. *The Metalogicon of John of
Salisbury*, trans. D. D. McGarry (Berkeley, 1962), pp. 44, 172.

24 *Otia Imperialia*, ed. F. Liebrecht (Hanover, 1856), pp. 49 ff.

25 *Des Adelard von Bath Traktat de eodem et diverso*, ed. H. Willner in *Beitraege zur
Geschichte der Philosophie des Mittelalters* 4 (Munster, 1903), p. 32, line 27.

26 C. H. Haskins and D. P. Lockwood, "The Sicilian Translators of the
Twelfth Century and the First Latin Version of Ptolemy's *Almagest*,"
Harvard Studies in Classical Philology 21 (1910), 89. On the Arabic name of
the *Almagest*, see F. Rosenthal, "Al-Kindi and Ptolemy" in *Studi in onore di
Giorgio Levi della Vida* (Rome, 1956), II, 438.

27 See Carlotta Labowsky, "Praefatio" in *Meno interprete Henrico Aristippo*, ed.
V. Kordeuter, *Corpus Platonicum Medii Aevi* (London, 1940), p. xi.

28 Preface to the Sicilian translation of the *Almagest* in Haskins, *Studies in the
History of Medieval Science*, p. 191, lines 22 ff., 27 ff.; p. 193, line 90.

29 V. Rose, "Die Luecke im Diogenes Laertius und der alte Uebersetzer,"

Hermes 1 (1866), 388; F. Bliemetzrieder, *Adelhard von Bath* (Munich, 1935), pp. 154 ff., 167 ff.

30 *Petri Blesensis Opera Omnia*, ed. I. A. Giles (Oxford, 1847), I, 194–95; cf. W. F. Schirmer and U. Broich, *Studien zum literarischen Patronat im England des 12. Jahrhunderts* (Cologne, 1961), pp. 193 ff.

31 P. de Gayangos, *The History of the Mohammedan Dynasties in Spain extracted from the Nafh-t-tib of al-Maqqari* (London, 1840), I, app. C, p. xl.

32 Ibid., I, pp. 34 ff.; on the breakup of the Umayyad Caliphate, see W. M. Watt, *A History of Islamic Spain* (Edinburgh, 1965), pp. 85 ff.

33 *Daniels von Morley Liber de naturis inferiorum et superiorum*, ed. Karl Sudhoff in *Archiv fuer die Geschichte der Naturwissenschaften und der Technik* 8 (Leipzig, 1918), p. 7.

34 Henri Pirenne, *Mohammed and Charlemagne* (New York, 1960), p. 162.

35 *Liber de naturis inferiorum et superiorum*, p. 33.

36 Kritzeck, pp. 210 ff.

37 V. Rose, "Ptolemaeus und die Schule von Toledo," *Hermes* 8 (1874), 346.

38 See A. González Palencia, *El Arzobispo Don Raimundo y la escuela de traductores de Toledo* (Barcelona, 1942).

39 Rose, "Ptolemaeus und die Schule von Toledo," p. 346.

40 See G. Strohmaier's article, "Ḥunayn b. Isḥāḳ," in *The Encyclopaedia of Islam*, new edition (Leyden, 1971), III, 578–81. Fuat Sezgin, *Geschichte des arabischen Schrifttums* (Leyden, 1967), III, 247–56.

41 See *The Cambridge History of Islam*, ed. P. M. Holt, Ann K. S. Lambton, and Bernard Lewis (Cambridge, 1970), II, 581–82.

CHAPTER 2

1 *King Alfred's West-Saxon Version of Gregory's Pastoral Care*, ed. Henry Sweet (London, 1934), see Preface. I discuss Adelard's travels later in this chapter.

2 "Id igitur quaerens violentes principes, vinolentos praesules, mercenarios iudices, patronos inconstantes, privatos adulatores, mendaces promissores, invidiosos amicos, ambitiosos fere omnes cum acceperim," *Die Quaestiones Naturales des Adelardus von Bath*, ed. M. Mueller, p. 1, lines 6–11.

3 Ibid., p. 1, line 14.

4 "Ut Arabum studia ego pro posse meo scrutarer," ibid., p. 4, line 32.

5 *De eodem et diverso*, ed. Willner, p. 32, line 27; quoted above, in chap. 1.

6 *Baedae Opera Historica*, ed. J. E. King (London, 1930), II, 368–69, book V, chap. 23.

7 R. W. Southern, *Western Views of Islam in the Middle Ages* (Cambridge, Massachusetts, 1962), p. 18.

8 D. M. Dunlop, "The British Isles according to Medieval Arabic Authors," *Islamic Quarterly* 4 (1957), 11–28; E. Lévi-Provençal, *Histoire de l'Espagne musulmane* (Paris, 1950–53), I, 219; G. Jacob, *Arabische Berichte von Gesandten an Germanische Fuerstenhoefe aus dem 9. und 10. Jahrhundert* (Berlin, 1927).

9 See J. Hunter, *English Monastic Libraries* (London, 1831), p. 29. On the York Cathedral library, see J. Leland, *Collectanea* (Oxford, 1715), IV, 14, 37.

10 The metrical catalogue of the library at York as translated by A. F. West,

Alcuin and the Rise of the Christian Schools (New York, 1892), p. 34; A. F. Leach, *The Schools of Medieval England* (London, 1915), p. 60; "Versus de Patribus Regibus et Sanctis Euboricensis Ecclesiae," lines 1535 ff. in *Poetae Latini Aevi Carolini*, I, ed. E. Duemmler, in *Monumenta Germaniae Historica* (Berlin, 1881), p. 203.

11 Ibn 'Abd al-Hakam, *Futūḥ Ifrīqiyah wa al-Andalus*, ed. and trans. A. Gateau (Algiers, 1942), pp. 44–45.

12 Pirenne, *Mohammed and Charlemagne*, p. 93; E. Ashtor, "Nouvelles réflexions sur la thèse de Pirenne," *Schweizerische Zeitschrift fuer Geschichte* 20 (1970), 602–04. But see R. S. Lopez, "Muhammed and Charlemagne: A Revision," *Speculum* 18 (1943), 15; F. J. Himly, "Y a-t-il emprise musulmane sur l'économie des états européens du VIIIe au Xe siècle?" *Schweizerische Zeitschrift fuer Geschichte* 5 (1955), 31–81. Cf. *The Pirenne Thesis, Analysis, Criticism, and Revision*, ed. A. E. Havighurst (Boston, 1958), where Lopez's "Muhammed and Charlemagne" and "East and West in the Early Middle Ages" are also to be found.

13 *Epistolae*, ed. W. Wattenbach and E. Duemmler in *Monumenta Alcuiniana (Bibliotheca Rerum Germanicarum 6)* (Berlin, 1873), ep. XIV, p. 167; Eleanor S. Duckett, *Alcuin, Friend of Charlemagne* (New York, 1951), pp. 136 ff.

14 Wattenbach and Duemmler, ep. IX, ii, 57.

15 Wattenbach and Duemmler, ep. CXII, p. 458.

16 *Isidori Etymologiae Codex Toletanus*, phototypice editus Rudolphus Beer (Leyden, 1909), see 11r, 19r, 28r, 33v, 34r, 35r, 35v, and passim. On the use of Isidore by Ibn Juljul, a Cordovan court physician of the tenth century, see F. E. Peters, *Aristotle and the Arabs* (New York, 1968), pp. 215, 268.

17 Wattenbach and Duemmler, ep. XCIX, p. 417. Ibid., "Versus de Sanctis," p. 125. lines 1439 ff., *Poetae Latini Aevi Carolini*, I, p. 201.

18 M. L. W. Laistner, *Thought and Letters in Western Europe, A.D. 500 to 900* (Ithaca, 1966), p. 229.

19 *Epistolae Merowingici et Karolini Aevi I* in *Monumenta Germaniae Historica* (Berlin, 1892), p. 413.

20 C. A. Nallino, *Raccolta di scritti* (Rome, 1944), V, 263 ff.

21 C. F. Seybold, *Glossarium Latino-Arabicum ex unico qui exstat codice Leidensi unidecimo saeculo in Hispania conscripto* [*Semitistische Studien* 15–17] (Berlin, 1900); cf. C. Schiaparelli, *Vocabulista in Arabico* (Florence, 1871), which dates from the thirteenth century.

22 See G. Neugebauer, "The Early History of the Astrolabe," *Isis* 40 (1949), 240–56.

23 ". . . causa sophiae primo (a) Franciam dein (b) Cordubam lustrans," Adémar de Chabannes, *Chronique*, ed. J. Chavanon (Paris, 1897), p. 154; *Gerberti Opera Mathematica*, ed. N. M. Bubnov (Berlin, 1899), p. 109 ff.; *Sbornik Pissem Gerberta* (St. Petersburg, 1888–90), part II, eps. 17, 24, 25, pp. 204, 221. Cf. *The Letters of Gerbert*, trans. Harriet P. Lattin (New York, 1961), pp. 64, 69, 70.

24 William of Malmesbury, *De Gestis Regum Anglorum*, ed. W. Stubbs (London, 1887), lib. II, 194.

25 Haskins, quoting from MS. Bodleian Auct. F.1.9, f. 90, in *Studies in the*

History of Medieval Science, p. 114, note 8. *A Treatise on the Astrolabe in the Works of Geoffrey Chaucer*, ed. F. N. Robinson (Cambridge, Massachusetts, 1957), Part I, 18, line 2; 19, line 6: 21, line 90, pp. 548–49, 869. On Walcher, see also A. C. Crombie, *Augustine to Galileo* (Cambridge, Massachusetts, 1961), I, 91.

26   For Walcher's account, see "De experientia scriptoris" in Haskins, *Studies in the History of Medieval Science*, pp. 114–15. J. K. Wright, "Notes on the Knowledge of Latitudes and Longitudes in the Middle Ages," *Isis* 5 (1923), 75–98, 81.

27   "De experientia scriptoris," Haskins, *Medieval Science*, p. 115.

28   C. Schoy, article "al-Ḳamar ('the moon')," in *The Encyclopedia of Islam* (Leyden, 1927), II, 705–06.

29   *The Complete Works of Venerable Bede*, ed. J. A. Giles, 12 vols. (London, 1843), vol. VI, "De Temporum Ratione," cap. XV, p. 178.

30   *Die Disciplina Clericalis des Petrus Alfonsi*, ed. A. Hilka and W. Soederhjelm (Heidelberg, 1911), "Prologus," pp. 1–2.

31   H. Schwarzbaum, "International Folklore Motifs in Petrus Alfonsi's *Disciplina Clericalis*," *Sefarad* 21 (1961), 267–99; 22 (1962), 1–59; 23 (1963), 55–73.

32   "The Tale of Melibee," B 2248, 2402, 2496, 2752 in *The Works of Geoffrey Chaucer*, ed. Robinson, pp. 170, 174, 176, 182.

33   J. M. Millás Vallicrosa, "La aportación astronómica de Pedro Alfonso," *Sefarad* 3 (1943), 65 ff.; "Avodato shel Moshe Sefaradi al hokhmat ha-tkhunah," *Tarbiz* 9 (1937–38), 55–64.

34   "Petri Alphonsi ex Judaeo Christiani Dialogi," *Praefatio*, Migne, *P.L.* 157, col. 538A: "Fuit autem pater meus spiritualis Alfunsus, gloriosus Hispaniae imperator . . ."; also in *Maxima Bibliotheca Veterum Patrum* 21 (Lyons, 1677), p. 172G.

35   Y. Baer, *A History of the Jews in Christian Spain*, trans. L. Schoffman (Philadelphia, 1966), I, 52.

36   Cecil Roth, *A History of the Jews in England* (Oxford, 1941), p. 6.

37   Praefatio in *Maxima Bibliotheca* 21, 172H. See A. Lukyn Williams, *Adversus Judaeos* (Cambridge, 1935), pp. 233–40.

38   Baer, *The Jews in Christian Spain*, I, 59.

39   *Dialogi*, Titulus V, in *Maxima Bibliotheca* 21, 195A; Daniel, *Islam and the West*, p. 217.

40   See the discussion of "Elohim" in Titulus VII, *Maxima Bibliotheca* 21, pp. 198 ff.

41   M. R. James, *The Ancient Libraries of Canterbury and Dover, The Catalogues of the Libraries of Christ Church Priory and St. Augustine's Abbey at Canterbury and of St. Martin's Priory at Dover* (Cambridge, 1903), p. 301; R. W. Hunt, "The Disputation of Peter of Cornwall against Symon the Jew" in *Studies in Medieval History Presented to F. M. Powicke*, ed. R. W. Hunt, W. A. Pantin, and R. W. Southern (Oxford, 1948), p. 147, n. 1, p. 151, n. 6; Beryl Smalley. *The Study of the Bible in the Middle Ages* (Oxford, 1952), p. 340; Dorothee Metlitzki, "*The Pearl*—poet as Bezalel," *Medieval Studies* 35 (1973), 413–32.

42   Hunt, "The Disputation of Peter of Cornwall," pp. 147, 151.

43 Ibid., pp. 150–51; R. Loewe, "The Medieval Christian Hebraists of England: Herbert of Bosham and Earlier Scholars," *Transactions of the Jewish Historical Society of England* 17 (1953), 232.

44 Hunt, "The Disputation of Peter of Cornwall," p. 151.

45 Loewe, "Medieval Christian Hebraists," p. 232.

46 Titulus I, *Maxima Bibliotheca* 21, p. 175E.

47 The Vulgate reads "et exercitus caeli te adorat." The name Esdras, in the Vulgate, has been adopted for the canonical Ezra and Nehemiah and is to be distinguished from the apocryphal Esdras. See *A Dictionary of the Bible*, ed. J. Hastings (New York, 1898), I, 763.

48 Titulus I, *Maxima Bibliotheca* 21, pp. 175 ff. See Wright, "Notes," *Isis* 5, 82; C. R. Beazley, *The Dawn of Modern Geography* (New York, 1949), II, 575. On "Arin," a misreading of the Arabic transliteration of an Indian town where there had been an astronomical observatory, see J. H. Kramers, "Geography and Commerce," *The Legacy of Islam*, p. 93. On the Indian origin of the whole conception, see D. Pingree, *The Thousands of Abu Ma'shar* (London, 1968), p. 45.

49 See Beazley, II, 576, 626ff.

50 "De Temporum Ratione," cap. XXXIV; cf. Macrobius, *Commentary on the Dream of Scipio*, trans. W. H. Stahl (New York, 1952), book II, chap. 6, p. 207; Beazley, II, 574.

51 MS. B. M. Arundel 270, fols. 40v–44v; see L. Thorndike, *A History of Magic and Experimental Science* (New York, 1923), II, 70–72; J. M. Millás Vallicrosa, *Tarbiz* 9, 60–61: "ut preparemus nobis etiam post mortem nomen perpetuum."

52 Millás Vallicrosa, *Tarbiz* 9, p. 61.

53 Beazley, *Dawn of Modern Geography*, I, 404–14.

54 Millás Vallicrosa, *Tarbiz* 9, p. 55. Petrus Alfonsi's dates are given as ca. 1062–1110 by Roth, *A History of the Jews in England*, p. 6.

55 *Llibre Revelador*, trans. J. M. Millás Vallicrosa (Barcelona, 1929), pp. 12 ff.

56 *Forma de la tierra*, trans. J. M. Millás Vallicrosa (Madrid, 1956), pp. 28, 47.

57 *Claudii Ptolemaei Opera quae exstant omnia*, ed. J. L. Heiberg, vol. II (*Opera astronomica minora*), pp. clxxxiii–clxxxvi; M. Steinschneider, *Abraham Judaeus, Savasorda und Ibn Esra zur Geschichte der mathematischen Wissenschaften im 12. Jahrhundert* (Berlin, 1925), pp. 327–87.

58 Abraham ibn Ezra's Sabbath Epistle is found in J. Jacobs, *The Jews of Angevin England* (New York, 1893), p. 35.

59 Haskins, *Medieval Science*, p. 115.

60 Ibid., pp. 114, 116.

61 Millás Vallicrosa, *Tarbiz* 9, p. 56.

62 Ibid., p. 60, n. 24.

63 Haskins, *Medieval Science·* p. 117.

64 O. Neugebauer, *The Astronomical Tables of al-Khwarizmi, Translation with Commentaries of the Latin Version*, edited by H. Suter, supplemented by Corpus Christi College MS. 283 (Copenhagen, 1962), see especially p. 232.

65 Haskins, *Medieval Science*, pp. 117–18; Neugebauer, *Astronomical Tables*,

pp. 213, 218–19, 231; Millás Vallicrosa, *Tarbiz* 9, 62–63; see G. Toomer's review of Neugebauer in *Centaurus* 10 (1964), 203 ff.

66   Haskins, *Medieval Science*, p. 118.

67   Neugebauer, *Astronomical Tables*, p. 232.

68   Ibid., pp. 133–34.

69   Millás Vallicrosa, *Tarbiz* 9, 62–64.

70   J. M. Millás Vallicrosa, *Nuevos estudios sobre historia de la ciencia española* (Barcelona, 1960), p. 106.

71   Haskins, *Medieval Science*, p. 117.

72   J. W. H. Atkins, *English Literary Criticism, the Medieval Phase* (Cambridge, 1943), p. 148.

73   *Opera*, Migne, *P.L.* 199, ep. 169; George Stephens, *The Knowledge of Greek in England in the Middle Ages* (Philadelphia, 1933), pp. 56–57.

74   M. R. James, *The Ancient Libraries of Canterbury and Dover*, p. lxxxv; N. R. Ker, *Medieval Libraries of Great Britain: A List of Surviving Books* (London, 1941), pp. 46, 77.

75   Roger Bacon knew no Arabic. See M. Bouyges, "Roger Bacon a-t-il lu les livres arabes?" *Archives d'histoire doctrinale et littéraire du Moyen âge* 54 (1930), 311–15; S. A. Hirsch, "Roger Bacon and Philology" in *Roger Bacon Essays*, ed. A. G. Little (Oxford, 1914); B. Altaner, "Zur Kenntnis des Arabischen im 13. und 14. Jahrhundert," *Orientalia Christiana Periodica* 2 (Rome, 1936), pp. 29–452; S. C. Easton, *Roger Bacon and His Search for a Universal Science* (New York, 1952), pp. 26, 86, 105; M. Manzalaoui, "The Pseudo-Aristotelian *Sirr al-Asrār* and Three Oxford Thinkers of the Middle Ages" in *Arabic and Islamic Studies in Honor of Hamilton A. R. Gibb*, ed. G. Makdisi (Leyden, 1965), pp. 481–82.

76   H. Suter, *Die astronomischen Tafeln des Muhammed ibn Musa al-Khwarizmi in der Bearbeitung des Maslama ibn Ahmed al-Madjriti und der lateinischen Uebersetzung des Athelhard von Bath* (Copenhagen, 1914), pp. 32, 167.

77   Millás Vallicrosa, *Tarbiz* 9, p. 64.

78   Suter, *Die astronomischen Tafeln*, pp. 241 ff.

79   "Incipit liber Ezeig id est chanonum Alghoarizmi per Adelardum Bathoniensem ex arabice sumptus et per Rodbertum Cestrensem ordine digestus" (Madrid, Biblioteca Nacional, MS. 10016, f. 8 in Haskins, *Medieval Science*, p. 123).

80   Ibid., p. 118.

81   Millás Vallicrosa, *Tarbiz* 9, p. 64.

82   *Regulae Abaci*, ed. B. Boncompagni in *Bulletino di bibliographia e di storia delle scienze mathematiche e fisiche* 14 (1881), 91–134; on "H. suo," see Bliemetzrieder, *Adelhard von Bath*, p. 341.

83   *The Pipe Roll of 31 Henri I* (London, 1929), p. 22.

84   J. Pits, *Relationum Historicarum de Rebus Anglicis* (Paris, 1619), p. 200; J. Leland, *Commentarii de Scriptoribus Britannicis* (Oxford, 1709), I, 201–02; Th. Tanner, *Bibliotheca Britannico-Hibernica* (London, 1748), p. 55.

85   "Cum in Angliam nuper redierim Henrico Wilhelmi Anglis imperante, quoniam a patria causa studii diu me exceperam, occursus amicorum et

iocundus mihi fuit et commodus." *Quaestiones Naturales*, ed. Mueller, p. 1; *De eodem et diverso*, ed. Willner, pp. 4, 5, 7.

86   *De eodem et diverso*, p. 33, lines 18–20.

87   Haskins, *The Normans in European History*, p. 238.

88   Haskins, *Medieval Science*, pp. 31–32.

89   Ibid., p. 32.

90   "Euclidis philosophi socratici incipit liber Elementorum artis geometricae translatus ab Arabice per Adelardum Gothum Bathoniensem . . . ." *Die Uebersetzung des Euklid aus dem Arabischen in das Lateinische durch Adelhard von Bath*, ed. H. Weissenborn in *Zeitschrift fuer Mathematik und Physik* 25 (1880), Supplement, pp. 143–66, see p. 144.

91   *De cura accipitrum, a medieval Latin treatise*, ed. A. E. H. Swaen (Amsterdam, 1937).

92   Haskins, *Medieval Science*, pp. 28–29. Gervase of Canterbury, *Historical Works*, ed. W. Stubbs (London, 1880), I, 125.

93   Preface in Haskins, *Medieval Science*, p. 29.

94   *Dodi Ve-Nechdi, The Work of Berachya Hanakdan*, ed. and trans. H. Gollancz (London, 1920). On Berachyah, who was also the author of "Fox Fables," see Cecil Roth, *The Jews of Medieval Oxford* (Oxford, 1950), pp. 49, 118, n. 1; J. Jacobs, *The Fables of Aesop* (London, 1889), I, 167–68. According to Habermann, editor of the "Fox Fables," Berachyah was from Normandy and spent some time in England—A. Habermann, *Mishlei Shualim* (Jerusalem, 1946), p. vi. Berachyah, at any rate, echoes Adelard's complaint about the state of corruption he found in England: "In the Isle of the Sea the mind of the childless one is disturbed, and he is surrounded by shame. His descent and kin are cast down. The ear of the multitude of rich is closed to all who ask . . . . The crowd of sycophants rejoice and are glad; their voice is heard even in the company of the good; they praise the mouth that uttereth falsehood, and he that speaketh truth is cursed. And good turns to ill, sweet to bitter, light to darkness, and Berachyah cursed the time . . . . I would prefer a piece of dry and mouldy bread without them rather than share their heritage with them. And when I dwell upon such thoughts of ill my mind is disturbed and sleep is removed from mine eyes . . . " (Jacobs, *Fables*, p. 280).

95   "Ketenensis," see in MS. Arsenal 1162, Marie-Thérèse d'Alverny, "Deux traductions latines du Coran au Moyen âge," *Archives d'histoire doctrinale et littéraire du Moyen âge* 22–23 (1947–48), 71.

96   Ibid., p. 87.

97   Robert's works on alchemy, algebra and astronomy, including a treatise on the astrolabe, dated London 1147, regularly have "Cestrensis." See L. C. Karpinski, *Robert of Chester's Latin Translation of the Algebra of Al-Khowarizmi* (New York, 1915). Haskins, *Medieval Science*, p. 120, note 19; Thorndike, *History of Magic*, II, 83.

98   See *Epistola de translatione sua* in Migne, *P.L.* 189, ep. VII, cols. 339–40; in Kritzeck, *Peter the Venerable*, p. 212.

99   Cf. G. Constable, *The Letters of Peter the Venerable* (Cambridge, Massachusetts, 1967), I, 294; II, 279; Kritzeck, pp. 59–61.

100 See Robert's preface to his Koran translation in Th. Bibliander, *Machvmetis saracenorum principis, eivsque successorum vitae, ac doctrina, seque Alcoran* (Basel, 1543), pp. 7–8. Migne, *P.L.* 189, cols. 657–59. Herman of Dalmatia (Kritzeck, pp. 66–67) mentions Robert in the preface to three of his works, in particular in the preface to *De essentiis* dedicated to "optime Rodberte": "Meministi, opinor, dum nos ex aditis nostris in publicam Minerve pompan prodeuntes circumflua multitudo inhianter miraretur, non tanti personas pensans quantum cultus et ornatus spectans quos ex intimis Arabum thesauris diutine nobis vigilie laborque gravissimus acquisierat . . ." (reprinted in Haskins, *Medieval Science*, pp. 48–49).

101 D'Alverny, "Deux traductions latines du Coran au Moyen âge," pp. 85, 114 ff.; for a criticism of Robert's Koran translation, see also A. Arberry, *The Koran Interpreted* (London, 1955), I, 7.

102 Migne, *P.L.* 189, cols. 637C–658D; Bibliander, *Machvmetis . . . eivsque successorum vitae,* p. 7; J. Leclercq, *Pierre le Vénérable* (Paris, 1946), p. 245.

103 "Prohemium," reprinted in Karpinski, *Robert of Chester's Latin Translation,* p. 31.

104 "Introductorium in astronomicam Albumasaris" in ibid., p. 32.

105 J.J. Manget, *Bibliotheca Chemica Curiosa* (Geneva, 1702), I. 509; Karpinski, *Robert of Chester's Latin Translation,* p. 30.

106 Thorndike, *History of Magic,* II, 83–84. For the date of Herman's *Zaelis Fatidica,* see Haskins, *Medieval Science,* p. 44.

107 *Claudii Ptolemaei Opera quae existant omnia,* ed. J. L. Heiberg, *Opera astronomica minora,* pp. clxxxiii-vi.

108 *Epistola Petri Pictavensis ad dominum Petrum Abbatem* in Kritzeck, pp. 215 ff.

109 Constable, *Letters of Peter the Venerable,* I, 294; II, 279.

110 Daniel, *Islam and the West,* p. 330; d'Alverny, "Deux traductions latines du Coran . . . ," pp. 87 ff.

111 Bibliander, *Machvmetis . . . eivsque successorum vitae,* p. 201.

112 Ibid., p. 189.

113 Ibid., pp. 1–6; reprinted in Kritzeck, pp. 204–11, 212–14.

114 Ibid., pp. 213–23.

115 Migne, *P.L.* 189, col. 671C; Kritzeck, pp. 33, 229.

116 Arsenal 1162, reprinted in d'Alverny, p. 87.

117 Bibliander, *Machvmetis . . . eivsque successorum vitae,* p. 509; J. W. Fueck, "The Arabic Literature on Alchemy according to an-Nadim (A.D. 987)," *Ambix* 4 (February 1951), 81–144. *The Fihrist of al-Nadim,* ed. and trans. B. M. Dodge (New York, 1970), II, 581, 1040.

118 Thorndike, *History of Magic,* II, 215.

119 Manget, *Bibliotheca Chemica Curiosa,* I, 519.

120 *Epistola Petri Cluniancensis ad Bernardum Claraveallis* in Kritzeck, p. 212. Cf. *Roberti Retenensis Praefatio in libro legis Saracenorum, quam Alcoran Vocant* in Migne, *P.L.* 189, cols. 657–60.

121 Haskins, *Medieval Science,* p. 122; Karpinski, *Robert of Chester's Latin Translation.*

122 Karpinski, *Robert of Chester's Latin Translation,* p. 66.

123 Ibid., p. 125.

124   Haskins, *Medieval Science*, p. 122.

125   H. E. Watts, *The Christian Recovery of Spain* (New York, 1894), pp. 14, 117.

126   K. Sudhoff, "Die kurze Vita und das Verzeichnis der Arbeiten Gerhards von Cremona, von seinen Schuelern und Studiengenossen kurz nach dem Tode des Meisters (1187) zu Toledo verabfasst," *Archiv fuer Geschichte der Medizin* 8 (1915), 79.

127   Rose, "Ptolemaeus und die Schule von Toledo," p. 328; Roger Bacon, *Compendium studii philosophiae*, ed. J. S. Brewer (London, 1859), p. 471.

128   Rose, "Ptolemaeus und die Schule von Toledo," p. 343; Thorndike, *History of Magic*, II, 73–78.

129   Haskins, *Medieval Science*, p. 13, note 39, citing MS. 188 at St. John's College, Oxford, first referred to by Thorndike, *History of Magic* II, 76, note 3: "Scire oportet vos, karissimi lectores, quod debetis aliquos annos scire super quod cursus planetarum valeatis ordinare vel per quos possitis ordinatos cursus in libro quem ego Johannis Yspalensis interpres existens rogatu et ope duorum Angligenarum, Gauconis scilicet et Willelmi, de arabico in latinum transtuli."

130   Sudhoff, "Die kurze Vita," p. 76.

131   "Prohemium" to "iudicia Alkindi astrologi" in Karpinski, *Robert of Chester's Latin Translation*, p. 31.

132   Sudhoff, "Die kurze Vita," p. 75.

133   "Philosophia magistri danielis de merlai ad iohannem Norwicensem episcopum," in Rose, "Ptolemaeus und die Schule von Toledo," p. 348. The works were *liber coeli et mundi, de auditu naturali, de sensu et sensato,* and *de generatione et corruptione. De sensu et sensato* is not in the list compiled by Gerard's pupils; see Sudhoff, "Die kurze Vita," p. 78.

134   "Philosophia," in Rose p. 347: ". . . doctrina Arabum, que in quadruvio fere tota existit, maxime his diebus apud Toletum celebratur . . . ." Cf. *Daniels von Morley Liber de naturis inferiorum et superiorum,* ed. Karl Sudhoff, *Archiv fuer die Geschichte der Naturwissenschaften und der Technik* 8, pp. 6–7.

135   M. Mueller, "Die Stellung des Daniel von Morley in der Wissenschaft des Mittelalters," *Philosophisches Jahrbuch* 41 (1928), 304, n. 5: "Die Respektlosigkeit wird dadurch gemildert, dass der Ausdruck bestiales Adelard von Bath entnommen ist."

136   Thorndike, *History of Magic*, I, 179.

137   A. Birkenmajer, "Eine neue Handschrift des Liber de naturis inferiorum et superiorum des Daniel von Merlai," *Archiv fuer die Geschichte der Naturwissenschaften und der Technik* 9 (1918), 47. On the importance of Northampton in the movement of secession from Oxford and Cambridge in 1261, see H. Rashdall, *The Universities of Europe in the Middle Ages,* ed. F. M. Powicke and A. B. Emden, new edition (Oxford, 1936), III, 86–89.

138   *Les Oeuvres de Simund de Freine,* ed. J. E. Matzke (Paris, 1909), p. vii. See J. C. Russell, "Hereford and Arabic Science in England about 1175–1200," *Isis* 18 (1932), 19 ff.

139   K. Miller, *Die aeltesten Weltkarten: Die Herefordkarte* (Stuttgart, 1896), p. 48: "Mit Orosius (um 418 n. Chr.) ist die Verwandtschaft so gross, dass man nach Ausscheidung des juengeren Materials die Karte geradezu als Erlaeu-

terung der Kosmographie des Orosius ansehen kann." See also R. Benedict, "The Hereford Map and the Legend of St. Brandan," *Bulletin of the American Geographical Society* 24 (1892), 329: "Passing around to the east we find not a trace of all that immense extent of Asia to the north and east, the marvels of which had been so recently brought back by Marco Polo, that nothing of them had reached the ears of Richard de Haldingham."

140 Dom A. Morey and C. N. L. Brooke, *Gilbert Foliot and His Letters* (Cambridge, 1905), p. 197; Russell, "Hereford and Arabic Science in England," p. 21.

141 A. Th. Bannister, *A Descriptive Catalogue of the Manuscripts in the Hereford Cathedral Library*, with an Introduction by M. R. James (Hereford, 1927), pp. 10, 118.

142 British Museum, Arundel MS. 377, ff. 86v–87: "Anni collecti omnium planetarum compositi a magistro Rogero super annos domini ad mediam noctem Herefordie anno ab incarnatione domini m.c.lxx.viii. post eclipsim que contigit Hereford eodem anno." See Haskins, *Medieval Science*, p. 125; T. Wright, *Biographia Britannica Literaria* (London, 1846), II, 219: "Maluimus enim haec quam annos Arabum et eorum menses propter difficultatem sequi, eo quod inusitati apud nostrates."

143 Tanner, *Bibliotheca Britannico-Hibernica*, pp. 641, 788; Wright, *Biographia Britannica*, pp. 89–91, 218 ff.; Haskins, *Medieval Science*, pp. 124–25.

144 Bannister, *Manuscripts in the Hereford Cathedral Library* p. 50; J. Price, *An Historical Account of the City of Hereford* (Hereford, 1796), p. 108.

145 Pipe Roll 31, Henri II, p. 146; Haskins, *Medieval Science*, p. 126.

146 Haskins, *Medieval Science*, pp. 123 ff. For a complete list of Roger of Hereford's works, see L. Thorndike and P. Kibre, *A Catalogue of Incipits of Mediaeval Scientific Writings in Latin* (Cambridge, Massachusetts, 1963), p. 1903.

147 MS. Digby, 40 ff. 21r–50v, cited in Haskins, *Medieval Science*, p. 124. In an acrostic of the table of twenty-six chapters which make up the five books of the work we have the following: "Gilleberto Rogerus Salutes H D." Haskins takes "H D" to stand for "Hic Dicit," but the letters probably stand for HereforD. Roger signs himself as "Rogerius de Hereford" in attesting Gilbert's documents. See *The Letters and Charters of Gilbert Foliot*, ed. Dom A. Morey and C. N. L. Brooke (London, 1967), pp. 422, 426, 436. Roger seems to have been a member of Gilbert's establishment when the latter was bishop of London. See Morey and Brooke, *Gilbert Foliot and His Letters*, p. 291.

148 "Ut exempli gratia circa tempus huius compositionis huius tractatus anno scilicet Domini m.c.lxx.vi . . . anni illius nona die septembris," Haskins, *Medieval Science*, p. 124.

149 "Sed et otium quod mihi contingit pro regimine scholarum quibus jam pluribus annis desudavi, et pro destrictione rei familiaris quod non facile relinquit me immemorem sui, malebam in studendo mihi quam aliis consumere," Wright, *Biographia Britannica*, p. 90.

150 Thorndike, *History of Magic*, II, 182–83.

151 "Incipit liber de plantis quem Alveredus de arabico transtulit in latinum mittens ipsum magistro Rogero de Herfodia"; H. Schipperges, *Die Assimilation der arabischen Medizin durch das lateinische Mittelalter* (Wiesbaden, 1964),

p. 73. See *Preface* reprinted in A. Jourdain, *Recherches critiques sur l'âge et l'origine des traductions latines d'Aristote* (Paris, 1843), app. N. xxi, p. 430. The author of this pseudo-Aristotelian treatise was a certain Nicolaus Damascenus (about 40 B.C.). It was translated from the original Greek into Syriac by Hunain ibn Ishaq, turned into Arabic by Hunain's son, and revised by Thabit ibn Qurrah (899–901). Neither the Greek text nor the Arabic version is extant. See H. F. Wuestenfeld, "Die Uebersetzung arabischer Werke ins Lateinische seit dem XI. Jahrhundert," *Abhandlungen der koeniglichen Gesellschaft der Wissenschaften* 22 (Goettingen, 1877), pp. 85 ff.

152   *Excerpta e Libro Alfredi Anglici De Motu Cordis item Costa-Ben-Lucae De Differentia Animae et Spiritus Liber translatus a Johanne Hispalensi*, ed. C. S. Barach (Innsbruck, 1878); *Des Alfred von Sareshel Schrift de Motu Cordis*, ed. Clemens Baeumker (Munster, 1923).

153   *Summa Philosophiae, Die philosophischen Werke des Robert Grosseteste, Bischofs von Lincoln*, ed. L. Baur in *Beitraege zur Geschichte der Philosophie des Mittelatlers* 9 (Munster, 1912), p. 280, line 5; Clemens Baeumker, "Die Stellung Alfred von Sareshel (Alfredus Anglicus) und seiner Schrift *De motu cordis* in der Wissenschaft des beginnenden 13. Jahrhunderts" in *Sitzungsberichte der bayerischen Akademie der Wissenschaften, philos.-hist. Klasse* (Munich, 1913), p. 24.

154   Bacon, *Compendium studii philosophiae*, p. 47.

155   Bannister, *Manuscripts in the Hereford Cathedral Library*, p. 19.

156   Baeumker cites the manuscript forms in "Die Stellung Alfred von Sareshel," p. 23. "Sarewel" seems to me to suggest Charwelton on the Cherwell in the county of Northampton. Cf. "Ceruelle" in *The Concise Oxford Dictionary of English Place-Names*, ed. E. Ekwall (Oxford, 1936), p. 95.

157   Ingeborg Hammer-Jensen, "Das sogennante IV. Buch der *Meteorologie* des Aristoteles," *Hermes* 50 (1915), 131. The following marginal note was found by Rose in a Nuremberg manuscript containing the complete Latin *Meteorology*: "Completus est liber metheororum cuius tres primos libors transtulit magister Gerardus Lumbardus summus philosophus de arabico in latinum. Quartem autem transtulit Henricus Arstippus de greco in latinum. Tria ultima capitula transtulit Aluredus Anglicus sarelensis de arabico in latimun" (V. Rose, "Die Luecke im Diogenes Laertius und der alte Uebersetzer," *Hermes* 1, 385).

158   A. Pelzer, "Une Source inconnue de Roger Bacon, Alfred Sareschel commentateur des *Météorologiques* d'Aristote," *Archivum Franciscanum Historicum* 12 (1919), 44–67.

159   Ibid., p. 44; cf. *The Opus Majus of Roger Bacon*, ed. J. H. Bridges (Oxford, 1897–1900), I, 55, 213; III, 67.

160   Bacon, *Compendium studii philosophiae*, p. 471.

161   Ibid., pp. 467 ff.

162   Baeumker, "Die Stellung Alfred von Sareshel . . . ," p. 23. "Arrova" is (a) a weight of 25 pounds, each containing 16 ounces; (b) a measure, containing 32 pints. G. J. Baretti, *A Dictionary, Spanish-English* (London, 1794), s.v. "arroba."

163   For an account of the activities at Toledo, see R. P. G. Théry. *Tolède, grande ville de la Renaissance médiévale* (Oran, 1944).

164   Henry of Avranches, "Drei Gedichte Heinrichs von Avranches an Kaiser
      Friedrich II" in *Forschungen zur deutschen Geschichte* 18 (1878), 486, lines 57–58.
165   Bacon, *Compendium Studii Philosophiae*, p. 472.
166   Thorndike, *History of Magic*, II, 84; M. Grabmann, *Forschungen ueber die
      lateinischen Aristoteles-Uebersetzungen des XIII. Jahrhunderts*, Beitraege zur
      Geschichte der Philosophie des Mittelalters, 7 (Munster, 1916), pp. 208 ff.
167   M. Steinschneider, *Die europaeischen Uebersetzungen aus dem Arabischen bis
      Mitte des 17. Jahrhunderts*, Sitzungsberichte der philos.-hist. Klasse der
      kaiserlichen Akademie der Wissenschaften, 149 (Vienna, 1905), pp. 32–35.
168   H. Denifle, *Chartularium Universitatis Parisiensis* (Paris, 1889), I, 105, n. 48;
      p. 110, n. 54.
169   Haskins, *Medieval Science*, p. 285.
170   M. Steinschneider, *Die hebraeischen Uebersetzungen des Mittelalters und die Juden
      als Dolmetscher* (Berlin, 1893), p. 523.
171   Jourdain, *Recherches critiques sur l'âge et l'origine des traductions latines d'Aristote*,
      p. 133: "Perfectus est liber Avenalpetrardi. Laudetur Jesus Christus qui
      vivit in aeternum per tempora. Translatus est a magistro Michaele Scoto,
      Tholeti in 18. die Veneris augusti hora tertia, anno incarnationis Christi
      MCCXVII."
172   There are two full-fledged biographies of Scot: J. Wood Brown, *An Enquiry
      into the Life and Legend of Michael Scot* (Edinburgh, 1895) and Lynn Thorn-
      dike, *Michael Scot* (London, 1965).
173   Brown, *Michael Scot*, p. 234: "Explicit nicromantiae experimentum illus-
      trissimi doctoris Domini Magistri Michaelis Scoti, qui summus inter alios
      nominatur Magister, qui fuit Scotus, et servus praeclarissimo Domino suo
      Domino Philipo Regis Ceciliae coronato; quod destinavit sibi dum esset
      aegrotus in civitate Cordubae. . . ." According to Brown, the Philip of this
      note is identical with Philip of Salerno who appears in Sicilian registers in 1200
      and 1213 and with Philip of Tripoli, the translator of the *Secret of Secrets* (pp.
      18 ff.), but see Haskins, *Medieval Science*, pp. 138–40; "Michael Scot in
      Spain," *Estudios eruditos in Memoria de Adolfo Bonilla y San Martín* (Madrid,
      1930), II, 129–34. See below, chapter 5.
174   M. Grabmann, *Die Geschichte der scholastischen Methode* (Freiburg, 1909), I,
      187; Brown, *Michael Scot*, p. 52.
175   S. D. Wingate, *The Mediaeval Latin Versions of the Aristotelian Scientific Corpus*
      (London, 1931), pp. 74–75; *Alexandri Neckam De naturis rerum libri duo*, ed.
      T. Wright (London, 1963), pp. 156, 265.
176   Thorndike, *Michael Scot*, p. 24. On William of Moerbeke (ca. 1215–86), see
      Wingate, *Versions of the Aristotelian Corpus*, pp. 87 ff.
177   F. E. Peters, *Aristoteles Arabus* (Leyden, 1968), p. 36; *Aristoteles Latinus*, ed.
      G. Lacombe et al. (Rome, 1939), I, 104–05. Cf. R. Arnaldez, "Ibn Rushd"
      Encyclopaedia of Islam, new edition III, 911.
178   "Tibi Stephano de Pruvino hoc opus, quod ego Michael Scotus dedi latini-
      tate ex dictis Aristotelis, specialiter commendo" (Jourdain, *Recherches criti-
      ques*, pp. 127 ff.)
179   M. R. James, *A Descriptive Catalogue of the Manuscripts in the Library of Gon-
      ville and Caius College* (Cambridge, 1907), I, 112, MS. 109: "Et iuro ego

michael scotus qui dedi hunc librum latinitati quod in anno m.cc.xxl.xll
kal. novembr. die mercurii accessit nobilior domina totius civitatis bononi-
ensis qui erat hospita mea . . . dicta uxor alberti galli . . . et adduxit ad
me discretam mulierem et sapientem, mariam nomine, habentem nobile
domicilium in vicinia iuxta me. . . ." See Haskins, *Medieval Science*, p. 274,
who points out that Scot is using the Pisan calendar by which the sworn note
is dated 12th November 1221. Thorndike gives the year as 1221, remarking
that there is "something wrong with the date" (*History of Magic*, II, 311).

180   Kantorowicz, *Frederick the Second*, p. 340.

181   W. H. Bliss, *Calendar of Entries in the Papal Registers relating to Great Britain and
      Ireland* (London, 1893), I, 96, 102.

182   Ibid., p. 98.

183   Haskins, *Medieval Science*, p. 273; Thorndike, *Michael Scot*, pp. 6–8, 94 ff.;
      cf. *Bede*, vol. VI "*De Temporum Ratione*," cap. XV, p. 178.

184   Denifle, *Chartularium Universitatis Parisiensis*, I, 110.

185   *Il Liber Abbaci di Leonardo Pisano* in *Scritti di Leonardo Pisano*, ed. B. Boncom-
      pagni (Rome, 1857), I, 1; Thorndike, *Michael Scot*, p. 34.

186   "Completus est liber Avicennae de animalibus, scriptus per magistrum
      Heinricum Coloniensem; ad exemplar magnifici imperatoris nostri domini
      Frederici apud Melfiam civitatem Apulie ubi Dominus imperator eidem
      magistro hunc librum premissum commodavit anno Domini MCCXXXII
      . . ." (*Historia diplomatica Frederici Secundi*, ed. J. L. A. Huillard-Bréholles
      [Paris, 1852–61], p. 382). The translation consisted of a portion of Ibn
      Sīnā's *Kitāb al-Shifā'*; see Haskins, "Michael Scot and Frederick II," *Isis* 4
      (1921–22), 257; Peters, *Aristoteles Arabus*, p. 47.

187   "Drei Gedichte," *Forschungen zur deutschen Geschichte* 18 (1878), 486, line 84.

188   It has been suggested that Scot spent the rest of his life at the court of Ed-
      ward I, to which he repaired after the death of Frederick II in 1250. See M.
      Cantor, *Vorlesungen ueber die Geschichte der Mathematik* (Leipzig, 1900), II, 7;
      Dante's Inferno in Italian and English, ed. Terence Tiller (New York, 1966), p.
      175.

189   "Inferno," II, 115–17; *Decameron*, Eighth Day, Ninth Story.

190   Canto II, 12; n. 28 in Sir Walter Scott, *The Poetical Works, with the Author's
      Introduction and Notes*, ed. L. J. Robertson (London, 1913), pp. 64 ff.

191   Thorndike, *Michael Scot*, pp. 116–17.

192   *The Didascalicon of Hugh of St. Victor*, trans. J. Taylor (New York, 1961), p.
      154.

193   Ibn Khaldūn, *The Muqaddimah*, trans. F. Rosenthal (Princeton, 1958), III,
      156–57, 116.

CHAPTER 3

1   *Opus Majus*, I, 55.

2   Ibid. John of Salisbury "knew nothing of Aristotle but his logic, and that
    imperfectly," "Introduction," p. xxxvii.

3   Denifle, *Chartularium Universitatis Parisiensis*, I, 70.

4   Ibid., pp. 78–79; "Non legantur libri Aristotelis de *methafisica* et de *naturali philosophia*, nec *summe* de eisdem. . . ."

5   Edicts were issued by Gregory IX in 1231 and Urban IV in 1264 (ibid., I, 136–39, 427). In 1255, Aristotle's *Physics*, *Metaphysics*, and *De animalibus* are listed among the required texts (ibid., I, 278). For an account of the prohibition of Aristotle, see F. van Steenberghen, *Aristote en Occident* (Louvain, 1946), pp. 63 ff.; F. E. Peters, *Aristotle and the Arabs* (New York, 1968), pp. 226 ff.

6   H. Schipperges, *Die Assimilation der arabischen Medizin durch das lateinische Mittelalter* (Wiesbaden, 1964), p. 69. On the Aristotelianism of Albertus Magnus, see F. Ueberweg-Heinze, *Grundriss der Geschichte der Philosophie*, ed. B. Geyer (Berlin, 1928), II, 410 ff.

7   Schipperges, *Die Assimilation der arabischen Medizin*, p. 74: "Incipit primus liber de animalibus Aristotelis translatus a Magistro Michaelo scotto in toleto de arabico in latinum" (Codex Cusanus 182, f. 117r).

8   ash-Shahrastānī, *Book of Religious and Philosophical Sects*, ed. W. Cureton (London, 1842), p. 311.

9   *Divine Comedy*, "Inferno," IV, 131: "il maestro di color che sanno." Maimonides calls Aristotle "the Chief of the Philosophers" (*Guide of the Perplexed*, I, 5), while Moses is the "Master of those who know" (I, 54; III, 12, 54). S. Pines suggests that Dante may have encountered the title in a Latin translation of the *Guide* (*The Guide of the Perplexed*, trans. S. Pines [Chicago, 1963], p. lxi).

10 Letter to Samuel Ibn Tibbon as quoted in Pines, p. lix.

11 Pines, p. lxi.

12 *Des Adelard von Bath Traktat de eodem et diverso*, ed. Willner, p. 13, line 20.

13 Ibid., p. 4, lines 1–2.

14 Ibid., p. 3, line 27 ff.; p. 4, line 1; p. 4, line 25; p. 5, line 20.

15 Ibid., p. 6, lines 15–16. Cf. Bertolt Brecht's "Erst kommt das Fressen, dann kommt die Moral," *Die Dreigroschenoper* in *Gesammelte Werke* (Frankfurt, 1967), II, 458.

16 *De eodem*, p. 7, lines 6–9.

17 See Willner's "Einleitung," pp. 42, 59. On a refutation of the assumption that there was a "School of Chartres," see R. W. Southern, *Medieval Humanism and Other Studies* (Oxford, 1970), pp. 61–85.

18 *De eodem*, p. 18, line 31.

19 Ibid., p. 13, lines 19–21.

20 Haskins, *Medieval Science*, p. 36; *De eodem*, p. 33, lines 12 ff.; lines 18 ff.

21 *De eodem*, p. 32, lines 27–29.

22 Ibid., p. 33, lines 18–22.

23 *Quaestiones Naturales des Adelardus von Bath*, p. 22, line 23; p. 381, line 20; p. 5, line 14.

24 *Quaestiones Naturales*, p. 1, cf. lines 6–10 as translated by Thorndike, *History of Magic*, II, 23.

25 *Quaestiones Naturales*, p. 4, lines 29–33.

26 Ibid., p. 5, lines 2–7; lines 10–17.

27 "Incipit libellus magistri Alardi bathoniensis de opere astrolapsus," reprinted in Haskins, *Medieval Science*, pp. 28–29.

28 A. Badawi, *Alaflaṭūniyah al muḥadathatu ʿinda alʿarab (Darāsāt islāmīyah 19)* (Cairo, 1955), pp. 36–37, 43–49. The author of the questions appears as "Faraglis."

29 See Schipperges, *Die Assimilation der arabischen Medizin*, pp. 17–46. On Chaucer's references to "daun Constantyn," see *General Prologue to the Canterbury Tales*, I, l. 433 and *The Merchant's Tale*, IV, l. 1810, in *The Works of Geoffrey Chaucer*, ed. Robinson, pp. 21, 121.

30 See Ibn Khaldūn, *Muqaddimah*, trans. Rosenthal, III, p. 35.

31 *Quaestiones Naturales*, p. 12, line 14; p. 9, line 31.

32 Ibid., p. 69, lines 3–4.

33 Ibid., Quaest. XV and Quaest. XIX.

34 Ibid., Quaest, XLVIII, pp. 47–48.

35 Ibid., p. 9, lines 20–33: "Et meo certe iudico in hoc sensibili mundo nihil omnino moritur, nec minor est hodie quam cum creatus est. Si qua enim pars ab una coniunctione solvitur, non perit, sed ad aliam societatem transit."

36 Ibid., p. 49, lines 25–29.

37 Ibid., p. 53, line 27; p. 54, line 3.

38 See translation of Adelard's "Quaestiones Naturales" in Berachya Hanakdan, *Dodi Ve-Nechdi*, ed. and trans. H. Gollancz, chapters I, L, LXIV, LXV, XLIX.

39 R. W. Chambers, *Thomas More* (London, 1935), p. 180. *The Confutation of Tyndale's Answer* in *The Complete Works of St. Thomas More*, ed. L. A. Schuster et al. (New Haven, 1973), VIII, 605, 1618; *Quaestiones Naturales* XLIX, pp. 48–49; *Dodi Ve-Nechdi* pp. 138–39; Vincent de Beauvais, *Speculum Naturale*, lib. V, 13, 31; and lib. VI, 6, 7, 40.

40 See Thorndike, *History of Magic*, II, 196; Wright, *Alexandri Neckam De naturis rerum*, pp. 56, 164, 288: caps. XVI (cf. *Quaestiones Naturales* XLIX), LVII (cf. *Quaestione Naturales* I), CLXII (cf. *Quaestiones Naturales* VII, VIII).

41 *De naturis rerum*, I, 93; Schipperges, *Die Assimilation der arabischen Medizin*, pp. 28 ff.

42 *De naturis rerum*, II, cap. XLIX, p. 159; *Legacy of Islam*, p. 381; F. J. Carmody, *Arabic Astronomical and Astrological Sciences in Latin Translation* (Berkeley, 1956), pp. 119, 155.

43 *Opus Majus*, I, pp. 5–6.

44 Alfred's *De motu cordis* is dedicated to Neckam: "Liber Magistri Alfredi Anglici ad Magistrum magnum Alexandrum Neckam"; see below, chapter 4.

45 *Quaestiones naturales*, p. 19, lines 21–30; *Dodi Ve-Nechdi*, p. 107.

46 Thorndike, *History of Magic*, II, 30. For a similar discussion, see *Didascalicon of Hugh of St. Victor*, p. 56.

47 *Quaestiones Naturales*, p. 20, lines 6–9; *Dodi Ve-Nechdi*, p. 107.

48 F. C. Copleston, *Medieval Philosophy* (New York, 1961), p. 65.

49 *Quaestiones Naturales*, p. 20, lines 16–21, 33; p. 21, line 4; *Dodi Ve-Nechdi*, pp. 107–08.

50 *Quaestiones Naturales*, p. 34, lines 21–23.

51 Ibid., p. 12, lines 9–11: "Quare si quid amplius a me audire desideras, rationem refer et recipe. Non enim ego ille sum, quem pellis pictura pascere possit." The vigorous metaphor of a beefsteak, which is Thorndike's translation (*History of Magic*, II, 29), gives a Chaucerian flavor to Adelard's "Englishness."

52 *Quaestiones Naturales*, p. 12, lines 11–12; *Dodi Ve-Nechdi*, p. 99.

53 *Quaestiones Naturales*, p. 6, lines 6–7; p. 8, lines 29–34; p. 69, lines 10–11, 17–20.

54 *Opus Majus*, I, 5–6.

55 *Quaestiones Naturales*, VI, p. 11, line 23; p. 12, line 6; *Dodi Ve-Nechdi*, pp. 98–99.

CHAPTER 4

1 In an acrostic of the table of chapters of the *Compotus* we read: "Gilleberto Rogerus Salutes H[ic?] D[icit?]," Haskins, *Studies in Medieval Science*, p. 124; see above, chap. 2, n. 148.

2 A. C. Cawley, "Astrology in *The Owl and the Nightingale*," *Modern Language Review* 46 (1951), 161–74.

3 *The Owl and the Nightingale*, ed. E. G. Stanley (New York, 1960), p. 85, line 1256. The translation of the Middle English text is quoted from J. W. H. Atkins, *The Owl and the Nightingale* (Cambridge, 1922); cf. *The Owl and the Nightingale*, trans. into verse by Graydon Eggers (Durham, 1955), p. 34.

4 L. Thorndike, "The True Place of Astrology in the History of Science," *Isis* 46 (1955), 273, 277; cf. E. Cassirer, *Individuum und Kosmos in der Philosophie der Renaissance* (Darmstadt, 1963), p. 105.

5 Beginning of the preface as reprinted in Th. Wright, *Biographia Britannica Literaria* (London, 1846), pp. 90–91.

6 *Daniels von Morley Liber de naturis inferiorum et superiorum*, ed. Sudhoff, p. 40.

7 Richard C. Dales, "Robert Grosseteste's Views on Astrology," *Medieval Studies* 29 (1967), 360, 362–63.

8 Quoted from MS. "Liber introductorius," cod. lat. 10268 in Staatsbibliothek, Munich, in Thorndike, *Michael Scot*, p. 93.

9 R. Lemay, *Abū Ma'shar and Latin Aristotelianism in the Twelfth Century* (Beirut, 1962), p. 69.

10 Ibid., p. 3, note 2.

11 *Liber de naturis inferiorum et superiorum*, ed. Sudhoff, pp. 17, 39.

12 Ibid., p. 32.

13 On Daniel's use of Alfraganus in the translation of John of Spain, see Theodore Silverstein, "Daniel of Morley, English cosmogonist and student of Arabic science," *Medieval Studies* 10 (1948), 182–83.

14 *Alexandri Neckam De naturis rerum*, p. 159; Alain de Lille, *Anticlaudianus*, ed. R. Bossuat (Paris, 1955), lib. IV, p. 108, l. 63; cf. *The Anticlaudianus of Alain de Lille*, trans. W. H. Cornog (Philadelphia, 1935), p. 92.

15 Lemay, *Abū Ma'shar*, p. 113.

16 Ibid., p. 59, note 3.

17 Ibid., pp. 68–69, 148–49.

18 See *The Astrological History of Māshā'allāh*, trans. E. S. Kennedy and D. Pingree (Cambridge, Massachusetts, 1971), p. 131: "but if God wishes it so, the evil planets will not harm him."

19 *The Muqaddimah*, III, p. 157.

20 "Petri Abaelardi Expositio in Hexameron," ed. Victor Cousin in *Opera* (Paris, 1849–59), I, 649–51.

21 Lemay, *Abū Ma'shar*, pp. 123, 127 ff.

22 Cf. Albumasar, *Flores astrologiae* (Augsburg, Erhard Ratdolt, 1488), b3-b4; *The Astrological History of Māshā'allāh*, pp. 43, 63, 64; Franz Boll, *Sternglaube und Sterndeutung* (Leipzig, 1926), pp. 44, 54, 564, 134, especially p. 112. The "incipit" of Robert Grosseteste's treatise *de prognosticatione* is cited by Baur, *Die philosophischen Werke des Robert Grosseteste*, p. 72: "Ad prognosticandam diversam dispositionem aeris futuram. . . ." Baur describes weather predictions in the treatise as founded on Arabian meteorology and resting solely on the positions of stars (p. 74).

23 Thorndike, *Michael Scot*, p. 117.

24 *Didascalicon* VI, 15; Migne, *P.L.* 176, col. 810, as cited in Thorndike, *History of Magic*, II, 13–14; *The Didascalicon of Hugh of St. Victor*, trans. J. Taylor, pp. 154–55.

25 Lib. II, cap. 4, in *P.L.* 176, col. 753.

26 *Policraticus*, lib. II, cap. 18, trans. J. Pike (Minneapolis, 1938), p. 88.

27 Th. Wedel, *The Mediaeval Attitude toward Astrology* (New Haven, 1920), p. 39.

28 Lemay, *Abū Ma'shar*, p. 303.

29 *Policraticus*, Lib. II, cap. 19; Pike, p. 97.

30 Ibid.

31 Lemay, *Abū Ma'shar*, p. 111.

32 Atkins, *The Owl and the Nightingale*, p. 167; Middle English text in Stanley, p. 76.

33 Baeumker, "Die Stellung Alfred von Sareshel (Alfredus Anglicus) und seiner Schrift *De motu cordis* in der Wissenschaft des beginnenden 13. Jahrhunderts," *Sitzungsberichte der bayerischen Akademie der Wissenschaften, philos.-hist. Klasse* 9 (Munich, 1913), pp. 1–64.

34 *Excerpta e Libro Alfredi Anglici De Motu Cordis item Costa-Ben-Lucae De Differentia Animae et Spiritus Liber translatus a Johanne Hispalensi*, ed. C. S. Barach (Innsbruck, 1878), pp. 51, 54; *Des Alfred von Sareshel Schrift de Motu Cordis*, ed. Baeumker (Munster, 1923), p. 14.

35 *Alexandri Neckam De naturis rerum*, p. 494; see "Preface," p. lxxiv.

36 Ibid., pp. 346 ff.

37 See E. J. Holmyard and D. C. Mandeville, *Avicennae De congelatione et conglutinatione lapidum; Being Sections of the Kitāb al-Shifā'* (Paris, 1927), p. 10.

38 F. Rahman, *Avicenna's Psychology, An English Translation of Kitāb-al-Najāt, Book II, Chapter VI* (Oxford, 1952), p. 66. The *Kitāb-al-Najāt*, the "Book of Salvation," is Avicenna's own abridgement of the *Kitāb ash-Shifā'*.

39 J. Willis, *Ambrosii Theodosii Macrobii Saturanalia* (Leipzig, 1963), p. 431; Macrobius, *Commentary on the Dream of Scipio*, trans. W. H. Stahl (New York, 1952), chapter 10, p. 239; chapter 14, pp. 143–44.

40 See Barach, pp. 19–20; *Chalcidii Timaeus de Platonis translatus item ejusdem in eundem Commentarius,* ed. J. Heursius (Leyden, 1617), p. 306.

41 See Heinrich Flatten, *Die Philosophie des Wilhelm of Conches* (Coblenz, 1929), "Einleitung"; Tullio Gregory, *Anima Mundi—la Filosofia di Gugliemo di Conches e la scuola di Chartres* (Florence, 1955), p. 165; Lemay, *Abū Ma'shar* pp. 157–95.

42 *Philosophia,* I. 21 in Migne, *P.L.* 172, col. 46; cf. Gregory, p. 165. M. Steinschneider, "Constantinus Africanus und seine arabischen Quellen" in *Virchows Archiv fuer pathologische Anatomie und Physiologie und fuer klinische Medizin* 37 (Berlin, 1866), 356–57. "Pantechni" is the Greek rendering of the Arabic subtitle "The Whole Medical Art" adopted by Constantine, probably on the model of Galen's Macro- and Microtechni (Steinschneider, p. 358). The *Liber Pantegni,* which was well known to Alexander Neckam, was a Latin version of a medical anthology by 'Alī ibn al-'Abbās al-Majūsī (the Magian), or Haly (d. 994), entitled *Kitāb Al-Malikī* or Royal Book, subsequently known to the Latins as *Liber Regius* (M. Meyerhof, "Science and Medicine" in *The Legacy of Islam,* p. 329; E. G. Browne, *Arabian Medicine* [Cambridge, 1921], pp. 119–25). Cf. *De naturis rerum,* chapter 157: "Ut enim docetur in Pantegni"; chapter 161: "id quod legitur in Tegni"; ed. Wright, pp. 257, 267.

43 *Dragmaticon Philosophiae,* 44, as cited in Flatten, p. 165, n. 984.

44 Barach, pp. 121, 130; cf. *Galen on the Passions and Errors of the Soul,* trans. P. W. Harkins, with an Introduction and Interpretation by W. Riese (Columbus, 1963), pp. 15–16.

45 Canon 168 in O. Cameron Gruner, *A Treatise on the Canon of Medicine of Avicenna incorporating a Translation of the First Book* (London, 1930), p. 123.

46 See H. A. Wolfson, "The Internal Senses in Latin, Arabic, and Hebrew Philosophic Texts," *Harvard Theological Review* 28 (1935), 69–133.

47 *Des Alfred von Sareshel Schrift,* ed. Baeumker, p. 4.

48 Ibid., p. 14; p. 43, l. 2; p. 84, l. 15; p. 28, l. 9.

49 Barach, cap. X, pp. 99–100; *Des Alfred von Sareshel Schrift,* ed. Baeumker, pp. 44–45.

50 *Des Alfred von Sareshel Schrift,* ed. Baeumker, p. 43, l. 10.

51 F. M. Cornford, *Plato's Cosmology, The Timaeus of Plato translated with a running commentary* (London, 1956), p. 283.

52 Aristotle, *History of Animals,* trans. Richard Creswell (London, 1891), book 9, chapter 8, p. 239.

53 "De animalibus" is a summary title. See Schipperges, *Die Assimilation der arabischen Medizin durch das lateinische Mittelalter,* p. 74.

54 *Des Alfred von Sareshel Schrift,* ed. Baeumker, p. 36, note 3; *Nicomachean Ethics,* trans. D. P. Chase (London, 1911), book 3, 1111b, p. 49.

55 Wolfson, "The Internal Senses," pp. 28, 31, 73.

56 *Galen on the Passions and Errors of the Soul,* pp. 28, 31, 73.

57 Cornford, *Plato's Cosmology,* p. 283.

58 *Aristotle on the Soul; Parva Naturalia; on Breath,* trans. W. S. Hett (Cambridge, Massachusetts, 1935), p. 475.

59 See J. Prendergast, "Galen's View of the Vascular System in Relation to

that of Harvey," *Proceedings of the Royal Society of Medicine* (London, 1928), p. 1845; cf. Plato, *Timaeus*, XXXV; Aristotle, *De partibus animalium*, III, 5.

60   Karl Sudhoff, *Tradition und Naturbeobachtung in den Illustrationen medizinischer Handschriften und Fruehdrucke vornehmlich des 15. Jahrhunderts* (Leipzig, 1907), pp. 54 ff.

61   Gruner, *A Treatise on the Canon of Medicine of Avicenna*, p. 104.

62   Sudhoff, *Tradition und Naturbeobachtung*, p. 56.

63   *Galen on Anatomical Procedures: The Later Books*, trans. W. L. H. Duckworth (Cambridge, 1962), p. 156.

64   Gruner, p. 162.

65   Ibid., pp. 321, 535.

66   Ibn Sīnā, *Kitāb al-Qānūn fī al-Ṭibb* (Rome, 1593), second "fan," chap. 18, p. 28; Gerard of Cremona, *Primus Canonis Avicenne Principis* (Lyon, 1498), "fen" 2, doctrina III, cap. XVIII. The terminology of "rūḥ" and "spiritus" is complicated by the semantic development and metaphysical complexities of Greek *pneuma*. In a chapter on the complexion of the heart, Constantine the African seems to be using "spiritus" in the literal sense of breathing: "Si pulsus at spiritus sunt vehementissimi in homine: ipse vero magne audacie vel iracundiae" (*Pantechni*, liber IV, cap. 12); cf. "Wind waxeth in the heart" in O. Cockayne, *Leechdoms, Wortcunning and Starcraft* (London, 1864–66), II, 60, 61. I owe this reference to F. C. Robinson.

67   See article on "breth" in Hans Kurath, *Middle English Dictionary* (Ann Arbor, 1952), part B, pp. 1154–56.

68   *OED*, s.v. "breath," 3a.

69   On the diverse senses of "spiritus" in the twelfth century, see M.-D. Chenu, " 'Spiritus,' le vocabulaire de l'âme au XIIe siècle," *Revue des sciences philosophiques et théologiques* 41 (1957), 209–32.

70   Gruner, p. 126.

71   Ibid., pp. 543–45.

72   Ibid., p. 321.

73   Boyd H. Hill, "The Grain and the Spirit in Mediaeval Anatomy," *Speculum* 40 (January, 1965), 64–73, discusses the evidence of the new psycho-physiology of the heart in the thirteenth century and in Chaucer's *Prioress's Tale* and *Knight's Tale*. The Middle English "heorte blod," as has been pointed out to me by F. C. Robinson, is a carry-over from Old English "heortan blod"; see "Salomo and Saturn," ed. R. P. Wuelker, *Bibliothek der angelsaechsischen Poesie* 3 (Leipzig, 1898), p. 66, line 156.

74   Schipperges, *Die Assimilation der arabischen Medizin*, pp. 142 ff.; also *Ideologie und Historiographie des Arabismus* (Wiesbaden, 1961), p. 2.

75   For the most comprehensive history of medieval Sarai, see B. Spuler, *Die goldene Horde: die Mongolen in Russland, 1223–1502* (Leipzig, 1943; second ed. 1965), pp. 266–69; Leonardo Olschki, *Marco Polo's Asia* (Berkeley, 1960), p. 80.

76   H. Yule, *The Book of Ser Marco Polo* (New York, 1926), book II, chapter 2.

77   Monneret de Villard, *Il Libro della Peregrinazione nelle parti d'Oriente di Frate Ricoldo da Montecroce* (Rome, 1948), p. 58; *Haithone Armeni Historia Orientalis: Quae & De Tartaris inscribitur* (Cologne, 1671), cap. XVI.

78 Cf. *Marco Polo*, book II, chapter 11; on "Kambala," cf. J. M. Manly, "Marco Polo and the Squire's Tale," *PMLA* 11 (1896), p. 358.

79 *Chaucer's Canterbury Tales: The Squire's Tale*, ed. A. W. Pollard (London, 1899), p. x.

80 *The Works of Geoffrey Chaucer*, ed. F. N. Robinson, "Explanatory Notes," p. 718; see *Canterbury Tales*, ed. J. M. Manly (New York, 1928), p. 598. Manly points out that, in the *Liber Astronomicus, qui dicitur Albion*, Elpheta is the thirteenth in a list of fifteen stars. On Richard of Wallingford (1292?–1336), abbot of St. Albans, see *DNB* 16, pp. 1091–1093. The literary occurrence of the name "Elphita" in a Catalan song cited by Braddy (*JEGP* 41, 284) and quoted by Robinson, refers to a poem by Andreu Febrer, a Catalan poet at the court of Aragon about 1425. "Elphita" is a diminutive of "Elpha," also in the poem. See Manuel de Montoliu, *Les Grans Personalitats de la literatura catalana* (Barcelona, 1957), "Poesías de Andreu Febrer," p. 53.

81 Robinson, "Explanatory Notes," pp. 545–46.

82 Ibid., p. 546. For a recent discussion of Chaucer's comments in the treatise, see Chauncey Wood, *Chaucer and the Country of the Stars* (Princeton, 1970), pp. 12 ff.

83 The Latin treatise of Messahalla is reprinted in Skeat's edition of Chaucer's *Astrolabe* (London, 1872), pp. 88–104; R. T. Gunther, trans., *Early Science in Oxford*, vol. V, *Chaucer and Messahalla on the Astrolabe* (Oxford, 1929), pp. 137 ff. Several Latin manuscripts attribute this work to Maslama al-Majriti, while the Arabic text of what has been known as Maslama's treatise on the astrolabe cites the author as Ibn al-Saffar, one of Maslama's disciples. See J. M. Millás Vallicrosa, "Los primeros tratados de astrolabio en la España árabe," *Revista del Instituto egipcio de estudios islámicos* (Madrid, 1955), pp. 35–39, 40–41, 45.

84 *A Treatise on the Astrolabe*, in *Works of Chaucer*, ed. Robinson, Part II, 45, line 2, p. 562. On Chaucer's "tables Tolletanes" (*Franklin's Tale*, l. 1273), see Robinson, "Explanatory Notes," p. 725; Derek J. Price, *The Equatorie of the Planetis* (Cambridge, 1955), pp. 79–80; E. Zinner, "Die Tafeln von Toledo,' *Osiris* 1 (1936), 747–74.

85 Robinson, pp. 546, 549, 550. On the meaning of the names and their derivation, see P. Kunitzsch, *Arabische Sternnamen in Europa* (Wiesbaden, 1959): "Aldebaran" (α Tauri, no. 16, pp. 109–10), Arabic *ad-dabarān*, probably from the root verb *dabara*, meaning "to follow," i.e., "one who follows." "Algomeysa" (α Canis Minoris, no. 93, pp. 160–61), Arabic [*ash-sh'irā*] *alghumayṣā*, i.e., [Sirius] "with eyes affected by weeping." "Alhabor" (α Canis Maioris, The Dog Star, Sirius, no. 26, pp. 117–19), Arabic [*ash-sh'irā*] *al-'abūr* [Sirius] who has crossed [the Milky Way].

86 P. Kunitzsch, *Typen von Sternverzeichnissen in astronomischen Handschriften des zehnten bis vierzehnten Jahrhunderts* (Wiesbaden, 1966), p. 10.

87 J. D. North, "Medieval Star Catalogues," *Archives internationales d'histoire des sciences* (janvier-juin 1967), p. 72.

88 The political struggles of the Duchess of Lancaster's learned ancestor were an important matter in 1386, the year of the final Lancastrian intervention in Spain. They were invoked by the Trastamara Pretender in a "complex

historical and genealogical discourse designed to shatter the claim of Lancaster and Dona Constanza that they represented the cause of legitimate monarchy" in their aspiration to the throne of Castile. See P. E. Russell, *The English Intervention in Spain and Portugal in the Time of Edward III and Richard II* (Oxford, 1955), p. 436. Constance, daughter of Don Pedro, became the wife of John of Gaunt in 1371. Beginning in 1372, Chaucer's wife Philippa was one of the attendants of the Duchess. In 1388 Catherine, daughter of the Duke and Duchess of Lancaster, married Henry, grandson of Trastamara, heir to the throne of Castile. Chaucer speaks of Don Pedro's "pitous deeth" in the *Monk's Tale* (l. 2377). Before these events, in 1366, Chaucer seems to have been in Spain himself; there is a safe-conduct, from 22 February to 24 May 1366, granted to Chaucer and three companions by the King of Navarre. See M. Crow and C. Olson, *Chaucer Life-Records* (Oxford, 1966), pp. 64–65, n. 2. The manuscript of *The Equatorie of the Planetis* ascribed to Chaucer contains sets of astronomical tables which are "a simple modification of the well-known Alfonsine tables" (Price, p. 75).   •

89 North, p. 72.

90 Kunitzsch, *Arabische Sternnamen in Europa*, no. 43, pp. 131–32; R. T. Gunther, *The Astrolabes of the World* (Oxford, 1932), II, 463, 466, 468, 475, 477, 479.

91 Gunther, *Chaucer and Messahalla on the Astrolabe*, p. 162, f. 70v and 71; Skeat, *A Treatise on the Astrolabe*, "Preface," p. xliv; Figure 2, cf. "tables of stars."

92 H. C. F. C. Schjellerup, *Description des étoiles fixes, composée . . . par l'astronome persan Abd al-Rahman al-Sufi* (St. Petersburg, 1874), pp. 207–08.

93 Kunitzsch, *Typen von Sternverzeichnissen*, p. 43.

94 Ibid., p. 39.

95 I owe this information to Professor Bernard Goldstein, who provided me with a photostat of the Almagest star catalogue in a fifteenth-century Arabic manuscript, British Museum Arabic Reg. 16. A VIII. My conclusion about the origin of Elpheta is confirmed by J. D. North, who has authoritatively discussed Chaucer's astronomical themes in a series of most important articles. North does not discuss Algarsif, and his derivation of Canacee from a star name is not entirely convincing in view of Chaucer's use of the name in the introduction to *The Man of Law's Tale*. See J. D. North, "Kalenderes Enlumyned Ben They: Some Astronomical Themes in Chaucer," *The Review of English Studies* 20 (1969), 129–54, 257–83, 418–44.

96 *Libros del saber de astronomia del Rey D. Alfonso X de Castilla*, ed. Manuel Rico y Sinobas (Madrid, 1863), I, 27 ff.

97 "The Tale of Saif al-Muluk and the Princess Badiat al-Jamal," Night 758 ff.

98 Kunitzsch, *Arabische Sternnamen*, no. 174, p. 202.

99 MS. British Museum Arabic Reg. 16. A VIII, 232b/118b.

100 *Libros del saber*, I, 138.

101 Kunitzsch, *Typen von Sternverzeichnissen*, pp. 111–13, "Typ XVII."

102 The form *liedideneba* is well attested and derives from the transposition of *deneb aliedi*, the Latin form of the Arabic *dhanab al-jady*, meaning the tail of the goat (γ Capricorn). The transliteration of the Arabic letter *jim* (*al-jady*) in medieval Latin appears both as *g* and *i* (*deneb algedi* or *deneb aliedi*). Cf. Skeat, "Stars marked on the Rete," *Treatise on the Astrolabe*, 40 Capricornus,

44 Aquarius, p. xxxix; see Kunitzsch, *Arabische Sternnamen*, p. 91; *Typen von Sternverzeichnissen*, p. 124. On the appearance of *b* as *v* and *u*, see A. Steiger, *Contribución a la fonética del hispano-árabe* (Madrid, 1932), pp. 108–09.

103   As quoted in G. K. Bauer, *Sternkunde und Sterndeutung der Deutschen im 9.–14. Jahrhundert* (Berlin, 1937), p. 66.

104   Cf. Kunitzsch, *Typen von Sternverzeichnissen*, p. 113.

105   *Libros del saber*, I, 92.

106   "Squire's Tale," lines 207–08; *Libros del saber*, I, 51–52.

107   Elias Ashmole, *Theatrum Chemicum Britannicum* (London, 1652), p. 470. See Gareth W. Dunleavy, "The Chaucer Ascription in Trinity College, Dublin, MS. D.2.8." *Ambix* 13 (1965), 12.

108   Edgar H. Duncan, "The Literature of Alchemy and Chaucer's 'Canon's Yeoman's Tale': Framework, Theme, and Characters," *Speculum* 43 (October, 1968), 633.

109   Robinson, p. 222.

110   J. L. Lowes, "The Dragon and his Brother," *Modern Language Notes* 28 (1931), 229; Duncan, p. 652.

111   The scheme originated in a theory of correspondence between the properties and colors of metallic substances and the planetary system (cf. *CYT* lines 826–29) which was developed by the star-worshipping Sabeans of early medieval Harran; it reached the scholars of the Muslim world in the guise of Babylonian and Greek learning, and the Latin Middle Ages in the Arabic writings of Muslim mystics and alchemists. Cf. D. Chwolsohn, *Die Ssabier und der Ssabismus* (St. Petersburg, 1856), I, 196.

112   J. Ruska and E. Wiedemann, "Alchemistische Decknamen," *Sitzungsberichte der Physikalisch-medizinischen Sozietaet in Erlangen* 56 (1924), 17–36; E. J. Holmyard, "Abu' l-Qāsim al-Irāqi," *Isis* 8 (1926), 402–24; Alfred Siggel, *Decknamen in der arabischen alchemistischen Literatur* (Berlin, 1951).

113   *Opus Minus (Opera quaedam hactemus inedita II)*, ed. J. S. Brewer (London, 1859), p. 313: "sicut dicit Hermes Mercurius, pater philosophorum."

114   Siggel, p. 32, citing al-Jildaki (d. 1342), Arabic MS. Gotha 1291, 73b, 10. On Aidamur ibn Ali al-Jildaki, see Fuat Sezgin, *Geschichte des arabischen Schrifttums*, I, 643–44.

115   Paul Kraus, *Jābir ibn Ḥayyān II* (Cairo, 1942), p. 1. Cf. F. Dieterici, *Die Naturanschauung und Naturphilosophie der Araber im zehnten Jahrhundert* (Posen, 1864), p. 97. The scientific analysis of the seven metals of the Sabean system, corresponding to the seven planets, proceeded on the principle of the balance of the four elements within them. See Paul Kraus, "Studien zu Jābir ibn Hayyān," *Isis* 15 (1931), 17.

116   *CYT* l. 1438. See list of "Decknamen" in Ruska and Wiedemann, pp. 28–32, "dragon," p. 32. Cf. Siggel, "Alphabetisches Verzeichnis der Decknamen," *Decknamen*, pp. 33–54, "tinnīn," p. 36.

117   *Kitāb al-kanz fī fakk ar-ramz*, Arabic MS. Berlin 4191 in Siggel, *Katalog der arabischen alchemistischen Handschriften Deutschlands* (Berlin, 1949), pp. 93–95; Siggel lists "serpent-dragon" in *Decknamen*, p. 36.

118   See Siggel, "Alphabetisches Verzeichnis," *Decknamen*, passim.

119   "Risālah fi'Ilm al-Kimiyah" (Arabic MS. Dresden 210) in Ruska and

Wiedemann, pp. 19, 31–32. "A list so similar as to point to a common origin" was found by Holmyard in an Arabic manuscript in the British Museum (MS. Add. 25724, ff. 15v–17r). The code words for mercury "show perfect agreement," E. J. Holmyard, "Alchemistische Decknamen," *Nature* 117 (January, 1926), 155–56.

120 *Three Arabic Treatises on Alchemy by Muhammad ibn Umail (10th Century* A.D.*)*, ed. M. Turāb 'Ali, with Excursus, and *Edition of the Latin Rendering of the Mā' al-Waraqī* by E. Stapleton and M. Hidāyat Husain (Calcutta, 1933), pp. 1–213; "tinnīn," p. 46; "draco," p. 191.

121 Ruska and Wiedemann, p. 32.

122 See Lynn Thorndike and P. Kibre, *A Catalogue of Incipits of Mediaeval Scientific Writings in Latin,* Index, column 1917; *Gebri Regis Arabum Philosophi Perspicacissimi Summa Perfectionis* in J. J. Manget, *Bibliotheca Chemica Curiosa* (Geneva, 1702), I, 519–57; German translation by E. Darmstaedter, *Die Alchemie des Geber* (Berlin, 1922).

123 J. Ruska, *Al Rāzī's Buch Geheimnis der Geheimnisse* in *Quellen und Studien zur Geschichte der Naturwissenschaften und der Medizin* 6 (Berlin, 1937), p. 40.

124 J. Ruska, *Das Buch der Alaune und Salze* (Berlin, 1935), p. 23.

125 Ruska and Wiedemann, pp. 34–35; Siggel, *Decknamen,* pp. 34, 39.

126 Abū'l-Qāsim Muḥammad ibn Aḥmad al-Irāqi, *Kitāb al-'Ilm al-Muktasab fi Zirā'at adh-Dhahab (Book of Knowledge Acquired concerning the Cultivation of Gold),* ed. and trans. E. J. Holmyard (Paris, 1923), p. 56.

127 J. Ruska, *Al-Rāzī's Buch Geheimnis der Geheimnisse,* p. 37.

128 Ibid., p. 105.

129 J. Ruska, *Turba Philosophorum* (Berlin, 1931), p. 162.

130 Ibid., pp. 324–28. The dream of Arisleus is also mentioned by Petrus Bonus, *Margarita Pretiosa* in Manget, II, 29.

131 *Speculum Doctrinale,* liber XI, cap. 127; *Speculum Naturale,* liber VII, cap. 26. On ascription to Razi, see J. Ruska, *Das Buch der Alaune und Salze,* pp. 13 ff.; *Uebersetzung und Bearbeitungen von al-Rāzīs Buch Geheimnis der Geheimnisse* in *Quellen und Studien zur Geschichte der Naturwissenschaften und der Medizin* 4 (Berlin, 1935), p. 4.

132 Ruska, *Das Buch der Alaune und Salze,* pp. 59, 92. For a similar debate between mercury and gold in Jabir's "Book of Seventy," see M. Berthelot, *Archéologie et histoire des sciences* (Paris, 1906), p. 351.

133 Printed in Manget, I, 626–33, cap. II, pp. 627–28.

134 Abū'l-Qāsim al-Irāqi, *Kitāb al 'Ilm al-Muktasab,* ed. and trans. E. J. Holmyard, p. 57.

135 J. Ruska, "Die Alchemie des Avicenna," *Isis* 21 (1934), 48.

136 Ruska, *Das Buch der Alaune und Salze,* pp. 18, 12; *Uebersetzung und Bearbeitungen von al-Rāzīs Buch Geheimnis der Geheimnisse,* p. 85.

137 The claim of Latin treatises to be translations from the Arabic when there is no Arabic original in the exact form is often substantiated by passages of direct translation, as in Robert of Ketton's *De compositione alchymiae;* see E. J. Holmyard, "Abū'l-Qāsim al-Irāqi," *Isis* 8 (1926), 424–25.

138 J. Ruska, "Chaucer und das Buch Senior," *Anglia* 61 (1937), 136–37; "Senior Zadith—Ibn Umail," *Orientalistische Literaturzeitung* 31 (1928),

665–66; "Muhammad ibn Umail al-Tamīmī's 'Kitāb al-mā' al-waraqī wa'l-arḍ an-najmiyya,' " *Orientalistische Literaturzeitung* 37 (1934), 593–96.

139   J. Ruska, "Studien zu Muhammad Ibn Umail al-Tamīmī's 'Kitāb al-Mā'al-Waraqī wa'l-Arḍ an-Najmīyah,' " *Isis* 24 (1936), 311–42; Stapleton and Husain, *Three Arabic Treatises on Alchemy by Muhammad ibn Umail*, "Excursus," p. 117. E. H. Duncan discusses passages from a Vienna manuscript of the "Epistola" in *"The Literature of Alchemy,"* pp. 653–54. The attribution of the *Epistola* to "Senior Calid filius Hahmil," which is found in medieval manuscripts, is a confusion of Ibn Umail with Khalid ibn Yazid, who, in the Latin text of the "book Senior," is quoted as "Calid filius Seid," or, more correctly, as "Calid filius Isid" (*Three Arabic Treatises*, pp. 153, 191). Khalid ibn Yazid, the first alchemist of Arab tradition, is said to have studied the science with a hermit, Maryanus, with whom he is associated in the "Book of the Monk" by Jabir ibn Hayyan, "king of medieval alchemy" (Ruska, *Arabische Alchemisten I. Chalid ibn Jazīd ibn Muʿā wija* [Heidelberg, 1924], pp. 48–49; Paul Kraus, *Jābir ibn Ḥayyān I* [Cairo, 1935], Arabic text, p. 569, line 14; "Studien zu Jābir ibn Ḥayyān," *Isis* 15 [1931], 8; Ibn Khaldūn, *Muqaddimah*, trans. Rosenthal, III, 229–30). The legendary association is clearly expressed in the title of an early alchemical treatise by Robert of Ketton: "Liber de compositione alchemiae, quem edidit Morienus Romanus, Calid Regi Aegyptiorum: quem Robertus Castrensis de Arabico in Latinum transtulit." Printed in Manget, I, 509–19; F. Wuestenfeld, "Die Uebersetzungen arabischer Werke in das Lateinische seit dem XI. Jahrhundert," *Abhandlungen der Koeniglichen Gesellschaft der Wissenschaften zu Goettingen* 20 (1877), 47.

140   For printed Latin text, see Stapleton and Husain in *Three Arabic Treatises on Alchemy by Muhammad ibn Umail*, pp. 147–97. The "book Senior" itself is attributed to Plato in one English fourteenth-century manuscript, Cambridge, Trinity College 1122, f. 35r, in which a hand contemporary with the handwriting of the manuscript has written above the second word of the *incipit* "Dixit senior: *i.e.* Plato" (Duncan, p. 653). Whatever the relationship of this superscription to Chaucerian usage, Ibn Umail's "book Senior" was to alchemy what Ptolemy's *Almagest* was to astrology. The disciple's reference to "his book Senior," which implies the authorship of Plato, is probably nothing more than an expression of thorough familiarity with a basic alchemical textbook, i.e., the disciple's alchemical "Bible."

141   *Three Arabic Treatises*, p. 39. Professor Joel Kraemer has helped me to clarify the neoplatonic meaning of this passage.

142   Ibid., p. 180.

143   The Arabic for Solomon is "Sulaimān." My suggestion is that Qālīmūs may have been mistakenly read as "Sālīmūn."

144   J. Ruska, "Chaucer und das Buch *Senior*," *Anglis* 61 (1937), 136–37.

145   Paul Kraus, *Jābir ibn Ḥayyān*, II, p. 48 and in *Mémories de l'Institut d'Egypte* 44 (Cairo, 1943), pp. 64–66.

146   *Three Arabic Treatises*, p. 39.

147   Ibid., p. 181.

148   Ibid., p. 41; Latin text, pp. 183–84.

149   Manget, I, 567.

150   *Kitāb al'Ilm al-Muktasab*, ed. E. J. Holmyard, p. 57.

151   *Opera Arnaldi de Villanuova* (Venice, 1505), p. 351.

152   K. Young, "The 'Secree of Secrees' of Chaucer's Canon's Yeoman," *MLN* 58 (1943), 98–105; Duncan, p. 653.

153   J. Ruska, *Al-Rāzī's Buch Geheimnis der Geheimnisse* in *Quellen und Studien z. Geschichte der Naturwissenschaften und der Medizin* 6 (1937), xii-240. Peter Bonus also mentions "Haly in suo. lib. de Secretis secretorum," *Margarita Pretiosa* in Manget, II, 80.

154   R. Foerster, "Handschriften und Ausgaben des pseudoaristotelischen 'Secretum Secretorum,' " *Centralblatt fuer Bibliothekswesen* 6 (Leipzig, 1889), pp. 3–10. See below, chapter 5.

155   Paul Kraus, "Dschābir ibn Hajjān und die Ismā'ilijja," *Dritter Jahresbericht, Forschungs-Institut fuer Geschichte der Naturwissenschaften* (Berlin, 1930), pp. 23–42, especially pp. 30–32, 41; Bernard Lewis, *The Origins of Ismā'ilism* (Cambridge, 1940) and *The Assassins* (New York, 1968); G. S. Hodgson, *The Order of the Assassins* (The Hague, 1955). On the Ikhwān aṣ-Ṣafā', see F. Dieterici, *Die Philosophie der Araber in IX. und X. Jahrhundert* (Berlin, 1865), III; (1868), IV; (1883), XI. For general information, see Stanley Lane-Poole, *Studies in a Mosque* (London, 1983), pp. 186–207; E. G. Browne, *A Literary History of Persia* (Cambridge, 1928), I, 292–93. For recent work on the tracts of the brotherhood, see M. Stern "The Authorship of the Epistles of the Ikhwān aṣ-Ṣafā," *Islamic Culture* 20 (1946), 367–72; A. L. Tibawi, "Ikhwān aṣ-Ṣafā and their Rasā'il, a Critical Review of a Century and a Half of Research," *Islamic Quarterly* 2 (1955), 28–46.

156   Kraus, "Dschābir Ibn Hajjān und die Ismā'ilijja," p. 35.

157   "Jābir ibn Ḥayyān" by M. Plessner in *Encyclopaedia of Islam*, new edition, II, 357.

158   Ruska, *Uebersetzung und Bearbeitungen von al-Rāzīs Buch Geheimnis der Geheimnisse*, pp. 85–87.

159   Ruska, *Al-Rāzī's Buch Geheimnis der Geheimnisse*, p. 13.

160   Siggel, *Decknamen*, p. 41.

161   "Studien zu Jābir ibn Ḥayyān," *Isis* 15 (1931), 7–30, 11–13.

162   Siggel, *Decknamen*, p. 9.

163   Arabic text translated by A. S. Fulton in *Opera hactenus inedita Rogeri Baconi Fasc. V (Secretum Secretorum)*, ed. R. Steele (Oxford, 1920), p. 258.

164   Ibid., p. 254.

165   Manget, II, 80; in Venice, 1546 edition, p. 84.

166   G. Kriesten, *Ueber eine deutsche Uebersetzung des pseudo-aristotelischen "Secretum Secretorum" aus dem 13. Jahrhundert* (Berlin, 1907), p. 63; Hiltgart von Huernheim, *Mittelhochdeutsche Prosauebersetzung des "Secretum Secretorum,"* ed. R. Moeller (Berlin, 1963).

167   Arabic text of "The Book of the Ancient" in Kraus, *Jābir ibn Ḥayyān I*, p. 546, lines 9–10.

168   Kraus, *Jābir ibn Ḥayyān, II*, p. 316.

169   M. Steinschneider, *Die hebraeischen Uebersetzungen des Mittelalters* (Berlin, 1893), I, 251; F. Dieterici, *Die Logik und Psychologie der Araber* (Leipzig, 1868),

pp. 113–16 contains a translated version of the tale from the "Rasā'il" of the "Brethren of Purity." Cf. John Gower, *Confessio Amantis*, liber VII, "Tale of the Jew and the Pagan," lines 3207–329; "The Story of the Jew and the Philosopher" in *Three Prose Versions of the Secretum Secretorum*, ed. R. Steele (London, 1898), pp. 165–67. See chap. 5, n. 77.

170 Ignaz Goldziher, "Ueber die Bennenung der Ichwān al-ṣafa," *Der Islam* 1 (1910), 22–26; G. von Grunebaum, *Medieval Islam* (Chicago, 1956), p. 42, note 50.

171 Arabic text in F. Dieterici, *Thier und Mensch* (Leipzig, 1881), p. 104.

172 Robert Steele, *Secretum Secretorum . . . Fratris Rogeri* (Oxford, 1920), p. 179.

CHAPTER 5

1 O. Eissfeldt, *The Old Testament, an Introduction* (New York, 1965), pp. 81–82.

2 W. G. Lambert, *Babylonian Wisdom Literature* (Oxford, 1960), pp. 1 ff.; C. C. Forman, "The Context of Biblical Wisdom," *The Hibbert Journal* 60 (1962), 125–32.

3 R. B. Y. Scott, *The Way of Wisdom in the Old Testament* (London, 1971), p. 26.

4 H. Gressman, *Israels Spruchweisheit im Zusammenhang der Weltliteratur* (Berlin, 1925), pp. 47–48.

5 *Die Disciplina Clericalis des Petrus Alfonsi nach allen bekannten Handschriften*, ed. A. Hilka and W. Soederhjelm in *Acta Societatis Scientiarum Fennice*, vols. 38 and 49 (Helsinki, 1911, 1922); *Peter Alfonse's Disciplina Clericalis, English translation from the fifteenth century Worcester Cathedral Ms. F 172*, trans W. H. Hulme (Cleveland, 1919); *Pedro Alfonso Disciplina Clericalis*, ed. and trans. A. González Palencia (Madrid, 1948), p. 2.

6 "Prologue" in González Palencia, pp. 1 ff.

7 H. Schwarzbaum, "International Folklore Motifs in Petrus Alfonsi's 'Disciplina Clericalis,' " *Sefarad* 21 (1961), 267–99; 321–44; 22 (1962), 1–59; 23 (1963), 55–73.

8 Hilka and Soederhjelm (vol. 49), pp. xii–xiii, 3 ff.; *Le Chastoiement d'un pere a son fils*, ed. E. D. Montgomery (Chapel Hill, 1971).

9 *Gesta Romanorum*, trans. Charles Swan (London, 1924), Tale CLXXI, p. 351: "Petrus Alphonsus relates . . ."; *The Early English Versions of the Gesta Romanorum*, ed. S. J. H. Herrtage (Oxford, 1962), "Summaries of Tales Not in the English Mss.," pp. 522, 523, 526, 628, 537.

10 Listed in Hilka and Soederhjelm, vol. 38, pp. i–xiv.

11 *Peter Alphonse's Disciplina Clericalis*, trans. Hulme, pp. 9–11. The plot of the *Merchant's Tale* is told in exemplum 35 which is extant in Spanish and French translations of the *Disciplina*. See Schwarzbaum, *Sefarad* 22 (1962), 340–41.

12 E. Stengel, *Codicem Manu Scriptum Digby 86 in Bibliotheca Bodleiana Asservatum descripsit* (Halle, 1871), pp. 11–17, 64, 68. The date of the manuscript may be as early as the reign of Edward I (1272–1307). See G. Mathew, *The Court of Richard II* (New York, 1968), p. 100.

13 Schwarzbaum, Num. 13, "Exemplum de Canicula Lacrimante," *Sefarad* 22

(1962), 24–28; *Tales of Sendebar*, ed. Morris Epstein (Philadelphia, 1967), pp. 123–41.

14 See K. Campbell, *The Seven Sages of Rome* (Boston, 1907), pp. xxxvi-lix; Epstein, p. 3.

15 *Middle English Humorous Tales in Verse*, ed. George H. McKnight (Boston, 1913), pp. 21–24; *Early Middle English Verse and Prose*, ed. J. A. W. Bennett and C. V. Smithers (Oxford, 1968), pp. 196–200.

16 Exemplum XIII, González Palencia, pp. 32–34; Schwarzbaum, *Sefarad* 22 (1962), 24–28.

17 Swan, Tale XXVIII, pp. 127–29.

18 Epstein, pp. 138–41.

19 McKnight, p. xxxvii.

20 McKnight, pp. 2–20, lines 67 ff., 109 ff., 127 ff., 224 ff., 199 ff., 205 ff., 229 ff., 355 ff., 361 ff., 425 ff., 445–50. My text is reprinted from "Dame Sirith" in *Early Middle English Verse and Prose*, pp. 80–95.

21 W. Elsner, *Untersuchungen zu dem mittelenglischen Fabliau Dame Siriz* (Berlin, 1887), pp. 2–4.

22 D. P. Cassel, *Mischle Sindbad* (Berlin, 1891), p. 100.

23 Epstein, p. 141. There is a Persian version in which the conclusion of the husband's return does not form part of the tale of the Weeping Bitch, but appears as a separate "Story of the Libertine Husband" (see W. A. Clouston, *The Book of Sindibad* [London, 1891], pp. 58–59). Cf. *Syntipas*, ed. J. F. Boissonade (Paris, 1828), p. 51; A. Eberhard, *Fabulae Romanenses Graece Conscriptae ex Recensione et cum Adnotationibus* (Leipzig, 1872), p. 39.

24 *The Exempla or Illustrative Stories from the Sermones Vulgares*, ed. Th. F. Crane (London, 1890), no. 251, p. 239. The moral is also ignored in the Middle English prose version in the fifteenth-century *Alphabet of Tales* (see the edition by Mary Macleod Banks, *EETS* orig. ser. 127, part II [London, 1905], p. 361).

25 Fernand Mossé, "*Le Roman de Renart* dans l'Angleterre du moyen âge," *Langues modernes* 45 (1951), 72–73.

26 Stengel, p. 11. The prominence of the *Disciplina Clericalis* in Digby MS. 86 refutes Mathew's view "that the animal stories that survive in literary form came seeping upwards from the medieval peasant culture" (*Court of Richard II*, p. 100).

27 "Renart," "Ysengris" in Hilka and Soederhjelm, vol. 49, pp. 60–61.

28 Exemplum XXIII; González Palencia, pp. 60–62; Schwarzbaum, *Sefarad* 22 (1962), 52–54.

29 Karl Warnke, *Die Quellen des Esope der Marie de France* (Halle, 1900), p. 46; cf. pp. 44–45.

30 McKnight, pp. 25–37.

31 See Rashi's commentary on Ezekiel 18:2 in *The Babylonian Talmud*, English edition, Soncino Press (London, 1935), "Neziḳin," III, 246–47; "Sanhedrin," 38b-39a.

32 Al-Maidani, *Majma'al-amthāl*, ed. Muhammad Muhyi al-Dīn 'Abd al-Hamīd (Cairo, 1959), II. 145, letter *Kaf*, no. 3045; G. W. Freytag, *Arabum Proverbia* (Bonn, 1839), II, 335.

33 A. M. Habermann, *Berachyah haNaqdan Mishlei Shualim* (Jerusalem, 1946), p. vii.

34 See Schwarzbaum, *Sefarad* 22 (1962), p. 54; *Babylonian Talmud*, "Nezikin," III, 246; "Sanhedrin," 38b-39a.

35 The exemplum of Marianus (XXV), a wise and holy man who prophesies the downfall of a cruel king, recalls the legend of Maryanus, a hermit philosopher and teacher of alchemy in Arabic literature. But Steinschneider connects it with the story of King Marinus in Yehudah Halevi's *Kuzari*, originally written in Arabic, and a popular work of moral and religious instruction in the form of a dialogue between a would-be convert to Judaism, the king of the Khazars, and a Jewish sage. See M. Steinschneider, *Die Hebraeischen Uebersetzungen des Mittelalters und die Juden als Dolmetscher* (Berlin, 1893), p. 849; *Manna* (Berlin, 1847), p. 114. The story of the hermit Marianus as a teacher of alchemy is related by Jabir ibn Hayyan in "The Book of the Monk," ed. P. Kraus, *Jābir ibn Ḥayyān, textes choisis* (Cairo, 1935), I. 529.

36 Stengel, pp. 17, 60; *English Lyrics of the XIIIth Century*, ed. Carleton Brown (Oxford, 1962), no. 48, pp. 85-87; James E. Cross, "*Ubi sunt* passages in Old English—Sources and Relationships," *Vetenskaps-Societetens i Lund Årsbok* (1956), pp. 25-44

37 González Palencia, pp. 86-87.

38 E. Barbazan, *Fabliaux et contes des poètes françois* (Paris, 1808), II, 182-83.

39 C. H. Becker, "Ubi sunt qui antes nos in mundo fuere" in *Aufsaetze zur Kultur- und Sprachgeschichte Ernst Kuhn gewidmet* (Munich, 1916), pp. 87-105. Petrus Alfonsi develops the theme from the reflection of philosophers at the tomb of Alexander (Exemplum XXXIII), as does Hunain ibn Ishaq. See A. Loewenthal, *Honein Ibn Ishak Sinnsprueche der Philosophen* (Berlin, 1896), p. 187.

40 Carleton Brown, *English Lyrics*, p. 70, lines 65 ff.

41 *Peter Alfonse's Disciplina Clericalis*, trans. Hulme, p. 65.

42 Becker, pp. 92-94.

43 Printed in the fifteenth-century work of ash-Sha'rani, *Mukhtaṣar tadhkirat al-Qurṭubī* (Cairo, 1939), p. 4, line 16, in a chapter on the need for remembering death and for being prepared for it.

44 González Palencia, pp. 87-88.

45 Banks, *An Alphabet of Tales*, pp. 359-63; *An Alphabet of Tales*, ed. R. T. Lenaghan (Cambridge, Massachusetts, 1967), pp. 193-213.

46 The names "Kalila" and "Dimna" were formed by the corruption of the Sanskrit names of two jackals, "Karataka" and "Damanaka," which are the two principal characters. The Pehlevi version is not extant, but it is known that it was made in the first half of the sixth century for the Sassanid prince Khusraw I Anusharwan by his physician Burzoye, who had brought it from India as part of the Panchatantra. See C. Brockelmann's article on "Kalila wa Dimna" in *The Encyclopaedia of Islam*, II, 694-98.

47 The phrase is John of Salisbury's; see *Metalogicon* I, 5 in Migne, *P.L.*, 199, col. 832B.

48 On the problem of identifying *rūmī*, a common word for "Roman" in the

sense of Byzantine, see M. Plessner's review of *Secretum secretorum cum glossis et notulis*, ed. R. Steele, in *Orientalistische Literaturzeitung* 28 (1925), 916; M. Bouyges, "Excursus d'un éditeur de textes arabes. 1. Roumiyy," in *Mélanges de l'Université Saint Joseph (Beyrouth)* 27 (1947–48), 123 ff. On the medieval identification of *rūmī* with "Chaldean," see "Incipit secundus prologus" in Schipperges, *Die Assimilation der arabischen Medizin durch das lateinische Mittelalter*, p. 78: "transtuli ipsum primum de greca lingua in caldeam et de hac in arabicam." For the problems of date, authorship, and structure of the Arabic *Secret of Secrets*, see M. Manzalaoui, "The Pseudo-Aristotelian *Kitāb Sirr Al-Asrār*," *Oriens* 24 (1974), 145–257.

49   Cf. *Secretum Secretorum (Pseudo-) Aristotelis, Fontes Graecae Doctrinarum Politicarum Islamicarum*, ed. A. Badawi (Cairo, 1954), "Introduction," p. 37 (Arabic text).

50   Steele, *Secretum Secretorum . . . Fratris Rogeri*, "Discourse," p. 226; *Three Prose Versions of the Secretum Secretorum*, ed. Steele, pp. 207–08: "the world is lyke a gardeyn . . ."; al-Mubashshir ibn Fatik, *Mukhtār al-ḥikam*, ed. A. Badawi (Madrid, 1958), p. 22; *Sirr al-Asrār*, p. 127. Ibn Khaldūn, *Muqaddimah*, trans. Rosenthal, I, 81–82.

51   G. Cary, *The Medieval Alexander* (Cambridge, 1957), pp. 14–16; Badawi, *Mukhtār al-ḥikam*, "Akhbār al-Iskandar," p. 236.

52   Bruno Meissner, "Mubassirs Ahbār el-Iskender," *Zeitschrift der deutschen morgenlaendischen Gesellschaft* 49 (1895), 598, 615, n. 3.

53   According to Noeldeke, the Syriac and Arabic legends of Alexander derive from a Pehlevi version of the Pseudo-Callisthenes. Th. Noeldeke, "Beitraege zur Geschichte des Alexanderromans," *Denkschriften der kaiserlichen Akademie der Wissenschaften, philos.-hist. Klasse* 38 (Vienna, 1890), Nr. V, pp. 1–56, 14 ff.

54   *Three Old English Prose Texts*, ed. Stanley Rypins (London, 1924), pp. 79–100; Dorothy Whitelock *The Audience of Beowulf* (Oxford, 1951), p. 51.

55   *Muqaddimah*, I, 81. Cf. J. Ruska, *Untersuchungen ueber das Steinbuch des Aristoteles* (Heidelberg, 1911), p. 43. Petrus Alfonsi quotes Aristotle's advice to Alexander on the subject of counsellors from a "letter" which seems to be a variation or paraphrase of Discourse IV of the *Secret of Secrets (Peter Alfonse's Disciplina Clericalis*, trans. Hulme, Ex. IV, p. 22; Steele, *Secretum Secretorum . . . Fratris Rogeri*, p. 237). Cf. R. Foerster, *De Aristotelis quae feruntur secretis secretorum commentatio* (Kiel, 1888), p. 25.

56   "Epistola Aristotilis ad Alexandrum cum Prologo Johannis Hispaniensis" in H. Suchier, *Denkmaeler provenzalischer Literatur und Sprache* (Halle, 1883), I, 531. Johannes Hispaniensis is believed to have been a Jew known as Ibn Daud (Avendauth or Avendehut) before his conversion to Christianity (Wuestenfeld, "Die Uebersetzungen arabischer Werke in das Lateinische," *Abhandlungen der koenigl. Gesellschaft der Wissenschaften zu Goettingen* 20 [1877], p. 25). Schipperges, however, makes a distinction between Johannes Hispaniensis and Avendehut, "Israelita philosophus" (*Die Assimilation der arabischen Medizin*, pp. 69–70). According to him, the reading "Joannes Avendehut" in the Latin translation of Avicenna's Aristotelian *De anima* is actually a dedication to Archbishop John of Toledo (1151–66) and should

read "Iohanni, Avendehut, Israelita philosophus, gratum debite servitudinis obsequium."

57 Suchier, p. 474.

58 R. Foerster, "Handschriften und Ausgaben des pseudoaristotelischen Secretum Secretorum," *Centralblatt fuer Bibliothekswesen* 6 (1889), 72–74.

59 M. Gaster, "The Hebrew Version of the 'Secretum Secretorum,' with an Introduction and an English Translation," *Journal of the Royal Asiatic Society* (London, 1908), pp. 111–62; Lloyd Kasten, " 'Poridad de las Poridades,' A Spanish form of the Western Text of the *Secretum Secretorum*," *Romance Philology* 5 (1951–52), 180–90.

60 Philip's prologue is reprinted in Foerster, *De Aristotelis quae feruntur secretis secretorum commentatio*, pp. 38–39, and Steele, *Secretum Secretorum . . . Fratris Rogeri*, pp. 25–27. See excerpt from a thirteenth-century manuscript in Schipperges, p. 79.

61 *De retardatione accidentium senectutis (Opera hactenus inedita Rogeri Baconi)*, Fasc. 9, ed. A. G. Little and E. Withington (Oxford, 1928), p. 29: ". . . ut Aristoteles dicit in libro Secreti Secretorum . . ."; Steele, *Secretum Secretorum . . . Fratris Rogeri*, p. xviii: cap. 2, "de accidentibus senectutis"; M. Manzalaoui, "The *Secreta Secretorum*: the Mediaeval European Version of 'Kitāb Sirr ul-Asrār,' " *Bulletin of the Faculty of Arts, Alexandria* 15 (1961), 91; "The Pseudo-Aristotelian *Sirr al-Asrār* and Three Oxford Thinkers of the Middle Ages" in *Arabic and Islamic Studies in Honor of Hamilton A. R. Gibb*, p. 483.

62 Foerster, *De Aristotelis . . . secretis secretorum*, pp. 29–30. It is more likely that Philip knew the portions on physiognomy in Michael's version and that his translation was a later work. A curious connection between Michael and Philip has been conjectured by Thorndike (*Michael Scot*, pp. 91, 121).

63 E. Kantorowicz, *Frederick II*, pp. 341, 357.

64 Steele, *Secretum Secretorum . . . Fratris Rogeri*, p. 39.

65 Ibid., p. xxiii.

66 Ibid., p. 28.

67 A. Badawi's edition of the Arabic text is based on eighteen manuscripts (*Sirr al-Asrār*, pp. 52–72); see list of manuscripts in Manzalaoui, "The Pseudo-Aristotelian *Kitāb Sirr al-Asrār*," pp. 148 ff.

68 H. Gaetje and H. Daiber, "Die arabische Handschrift Chester Beatty 4183 und das Kitāb Sirr al-Asrār," *Der Islam* 42 (1965), 71–78.

69 The catalogue of books, *al-Fihrist*, lists the subject of alchemy in a final tenth discourse. See J. W. Fueck, "The Arabic Literature on Alchemy according to an-Nadīm (A.D. 987)," *Ambix* 4 (1951), 81–144.

70 Steele, *Secretum Secretorum . . . Fratris Rogeri*, p. 26.

71 Ibid., pp. 114–23.

72 Ibid., pp. 173–75.

73 J. Ruska, *Untersuchungen ueber das Steinbuch des Aristoteles*, pp. 42–46.

74 Steele, pp. 115–17; J. Ruska, *Tabula Smaragdina* (Heidelberg, 1926), pp. 138, 160.

75 Albertus Magnus, *De somnio et vigiliis* in Ruska, *Tabula Smaragdina*, pp. 186–90, 193–94.

76 Badawi, p. 164; Steele, p. 259; Ruska, p. 109.

77 The parallels are listed in A. Verdenius, *Jacob von Maerlants Heimelijkheid* (Amsterdam, 1917), pp. 29–39; Manzalaoui, "The Pseudo-Aristotelian *Kitāb Sirr al-Asrār,*" pp. 175 ff.; Gower (*Confessio Amantis*, Book VII) has a different ending to his story where the Jew is killed by a lion. In the Arabic, Latin, Spanish and French versions, the Magian (or Oriental Christian in Spanish) takes pity on the Jew (who has been thrown by the Magian's ass after he has treacherously absconded with it in the desert, leaving the Magian behind), and brings him home to his relatives where the Jew dies. See Badawi, p. 142; Steele, *Secretum Secretorum*, pp. 145–46, 240–41; J. E. Keller, *Motif-Index of Mediaeval Spanish Exempla* (Knoxville, 1949), p. 66; P. de Gayangos, *El Libro de los enxemplos* in *Biblioteca de autores españoles* 51 (Madrid, 1860), no. 131, p. 479; Steele, *Three Prose Versions of the Secretum Secretorum*, pp. 105–06. On Gower's use of the *Secretum Secretorum*, see George L. Hamilton, "Some Sources of the Seventh Book of Gower's *Confessio Amantis*," *Modern Philology* 9 (1911–12), 338–39; A. H. Gilbert, "Notes on the influence of the *Secretum Secretorum*," *Speculum* 3 (1928), 84–98.

78 M. Stern, "The Authorship of the Epistles of the Ikhwān aṣ-Ṣafā," *Islamic Culture* 20 (1946), 367–72.

79 For an English version, see W. Knatchbull, *Kalila and Dimna* (Oxford, 1819), pp. 192 ff.

80 Ignaz Goldziher, "Ueber die Bennenung der Ichwan al-Safa," *Der Islam* 1 (1910), 22–26; G. von Gruenebaum, *Medieval Islam* (Chicago, 1956), p. 42, n. 50.

81 Al-Mubashshir ibn Fatik, *Mukhtār al-ḥikam*, pp. 179, 181; *Dicts and Sayings of the Philosophers*, ed. Curt F. Buehler (London, 1941), pp. 150, line 4; 152, line 13.

82 Steele, *Secretum Secretorum . . . Fratris Rogeri*, p. 24, lines 10–11; see p. xii. Cf. M. Plessner, *Orientalistische Literaturzeitung* 28 (1925), 918–19. According to Hunain ibn Ishaq, Aristotle followed the custom of wise philosophers in teaching his pupils ten sciences in ten years (Loewenthal, *Honein Ibn Ishak, Sinnsprueche der Philosophen*, p. 69). A fifteenth-century manuscript of the Western Arabic form of the *Secret of Secrets* also bears a title hitherto unknown: "Counsels of Alexander" (Gaetje and Daiber, p. 71).

83 Easton, *Roger Bacon and His Search for a Universal Science*, pp. 24, 81.

84 Foerster, "Handschriften und Ausgaben des pseudoaristotelischen Secretum Secretorum," pp. 4–10, 58–71.

85 Steele, *Three Prose Versions of the Secretum Secretorum*, pp. 121 ff.; *Lydgate and Burgh's Secrees of Old Philisoffres*, ed. R. Steele (London, 1894), p. xii.

86 Steele, *Three Prose Versions of the Secretum Secretorum*, pp. 3–4.

87 *WB Prol.*, lines 180–83; 323–27 in *The Works of Geoffrey Chaucer*, ed. Robinson, pp. 77, 79.

88 *Le Roman de la Rose*, ed. F. Lecoy (Paris, 1965), I, 215, lines 7007–13; *The Romance of the Rose*, trans. H. W. Robbins (New York, 1962), p. 144.

89 F. Carmody, *Arabic Astronomical and Astrological Science in Latin Translation* (Berkeley, 1956), p. 15. For preface, see *Almagestu . . . Ptolemei . . . ductu Petri* (Venice, 1515).

90   The sayings which Chaucer used also appear in Hunain's collection. See A.
      Loewenthal, *Honein Ibn Ishak Sinnsprueche der Philosophen*, pp. 137, 139 (say-
      ings 39 and 62); cf. al-Mubashshir ibn Fātik, *Mukhtār al-ḥikam*, ed. Badawi,
      pp. 253–54, sayings of Ptolemy, 19, 30; *The Dicts and Sayings of the Philoso-
      phers*, ed. Curt F. Buehler (London, 1941), p. 226, line 7, for a version of the
      first saying: "a man that is to correct bi other may surely correct other."
      The second syaing is missing in the Middle English translations of al-
      Mubashshir's *Dicts*. Cf. B. J. Whiting, *Proverbs, Sentences and Proverbial Phrases
      from English Writings Mainly before 1500* (Cambridge, Massachusetts, 1968),
      p. 9, A. ll8; p. 377, M. 170, for the first saying, and p. 371, M. 100, for the
      second.

91   F. Rosenthal, "Al-Mubashshir ibn Fātik," *Oriens* 13–14 (1961), 135.

92   Ibid., pp. 147–48. Al-Mubashshir's original list includes Hermes Trisme-
      gistos, Aesculapius, Homer, Solon, Hippocrates, Pythagoras, Plato, Aris-
      totle, Alexander, Socrates, Diogenes, Ptolemy, and Galen. In the Spanish
      and Latin versions, as well as in the French and English, there is a curious
      philosopher named "Asaron" who does not appear in the Arabic original.

93   See Robinson, "Explanatory Notes," p. 699, note to line 180; p. 700, note to
      line 326.

94   *Roman de la Rose*, lines 13605–08, 18539–48; Robbins, pp. 284, 394. Cf.
      Badawi, *Mukhtār al-ḥikam*, pp. 252, 254, sayings of Ptolemy, 2, 3, 24.

95   Carmody, p. 15. See P. Kunitzsch, *Der Almagest* (Wiesbaden, 1974), 84–85.

96   *Almagestu . . . Ptolemei*, p. 1.

97   "Il 'Liber philosophorum moralium antiquorum,' " ed. Ezio Franceschini in
      Atti del Reale Istituto Veneto di Scienze, Lettere ed Arti 91 (1931–32), parte
      seconda, pp. 393–597.

98   Reprinted in H. Knust, *Mittheilungen aus dem Eskurial* (Tübingen, 1879), pp.
      66–414, 556.

99   The translation is ascribed to Procida in one manuscript where he is said to
      have made it from the Greek. Stylistic evidence has led Sabbadini to the
      conclusion that it was done by an Italian translator who worked from a
      Spanish text. See Ezio Franceschini, "Il 'Liber philosophorum moralium
      antiquorum,' " *Atti della Reale Accademia Nazionale dei Lincei* 3 (Rome, 1930),
      p. 397; Remigio Sabbadini, "Il traduttore latino del *Liber Philosophorum*,"
      Atti del Reale Istituto Veneto di Scienze, Lettere ed Arti 92 (1932–33), parte
      seconda, p. 538. However, "the connection of the work with John of Procida
      remains dubious," according to P. O. Kristeller, *Studies in Renaissance Thought
      and Letters* (Rome, 1956), p. 527, who cites G. Billanovich, "La tradizione
      del 'Liber de dictis philosophorum antiquorum' e la cultura di Dante del
      Petrarca e del Boccaccio," *Studi Petrarcheschi* 1 (1948), 111–23.

100   "Il *Liber philosophorum moralium antiquorum*," testo critico, Ezio Franceschini
      in *Atti del Reale Istituto Veneto di Scienze, Lettere ed Arti* 91 (1931–32), parte
      seconda, p. 533.

101   *The Dicts and Sayings of the Philosophers*, ed. Buehler, "Introduction," pp. xi,
      xviii-xix.

102   *Disciplina Clericalis*, ed. González Palencia, pp. xxxiii-xxxv; Schwarzbaum,
      Sefarad 21 (1961), 271–73 and passim.

103 Robinson, p. 170, "Explanatory Notes," p. 741, line 1053. In the *Disciplina Clericalis* the proverb appears at the conclusion of Ex. XXIV, the tale of a thief and the moonbeam which Petrus Alfonsi translated from *Kalīla wa-Dimna*; see Schwarzbaum, *Sefarad* 22 (1962), fasc. 1, p. 55.

104 Robinson, p. 174, "Explanatory Notes," p. 743, line 1218. From an exhortation "on lying" attached to Ex. IV, an Aesopian story of a mule and a fox which illustrates the folly of boasting about one's pedigree. A medieval version, contemporary with Petrus Alfonsi, is found in the Hebrew collection of Fox Fables by Berachyah haNakdan; see Schwarzbaum, *Sefarad* 21 (1961), 295; *Mishle Shu'alim*, ed. A. M. Habermann, p. 73.

105 Robinson, p. 182, "Explanatory Notes," p. 744, line 1566. From a list of sayings "On Counsel" following Ex. II, the Arabian tale of two faithful friends celebrated in the Middle English metrical romance *Amis and Amiloun*.

106 *Speculum Historiale*, III, 58. Vincent lists Eusebius, St. Augustine, Hugh of St. Victor, St. Jerome, Cassian, Gellius, Tertullian, and Seneca.

107 Buehler, *Dicts*, p. 86, line 33.

108 H. Knust, *Gualteri Burlaei Liber de Vita et Moribus Philosophorum* (Tübingen, 1886), p. 128: "Principium amicicie est bene loqui; maledicere autem est inimiciciarum exordium."

109 *Speculum Historiale*, III, 86: "Flores eiusdem morales ex Ethicis"; cf. *Nicomachean Ethics*, trans. D. P. Chase (London, 1911), II, 1105b, p. 32.

110 Buehler, *Dicts*, p. 170, line 34 to p. 173, line 4. Cf. *Speculum Historiale*, III, 86: "Sed multi haec quidem quae secundum virtutes sunt non faciunt, ad rationem autem confugientes existimant philosophari & esse boni, simile aliquid facientes aegrotantibus: qui medicos audiunt quidem studiose, & ipsi nihil faciunt operandorum: igitur nec illi bene habebunt corpus, nec isti animam sic philosophantes." *Nicomachean Ethics*, II, 1105b: "Yet people in general do not perform these virtuous actions, but taking refuge in talk they flatter themselves they are philosophising, and that they will so be good men: acting in truth very like those sick people who listen to the doctor with great attention but do nothing that he tells them: just as these then cannot be well bodily under such a course of treatment, so neither can those be mentally by such philosophising." While the main part of the saying, in particular the simile of the doctor and the sick, closely corresponds to al-Mubashshir's original version, the conclusion does not.

111 Buehler, p. 172, line 6; *Nicomachean Ethics*, II, 1106b; Chase, p. 35; cf. *Speculum Naturale*, III, 87: "facile quidem diverti a signo, difficile autem invenire." Vincent has clearly followed the *Nicomachean Ethics* in separating this saying from the first. In al-Mubashshir's *Mukhtār al-ḥikam* the two sayings are continuous (Badawi, p. 211). The continuous sequence of the Arabic original is maintained in the Latin, French and Middle English translations of al-Mubashshir. The brief discussion of Vincent's sayings by Franceschini has incomplete quotations and inaccurate references ("Il 'Liber philosophorum moralium antiquorum,' " *Atti della Reale Accademia Nazionale dei Lincei* 3 [1930], p. 383, A. 21.040/vi.3).

112 Buehler, *Dicts*, p. xii–xiii, 2.

113 William Caxton, *The Dictes and Sayings of the Philosophers*. A facsimile re-

production of the first book printed in England with a preface by William Blades (London, 1877), ff. lr and v, 2r. Blades, who compared Earl Rivers's version with that of Scrope, was of the opinion that "there seems reason for supposing that the Earl may have cast a glance over the performance of his predecessor while making his own translation" (W. Blades, *The Life and Typography of William Caxton* [London, 1863], II, 37). But see Buehler, *Dicts,* "Introduction," pp. xlix-lix.

CHAPTER 6

1 Ramón Menéndez Pidal, *La Chanson de Roland et la tradition épique de France* (Paris, 1960), pp. 503, 273 ff.

2. *The Song of Roland,* trans. W. S. Merwin (New York, 1970), p. 3.

3 Ibn al-Athīr, *Chronicon quod perfectissimum inscribitur,* ed. C. J. Tornberg (Leyden, 1851–74), VI, 1, 7–8; Menéndez Pidal, pp. 520–21; *Annales Mettenses Posteriores* (entry 778) in Menéndez Pidal, p. 524; *Historiae Francorum Scriptores,* ed. F. Duchesne (Paris, 1641), III, 282.

4 Menéndez Pidal, p. 182; cf. Eginhard, *Vie de Charlemagne,* ed. L. Halphen (Paris, 1947), pp. 28–30.

5 Ibn al-Athīr in Menéndez Pidal, p. 520.

6 *Firumbras and Otuel and Roland,* ed. Mary I. O'Sullivan (London, 1935), p. 112, lines 1692–96.

7 Ibid., p. 122, lines 2014–24.

8 D. Douglas, "Song of Roland and the Norman Conquest of England," *French Studies* 14 (1960), 99–114.

9 *Laȝamon: Brut,* ed. G. L. Brook and R. F. Leslie (Oxford, 1963), I, 378, line 7279. The etymology of *Saracen* is doubtful. It may derive from Arabic *sharqī,* "eastern," (*OED* IX, 106). On the medieval association with Sara, see Isidore of Seville, *Etymologiarum sive Originum Libri XX,* IX, 2.

10 Ronald N. Walpole, *Charlemagne and Roland* (Berkeley, 1937–44).

11 *The Romance of Sir Beues of Hamtoun,* ed. E. Koelbing (London, 1885, 1886, 1894), p. 42, line 888; p. 81, line 1566; p. 90, line 1782.

12 D. M. Dunlop, "The British Isles according to Medieval Arabic authors," *Islamic Quarterly* 4 (April, 1957), 13–14.

13 R. Dozy, *Recherches sur l'histoire et la littérature de l'Espagne pendant le Moyen âge* (Leyden, 1881), II, 270.

14 Dunlop, pp. 12–14.

15 Dozy, pp. 270, lxxxii.

16 R. Dozy, *Spanish Islam* (London, 1913), p. 517.

17 Dozy, *Recherches,* pp. 272–78, lxxxiv-lxxxviii; E. Lévi-Provençal, *Histoire de l'Espagne musulmane* (Paris, 1953), III, 108.

18 Dunlop, pp. 19–20; al-Qazwīnī, *Kosmographie,* ed. F. Wuestenfeld (Goettingen, 1849), II, 388–89.

19 Dunlop, pp. 18, 23; al-Mas'ūdī, *Les Prairies d'or,* ed. and trans. C. Barbier de Meynard et Pavet de Courteille (Paris, 1861), I, 258–89.

20 Dunlop, p. 18.

21 M. Reinaud, *Invasions des Sarrazins en France* (Paris, 1836), p. 134; *Recueil des*

historiens des Gaules et de la France, ed. Dom M. Bouquet (Paris, 1749), VI, 308.

22   Dunlop, p. 23.

23   P. A. Jaubert, *Géographie d'Edrisi* (Paris, 1840) in *Recueil de voyages et de mémoires*, VI, 27–29.

24   Marc Bloch, *Feudal Society* (Chicago, 1963), p. 5.

25   J. Lacam, *Les Sarrazins dans le haut Moyen âge français* (Paris, 1965), p. 11.

26   Bloch, p. 6.

27   *Historia compostelana* in *España sagrada*, ed. H. Florez (Madrid, 1791), XX, 133–34.

28   Dozy, *Recherches*, II, 318; al-Maqqarī, *Kitāb Nafḥ aṭ-Ṭib*, ed. R. Dozy, G. Dugat, L. Krehl, W. Wright in *Analectes sur l'histoire et la littérature des Arabes d'Espagne* (Leyden, 1855–60), I, 104.

29   *Middle English Dictionary* ed. Hans Kurath (Ann Arbor, 1954), I, 252.

30   Line 27668.

31   H. Suchier, "Nachtrag" (p. cxcv) in Albert Stimming, *Der anglonormannische Boeve de Haumtone, Bibliotheca Normannica 7* (Halle, 1899).

32   Albert Stimming, *Der festlaendische Bueve de Hantone* (Dresden, 1911 [Fassung I], 1912 [Fassung II], 1920 [Fassung III]); *Der anglonormannische Boeve de Haumtone*, p. 15, line 355.

33   *The Canterbury Tales*, "General Prologue," line 58.

34   See W. von Heyd, *Geschichte des Levanthandels im Mittelalter* (Stuttgart, 1879), II, 714.

35   H. Jankuhn, *Haithabu, ein Handelsplatz der Wikingerzeit* (Neumunster, 1956), p. 147.

36   *A Description of Europe, and the Voyages of Ohthere and Wulfstan*, ed. and trans. J. Bosworth (London, 1855), p. 5; G. Jacob, *Arabische Berichte von Gesandten an germanische Fuerstenhofe aus dem 9. und 10. Jahrhundert* (Berlin, 1927), p. 3; Jankuhn, p. 139; al-Qazwīnī, *Kosmographie*, ed. F. Wuestenfeld, II, 408. See reference in B. Lewis, "Politics and War," *The Legacy of Islam*, second edition, ed. J. Schacht with C. E. Bosworth (Oxford, 1974), pp. 190–91.

37   J. H. Kramers, "Geography and Commerce," *The Legacy of Islam*, ed. Arnold and Guillaume, p. 106; G. Jacob, *Der Nordisch-baltische Handel der Araber im Mittelalter* (Leipzig, 1887), p. 39; Jankuhn, pp. 182 ff.

38   G. Waldron, *A Description of the Isle of Man* (Douglas, 1865), p. 11.

39   *The Romance of Sir Beues of Hamtoun*, ed. E. Koelbing (London, 1885–94).

40   G. Le Strange, *The Lands of the Eastern Caliphate: Mesopotamia, Persia, and Central Asia from the Moslem Conquest to the Time of Timur* (Cambridge, 1905), pp. 139 ff. Cf. Lillian H. Hornstein, "The Historical Background of the King of Tars," *Speculum* 16 (1941), 404–14. For a general history of the Tartars, see J. J. Saunders, *The History of the Mongol Conquests* (London, 1971); B. Spuler, *History of the Mongols based on Eastern and Western Accounts of the Thirteenth and Fourteenth Centuries* (Berkeley, 1972).

41   *Haithoni Armeni Historia Orientalis: quae & De Tartaris inscribitur* (Cologne, 1671).

42   *The Cambridge Medieval History*, ed. J. M. Hussey (Cambridge, 1966), IV, part I, chapter XIV, pp. 632–36; May McKisack, *The Fourteenth Century: 1307–1399* (Oxford, 1959), p. 441.

43 Stimming, *Der anglonormannische Boeve de Haumtone*, p. 59, lines 1519–23.

44 *The Itinerary of Rabbi Benjamin of Tudela*, trans. and ed. A. Asher (New York, 192–?), I, 159.

45 Le Strange, *The Lands of the Eastern Caliphate*, p. 141.

46 *Wilbrandus de Oldenborg*, ed. J. C. M. Laurent (Leipzig, 1864), p. 180, Lib. I, XII, line 6; p. 170, Lib. I, XI, lines 12, 14; p. 187, Lib. II, VI, line 4. On Wilbrand, see J. C. M. Laurent, *Wilbrands von Oldenburg Reise nach Palaestina und Kleinasien* (Hamburg, 1859), pp. 33 ff.

47 Baha ad-Din, *The Life of Saladin*, trans. A. W. Wilson (London, 1897), chap. 35, pp. 110 ff.; Andrew S. Ehrenkreutz, *Saladin* (Albany, 1972), pp. 200–02. See also R. Roehricht, *Geschichte des Koenigreichs Jerusalem, 1100–1291* (Innsbruck, 1898), pp. 463, 754.

48 *Regesta Honorii Papae III*, ed. P. Pressutti (Rome, 1888), I, An. 1217, reg. 672, p. 117; Albert von Stade, *Chronik*, trans. F. Wachter (Leipzig, 1896), p. 47.

49 Francesco Gabrieli, *Arab Historians of the Crusades* (London, 1969), pp. 139–61; Runciman, *History of the Crusades*, II, 468.

50 Ambroise, *L'Estoire de la Guerre Sainte*, ed. G. Paris (Paris, 1897); Ambroise, *The Crusade of Richard Lion-Heart*, trans. M. J. Hubert (New York, 1941).

51 Ambroise, *The Crusade*, p. 228, lines 5531 ff.

52 *Itinerarium Peregrinorum et Gesta Regis Ricardi*, ed. W. Stubbs (London, 1864).

53 *Flores Historiarum*, ed. H. R. Luard, 3 vols. (London, 1890), II, 197–98; cf. *Matthaei Parisiensis Chronica Majora*, ed. H. R. Luard (London, 1876), III, 172 ff.

54 Albertus Stadensis, *Chronicon* (Helmstadt, 1587), folio 198 verso.

55 *Chronica Albrici Monachi Trium Fontium*, ed. G. H. Pertz in *Monumenta Germaniae Historica* 23 (Hannover, 1874), p. 936.

56 Jules de Saint-Genois, *Voyages faits en Terre-Sainte par Thietmar, en 1217* in *Mémoires de l'Académie royale des sciences, des lettres et des beaux-arts de Belgique* 26 (Brussels, 1851), pp. 19–61.

57 Ibid., p. 45.

58 Al-Sirāfī, *Akhbār as-Ṣīn wa l'Hind, rédigée en 851*, ed. and trans. J. Sauvaget (Paris, 1948).

59 *Flores Historiarum*, I, 456.

60 *Alberuni's India*, trans. E. C. Sachau and ed. Ainslie T. Embrec (New York, 1971).

61 *Three Old English Prose Texts in Ms. Cotton Vitellius A xb*, ed. S. Rypins (London, 1924), pp. 1–50, 79–100.

62 See summary of the plot in J. Burke Severs, *A Manual of the Writings in Middle English, 1050–1500* (New Haven, 1967), p. 130.

63 Thomas Walsingham, *Quondam Monachi S. Albani, Historia Anglicana*, ed. H. Thomas Riley (London, 1863), I, 77; *Flores Historiarum*, III, 107–08.

64 See Lillian H. Hornstein, "The Historical Background of the *King of Tars*," *Speculum* 16 (1941), 404–14; "New Analogues to the 'King of Tars,'" *Modern Language Review* 36 (1941), 433–42; "Trivet's Constance and the *King of Tars*," *Modern Language Notes* 55 (1940), 354–57.

65 Walsingham, p. 77.

66 Hornstein, "New Analogues to the 'King of Tars,'" 438–39, citing Gilles Le Muisit, *Chronique et annales*, ed. Henri Lemaître (Paris, 1906), pp. 114–15;

also in *Chronicon Meuvini, Recueil des Chroniques de Flandre*, ed. J. J. de Smet (Brussels, 1841), p. 470.

67 *Digenes Akrites*, ed. and trans. John Mavrogordato (Oxford, 1956). On date, see H. Grégoire and R. Goossens, "Byzantinisches Epos und arabischer Ritterroman" in *Zeitschrift der Deutschen Morgenlaendischen Gesellschaft*, Neue Folge 13 (1934), 213; H. Grégoire, "L'Epopée byzantine et ses rapports avec l'épopée turque et l'épopée romane," *Bulletin de la classe des lettres de l'Académie royale de Belgique* 17 (1931), 463 ff., 466, 473.

68 Mavrogordato, pp. 45, 51–53.

69 "Kleine Publicationen aus der Auchinleck-hs.," ed. F. Krause, *Englische Studien* 11 (1888), 55, lines 835–40.

70 Gilles Le Muisit, *Chronique et annales*, pp. 114–15; *Chronicon Muevini*, p. 470.

71 Richard F. Burton, *The Book of the Thousand Nights and a Night*, 12 vols. (London, 1894), II, 77–283.

72 Girard d'Amiens, *Le Roman du cheval de fust ou de Méliacin*, ed. P. Aebischer (Geneva, 1974), p. 4. See G. J. Brault, "Les Manuscrits des oeuvres de Girart d'Amiens," *Romania* 80 (1959), 433–46, in particular pp. 434–37; E. Krueger, *Das Verhaeltnis der Handschriften von Girards d'Amiens Roman Cheval de fust* (Greifswald, 1910); *Li Roumans de Cléomades par Adenes li Rois*, ed. A. van Hasselt (Brussels, 1865), I, xv–xvi, xix, xxi, xxvii.

73 Georg Graf Vitzthum, *Die Pariser Miniaturmalerei von der Zeit des Hl. Ludwig bis zu Philipp von Valois* (Leipzig, 1907), pp. 24–32, 55–56, plate X.

74 Burton, II, 283–97; *Sources and Analogues of Chaucer's Canterbury Tales*, ed. W. F. Bryan and G. Dempster (New York, 1958), pp. 375–76.

75 Burton, V, 189 ff.

76 Ibid., II, 77–282.

77 Ibid., V, 1–32; Bryan and Dempster, pp. 364–65.

78 Bryan and Dempster, p. 366; J. Froissart, *L'Espinette amoureuse*, ed. A. Fourrier (Paris, 1972), p. 68, line 705.

79 Claude Fauchet, *Recueil de l'origine de la langue et poésie françoise* (Paris, 1581), p. 180; *Premier Volume de la Bibliothèque du sieur La Croix du Maine* (Paris, 1584), p. 131.

80 See E. Stengel, "Die altfranzoesischen Liedercitate aus Girardins d'Amiens Conte du cheval de fust," *Zeitschrift fuer romanische Philologie* 10 (1887), 460–76; Mavrogordato, Introduction, p. liii.

81 Al-Istakhri, *Das Buch der Laender*, trans. A. D. Mordtmann (Hamburg, 1845), p. 38.

82 Abulfeda (Abū al-fidā), *al-Mukhtaṣar fī akhbār al-bashar* (Beirut, 1956–61), part 7, *futūḥ malaṭiyah*, p. 88.

83 Grégoire and Goossens, "Byzantinisches Epos und arabischer Ritterroman," p. 221; R. Goossens, "Autour de Digenis Akritas: le 'Geste d'Omar' dans les Mille et une nuits," *Byzantion* 7 (1932), 311; Grégoire, "Le Tombeau et la date de Digenis Akritas," *Byzantion* 6 (1931), 497; Goossens, "Les Recherches sur l'épopée byzantine," *L'Antiquité classique* 2 (1933), 451.

84 Grégoire, "Echanges épiques arabo-grecs," *Byzantion* 7 (1932), 378.

85 Grégoire and Goossens, "Les Recherches récentes sur l'épopée byzantine," *L'Antiquité classique* 1 (1932), 429.

86   Goossens, "Autour de Digenis Akritas," pp. 306–07.

87   Grégoire, "L'Epopée byzantine et ses rapports avec l'épopée turque et l'épopée romane," pp. 463 ff.; Mavrogordato, *Digenes Akritas*, Introduction, pp. lxxix, lxxxiv.

88   Mavrogordato, p. lxxix.

89   K. Krumbacher, *Geschichte der byzantinischen Litteratur* (Munich, 1897), pp. 827–28, 832.

90   J. B. Bury, *A History of the Eastern Roman Empire* (London, 1912), pp. 17–18.

91   Goossens, "Les Recherches récentes sur l'épopée byzantine," *L'Antiquité classique* 2, pp. 516–17; Grégoire, "Etudes sur l'épopée byzantine," *Revue des études grecques* 46 (1933), 48–69; Grégoire and Goossens, "Byzantinisches Epos und arabischer Ritterroman," p. 217.

92   Goossens, "Les Recherches récentes sur l'épopée byzantine," p. 471.

93   Grégoire and Goossens, "Byzantinisches Epos und arabischer Ritterroman," p. 228.

94   Ibid., p. 226.

95   Burton, V, 31.

96   W. P. Ker, *The Dark Ages* (New York, 1904), p. 345.

97   *The Works of Geoffrey Chaucer*, ed. Robinson, p. 304.

98   D. J. Geanakoplos, *Greek Scholars in Venice* (Cambridge, Massachusetts, 1962), pp. 20–22; *Byzantine East and Latin West* (Oxford, 1966), p. 29.

99   "Byzantinisches Epos und arabischer Ritterroman," p. 230.

100 Mavrogordato, p. xxvii.

101 Burton, II, 77–78, 81–82.

102 Burton, III, 60, 72, 79.

103 M. Schlauch, "The Man of Law's Tale" in Bryan and Dempster, *Sources and Analogues*, pp. 155 ff.

104 Cf. M. Schlauch, *Chaucer's Constance and Accused Queens* (New York, 1927).

105 Reprinted in Bryan and Dempster, p. 165. Chaucer's use of Trivet is examined in detail by E. A. Block, "Originality, Controlling Purpose, and Craftsmanship in Chaucer's *Man of Law's Tale*," *PMLA* 68 (1953), 572–616.

106 Burton, V, 189–245. On Western versions of the name, see W. Suchier, *L'Enfant sage* (Dresden, 1910), pp. 127, 216, 221. Teodor is derived from the Arabic Tudur, as the name actually runs in one Arabic manuscript through alteration of the terminal *d* into *r* (J. Horovitz, "The Origins of 'The Arabian Nights,'" *Islamic Culture* 1 [1927], p. 51).

107 M. Menéndez y Pelayo, "La Doncella Teodor" in *Homenaje a Don Francisco Cordera en su jubilación del profesorado* (Zaragoza, 1904), p. 489; quoted in J. V. Ruiz, "Una nueva versión árabe del Cuento de la Doncella Teodor" in *Miscelánea de estudios árabes y hebráicos* (1952), I, 150. I owe the knowledge and translation of the article to Charles Faulhaber.

108 E. Littmann, *Die Erzaehlungen aus den Tausendundein Naechten* (Wiesbaden, 1953), VI, 726.

109 G. von Gruenebaum, "Greek Form Elements in the Arabian Nights," *Journal of the American Oriental Society* 62 (1942), 291, n. 129; see also "Creative Borrowing: Greece in the 'Arabian Nights'" in *Medieval Islam* (Chicago,

1969), pp. 294 ff.; A. Wesselski, "Die gelehrten Sklavinnen des Islams und ihre byzantinischen Vorbilder," *Archív Orientálni* 9 (1937), 353–78.

110   W. Mettmann, *La Historia de la Donzella Teodor, ein Volksbuch arabischen Ursprungs* (Wiesbaden, 1962), pp. 76 ff.

111   Mettmann, p. 76; W. Suchier, *L'Enfant sage*, pp. 466–91. See H. Gruber, "Beitraege zu dem mittelenglischen Dialoge 'Ipotis,' " *Anglia* 18 (1896), 56–82.

112   W. Suchier, p. 127; Mettmann, p. 103, lines 1–11. The Spanish text has been translated by Charles Faulhaber.

113   Mettmann, pp. 108, 109, lines 105–37.

114   Ibid. p. 82.

115   *Chaucer Life-records*, ed. M. M. Crow and C. C. Olson (Oxford, 1966), p. 64.

116   Bryan and Dempster, p. 156.

117   On the dating of the *Man of Law's Tale*, in particular the views of Skeat and Pollard, see J. S. P. Tatlock, *The Development and Chronology of Chaucer's Works* (London, 1906), p. 175, n. 3. Cf. W. W. Skeat, *The Complete Works of Geoffrey Chaucer* (Oxford, 1894–1900), V, 409, 413; A. W. Pollard, *The Works of Geoffrey Chaucer* (London, 1919), pp. xxvi-xxvii.

118   A. W. Pollard, *The Squire's Tale* (London, 1899), p. x.

119   E. Littmann, "Alf Layla wa Layla" in *Encyclopaedia of Islam*, new edition, I, 358 ff.

120   Dorothy Everett, *Essays on Middle English Literature* (Oxford, 1955), p. 13.

121   *La Chanson de Roland*, line 1015: "Païen unt tort e chrestiens unt dreit."

122   Jessie Crosland, *The Old French Epic* (Oxford, 1951), p. 1.

123   Ibid., pp. 70–91.

124   Ordericus Vitalis, *The Ecclesiastical History of England and Normandy*, trans. Th. Forester (London, 1853–56), III, 307 ff.

125   Runciman, *History of the Crusades*, II, 38; H. A. R. Gibb, *The Damascus Chronicle of the Crusades, Extracted and Translated from the Chronicle of Ibn al-Qalanisi* (London, 1932), pp. 91 ff.

126   *Acta Sanctorum Novembris tomus tertius*, p. 163A, citing 1 Cor. 7, 14.

127   Orderic, III, book IX, p. 59.

128   Gibb, *Damascus Chronicle*, pp. 49–50; cf. Kamāl ad-Dīn ibn al-'Adīm, *Chronicle of Aleppo* in *Recueil des historiens des Croisades, Historiens orientaux* (Paris, 1884), III, 589.

129   Orderic, III, book X, pp. 310–22.

130   Albertus Aquensis in *Recueil des historiens des Croisades, Historiens occidentaux* (Paris, 1879), IV, 524 ff.

131   Runciman, II, 38.

132   Fulcher of Chartres, *A History of the Expedition to Jerusalem (1095–1127)*, trans. F. R. Ryan (Knoxville, 1969), book III, p. 227.

133   Burton, V, 277–83. See also F. M. Warren, "The Enamoured Moslem Princess in Orderic Vital and the French Epic," *PMLA* 19 (1914), 341–58.

134   Burton, V, 280, 282.

135   *The Romance of Sir Beues of Hamtoun*, ed. E. Koelbing (London, 1894), p. 24, lines 519–26.

136   Ibid., lines 585–644, 655–72, 725–30, 963–1082.

137 *The Romaunce of the Sowdone of Babylone and of Ferumbras his Sone who conquered Rome*, ed. E. Hausknecht (London, 1881); *Sir Ferumbras*, ed. S. J. Herrtage (London, 1879).

138 *The Sowdone of Babylone*, p. 91, line 3171.

139 Crosland, p. 237.

140 Runciman, II, 45.

141 *Orderici Vitalis Historiae Ecclesiasticae Libri Tredecim* (Paris, 1852), IV, 253. Cf. Orderic, *Ecclesiastical History*, III, 399.

142 *Orderici Vitalis Historiae Ecclesiasticae Libri Tredecim*, IV, 255.

143 Runciman, II, p. 45; Albertus Aquensis, lib. IX, cap. XLVI, pp. 619–20.

144 Klaus Heitmann, "Das Verhaeltnis von Dichtung und Geschichtschreibung in aelterer Theorie," *Archiv fuer Kulturgeschichte* 51 (1969), 260.

145 Isidore of Seville, *Etymologiarum sive Originum Libri XX*, I, 40; see J. Fontaine, *Isidore de Séville et la culture classique dans l'Espagne wisigothique* (Paris, 1959), I, 174–85; Arno Borst, "Das Bild der Geschichte in der Enzyklopaedie Isidors von Sevilla," *Deutsches Archiv fuer Erforschung des Mittelalters* 22 (1966), 20, 33–34.

146 Nathaniel E. Griffin, "The Definition of Romance," *PMLA* 38 (1923), 57; Gerhard Schoebe, "Was gilt im fruehen Mittelalter als geschichtliche Wirklichkeit?" in *Festschrift Hermann Aubin* (Wiesbaden, 1965), II, 635.

147 See P. Aebischer, *Etudes sur Otinel* (Bern, 1960), pp. 117 ff.

148 *Otuel and Roland*, lines 1157–62, in *Firumbras and Otuel and Roland*, ed. Mary I. O'Sullivan from MS. Brit. Mus. Addit. 37492 (the Fillingham MS.) (London, 1935), pp. 59 ff.

149 *Otuel and Roland*, see above; *Otuel*, ed. S. J. Herrtage in *The Taill of Rauf Coilyear, with the Fragments of Roland and Vernagu, and Otuel* (London, 1882), pp. 65–116; *The Romance of Duke Rowland and Sir Otuell of Spayne*, ed. S. J. Herrtage in *The Sege off Melayne, The Romance of Duke Rowland and Sir Otuell of Spayne* (London, 1880), pp. 55–104.

150 See R. N. Walpole, *Charlemagne and Roland, A Study of the Source of Two Middle English Metrical Romances, Roland and Vernagu and Otuel and Roland* (Berkeley, 1944), pp. 385, 390.

151 Book III, line 437; *The Bruce . . . compiled by Master John Barbour*, ed. W. W. Skeat (London, 1894), II, 67.

152 *Sir Ferumbras*, ed. S. J. Herrtage from the unique paper manuscript, about A.D. 1380, in the Bodleian Library (Ashmole MS. 33) (London, 1879), p. 2, lines 46–55.

153 Ibid., pp. 25–26. lines 615–19.

154 Crosland, p. 138.

155 *Li romans de Floire et Blancheflor*, ed. F. Krueger (Berlin, 1938), p. xv.

156 *Floris and Blancheflour*, lines 1056–67 in *Middle English Verse Romances*, ed. D. B. Sands (New York, 1966), p. 308.

157 Richard Bernheimer, *Wild Man in the Middle Ages* (Cambridge, Massachusetts, 1951), p. 44 and passim.

158 E. H. Ahrendt, *Der Riese in der mittelhochdeutschen Epik* (Guestrow, 1923), p. 14.

159 Cf. Isidore of Seville: "Falso autem opinantur quidam inperiti de Scrip-

turis sanctis praevaricatores angelos cum filiabus hominum ante diluvium concubuisse, et exinde natos Gigantes, id est nimium grandes et fortes viros, de quibus terra conpleta est" (*Etymologiarum* . . . Libri XX, XI, 3, 14–15).

160   *The Taill of Rauf Coilyear.*

161   *The Pseudo-Turpin, edited from Bibl. Nat. Ms. 17656* by H. M. Smyser (Cambridge, Massachusetts, 1937), p. 75, lines 18–20.

162   *Sir Ferumbras,* ed. Herrtage; *Firumbras and Otuel and Roland,* ed. O'Sullivan.

163   On the etymology of *Achopart,* see H. Grégoire, "L'Etymologie de Tervagant" in *Mélanges d'histoire du théâtre du Moyen-âge et de la Renaissance offerts à Gustave Cohen* (Paris, 1950), pp. 68–69, 70–71, in particular p. 68, n. 4. On *amirant,* see p. 69.

164   *Guy of Warwick nach Coplands Druck (Palaestra 139),* ed. G. Schleich (Leipzig, 1923), p. 196, line 6478; "Ameraunt he hight of Ethiopy." Cf. Robert Copland (1508–47), *Book of the Most Victoryous Prince Guy* (London, ca. 1560).

165   *The Romance of Guy of Warwick,* ed. J. Zupitza (London, 1883, 1887, 1891), p. 430, stanza 62.

166   *The Romance of Guy of Warwick, the Second or 15th-century Version,* ed. J. Zupitza (London, 1875–76), p. 217, line 7577.

167   While, in the Auchinleck manuscript, the sultan has promised the giant both land and daughter as a prize, the idea is developed into a love affair in the fifteenth-century version: "Y loue hur well, se dothe sche me: / The sowdan þynkyth to geue hur me" (p. 235, lines 8203 ff.).

168   The giant is "four fot, sikerly, / More þan ani man stont him bi," in the Auchinleck manuscript (Zupitza, p. 430, stanza 63); "a fote and a halfe more / Than eny man that euer was bore" in MS. 107, Caius College, Cambridge (Zupitza, p. 431, lines 7767–68); "two fote and more / Hyer, then any, that was þore," in the fifteenth-century version (Zupitza, p. 217, lines 7585–86).

169   *The Travels of Sir John Mandeville, with Three Narratives in Illustration of It: The Voyage of Johannes de Plano Carpini, The Journal of Friar William de Rubruquis, The Journal of Friar Odoric,* (New York, 1964), pp. 187–88.

170   *The Vision of William concerning Piers the Plowman, in Three Parallel Texts,* ed. W. W. Skeat (Oxford, 1886), I. 98, B III, 327: "For Makomet and Mede. myshappe shal that tyme." All quotations of *Piers Plowman* are from Skeat's edition.

171   See *Liber contra sectam sive haeresim Saracenorum,* Prologue, reprinted in Kritzeck, p. 227: "Si hereticos dixeris, probatum est supra, omnibus hereticis uel heresibus obuiandum. Si paganos uocaueris, probo idque patrum auctoritate ostendo, non minus et illis resistendum."

172   Daniel, pp. 229–41.

173   Olschki, *Marco Polo's Asia,* p. 239, n. 19.

174   Kritzeck, pp. 143 ff., 227.

175   See A. Abel, "Baḥīrā," in *The Encyclopaedia of Islam,* new edition, I, 922–23.

176   "Guilelmi Tripolitani Ordinis Praedicatorum Tractatus de statu Saracenorum et de Mahomete pseudo-propheta et eorum lege et fide incipit" reprinted in H. Prutz, *Kulturgeschichte der Kreuzzuege,* pp. 575–98.

177   Ibid., p. 576.

178   *Vita Mahumeti,* ed. F. Huebner in *Historische Vierteljahrschrift* 29 (Dresden, 1935), 441–90; on the question of authorship, see G. Cambier, "Embricon de Mayence (1010?–77) est-il l'auteur de la *Vita Mahumeti?*" *Latomus* 16 (1957), 468–79.

179   Huebner, p. 473, line 660.

180   *The Vision of William concerning Piers the Plowman,* II, 233, note to C XVIII, 241.

181   *Petri Alphunsi ex Iudaeo Christiani Dialogi* in *Maxima Bibliotheca Veterum Patrum* 21, p. 194, Titulus V: "Semper enim ut dixi cum eis conversatus & enutritus es, libros legisti, linguam intellegis. . . ."

182   "Sed cum paternam reliqueris fidem, miror cur Christianorum & non potius Sarracenorum cum quibus semper conversatus atque nutritus es delegeris fidem" (ibid.).

183   Ibid., p. 196.

184   Ibid., p. 195 H.

185   *The Apology of al Kindy,* ed. Sir W. Muir (London, 1887); d'Alverny, "Deux traductions latines du Coran," pp. 87 ff. The "epistola" is mentioned by Peter in his letter to Bernard of Clairvaux, printed in Kritzeck, p. 212.

186   *Speculum Historiale,* lib. XXIII, cap. XL, Photomechanischer Nachdruck der Akademischen Druck- und Verlagsanstalt (Graz, 1965), p. 913: "Hic enim pauca libet inserere de libello disputationis cuiusdam Saraceni, & cuiusdam Christiani de Arabia super lege Sarracenorum & fide Christianorum inter se."

187   *Epistola Petri Cluniacensis ad Bernardum Claraevallis* in Kritzeck, p. 212.

188   *Roman de Mahomet en vers du XIIIème siècle, par Alexandre du Pont,* ed. F. Michel (Paris, 1831), pp. 1 ff., 84. On the Latin source of Alexandre, Waltherius (Gautier), and the abbot Warnerius (Gravier), see Alessandro d'Ancona, "La leggenda di Maometto in Occidente," *Giornale storico della letteratura italiana* 13 (1889), 233; B. Ziolecki, *Alixandre du Pont's roman de Mahomet: ein altfranzoesisches Gedicht des XIII. Jahrhunderts* (Oppeln, 1887), pp. xx, xxiii.

189   *Matthaei Parisiensis Chronica Majora,* V. 425.

190   D'Ancona, p. 245; also A. Mancini, "Per lo studio della leggenda di Maometto in Occidente," *Rendiconti della R. accademia nazionale dei lincei* 10 (1934), 327 ff.; Ziolecki, p, xvi.

191   Excerpt from Latini's *Tesoro* in d'Ancona, p. 200.

192   M. Asín Palacios, *Islam and the Divine Comedy* (New York, 1926), p. 260.

193   Cf. Dante Alighieri, *Die Goettliche Komoedie,* trans. H. Gmelin (Stuttgart, 1954), Kommentar I, Inferno XXVIII, pp. 411–12.

194   *Le Roman de Renart le Contrefait,* ed. G. Raynaud and H. Lemaître (Paris, 1914). I, v; A. C. M. Robert, *Fables inédites des XIIe, XIIIe et XIVe siècles* (Paris, 1825), I, cxxxiii ff.

195   Robert, p. cxiv.

196   Raynaud and Lemaître, "deuxième branche," I, 260.

197   *The Golden Legend of Master William Caxton,* ed. F. S. Ellis (London, 1892), III, 1170; cf. "hocquidem vulgariter dicitur. Sed verus est quod inferius habetur," Jacobus de Varagine, *Legenda aurea* (Nuremberg, Anton Koberger, 1478), pp. 239 ff.

198   *Polychronicon Ranulphi Higden Monachi Cestrensis,* ed. J. R. Lumby (London, 1876), VI, 20, lib. V, cap. xiv.
199   Ibid., pp. 19–23.
200   Ibid., p. 25.
201   Cf. Vincent of Beauvais, *Speculum Historiale,* lib. XXIII, caps. XLIII, LXV, LXVI, pp. 914, 921, 922.
202   Ibid., cap. XL, p. 913.
203   Muir, p. 57.
204   Cap. XL, p. 913.
205   *Chronica Majora,* II, 343.
206   Daniel, p. 231.
207   R. Reilly, "A Middle English Summary of the Bible: an Edition of Trinity College (Oxon) Ms. 93," Ph.D. dissertation, University of Washington, 1966, p. 226.
208   *Roland and Vernagu,* ed. Herrtage, pp. 56–59, lines 677–786.
209   Daniel, p. 309.
210   H. Grégoire, "Les Dieux Cahu, Baraton, Tervegant . . . et de maints autres dieux non moins extravagants," *Annuaire de l'Institut de philologie et d'histoire orientales et slaves* 7 (1939–44), 461–62.
211   Ibid., p. 455; see W. Tavernier, *Zur Vorgeschichte des altfranzoesischen Rolands-liedes* (Berlin, 1903), pp. 22–23.
212   *Anonymi gesta Francorum et aliorum Hierosolyminatorum,* ed. H. Hagenmeyer (Heidelberg, 1890), p. 322, XXI, 9: "iuro vobis per Machomet et per omnia Deorum nomine"; p. 324, XXII, 1; p. 498, XXXIX, 17.
213   Daniel, p. 310.
214   Cf. the interpolation in Thomas of Kent's *Roman de toute cheualerie*:

> D'une noire pere vn ymage esgarda—
> En mye du marche sur vne voute esta.

[D 1128–29]

We have the same image in so "historical" a romance as *Richard Coeur de Lion*:

> Kyng Richard askyd at the fyrst word
> Of þat cyte where was þe lord,
> And þey answede to þe kyng
> Þat þey hadde non oþir lordyng
> But the ymage of marbyl fyn,
> And Mahoun, here God, and Appolyn.

[6259–64]

Both references are discussed in *Kyng Alisaunder,* ed. G. V. Smithers, 2 vols. (London, 1952), II, 88–89.
215   Daniel, p. 310, citing Peter de Pennis's manuscript ("Appendix A," p. 389, n. 9).
216   See poem of Dracontius (sixth century) cited in Grégoire, "Les Dieux Cahu . . . ," p. 460.
217   Brook and Leslie, *Laȝamon: Brut,* p. 361, line 6942.

218 *Petri Alphunsi ex Iudaeo Christiani Dialogi* in *Maxima Bibliotheca Veterum Patrum* 21, Titulus V, "De Sarracenorum lege destruenda, & sententiarum suarum stultitia confutanda," p. 195, section D.

219 Surah "al-Haqqah," verses 21–24, *The Holy Qur-án*, containing the Arabic text with English translation and commentary by Maulvi Muhammad Ali (Surrey, England, 1917), p. 1111.

220 "To be concerned about what will happen to you after death, or to let your thought dwell much upon the joys which you hope will then await you, may obviously be the most extreme form of this-worldliness" (A. O. Lovejoy, *The Great Chain of Being* [New York, 1960], p. 24).

221 *Summa Totius Haeresis Saracenorum* in Kritzeck, p. 207.

222 Both the French and Dutch poems are reprinted in V. Vaananen, "Le Fabliau de Cocagne," *Neuphilologische Mitteilungen* 48 (1947), 20–29, 33–36. For the Middle English version, see W. Heuser, *Die Kildare-Gedichte* in *Bonner Beitraege zur Anglistik* 14 (1904), 141–50 and *Early Middle English Verse and Prose*, ed. J. A. W. Bennett and G. V. Smithers, pp. 138–44.

223 A. L. Morton, *The English Utopia* (London, 1952), pp. 11 ff. "And he seiþ þat who þat holdeþ al þis and oþere hestes of his lawe God Almyȝti byhoteþ hym paradys, þe orchard of likynge, þere is noon distemperure noþer peyne, þere is no manere greef, but al manere of welþe and of likynge; þere is likynge mete for to ete, and cloþes to werie, and maydens to beclippe faire schal serve him þere; þe aungels beeþ so huge and so greet þat from þe oon yȝe to þat oþer is þe space of a day his jornay" (*Polychronicon Ranulphi Higden*, VI, 31 ff.).

224 *Early Middle English Verse and Prose*, ed. Bennett and Smithers, "The Land of Cockayne," pp. 138–44, lines 7–14. For traditional Christian accounts of the earthly paradise, see A. B. Giamatti, *The Earthly Paradise and the Renaissance Epic* (Princeton, 1969), pp. 67–85.

225 "The Fox and the Wolf," *Early Middle English Verse and Prose*, p. 71, lines 140–47.

226 For "A True Story," see *Selected Satires of Lucian*, ed. and trans. Lionel Casson (Chicago, 1962), pp. 13–57, "Isle of the Blest," pp. 37 ff.

227 "The Land of Cockayne," p. 138, line 1.

228 Chaucer's Shipman "knew alle the havenes, as they were, / Fro Gootland to the cape of Fynystere" (*General Prologue to the Canterbury Tales*, I, 408, Robinson, "Explanatory Notes," p. 661).

229 For *coco = gâteau*, see S. J. Honnorat, *Dictionnaire provençal-français* (Digne, 1846), I, 514; "Abbas Cucaniensis" appears in *Carmina Burana*, ed. J. A. Schmeller (Stuttgart, 1847), p. 254, no. 196. See full discussion in Vaananen, p. 5; J. Poeschel, "Das Maerchen vom Schlaraffenlande," *Beitraege zur Geschichte der deutschen Sprache und Literatur* 5 (1878), 406.

230 The complete French and Latin texts are found side by side in *La Escala de Mahoma*, ed. José Múñoz Sendino (Madrid, 1949) and in Enrico Cerulli, *Il "Libro della Scala" e la questione delle fonti arabo-spagnole della Divina Commedia* (Rome, 1949).

231 Múñoz Sendino, p. 251.

232 Ibid., p. 265.

233   Ibid., p. 337. My inconsistency in using both Latin and French texts for quotation is not only a matter of variety, but to show the importance of the word *coc* in the portrayal of the Muslim paradise in thirteenth-century French.

234   Muḥammad ibn Mūsā ad-Damīrī, *Ḥayāt al-Ḥayawān*, trans. A. S. G. Jayakar (London, 1906), I, 802.

235   *Islam and the Divine Comedy*, pp. 29–30, 72. Cf. Cerulli's critical comment "L'Aquila ed il gallo" in *Il Libro della Scala* pp. 527–28, and on the question of Dante's knowledge of the *Liber Scalae*, see *Nuove ricerche sul "Libro della scala" e la conoscenza dell'Islam in Occidente* (Vatican City, 1972), pp. 317 ff.

236   Chapter XXXIV. Cerulli, *Il "Libro della Scala"*, §83, pp. 109–11, with explanation of the Arabic designations, p. 233.

237   See A. A. Bevan, "Mohammed's Ascension to Heaven," *Studien zur semitischen Philologie und Religionsgeschichte Julius Wellhausen zum 70. Geburtstag gewidmet* (Giessen, 1914), pp. 52–53.

238   Chapter XXX, Cerulli §72, p. 103: "Ego vero quaesivi a Gabriele et dixi: 'Quid est hoc quod video?' et ipse respondens dixit: 'Scias, nuncie Dei, quod hii sunt murus et turres Paradisi; . . . et scias quod, quicquid homo dicat quod non est nisi unicus Paradisus, verum est in eo quod Paradisus nichil aliud quam delectatio nuncupatur; sed delectacionem istam divisit Deus maneriebus quam plurimis et eam suis donat juxta meritum cujusque ipsorum. Vult namque Deus quod tu scias et videas quomodo hujusmodi delectacionis maneries sunt distincte; et quid eciam ipse tibi et populo tuo duxerit eligendum."

239   Chapter XXVIII, Cerulli §67, p. 99.

240   Chapters XXXI, XXXII, Cerulli §74, p. 104; §78, p. 106.

241   See chapter XLIII on the riverbed of precious stones (Cerulli, p. 133) and especially chapters XL and XLIII (Cerulli, pp. 125, 133).

242   Chapter XXXVI, Cerulli §90, pp. 114, 116.

243   M. Manzalaoui, "English Analogues to the *Liber Scalae*," *Medium Aevum* 34 (1965), 21–35.

244   Ibid., p. 25.

245   *Sir Orfeo*, ed. A. J. Bliss (Oxford, 1966), Auchinleck Ms., lines 355–76, pp. 32–33.

246   Chapter XXXVII, Cerulli §94, p. 118.

247   From the Arabic *ṭūba*, "happiness." The tree is described in chapter XXXIX, Cerulli §99, p. 122.

CHAPTER 7

1   Dorothee Metlitzki, *Melville's Orienda* (New Haven, 1961), pp. 59–91.

2   *Mandeville's Travels*, ed. M. C. Seymour (Oxford, 1967), p. xiv.

3   L. Olschki, *Marco Polo's Precursors* (Baltimore, 1943), p. 13.

4   See the most recent effort at identification by Barbara Nolan and David Farley-Hills, "The Authorship of *Pearl*: Two Notes," *The Review of English Studies* 22 (1971), 295–302; on the *Pearl*-poet's use of Mandeville's *Travels*, see *Purity*, ed. R. J. Menner (New Haven, 1971), p. xli.

5   Seymour, p. 3; cf. *Mandeville's Travels*, ed. P. Hamelius (London, 1919), p. 3, lines 13–36.

6   *L'Extrême Orient au Moyen-âge, d'après les manuscrits d'un Flamand de Belgique, moine de Saint Bertin à Saint-Omer* (Paris, 1877), p. 7.

7   Olschki, *Marco Polo's Precursors*, pp. 32–33; Seymour, xv, 244, 252, 277.

8   Seymour, p. 277.

9   Ibid., p. 4; Hamelius, p. 4, lines 1–12.

10 Seymour, p. 2; Hamelius, p. 2.

11 G. Cary, *The Medieval Alexander* (Cambridge, 1956), p. 15.

12 Seymour, pp. 195–200; Hamelius, pp. 179–86.

13 Dante Alighieri, *Inferno, the Italian text with translation by A. Gilbert* (Durham, North Carolina, 1969), canto 19, line 50, pp. 152–53.

14 F. M. Chambers, "The Troubadours and the Assassins," *Modern Language Notes* 64 (1949), pp. 245–47.

15 Lewis, *The Assassins*, pp. 109, 117–18.

16 *The Itinerary of Benjamin of Tudela*, ed. and trans. M. N. Adler (London, 1907), p. 16.

17 Lewis, p. 31; *Chronica Slavorum Arnoldi Abbatis Lubecensis* (Lubeck, 1659), lib. VII, cap. X, p. 523.

18 William of Tyre, *Historia rerum in partibus transmarinis gestarum* in Migne, *P.L.* 201, cap. XXXI, 810–11; see Ch. E. Nowell, "The Old Man of the Mountain," *Speculum* 22 (1947), 505.

19 *Matthaei Parisiensis Chronica Majora*, ed. H. R. Luard, 7 vols. (London, 1872–73), III, xiii, 488–89.

20 Gibb, *Damascus Chronicle*, p. 191; Ibn al-Athir, ed. C. J. Tornberg, X, 215; F. Gabrieli, *Arab Historians of the Crusades* (London, 1957), pp. 16, 47, 50.

21 Gibb, *Damascus Chronicle*, p. 57.

22 *Chronica Magistri Rogeri de Houidene*, ed. W. Stubbs (Cambridge, 1870), III, 181.

23 See Lewis, p. 142; J. de Vitry, *Histoire des Croisades* in *Collection des mémoires relatifs à l'histoire de France* (Paris, 1825), pp. 47–50; Latin text *Iacobide Vitiaco Historia Hierosolimitana* in J. Bongars, *Gesti Dei per Francos* (Hanovia [Hainaut], 1611), lib. I, cap. XIV, pp. 1062 ff.

24 Olschki, *Marco Polo's Asia*, p. 363; Lewis, p. 6.

25 Yule, *The Book of Ser Marco Polo*, chaps. 23 and 24, pp. 140, 143.

26 J. von Hammer, *Mines de l'Orient* (Vienna, 1813), III, 202–06; M. G. S. Hodgson, *The Order of the Assassins* (The Hague, 1955), pp. 134–35.

27 On a tradition of the confinement of the Assassins underground, see Hans R. Runte, "A Forgotten Old French Version of the Old Man of the Mountain," *Speculum* 49 (July 1974), 542–45.

28 Seymour, pp. 200–02; Hamelius, p. 184, line 32; p. 186, line 33.

29 G. F. Warner, *The Buke of John Maundeuill* (London, 1889), p. xxvii.

30 Hodgson, pp. 41 ff.

31 Lewis, p. 95; P. Willey, *The Castles of the Assassins* (London, 1963), appendix A, p. 297.

32 Lewis, p. 121.

33 Odoric of Pordenone, *Relatio in Sinica Franciscana* (Florence, 1929), chap. XXXV, p. 489. English version in *The Travels of Sir John Mandeville, with*

Three Narratives in Illustration of It: The Voyage of Johannes de Plano Carpini, The Journal of Friar William de Rubruquis, The Journal of Friar Odoric, p. 357.

34 Seymour, p. 201; Hamelius, p. 185, line 14.

35 "Catolonabes" seems to contain the Arabic word *qatala,* "to kill," suggesting *qātil an-nafs,* "murderer" or *qātil nafsī,* "one who commits suicide," an appropriate term for an assassin fedawi. It also suggests *abū l-qātilīn,* "father of those who kill," in what looks like a typical Latin transposition of *catolon-abes.* On the terminology of suicide, see F. Rosenthal's article: "Intiḥār—suicide" in *The Encyclopaedia of Islam,* new edition, III, 1246–48.

36 Hodgson, p. 136. On the use of hashish in medieval Muslim society, see F. Rosenthal, *The Herb* (Leyden, 1971).

37 Daniel, pp. 88–89.

38 Seymour, pp. 102–03; Hamelius, p. 90. line 13; p. 92, line 4.

39 Cf. Seymour, p. 24; Hamelius, p. 21, lines 14–23.

40 Seymour, pp. 25–26; Hamelius, p. 22, lines 4–23, line 22.

41 See *Haithoni Armeni Historia Orientalis* (Cologne, George Schulz, 1672), pp. 75–76, cap. XLVI: "de distinctionibus hujus operis, & qualiter habuit originem."

42 *Historia Orientalis,* cap. LI, p. 84.

43 Ibid., cap. LII, p. 87.

44 W. Muir, *The Mameluke or Slave Dynasty of Egypt, 1260–1715* A.D. (London, 1896), pp. 66 ff.; S. Lane-Poole, *A History of Egypt in the Middle Ages* (New York, 1901), pp. 306–20.

45 Muir, p. 86.

46 Hamelius, II, 40–42.

47 Cf. Seymour, pp. 26, 235.

48 Hamelius, II, 41.

49 Ibid., p. 42.

50 See F. Zarncke, "Der Priester Johannes," *Abhandlungen der koeniglichen saechsischen Gesellschaft der Wissenschaften, philos-hist. Klasse* 7:8 (1879), chaps. 1–3 and 8:1 (1876), chaps. 4–6; L. Olschki, "Der Brief des Presbyters Johannes," *Historische Zeitschrift* 144 (1931), 1–14; Olschki, *Marco Polo's Asia,* pp. 381 ff.; V. Slessarev, *Prester John, the Letter and the Legend* (Minneapolis, 1959), pp. 67–79; Lane-Poole, p. 310.

51 See G. Weil, *Geschichte der Chalifen nach handschriftlichen, groesstentheils noch unbenuetzten Quellen bearbeitet* (Stuttgart, 1862), IV, 353, citing the Egyptian historian al-Maqrīzī (A.D. 1364–1442) and the encyclopaedist al-Nuwairī (d. 1332); cf. Ahmad 'Ali al-Maqrīzī, *Kitāb as-sulūk,* ed. Muḥammad Muṣṭafā Ziyādah (Cairo, 1957), II, 909 on Nasir's epistle on the Christians in his domain, as taken from Nuwairi.

52 Seymour, p. 241.

53 Louis de Backer, *L'Extrême Orient au Moyen-âge,* p. 223.

54 *Haithoni Armeni Historia Orientalis,* pp. 82–83.

55 Weil, pp. 369–71.

56 See Robert Fazy, "Jehan de Mandeville: ses voyages et son séjour discuté en Egypte," *Etudes asiatiques* 3 (1949), p. 54.

57 Fazy, p. 44; Seymour, p. 6, lines 13–16; Hamelius, p. 5, lines 15–21. An illustration of the statue is found in J. Ebersolt, *Constantinople byzantine et les voyageurs du Levant* (Paris, 1918), p. 30.

58 Fazy, p. 46; Seymour, p. 20, lines 17 ff.; p. 19, lines 23 ff.; Hamelius, p. 17, lines 29 ff. and 10–13.

59 Fazy, p. 50; Seymour, p. 31, line 18; p. 33, lines 14–17; Hamelius, p. 28, line 14; p. 29, lines 26–30.

60 Fazy, pp. 45–46, 48–49.

CHAPTER 8

1 Maud Bodkin, *Archetypal Patterns in Poetry* (New York, 1958), p. 102.

2 *The History of Hayy ibn Yaqzan*, trans. Simon Ockley (London, 1929); *Hayy ben Yaqdhan, roman philosophique d'Ibn Thofail*, ed. and trans. L. Gauthier (Beirut, 1936); *Ibn Tufayl's Hayy Ibn Yaqzan*, trans. L. E. Goodman (New York, 1972); A. Pastor, *The Idea of Robinson Crusoe* (Watford, England, 1930), p. 177.

3 "To put the matter conventionally and moderately, it is a paradox that a man who had Johnson's preference for both the homely and the abstract should undertake an oriental tale at all," W. K. Wimsatt, "In Praise of *Rasselas*" in *Imagined Worlds, Essays on some English Novels and Novelists in Honour of John Butt*, ed. Maynard Mack and Ian Gregor (London, 1968), p. 117. On Johnson's debt to the "Persian Tales," translated by Ambrose Philips from the French of Pétis de la Croix's "Mille et un jours," see G. Tillotson, *Essays in Criticism and Research* (Cambridge, 1942), pp. 113–16.

4 Thomas Warton, *The History of English Poetry* (London, 1824), I, i; cf. A. Johnston, *The Study of Medieval Romance in the Eighteenth Century* (London, 1964), p. 198. For a general view, see Martha P. Conant, *The Oriental Tale in England in the Eighteenth Century* (New York, 1908).

5 Warton, I, ii.

6 James Beattie, "On Fable and Romance," excerpt in I. Williams, *Novel and Romance, 1700–1800* (London, 1970), p. 312.

7 Ibid., p. 313.

8 G. von Grunebaum, *Medieval Islam*, p. 295.

9 *The Story of England by Robert Mannyng of Brunne*, ed. F. J. Furnivall (London, 1887), part II, p. 579, lines 16701–08; R. Hoops, *Der Begriff 'Romance' in der mittelenglischen und fruehneuenglischen Literatur* (Heidelberg, 1929), p. 13.

10 *The Romance of Guy of Warwick*, ed. J. Zupitza, p. 243, line 8486; Hoops, p. 22.

11 *OED* VIII, 767.

12 See Hoops, pp. 34–36, 85–92. For Chaucer's use of "romaunce," see J. S. P. Tatlock and A. G. Kennedy, *A Concordance to the Complete Works of Geoffrey Chaucer* (Washington, 1927), p. 752. Cf. "This romaunce is of Thebes, that we rede" (*TC* II, 100).

13 Dorothy Everett, *Essays on Middle English Literature* (Oxford, 1955), p. 3.

14 Warton, I, lxii.

15 *Floris and Blauncheflur*, ed. E. Hausknecht (Berlin, 1885), p. 8; *The Romance of Emaré*, ed. E. Rickert (London, 1906), p. 5, lines 145 ff.

16 Laura Hibbard Loomis, *Mediaeval Romance in England* (New York, 1963), p. 184; F. C. de Vries, *Floris and Blauncheflur, a Middle English Romance* (Groningen, 1966), p. 60.

17 See summary in Burke Severs, *A Manual of the Writings in Middle English: 1050–1500* (New Haven, 1967), p. 146.

18 *Floris and Blancheflour*, ed. A. B. Taylor (Oxford, 1927), p. 17.

19 G. Huet, "Sur l'origine de *Floire et Blanchefleur*," *Romania* 28 (1899), 348–59; "Encore *Floire et Blanchefleur*," *Romania* 35 (1906), 95–100. Cf. R. Basset, "Les Sources arabes de *Floire et Blancheflor*," *Revue des traditions populaires* 22 (1907), 241–45. See also N. Elisséeff, *Thèmes et motifs des Mille et une nuits* (Beirut, 1949).

20 Burton, I, 286, n. 1; IV, 229. Huet, "Sur l'origine . . . ," *Romania* 28, 350–51.

21 "The Story of the Sleeper and the Waker" in R. F. Burton, *Supplemental Nights to the Book of the Thousand and a Night* (London, 1886), I, 11; Huet, "Sur l'origine . . . ," *Romania* 28, 350.

22 "Ardashir and Hayat al-Nufus," in Burton, VII, 256, 264.

23 Burton, VII, 230; cf. "Tale of Taj al-Muluk and the Princess Dunya," Burton, I, 236. On the garden in *Floris and Blancheflour* as "Otherworld," see O. M. Johnston, "The Description of the Emir's Orchard in *Floire et Blancheflor*," *Zeitschrift fuer romanische Philologie* 32 (1908), 705–10. The description of the garden in *Floris and Blancheflour* is as follows:

> Then shull men bring doun of the toure
> All the maidens of grete honoure
> And bring hem into an orchard,
> The fairest of all midlerde,
> Therin is mony fowles song;
> Men might leve therin full long.
> About the orchard is a walle;
> The foulest stone is cristall;
> And a well springeth therinne
> That is made with much ginne.
> The well is of muche prise;
> The stremes com fo Paradise;
> The gravel of the ground is precious stoones
> And all of vertu for the noones.

[ll. 603–15]

24 "Ni'amah bin al-Rabi'a and Naomi his Slave-girl," Burton, IV, 1 ff. The names Ni'amah and Naomi correspond, like Floris and Blancheflur, the Arabic names being derivatives of "grace." Cf. also "The Tale of Aziz and Azizah," where the names mean "dear, excellent, honored" (Burton, II, 193). Cf. "The Loves of the Boy and Girl at School," Burton, V, 73.

25 "Tale of Ghanim Bin Ayyub, the Distraught, the Thrall of Love," Burton, II, 45 ff.

26 Elisséeff, pp. 107–08. This motif is most common in stories relating to the caliph Harun al-Rashid, e.g., "Tale of Harun al-Rashid and Abu Hasan, the Merchant of Oman," Burton, IX, 189.

27 "The Ebony Horse," Burton, V, 25.

28 "The Reeve's Tale," Burton, I, 283. A Buddhist story from *The Jataka* in which a lover is concealed in a flower-basket and introduced into "the seven-fold guarded house" of a virtuous girl is cited by J. W. Spargo, "The Basket Incident in *Floire et Blancheflor*," *Neuphilologische Mitteilungen* 28 (1927), 69–75.

29 Inconclusive theories of Arabian, Byzantine, and French origin have been set forth with much machinery. See L. Hibbard Loomis, *Medieval Romance in England*, pp. 189–93. On the present state of the problem of origin, see the most recent translation of the French poem by M. J. Hubert, *The Romance of Floire and Blanchefleur* (Chapel Hill, 1966), p. 20 and Bibliography, pp. 113–14; and de Vries, *Floris and Blauncheflur: a Middle English Romance*, pp. 63–66.

30 S. Singer, "Arabische und europaeische Poesie im Mittelalter" in *Abhand-lungen der preussischen Akademie der Wissenschaften, philos.-hist. Klasse* (Berlin, 1918), pp. 4–6.

31 On the present state of the Kyot-problem, see Joachim Bumke, *Die Wolfram von Eschenbach Forschung seit 1945* (Munich, 1970), pp. 243–50 and Index, p. 431.

32 Von Grunebaum, p. 340; cf. E. Lévi-Provençal, *Islam d'Occident* (Paris, 1948), pp. 292–304. But see the strongly-worded opposite view of S. M. Stern, expressed five years before his death at the 1964 Spoleto conference on 'L'Occidente e l'Islam nell'alto Medioevo': "Esistono dei rapporti letterari tra il mondo islamico e l'Europa occidentale nell'alto Medioevo?" published in the Centro italiano di studi sull'alto Medioevo's *Settimane di studio* 12 (1965), II, 661. For the most recent discussion of the problem by Arabists, see the articles by F. Gabrieli, "Islam in the Mediterranean World" and by F. Rosenthal, "Literature," in *The Legacy of Islam*, second edition, pp. 94–97, 332, 340–41.

33 On the state of research in troubadour studies, see R. Baehr, *Der proven-zalische Minnesang: ein Querschnitt durch die neuere Forschungsdiskussion* (Darm-stadt, 1967). For the result of musicological evidence which points to the important medieval influence of the Church, see Friedrich Gennrich, "Zur Ursprungsfrage des Minnesangs: ein literarhistorisch-musikwissenschaft-licher Beitrag," ibid., pp. 115–60.

34 A. R. Nykl, *Hispano-Arabic Poetry and Its Relations with the Old Provençal Trou-badours* (Baltimore, 1946), pp. 266–308. See also R. Menéndez Pidal, "La primitiva lírica europea: estado actual del problema," *Revista de filología española* 43 (1960), 279–354.

35 *El Cancionero del seih Aben Guzman*, ed. A. R. Nykl (Madrid, 1933).

36 M. Hartmann, *Das arabische Strophengedicht* (Weimar, 1897), pp. 2 ff. Ibn Quzman writes in the preface ot his *Diwan*: "I established the principles of

the art and made it difficult for dull brains to engage in it. At the same time I removed all roughness from it and polished it so that it became smooth, free from grammatical inflections and technicalities; yet, while apparently easy, it became difficult, and while apparently vulgar, it was full of *finesse*, and while apparently obvious, it was difficult to understand, so that now, when someone hears the abundance of its hemistichs and its verses, he is induced to imitate it" (Nykl, *Hispano-Arabic Poetry*, pp. 269–70).

37 *The Muqaddimah*, trans. Rosenthal, III, 454, I have omitted Rosenthal's brackets.

38 S. M. Stern, "Les Vers finaux en espagnol dans les muwassahs hispano-hébraiques," *al-Andalus* 13 (1948), 299–346, pp. 305 ff.

39 Ibid., pp. 303–05; Leo Spitzer, "Die mozarabische Lyrik und die Theorien von Theodor Frings" translated from *Comparative Literature* 4 (1952) in Baehr, *Der provenzalische Minnesang*, p. 206.

40 Stern, pp. 303–04.

41 Aurelio Roncaglia, "Die arabisch-spanische Lyrik und die Entstehung der romanischen Lyrik ausserhalb der iberischen Halbinsel" in Baehr, *Der provenzalische Minnesang*, p. 214.

42 Ibid., p. 243.

43 R. Menéndez Pidal, *Poesía árabe y poesía europea, con otros estudios de literatura medieval* (Buenos Aires, 1946), p. 46; Roncaglia, pp. 243 ff. For examples of *zajal*, see A. R. Nykl, *Hispano-Arabic Poetry*, pp. 273 ff.

44 Spitzer, p. 214; Roncaglia, pp. 250 ff. For the musicological aspect of the whole question, see F. Gennrich in Baehr, *Der provenzalische Minnesang*, pp. 115–60. On a recent modification of the theory of Arabic influence on medieval Western love poetry, see Peter Dronke, *Medieval Latin and the Rise of European Love-Lyric* (Oxford, 1968), I, 52 ff.

45 On Ibn Hazm, see the article by R. Arnaldez in *Encyclopaedia of Islam*, new edition, III, 790–98.

46 Andreas Capellanus, *The Art of Courtly Love*, trans. J. J. Parry (New York, 1959); see pp. 9–12 on a comparison of Ibn Hazm and Andreas.

47 Ibn Hazm, *The Ring of the Dove*, trans. A. J. Arberry (London, 1953), pp. 152, 110–11.

48 Ibid., p. 101.

49 Ibid., pp. 73 ff., 98 ff., 102 ff., 107 ff.

50 Ibid., pp. 128, 197 ff.

51 Ibid., p. 79

52 *La Chançun de Williame*, ed. E. S. Tyler (New York, 1919), p. 90, line 2118; Crosland, *The Old French Epic*, p. 141.

53 Ezra Pound, *The Spirit of Romance* (London, 1952), p. 161.

54 *Sir Thopas*, lines 807–13 in Robinson, *The Works of Geoffrey Chaucer*, p. 165.

55 Alain de Lille, *The Complaint of Nature*, trans. D. M. Moffat (New York, 1908), p. 40; Prose IV, lines 214–17.

56 Marc Bloch, *Feudal Society*, p. 94.

57 Beatrice White, "Saracens and Crusaders: from Fact to Allegory" in *Medieval Literature and Civilization*, ed. D. A. Pearsall and R. A. Waldron (London, 1969), p. 178.

58   Leo Spitzer, "Classical and Christian Ideas of World Harmony," *Traditio* 2 (1944), 455; *Traditio* 3 (1945), 325.

59   Stephan G. Kuttner, *Harmony from Dissonance* (Latrobe, 1960).

60   Kuttner, p. 14; Spitzer, *Traditio* 2,438. In his discussion of this concept in Boethius and Dante, Spitzer defines it as "the feeling of the group, of being united in one *concordia* or World Harmony, which extends from angel to star to man to bird" (*Traditio* 3, 325).

Index